Why Do You Need this New Edition?

If you're wondering why you should buy this new edition of *English Fundamentals*, here are 5 good reasons!

1. **All five drill and practice opportunities** in Lessons 1 through 25 (Practice Sheets, Exercises, MyWritingLab connections, Progress Tests, and Test Bank items) **align with the specific content of the individual lesson**, rather than combining content from several lessons as in previous editions. This new emphasis on coordinated content offers repeated opportunities to reinforce your learning and guarantee mastery.

2. **New Review questions** direct you to a concept covered in the previous lesson and help to drive home a newly learned concept so that—like an experienced athlete—your skills mastery becomes second nature.

3. **New Practice Sheets, Exercises, and Progress Tests** throughout support the new focus on coordination among all these elements and provide repeated practice opportunities.

4. **References to MyWritingLab throughout** send you to appropriate content in Pearson's premier learning site for developmental writing.

5. **A proven history**—more than eight decades—of offering clear, accessible explanations for grammar fundamentals underlies this edition's new emphasis on aligning content with every element of practice— Practice Sheets, Exercises, Progress Tests, and Review questions.

PEARSON

English Fundamentals

Sixteenth Edition

Donald W. Emery
Late of The University of Washington

John M. Kierzek
Late of Oregon State University

Peter Lindblom
Miami-Dade College

Longman
Boston Columbus Indianapolis New York San Francisco
Upper Saddle River Amsterdam Cape Town Dubai London Madrid
Milan Munich Paris Montreal Toronto Delhi Mexico City Sao Paulo
Sydney Hong Kong Seoul Singapore Taipei Tokyo

Senior Sponsoring Editor: Virginia L. Blanford
Senior Marketing Manager: Thomas DeMarco
Assistant Editor: Rebecca Gilpin
Senior Supplements Editor: Donna Campion
Senior Media Producer: Stefanie Liebman
Production Coordinator: Scarlett Lindsay
Project Coordination, Text Design, and Electronic Page Makeup: Nesbitt Graphics, Inc.
Cover Design Manager: John Callahan
Cover Designer: Maria Ilardi
Cover Image: © Stephan Zabel/iStockphoto
Senior Manufacturing Buyer: Dennis J. Para
Printer and Binder: RR Donnelley–Crawfordsville
Cover Printer: RR Donnelley–Crawfordsville

7 8 9 -V056- 16 15

Longman
is an imprint of

www.pearsonhighered.com

ISBN 13: 978-0-205-82597-4
ISBN 10: 0-205-82597-4

Contents

Part 3

Sentence Building 137
Lessons, Practice Sheets, and Exercises

Part 4

Punctuation 179
Lessons, Practice Sheets, and Exercises

Preface

*P*owerful, effective writing—that is the goal for every student who uses *English Fundamentals,* Sixteenth Edition.

The basic premise underlying this work is quite simple:

> Those students who work diligently through the twenty-eight lessons in this edition will master a wide range of writing strategies. Mastering those strategies will allow them to become power writers in every context: college, businesses and the professions, and personal life.

HOW THIS EDITION IS NEW AND DIFFERENT

To make the mastery of those strategies more permanent, the book has been re-structured in two important ways:

- **Closer coordination among its components**. Lessons 1 through 25 present five opportunities for drill and practice: Practice Sheets, Exercises, MyWritingLab connections, Progress Tests, and Test Bank items. In previous editions, the Progress Tests and Test Bank items addressed several lessons simultaneously—but in this edition, all five drill and practice opportunities align with the specific content of the individual lesson being taught. As a result, students have five coordinated opportunities to reinforce the concepts that they have learned in each lesson.

  Repeated drill and practice will embed these writing strategies so that the writer's use of the strategies becomes almost automatic. The highly skilled tennis player does not make a conscious decision in mid-stride to use a drop shot, or a lob, or a forehand smash to the far corner. Rather, constant, repeated practice dictates the choice of shot without any conscious thought on the part of the player. So it becomes for the skilled writer. At a certain point in the development of a writer, the choice of strategies becomes almost automatic—but only after extensive drill and practice.

- **Regular review**. Each lesson, either in the Practice Sheets or the Exercises, directs students to a concept covered in a previous lesson. The reviews are simple, a request, for example, to identify subjects and verbs in a lesson after subjects and verbs have been introduced. Simple but important, the reviews offer yet one more opportunity to fix a concept permanently.

  Repeated review, the act of looking back at a structure or strategy covered one or two lessons earlier, will help to drive home a newly learned concept. Reviewing allows students to gain access to the strategies they have learned with greater and greater ease, until the selection becomes almost automatic. Again, the benefit of all this practice and review is mastery of a large repertoire of strategies, all of which will be consistently accessible.

In creating this more targeted structure, I have been inspired by two books. In *Talent Is Overrated,* Geoff Colvin argues, with extensive research support, that accomplishment in any field (chess, mathematics, writing) results not from an inborn or "natural" talent but rather from hard, repeated work—what Colvin and others call *deliberate practice.*

(Malcolm Gladwell makes a similar argument in his best-selling *Outliers.*) This type of practice requires both diligent application by the learner and expert coaching. From this idea comes the strategy of close coordination within each lesson: Five opportunities for drill and practice, all focused on a single concept, all supervised by an expert instructor.

In his chapter called "Repeat to Remember" in *Brain Rules,* John Medina argues that repetition fixes material in the brain, and that review is critical to this process. So, in this book, each lesson presents a concept reinforced by five opportunities for practice, but each lesson also points backward, encouraging students to identify a relevant concept from an earlier lesson.

Together, these emphases on coordinated practice and on regular review offer your students powerful support in their journey toward becoming effective writers.

THE FUNDAMENTALS OF *ENGLISH FUNDAMENTALS*

The irreplaceable foundations of this textbook remain in this new edition.

- Step-by-step presentation of the structure and organization of the language moves students from passive recognition (a choice between two items) to active production (writing correct forms, inserting words, transforming sentences from one structure to another, writing complete sentences, composing entire paragraphs).

- A continuum of building blocks for the language takes students from the simplest, most basic concepts of subject–verb combinations to the production of entire essays.

- Two levels of drill work provide a range of practice opportunities: Practice Sheets offer simple versions of the concepts taught in each lesson, and Exercises offer more advanced sophisticated work. These practice opportunities make references to science, business, history, and other fields, so that every student can find some connection to the subject matter in the lessons.

- Brief Writing Assignments at the end of many chapters encourage students to create short paragraphs using specific sentence structures.

- Check Sheets at the end of each group of lessons provide concise overviews of the principles taught in the section. Students may use these for review and for reference during writing assignments.

- References at the end of each chapter point students to pertinent sections of MyWritingLab (www.mywritinglab.com), Pearson's robust site for online review and practice of the principles taught in *English Fundamentals.*

- Sentence-combining drills offer a different approach to the development of sentence skills and review the structures taught in the lessons.

- Sequences and connections are modeled in every chapter. The earliest lessons show how one word can change (*immediate* becomes *immediately,* or *immediacy* as one word is used in different forms for different purposes). In later lessons, compound sentences become complex sentences (main clause + adverbial clause), an illustration of the wide variety of sentence strategies available to good writers.

WHAT ELSE IS AVAILABLE

An Answer Key and Test Bank are available to adopters of *English Fundamentals,* Sixteenth Edition, from Pearson's online Instructor Resource Center. Ask your local Pearson Arts and Science sales representative about this, or register yourself at www.pearsonhighered.com/educator.

In addition to these book-specific supplements, Pearson offers a wealth of instructor and student ancillaries to complement all its offerings in developmental writing. Please visit our online catalogue at www.pearsonhighered.com/devenglish or consult your Pearson representative to learn about the options that best suit your interests.

mywritinglab ▍ **MyWritingLab (www.mywritinglab.com)** is Pearson's powerful online learning system for developmental writing students. A prompt to use MyWritingLab appears at the end of each lesson in *English Fundamentals*. The exercises in MyWritingLab are progressive, moving within each skill module from literal comprehension to critical application to demonstrating individual skills in students' own writing. The 9,000-plus exercises rehearse grammar, but they also extend into the writing process, paragraph development, essay development, and research. A thorough diagnostic test outlines where students have not yet mastered a skill, and easy-to-use tracking systems enable students and instructors to monitor all work. MyWritingLab can be packaged with this text at no additional cost to your students. Ask your Pearson representative for more information.

ACKNOWLEDGMENTS

Our thanks go to all those who offered advice and suggestions for this new edition: Linda Conry, Collin College; Thomas D'Angelo, Nassau Community College; Patricia DiMond, University of South Dakota; and Nabila Hijazi, University of Maryland, College Park.

Peter Lindblom

Basic Sentence Patterns

Lessons, Practice Sheets, and Exercises

Lesson 1 — *The Simple Sentence; Subjects and Verbs*

Powerful writers possess the ability to use the English language to explain, persuade, motivate, and accomplish any of the other purposes for which writing is used. The goal of this book is to assist you in becoming a powerful writer. To write effectively and powerfully, you need to master the fundamentals of the language: the way sentences are formed, the various structures that can be employed to make a point, the combinations of sentences that form paragraphs, and the ways in which paragraphs work together to create complete writing projects. These elements are the tools effective writers employ; learning to use these elements will help you to become a more effective, powerful writer.

In the first few lessons of this book, you'll examine the parts that make up a sentence and the distinctive characteristics of a few types of sentences that serve as the basic structures of more complicated units.

To begin, be sure you can recognize the two indispensable parts of a sentence:

1. The **subject**: the unit about which something is said.
2. The **predicate**: the unit that says something about the subject.

↳ predicate – verb

Although the predicate usually includes other modifying words and phrases, the indispensable part of a predicate is the **verb**, the word (or words) that says what the subject does or is. Here are a few things to remember about the subject–verb relationship:

1. In a sentence that reports a specific action, the verb is easily recognized. For instance, to find the subject and verb in *The rusty bumper on the front of my truck rattles noisily*, ask the question "What happens?" The answer, *rattles*, gives the verb. Then, by asking the question, "Who or what rattles?", you will find the subject, *bumper*. Notice that neither "front rattles" nor "truck rattles" makes the basic statement of the sentence.

2. Some sentences do not report an action. Instead, the sentence says something about the *condition* of the subject. It points out a descriptive quality of the subject or says that something else resembles or is the same thing as the subject. In this kind of sentence, you must look for verbs like *is, are, was, were, seem,* and *become.* Such verbs are often called *describing (linking) verbs.* These verbs serve as connectors; they join the subject to something that is said about the subject. They are words that are almost impossible to define because they lack the concrete exactness and action of verbs like *rattle, throw, smash,* and *explode.*

In a sentence using a describing verb, the subject usually reveals itself easily. For example, in the sentence "The long first chapter seemed particularly difficult," the verb

1

is *seemed*. The question "Who or what seemed?" provides the subject, *chapter*. The other possible choices—*long*, *first*, *particularly*, and *difficult*—do not make sense as answers to the question "Who or what seemed?"

3. Very often, the subject of a sentence has material between it and its verb:

> The *price* of potatoes *is* high. [The subject is *price*, not *potatoes*.]
> *Each* of my sisters *is* tall. [The subject is *each*, not *sisters*.]
> Only *one* of these watches *works*. [The subject is *one*, not *watches*.]

4. Most modern English sentences place the subject before the verb, but in some sentences, the verb precedes the subject:

> Behind the house *stood* [verb] an old *mill* [subject].
> Under the table *sat* [verb] a large *cat* [subject].

A very common type of sentence with the verb-subject arrangement uses *here* or *there* preceding the verb:

> There *are* [verb] three willow *trees* [subject] in our yard.
> Here *is* [verb] the *list* [subject] of candidates.

5. Casual, informal language often combines short verbs and subjects with apostrophes representing the omitted letters:

> I'm (I am)   It's (It is)   You've (You have)   They're (They are)

For your first practice work, you'll be using only a single subject for each sentence. Within this limitation, the subject is always a noun or a pronoun. Before the first practice, it would be wise to review a few facts about nouns, pronouns, and verbs so that you can recognize them easily.

NOUNS

A **noun** is a word that names something, such as a person, place, thing, quality, or idea. If the noun names just any member of a group or class, it is called a *common noun* and is not capitalized:

> man, city, school, relative

A noun is a *proper noun* and is capitalized if it refers to a particular individual in a group or class:

> Albert Lawson, Toledo, Horace Mann Junior High School, Aunt Louise

Most nouns have two forms; they show whether the noun is naming one thing (singular number) or more than one thing (plural number, which adds *s* or *es* to the singular form): one *coat*, two *coats*; a *lunch*, several *lunches*. Proper nouns are rarely pluralized, and some common nouns have no plural form—for example, *honesty, courage, ease,* and *hardness*.

Nouns often follow *the*, *a*, or *an*, words that are called **articles**. A descriptive word (an adjective) may come between the article and the noun, but the word that answers the question "What?" after an article is a noun:

Article $\left(\begin{matrix} optional \\ adjective \end{matrix} \right)$ noun

A (or The)   happy   girl.

Another way to identify nouns is to recognize certain suffixes. A **suffix** is a unit added to the end of a word or to the base of a word (see Supplement 1).[*] Here are some of the common suffixes found in hundreds of nouns:

age [break*age*]; ance, ence [resist*ance*, insist*ence*]; dom [king*dom*]; hood [child*hood*]; ion [prevent*ion*]; ism [national*ism*]; ment [move*ment*]; ness [firm*ness*]; or, er [invest*or*, los*er*]; ure [expos*ure*]

PRONOUNS

A **pronoun** is a word that substitutes for a noun. There are several classes of pronouns. (See Supplement 2.) The following classes can function as subjects in the basic sentences that you will examine in these early lessons:

Personal pronouns substitute for definite persons or things: *I, you, he, she, it, we, they.*

Demonstrative pronouns substitute for things being pointed out: *this, that, these, those.*

Indefinite pronouns substitute for unknown or unspecified things: *each, either, neither, one, anyone, somebody, everything, all, few, many,* and so on.

Possessive pronouns substitute for things that are owned: *mine, yours, his, hers, its, ours, theirs.*

VERBS

A **verb** is a word that expresses action, existence, or occurrence by combining with a subject to make a statement, to ask a question, or to give a command. One easy way to identify a word as a verb is to use the following test:

Let's _____
    (action word)

Any word that will complete the command is a verb: "Let's *leave*." "Let's *buy* some popcorn." "Let's *be* quiet." This test works only with the basic present form of the verb, not with forms that have endings added to them or that show action taking place in the past: "Let's *paint* the car" (not "Let's *painted* the car").

---

[*]In some lessons of this book, you will find notations referring you to a supplement that appears at the end of the lesson. Read the supplement *after* you have thoroughly studied the lesson. The lesson contains the essential information that is vital to your understanding of subsequent lessons and exercises. The supplement presents material that has relevance to some points of the lesson. The supplements at the end of this lesson are found on page 4.

Some verbs that do not convey action may not fit this particular test. *Let's seem*, for example, is not a regular English construction. In such cases, look for a connection between the first part of the sentence, the subject, and the second part. The word making the connection is the verb.

He seems happy.

SUPPLEMENT 1

Hundreds of nouns have distinctive suffix endings. The definitions of some of these suffixes are rather difficult to formulate, but you can quite readily figure out the meanings of most of them: *ness*, for instance, means "quality or state of" (thus *firmness* means "the state or quality of being firm"); *or* and *er* show the agent or doer of something (an *investor* is "one who invests").

A unit added to the beginning of a word is called a **prefix**. Thus, to the adjective *kind*, we add a prefix to derive another adjective, *unkind*, and a suffix to derive the nouns *kindness* and *unkindness*. An awareness of how prefixes and suffixes are used will do far more than just refine your ability to recognize parts of speech: Your spelling will improve and your vocabulary will expand.

SUPPLEMENT 2

Two classes of pronouns, the **interrogative** and the **relative**, are not listed here. Because they are used in questions and subordinate clauses but not in simple basic sentences, they will not be discussed until later lessons.

Another type of pronoun that you use regularly (but not as a true subject) is the **intensive** or **reflexive** pronoun, the "self" words used to add emphasis:

You *yourself* made the decision.

These pronouns also name the receiver of an action when the doer is the same as the receiver:

The boy fell and hurt *himself*.

The first example is the intensive use; the second is the reflexive. Pronouns used this way are *myself, yourself, himself* (not *hisself*), *herself, itself, ourselves, yourselves*, and *themselves* (not *themself, theirself*, or *theirselves*).

The "self" pronouns are properly used for these two purposes only. They should not be substituted for regular personal pronouns:

Mary and I [not *myself*] were invited to the dance.
Tom visited Eric and me [not *myself*] at our ranch.

A fourth type of pronoun is the **reciprocal pronoun**, which denotes a mutual relationship—for example, *one another, each other*:

We try to help *each other* with our homework.

English Fundamentals Online

After you have completed the Practice Sheets and Exercises in this lesson, you can find additional help and drill work at **MyWritingLab.com**, in the section on Subjects and Verbs.

NAME _____ SCORE _____

Directions: In the space at the left, copy the word that is the verb of the italicized subject.

_____ 1. *June* runs three miles before class every morning.

_____ 2. *Sam* works in the library on Saturdays.

_____ 3. The *bells* chime at the beginning of each hour.

_____ 4. There are tall *trees* along the walkway to that classroom building.

_____ 5. The *effects* of that windstorm appear everywhere on campus.

_____ 6. That first *chapter* in the textbook was very difficult.

_____ 7. The three *concepts* in that chapter seemed extremely complex.

_____ 8. The next *stretch* of road goes through a beautiful valley.

_____ 9. That *valley* stretches for almost five miles along that river.

_____ 10. The *mouth* of the river opens into a broad, beautiful lake.

_____ 11. Along the shores of the lake there are two small *towns*.

_____ 12. Beyond one of the towns stands a small *college*.

_____ 13. A *stand* of tall trees hides part of the campus from view.

_____ 14. *I* see the small college every morning on my way to class.

_____ 15. The *classes* in my schedule this term seem very challenging.

_____ 16. *Each* of the students in my classes was nervous on the first day of class.

_____ 17. Each *class* presents a special challenge to us students.

_____ 18. *Some* of the students grasp the material quite easily.

_____ 19. *Others* seek help from their fellow students.

_____ 20. A decent *grade* in each of my classes is my goal for the term.

Directions: In the space at the left, copy the word that is the subject of the italicized verb.

_____ 1. No one ever *laughs* at my jokes.

_____ 2. The lack of laughter from my friends always *hurts* my feelings.

_____ 3. Our collection of food for the trip *lacked* both snacks and soft drinks.

_____ 4. There *is* not enough room in my backpack for all the books for my classes.

_____ 5. The coach's assistant *books* the rooms for all the baseball trips.

_____ 6. James *tripped* on that rock in the middle of the trail.

_____ 7. Even in that dense fog, the dogs *trailed* the lost child for two whole hours.

_____ 8. Yesterday, I *lost* my chemistry book and the notes from the last two classes.

_____ 9. Unfortunately, the loss of that textbook *cost* me $75.00 for its replacement.

_____ 10. The entire team *seems* sad and frustrated after that loss in the bottom of the last inning.

_____ 11. The trail, for that last mile, *was* a pleasant downhill walk.

_____ 12. My grandmother, along with several of her friends, often *walks* to town on Friday afternoon.

_____ 13. Some of her friends *sit* contentedly in their rocking chairs on the porch.

_____ 14. Those two women *buy* new cars every year.

_____ 15. Two of the women among my grandmother's friends *purchase* new cars every year.

_____ 16. Those purchases *are* always their largest for the entire year.

_____ 17. My brother, with a little help from me, *bought* an older used car last year.

_____ 18. Because of its lack of reliability, we *use* it only for trips to class and back to our apartment.

_____ 19. The uses for any type of unreliable car *are* very limited.

_____ 20. That unreliable old car *limits* our opportunities for any kind of long trip.

Subjects and Verbs

NAME _____ SCORE _____

In the first space at the left, copy the subject of the sentence. In the second space, copy the verb.

members/
team   1. The members of our drafting team worked late last night on the
worked   drawings for the new building.

they   2. Yesterday afternoon they weren't quite ready for the presentation
were   to the developers of the project.

presentation 3. But today the presentation worked both smoothly and successfully
worked   to the delight of the developers.

moments 4. During the presentation, there were brief moments of applause
were   and general approval for the quality of the work by the drafting team.

work   5. The work of the designers and architects also received high marks
received   from the developers.

★ _time_   6. Now is the time for invitations for bids from contractors.
_is_   *P Phrase*

~~time frame~~ 7. The time frame for the submission of bids by contractors is
_is_   usually 60 days.

member   8. During construction, one member of our firm serves as the
serves   supervising architect.

oversight 9. That person's oversight of the project insures the quality of the
ensures   work by the contractor and subcontractors.

member 10. Every member of our firm feels grateful for this work during
feels   these difficult economic times.

family 11. Years ago, my family watched with keen interest the construction
watched   of an office building near our house.

sister 12. My little sister, all of eleven years old, paid very careful attention
paid   to the whole building process.

hours 13. Usually there were several hours a week for observations and
were   commentary on the work.

family 14. The rest of the family heard these reports around the dinner table.
heard

stories 15. Sometimes the stories of the activities of the workers and the
carried   progress on the job carried into the evening hours.

completion 16. The completion of the building left her with a great deal of time
left   on her hands.

She 17. At first, she walked through the empty building on inspection tours.
walked

observations 18. Then at dinner, there were detailed observations on the
were   workmanship and any mistakes by the workers.

occupants 19. Finally, the occupants of the various offices moved into the building.
moved

opportunities 20. At that point, to the great relief of the rest of the family, there
were   weren't any more opportunities for observation and criticism.

7

sister
recorded
21. Without the knowledge of the rest of the family, my sister very carefully recorded all her observations on the building process.

she
wrote
22. She faithfully wrote down these very detailed observations in a file in her computer.

she
imported
23. Along with her observations, she imported pictures of each stage of the construction into the file.

production
was
24. After weeks of work, the entire production from the beginning of the work to the end was ready for presentation.

she
set
25. After dinner one night, she set her computer very carefully at the end of the dining room table.

presentation
began
26. Then began a long presentation about the construction of "her" building.

drifted
27. The rest of us, after about an hour, drifted quietly away to our other evening activities.

member
was
28. To her surprise, there wasn't a single family member present at the table at the end of the presentation.

lack
diminished
29. Our lack of interest, however, in no way diminished her enthusiasm for every aspect of construction.

girl
got
30. That same girl, at the age of fourteen, got herself a job at a local engineering firm.

31. Actually, it was more of a volunteer position than a real job.

32. There wasn't any pay for the work every afternoon in the office.

33. In exchange for clean-up work, she observed the engineers at their work.

34. After a few months, she found opportunities for questions for the engineers and the computer operators.

35. These computer operators, highly skilled at their work, ran the CAD programs for the design of buildings.

36. Their skill with these design programs constantly amazed my sister.

37. One day a particularly kind engineer gave my sister initial instructions in the use of a simple program.

38. On that day, the door to an entire career opened for my sister.

39. My sister, her enthusiasm at an all time high, babbled almost incoherently through dinner about the joys of her experience.

40. Today my sister works happily at an engineering firm as a professional engineer.

In Lesson 1 you learned how to recognize a verb. Every verb has a **base** or **infinitive**. This form of the verb "names" the verb. But verbs change their form according to various conditions, three of which are person, number, and tense. You should learn these forms because they occur in nearly every sentence that you speak or write.

Person specifies the person(s) speaking (first person: *I, we*); the person(s) spoken *to* (second person: *you*); and the person(s) or thing(s) spoken *about* (third person: *he, she, it, they*).

Number shows whether the reference is to *one* thing (*singular* number) or to more than one thing (*plural* number).

Tense refers to the time represented in the sentence, whether it applies to the present moment (I *believe* him) or to some other time (I *believed* him, I *will believe* him).

To demonstrate these changes in form, you can use a chart or arrangement called a ***conjugation***. In the partial conjugation that follows, three verbs are used: *earn, grow,* and *be*. The personal pronoun subjects are included to show how the person and number of the subject affect the form of the verb.

Indicative Mood
Active Voice*

Present Tense

	Singular	*Plural*
1st person	I earn, grow, am	We earn, grow, are
2nd person	You earn, grow, are	You earn, grow, are
3rd person	He earns, grows, is†	They earn, grow, are

Past Tense

1st person	I earned, grew, was	We earned, grew, were
2nd person	You earned, grew, were	You earned, grew, were
3rd person	He earned, grew, was	They earned, grew, were

---

*Indicative mood signals that the verb expresses a fact as opposed to a wish, command, or possibility. *Active voice* indicates that the subject of the verb is the *doer*, rather than the *receiver*, of the action of the verb.

†The pronoun *he* is arbitrarily used here to represent the third-person singular subject, which may be any singular pronoun (*she, it, who, nobody*); singular noun (*girl, neighbor, elephant, misunderstanding, Alice, Christopher Robert Klein III*); or word groups constituting certain types of phrases or clauses that will be studied in later lessons.

Future Tense

1st person	I will earn, grow, be*	We will earn, grow, be
2nd person	You will earn, grow, be	You will earn, grow, be
3rd person	He will earn, grow, be	They will earn, grow, be

Present Perfect Tense

1st person	I have earned, grown, been	We have earned, grown, been
2nd person	You have earned, grown, been	You have earned, grown, been
3rd person	He has earned, grown, been	They have earned, grown, been

Past Perfect Tense

1st person	I had earned, grown, been	We had earned, grown, been
2nd person	You had earned, grown, been	You had earned, grown, been
3rd person	He had earned, grown, been	They had earned, grown, been

Future Perfect Tense

1st person	I will have earned, grown, been	We will have earned, grown, been
2nd person	You will have earned, grown, been	You will have earned, grown, been
3rd person	He will have earned, grown, been	They will have earned, grown, been

Notice that in the past tense, *earn* adds an *ed* ending, but *grow* changes to *grew*. This difference illustrates **regular** and **irregular verbs**, the two groups into which all English verbs are classified. *Earn* is a regular verb; *grow* is an irregular verb. (Lesson 21 discusses irregular verbs in more detail.)

Notice also that some verb forms consist of more than one word (*will earn*, *have grown*, *had earned*, *will have been*). In such uses, *will*, *have*, and *had* are called **auxiliary verbs**. More auxiliary verbs are examined in Lesson 5.

With the "naming" words (nouns and pronouns) and the "action" and "linking" words (verbs), you can construct true sentences:

Janice arrived.

He laughed.

Power corrupts.

But to make sentences more varied and complete, you need modifiers or "describing" words (adjectives and adverbs) and prepositional phrases.

---

*Earlier, some writers made distinctions in the use of *shall* and *will* in the future and future perfect tenses. *Shall* was always used with the first person singular and *will* was used in the second and third person plural. In addition, there was an emphatic mood created by reversing *shall* and *will*. So in the emphatic mood, people employed *I will* and *you* or *he shall*. In recent years, those distinctions have been lost, and we now employ *will* for all three persons in both tenses.

ADJECTIVES

An **adjective** is a word that describes or limits—that is, gives qualities to—a noun. Adjectives are found in three positions in a sentence:

1. Preceding a noun that is in any of the noun positions within the sentence

   The *small* child left. He is a *small* child. I saw the *small* child. I gave it to the *small* child.

2. Following a describing (linking) verb and modifying the subject

   The child is *small*. Mary looked *unhappy*. We became *upset*.

3. Directly following the noun (less common than the two positions described above)

   He provided the money *necessary* for the trip. The hostess, *calm and serene*, entered the hall.

Certain characteristics of form and function help you recognize adjectives. There are several suffixes that, when added to other words or roots of other words, form adjectives. Here again, an understanding of the meaning of a suffix can save trips to the dictionary. For instance, in the hundreds of adjectives ending in *able* (*ible*), the suffix means "capable of" or "tending to"; thus, *usable* means "capable of being used" and *changeable* means "tending to change."

able, ible [read*able*, irresist*ible*]; al [internation*al*]; ant, ent [resist*ant*, diverg*ent*]; ar [lun*ar*]; ary [budget*ary*]; ful [meaning*ful*]; ic, ical [cosm*ic*, hyster*ical*]; ish [fool*ish*]; ive [invent*ive*]; less [blame*less*]; ous [glamor*ous*]; y [greas*y*]

One note of warning: Many other words in English end with these letters, but you can easily see that they are not employing a suffix. T*able*, ferm*ent*, arr*ive*, d*ish*, and pon*y*, for instance, are not adjectives. (See Supplement 1 for more information on adjectives.)

ADJECTIVES USED IN COMPARISONS

Nearly all adjectives, when they are used in comparisons, can be strengthened or can show degree by changing form or by using *more* and *most*:

great trust, *greater* trust, *greatest* trust
sensible answer, *more sensible* answer, *most sensible* answer

The base form (*great* trust, *sensible* answer) is the **positive degree**. The second form (*greater* trust, *more sensible* answer) is the **comparative degree**: it compares two things. The third form (*greatest* trust, *most sensible* answer) is the **superlative degree** and distinguishes among three or more things. (See Supplement 2.)

ADVERBS

Another modifier is the **adverb**, a word that modifies anything except a noun or a pronoun. Most adverbs modify verbs (She walked *quickly*). Some adverbs modify adjectives and other adverbs (The *very* old man walked *quite slowly*). Some adverbs modify whole sentences (*Consequently*, we refused the offer).

Adverbs tell certain things about the verb, the most common being:

1. **Manner:** John performed *well*. We worked *hard*. The child laughed *happily*. I would *gladly* change places with you.
2. **Time:** I must leave *now*. I'll see you *later*. *Soon* we shall meet *again*.
3. **Frequency:** We *often* go on picnics, *sometimes* at the lake but *usually* in the city park.
4. **Place:** *There* he sat, alone and silent. *Somewhere* we shall find peace and quiet.
5. **Direction:** The police officer turned *away*. I moved *forward* in the bus.
6. **Degree:** I could *barely* hear the speaker. I *absolutely* refuse to believe that story.

The most frequently used adverbs answer such questions as "How?" (manner or degree), "When?" (time or frequency), and "Where?" (place or direction).

Adverbs of a subclass called **intensifiers** modify adjectives or adverbs but not verbs—for example, a *very* good meal, his *quite* surprising reply, *too* often, *somewhat* reluctantly.

Many adverbs change form the way adjectives do, to show degree:

to drive *fast*, to drive *faster*, to drive *fastest*

to perform *satisfactorily*, to perform *more satisfactorily*, to perform *most satisfactorily*

See Supplement 2 for details on some common irregular intensifiers.

PREPOSITIONS

A **preposition** is a word that introduces a phrase and shows the relationship between the object of the phrase and some other word in the sentence. Notice that many prepositions show a relationship of space or time. Here are some common prepositions; those in the last column are called *group prepositions*:

about	beside	inside	through	according to
above	besides	into	throughout	because of
across	between	like	till	by way of
after	beyond	near	to	in addition to
against	by	of	toward	in front of
around	down	off	under	in place of
at	during	on	until	in regard to
before	except	out	up	in spite of
behind	for	outside	upon	instead of
below	from	over	with	on account of
beneath	in	since	without	out of

A preposition always has an object; with its object and any modifiers, the preposition makes a **prepositional phrase**. You can easily illustrate the function of prepositions by constructing sentences like the following:

After breakfast I walked *to* town *without* my friend. [Objects: *breakfast, town, friend.*]

On account of the rain, I canceled my plans *for* a game *of* tennis *at* the park *with* John. [Objects: *rain, game, tennis, park, John.*]

The trees *outside* the window *of* the kitchen are full *of* blossoms *during* the spring. [Objects: *window, kitchen, blossoms, spring.*]

SUPPLEMENT 1

Besides what could be called true adjectives, there are other classes of words that modify nouns. If you concentrate on the *functions* of the various kinds of words, however, you can safely classify as adjectives all words that precede nouns and limit their meaning. Such adjectives include articles, numerals, and possessives (*an* apple, *the* weather, *my three* room-mates); modifiers that can be used also as pronouns (*these* people, *some* friends, *all* workers); and nouns that modify other nouns (*basketball* players, *summer* days, *crop* failures).

Many words can be used as adjectives or as pronouns; the position of a word within the sentence determines which part of speech it is:

Several [*adj.*] classmates of mine [*pron.*] read this [*adj.*] report.
Several [*pron.*] of my [*adj.*] classmates read this [*pron.*].

SUPPLEMENT 2

A few commonly used modifiers form their comparative and superlative degrees irregularly:

good (*adj.*)	better	best
well (*adv.*)	better	best
bad (*adj.*)	worse	worst

English Fundamentals Online

After you have completed the Practice Sheets and Exercises in this lesson, you can find additional help and drill work at **MyWritingLab.com**, in the sections on Parts of Speech; Subjects and Verbs; Adjectives and Adverbs; Nouns; Verbs; Modifiers; Pronouns; and Prepositions.

Parts of Speech

NAME _____   SCORE _____

Directions: Identify the part of speech of each italicized word by writing one of the following numbers in each space at the left:

1. noun	3. verb	5. adverb
2. pronoun	4. adjective	6. preposition

Notice the changes in the forms of words as they change functions in the sentence.

_____   1. There was no *movement* in the darkness *outside* the house.

_____   2. There *has been* no sign of rain for *two* days.

_____   3. The man had been standing *quietly* at the *back* of the room for 30 minutes.

_____   4. The dog *will come* into the house through the *back* door.

_____   5. The *only usable* plan came to us from James McCoy.

_____   6. *According to* the weather report, a blizzard will arrive *here* on Thursday.

_____   7. We *have* not yet *heard* a *sensible* answer to Ms. Johnson's question.

_____   8. Unfortunately, the bus left shortly *after* Jim's arrival at the *bus* stop.

_____   9. *Few* members *of* the class remember the due date for that paper.

_____   10. *Few* of the members of the class *submitted* their papers on time.

_____   11. The field trip to the archeological dig will leave from the *classroom* building
                at 8:00 A.M. tomorrow *morning*.

_____   12. The mayor registered *his* opinion of that particular motion *with* a loud chuckle.

_____   13. *Several* of the people in the audience broke *into* spontaneous applause at the
                end of the movie.

_____   14. *I* will probably think of a *more* clever response to that question sometime later
                this afternoon.

_____   15. We *barely* heard the announcer *because of* the noise from the people in the
                back of the room.

_____   16. The instructor *gave* copies of his notes to the people *absent* from yesterday's
                class.

_____   17. Without any *further* delay, all of *us* students left the campus for the weekend.

_____   18. My absence from that small class was *quite noticeable*.

_____   19. The note to *us* from Jim was barely *legible*.

_____   20. I *will send* copies of that letter to a few *interested* people.

_____ 21. The *members* of the inspection team will walk *through* the factory this afternoon.

_____ 22. The *walk* from my office to the *coffee shop* takes about 10 minutes.

_____ 23. My *interest* in that event is far less than *yours*.

_____ 24. *That* jacket in the hall closet is not *mine*.

_____ 25. The *value* of my father's antique car *has appreciated* considerably in the last 5 years.

_____ 26. I have *always* valued your opinion on *financial* matters.

_____ 27. Marge *financed* her new car *with* the credit union.

_____ 28. The store *will credit* my account *for* the amount of the returned merchandise.

_____ 29. Your selection of music for our trip *includes* many of my *favorites*.

_____ 30. The *inclusion* of your name on the list of mayoral candidates is a *bit* of a surprise.

_____ 31. The sight of your name on that list *surprised me*.

_____ 32. The *appearance* of those dolphins *caused* great excitement among the passengers on our cruise.

_____ 33. The *causes* of my financial problems are clear to me *now*.

_____ 34. The first signs of trouble with *my* car *appeared* last week.

_____ 35. The presence of a new coach *troubled some* members of the team.

_____ 36. That development was *troublesome* to *some* of the people in the room.

_____ 37. The Secret Service took the *usual* precautions for the *visit* of the President.

_____ 38. *Usually*, I *visit* my grandmother at the end of every month.

_____ 39. My grandmother *always* bakes an apple *pie* for me.

_____ 40. My grandmother's great skills as a *baker have been* famous in our family for many years.

NAME _____   SCORE _____

Directions: Identify the part of speech of each italicized word by writing one of the following numbers in each space at the left:

1. noun   3. verb   5. adverb
2. pronoun   4. adjective   6. preposition

_____ 1. The weather this *morning* is *clear* and cold.

_____
_____ 2. The boats in the harbor *weathered* last week's storm *with* few problems.

_____ 3. The *angry* man stormed out of the room in the *middle* of the meeting.

_____ 4. *He obviously* disagreed with the statements of the chairperson.

_____ 5. A serious disagreement *had arisen* between the chair and one of the people
_____ *in* the audience.

_____ 6. I *have chaired* such unpleasant meetings in the *past*.

_____
_____ 7. In each meeting, the *unpleasantness* occurred because of a *disagreeable* person in the audience.

_____ 8. *Some* people *disagree* with others in a pleasant fashion.

_____ 9. *Some* of the people at those meetings take the issues *very* seriously.

_____ 10. *These* people sometimes become *angry* and disagreeable.

_____ 11. *Anger* in that kind of meeting is never very *productive*.

_____ 12. In fact, anger in the meetings often *produces negative* reactions in those in
_____ attendance at the meeting.

_____ 13. Anger in a meeting often *negates* any *progress* on an issue.

_____ 14. *One* of the people in the meeting *threatened* a boycott of any action of the
_____ council.

_____ 15. A security guard actually *escorted* one of the angry people *from* the room.

_____ 16. The people in the meeting cheered the *departure* of the angry, *unpleasant*
_____ person.

_____ 17. The chair of the meeting *departed* from the agenda *because of* the disruption
_____ of the meeting.

_____ 18. No one disrupted the meeting *after* that *one* outburst.

_____ 19. The council took two *important* actions *toward* the end of the meeting.

_____ 20. *None* of us *will know* the importance of the actions for several months.

_____ 21. *Few* of the people in town *remember* the day of the great blizzard of 1981.

_____ 22. My *father's* recollection of that day is still very clear in his *memory*.

_____ 23. With *some* of his friends, he *was clearing* a vacant lot down the street from
_____   his house.

_____ 24. *Because of* the thick underbrush, they were working *very* hard with axes,
            saws, and shovels.

_____ 25. *According to* his story, they worked all morning and into the afternoon
            without stopping *more* than a few minutes for lunch.

        26. Suddenly, the skies grew *very dark*.

_____ 27. Dark, *angry* clouds moved in over the town *along with* flurries of snow and
            hail.

_____ 28. Then snow *fell* heavily in *every* area of the town.

_____ 29. Every man on that job ran *quickly* to his house *because of* the wind, snow,
            and sudden drop in temperature.

_____ 30. In Texas, the sudden arrival of *such* heavy snow *in addition to* sudden drops
            in temperature is called a "Blue Norther."

        31. In *their* haste, the men dropped their tools in the *middle* of the vacant lot.

_____ 32. Two days after the end of the great blizzard, the men *returned* to the *lot* for
_____   their tools.

_____ 33. The tools, *under* two feet of snow, were *lost* to sight.

_____ 34. *After* a four-hour search, the men found *all* the tools.

_____ 35. In the search for the tools, the men walked *back and forth* across the lot in a
_____   *carefully* planned pattern.

        36. With the tools back in the *trunks* of their cars, they drove off *again*.

_____ 37. *They* did not return to *that* job until the first snow melt of the spring.

_____ 38. The snow *melted* about a month later after several days of *higher* temperatures.

_____ 39. *In spite of* the long delay, the men completed a *new* baseball field for the kids
_____   in the neighborhood.

_____ 40. At the first game, the kids *expressed* their gratitude to the men with a long
            round of applause.

Directions: Each of the following words is labeled as a noun, verb, adjective, or adverb. In the spaces following the words, write related words of the parts of speech indicated. (Do not use adjectives ending in *ing* or *ed*.) Consult a dictionary when necessary.

Example:

worry (n.)	*worry* (v.)	*worriedly*	(adv.)
1. argument (n.)	_____ (v.)	_____	(adj.)
2. brave (v.)	_____ (adv.)	_____	(adj.)
3. bashfully (adv.)	_____ (n.)	_____	(adj.)
4. casual (adj.)	_____ (adv.)	_____	(n.)
5. dirty (v.)	_____ (adj.)	_____	(n.)
6. charitable (adj.)	_____ (adv.)	_____	(n.)
7. deny (v.)	_____ (n.)	_____	(adj.)
8. embarrass (v.)	_____ (adv.)	_____	(n.)
9. emphasis (n.)	_____ (adj.)	_____	(v.)
10. fallen (adj.)	_____ (v.)	_____	(n.)
11. greedily (adv.)	_____ (n.)	_____	(adj.)
12. hearty (adj.)	_____ (adv.)	_____	(n.)
13. injurious (adj.)	_____ (v.)	_____	(n.)
14. lower (v.)	_____ (adj.)	_____	(n.)
15. luxurious (adj.)	_____ (v.)	_____	(adv.)
16. mysteriously (adv.)	_____ (n.)	_____	(adj.)
17. offend (v.)	_____ (adj.)	_____	(n.)
18. recognize (v.)	_____ (adv.)	_____	(n.)
19. scandal (n.)	_____ (v.)	_____	(adj.)
20. thankful (adj.)	_____ (adv.)	_____	(n.)

Exercise 2A   *Subjects and Verbs*

NAME _____   SCORE _____

Directions: Circle the subject and underline the verb of each sentence. (Some verbs may consist of more than one word.) Then, in the space at the left, identify the italicized parts of speech by writing one of the following numbers:

1. noun	3. verb	5. adverb
2. pronoun	4. adjective	6. preposition

Note that this exercise is an intensive review of the concepts taught in Lesson 1.

___1___ 1. The narrow *lanes* on that old bridge provide little margin *for* errors by a driver.

___6___
___2___ 2. *We* had gone *only* a short distance down the road past that intersection.
_B5_   adverb

___3___ 3. The *men* *will* not *have seen* all the displays by the end of *their* hour-long tour.
_4 3 4_   adj

___6___ 4. The *tears in* the girl's eyes were clear evidence of her *disappointment* with
___1___   her poor grade on that test.

___4___ 5. There is a large *swampy* area out *behind* my uncle's house.
___6___

___6___ 6. *Because of* all that study, *not* one of us made a grade lower than B on the exam.
___4___

___6___ 7. On Saturday I will walk down to the river *for* a swim and some *fishing*.
___4___
___4___ 8. The *fish* population in that river has increased *remarkably* over the past few years.
___5___

___4___ 9. In fact, the numbers of fish in *all* the nearby rivers have increased because of
___1___   the efforts of the people at the state's fish *hatcheries*.

_____ 10. A great *deal* of money has gone into projects for the restoration of *our* streams
_____   and rivers.

_____ 11. That game will stand out in our memories because of our *lopsided* defeat at
_____   the hands of the *other* team.

_____ 12. *Fortunately*, almost all of the rest of the games in that season were great
_____   victories for our side.

_____ 13. The need *for greater* trust among politicians has rarely been more *evident*.

_____ 14. My choice of a late afternoon class *over* an early morning class seemed to me
_____   the *lesser* of two evils.

_____ 15. Because of her high grade on that paper, Joan is probably the *happiest* person
_____   in that class.

_____ 16. With the sun behind the clouds all day long, *today* has been one of the *coolest*
_____   days this month.

_____ 17. Jim, with all his exams behind him, *seems very* happy and relaxed.
_____

21

_____ 18. Alexis appears very grim and determined *because of* the three papers *due* this week.

_____ 19. At the end of the term, we will be *free* of all assignments *for* a short time.

_____ 20. One of us family members has *always* cared for our elderly Aunt Lucy *during* the holidays.

_____ 21. My brother, strong and *handsome*, has always helped me with good advice and an *occasional* loan.

_____ 22. The wonderful aroma of the pizza made *it* an irresistible choice for a midnight *snack*.

_____ 23. The addition of that class to my schedule was *one* of my *better* choices last term.

_____ 24. The *earlier* edition of that novel will not be *usable* for our work this term.

_____ 25. Probably the *more sensible* course of action at that point will be a quick retreat from the scene of the conflict.

_____ 26. In spite of the odds *against* them, all the members of the team performed *admirably*.

_____ 27. Mary, *because of* her training and experience, has proved a *better* choice as treasurer than Jim.

_____ 28. *She* has kept the company's accounts *straight* from her first day on the job.

_____ 29. The problem, *according to* all the sources available to me, has never resolved *itself* in the opinion of most people.

_____ 30. Once inside the canyon, we stood *transfixed* by the *astonishingly* beautiful colors in the rocks on its walls.

_____ 31. *My* uncle's poodle, in comparison to our Great Dane, looks *extremely* small and vulnerable.

_____ 32. Uncle Jim, because of his small size, *has* always *selected* smaller dogs as *pets*.

_____ 33. Because of their *aloof*, independent attitude, I have *never* chosen a cat as a pet.

_____ 34. Dogs, on the other hand, *have* always *been* most faithful and *reliable* companions.

_____ 35. The workers, by the end of the work day, *had finished only* a small part of the stone wall.

____5____ 36. The work had been *very* slow because of the *intermittent* showers and sudden
____4____ downpours throughout the morning.
noun _1_ 37. The *rainstorms*, along with the thunder and lightning, slowed the work *on* the
prep _6_ wall.

_____ 38. *Possibly*, with better weather in the next two days, they *will have* finally *finished* their work.

_____ 39. Progress on *construction* projects is *often* difficult because of delays from weather and shortages of materials.

_____ 40. My friends have never understood my *choice* of construction work as a *career*.

As you know from Lesson 1, the sentence, which is a subject and predicate arranged to make a statement, is the basic unit of written and oral communication. There are just five sentence types or patterns, and learning to recognize those five patterns can help you become a more effective communicator. In this lesson and the following one, we look at the five patterns so that you can learn to use them in your writing.

The nature of the verb is the key to recognizing sentence patterns. There are two types of verbs, **transitive** and **intransitive**. The prefix *trans* means "across," and the letters *it* come from the Latin word meaning "to go," so *transit* means "to go across." The additional prefix *in* means "not," so *intransit* means "not to go across." (Don't confuse the Latin word with the colloquial *in transit*, which means "in the act of going somewhere.")

When an **intransitive verb** is used, the verb does not transfer its action to an object. In the sentence "John spoke softly," the action is *spoke* and the actor is *John*. The action does not "go across" to a noun that receives that action. The verb is intransitive. Some intransitive verbs do not express an action; they simply connect or link the subject to a noun that renames the subject or to an adjective that modifies the subject. These types of intransitive verbs are called **linking verbs**. In the following sentences there is no action:

> John *is* a genius.
> John *is* brilliant.

The subject *John* is simply linked by the verb to a word that identifies or modifies it.

Sentence Patterns 1 and 2 use intransitive verbs. Sentence Patterns 3, 4, and 5 use transitive verbs and are addressed in Lesson 4.

SENTENCE PATTERN 1

Sentence Pattern 1 contains an intransitive verb and is the only sentence pattern that does not require a word to complete the sense of the action. Some activity takes place in each of these sentences, but no completer is needed because the action of the verb is not transferred to anything.

> The child *runs*.
> The tree *fell*.
> The customer *complained* loudly.
> The professor *walked* into the room unexpectedly.

The action of the verb is complete within itself. Pattern 1 sentences nearly always contain modifiers that tell how, when, and where the action occurred:

> Yesterday the neighborhood children played noisily in the vacant lot.

Notice that the material associated with the verb is all adverbial: "When?" *Yesterday*. "How?" *Noisily*. "Where?" *In the vacant lot*. The important characteristic to recognize about a Pattern 1 sentence with an intransitive verb is that there is no noun answering the question "What?" after the verb.

In some Pattern 1 sentences, the purpose of the statement is simply to say that the subject exists. Usually some adverbial material is added to show the place or the time of the existence:

> The glasses *are* in the cabinet.
>
> Flash floods often *occur* in the spring.
>
> There *were* several birds around the feeder.

COMPLEMENTS

Now we need to define a term that identifies an important part of the sentences in the four remaining patterns. As you know, the two parts of any sentence are the subject and the predicate. The core of the predicate is the verb, but the predicate also often includes words that complete the thought of the sentence. Words that follow the verb and complete the thought of the sentence are called **complements**. Complements can be nouns, pronouns, or adjectives, but all serve the same purpose in the sentence: They complete the idea or sense of the sentence.

SENTENCE PATTERN 2

Pattern 2 includes two closely related kinds of sentences. The purpose of the first type of Pattern 2 sentence is to rename the subject, to say that the subject is the same as something else. In the sentence "John is a genius," the noun *genius* is called a **subjective complement** because it completes the verb and renames the subject. (See Supplement.) The intransitive linking verb used in Pattern 2 sentences is often a form of *be*.

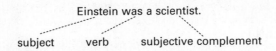

Einstein was a scientist.

subject   verb   subjective complement

Note that both words, *Einstein* and *scientist*, refer to the same thing. There is no action; rather, a connection is established between the subject and the verb.

In the second type of Pattern 2 sentence, the subjective complement is an adjective, a word that describes rather than renames the subject. For example, in the sentence "The child is clever," the subject is joined by the verb to an adjective, again called a subjective complement. Comparatively few verbs serve the linking function. For convenience, you can think of them in three closely related groups:

1. *Be*, the most commonly used linking verb and a few others meaning essentially the same thing (*seem, appear, prove, remain, continue,* and so forth):

> John *is* a talented musician.
>
> The performer *seemed* nervous.
>
> He *remained* calm.
>
> His words *proved* meaningless.

2. *Become*, and a few others like it (*turn, grow, work, get, wear*, and so forth):

> The fabric *wore* thin.
> Later she *became* an accountant.
> Soon he *grew* tired of the game.
> Billy *turned* red from embarrassment.
> The knot *worked* loose.

3. A few verbs referring to the senses (*look, smell, taste, feel, sound*), which can be followed by adjective subjective complements that describe the condition of the subject:

> The roses *look* beautiful in that vase.
> This milk *tastes* sour.

The ability to recognize Pattern 2 sentences will help you understand a few troublesome usage problems that are examined in a later lesson—to understand why, for instance, careful writers use "feel bad" rather than "feel badly": "I *feel* bad about the election results."

SUPPLEMENT

A note about grammatical terminology is needed here. A noun following a linking verb and renaming the subject is sometimes called a *predicate noun* or a *predicate nominative*; an adjective following a linking verb and describing the subject is sometimes called a *predicate adjective*.

> subjective complement (n.) = predicate noun
>   predicate nominative
> subjective complement (adj.) = predicate adjective

English Fundamentals **Online**

After you have completed the Practice Sheets and Exercises in this lesson, you can find additional help and drill work at **MyWritingLab.com**, in the section on Basic Sentence Patterns.

Sentence Patterns 1 & 2

NAME _____   SCORE _____

Directions: Each of the following sentences is either a Pattern 1 or a Pattern 2 sentence with a noun or pronoun subjective complement. If the sentence is a Pattern 1 sentence, write the numeral **1** in the space at the left. If the sentence is a Pattern 2 sentence, write the subjective complement in the space at the left.

_____   1. The two young boys ran quickly down the road.

_____   2. The young mother sang softly to the baby.

_____   3. By that time, I will have been gone for about three hours.

_____   4. My friend John will be a fine representative for the college.

_____   5. Over the years Sam has become an excellent musician.

_____   6. Joanne became an FBI agent after her service in the military.

_____   7. The fabric in that old sail has worn thin.

_____   8. By the end of the day, all of us had worked very hard on that project for several hours.

_____   9. Michelle seemed a perfect choice for that assignment in Alaska.

_____   10. Out on the end of the dock sat an old blue chair.

_____   11. My 5-year-old brother has always seemed a little man in that blue suit.

_____   12. We have been inside the house for two days now because of the blizzard.

_____   13. The lost dog sat on our porch for a whole day.

_____   14. Karen left on a plane for New York City last night about midnight.

_____   15. Under an old, dusty book on the corner of my desk lay a copy of last Monday's to-do list.

_____   16. The little girl toddled around the room with a delighted smile on her face.

_____   17. The limb on that old oak tree has sagged dangerously close to the roof of the garage.

_____   18. With any luck, Jimmy will prove a worthwhile addition to our pitching staff.

_____   19. Sandra, because she has weak public relations skills, is a serious liability to our company.

_____   20. In the past three hours, that light sprinkle of rain has become a downpour.

Directions: Most of the following sentences are Pattern 2 sentences with a noun, pronoun, or adjective subjective complement. If you find a Pattern 1 sentence, put the numeral **1** in the space at the left. If the sentence is a Pattern 2 sentence, write the subjective complement in the space at the left.

_____ 1. Jennifer has become quite successful in her new job.

_____ 2. On Monday Roger will have been here for two weeks.

_____ 3. On my front porch this morning sat the soggy morning paper.

_____ 4. The newspaper on my porch this morning was soggy from the rain.

_____ 5. Marilyn's acceptance in our office has grown very thin in the last few weeks.

_____ 6. Those children at the table in the back of the room seem very skilled at problem solving.

_____ 7. Barbara has always been a highly skilled mechanic.

_____ 8. The milk in my refrigerator will have turned sour by the end of the week.

_____ 9. The knot in the politician's tie had worked loose by the end of his speech.

_____ 10. The air in the room with the broken air conditioner smelled quite stale by the end of the class.

_____ 11. The frightened wild turkeys flew into the tops of the trees at the end of the field.

_____ 12. The notes from that old piano in the basement always sound off-key.

_____ 13. The chorus of that song has always seemed quite humorous to me.

_____ 14. The leaves on all those trees will have turned bright colors by the end of the month.

_____ 15. At the end of that long run, my legs got very shaky.

_____ 16. Max has always gotten seasick on our off-shore fishing trips.

_____ 17. Jan has remained faithful to her favorite baseball team in spite of its dreadful record this season.

_____ 18. For once, I was ready for any question from the teacher on that chapter in the textbook.

_____ 19. Robin, on the other hand, had not prepared very thoroughly for that oral quiz.

_____ 20. Soon, the little boy grew tired of the complex, silly game.

NAME _____ SCORE _____

Directions: These sentences are either Pattern 1 or Pattern 2 sentences. In the first space at the left, write the subject of the sentence. In the second space, write the verb. Many of the verbs consist of more than one word. If the sentence is a Pattern 2 sentence, circle the subjective complement. **Review:** In sentences 1–10, underline the adjectives and bracket the adverbs.

Pattern 1
arrived

1. Most of the members of the softball team arrived at the field about two hours before game time.

Pattern 1

2. The softball players have waited eagerly for this game against their archrivals.

3. This particular game has always been the most important of the season for our team.

Pattern 2

candidates

4. Two of our pitchers will probably be candidates for the USA softball team next year.

5. The anchor of our women's sports program has always been the women's softball team.

Pattern 1

6. At first glance, the questions on the first page of the test seemed quite simple.

7. Unfortunately, the second page, along with all the other pages on the test, proved very complex.

8. The third page, in fact, was almost impossibly difficult.

9. I had worked for the entire period on pages one and two.

Pattern 1

10. At the end of the hour, all of the members of the class remained totally frustrated by the difficulty of the test.

11. The dozen roses in that vase on the corner of the table certainly look beautiful.

12. The roses have continued a bright red for the past four days.

13. The roses, in a beautiful vase, appeared on that table early Monday morning.

14. The person responsible for the gift of the roses has remained anonymous for the entire week.

Pattern 1

15. By the end of the day on Friday, the roses, along with the vase, had quietly disappeared from the table.

16. My schedule of classes for next term will be much easier than this term's schedule.

Pattern 1

17. I have worked much too hard in my classes this term.

Pattern 2

good thing

18. For this next term, an easy schedule will be a good thing because of my heavy commitments to the marching band.

29

Pattern 2
high

19. With an easier schedule, my GPA will remain acceptably high.

20. Then, in the following term, I will return to a harder schedule with several required courses in it.

Pattern 1

21. Some of the people in my neighborhood are upset by the presence of a coyote in a nearby wooded area.

22. Coyotes have always been among the most adaptable mammals on the North American continent.

23. Coyotes originally lived on prairies and plains of the central United States, Canada, and Mexico.

24. With increased population and the spread of farms, these wily animals have adapted to life in the mountains, on islands, and even in cities.

25. The city of Los Angeles, as well as many other cities, has for years been a home to a large coyote population.

26. The diet of coyotes, originally made up of small animals and rodents, is now almost incredibly diverse.

Pattern 1
will dine

27. In cities, coyotes will dine on anything from garbage to small household pets.

Pattern 2
have become

28. Thus, city dwellers have become wary of the presence of coyotes, especially in packs.

Pattern 2
are

29. Although a danger to small animals, coyotes are little or no threat to humans.

30. Nevertheless, the sound of the howls of a pack of coyotes in the hills is a source of fear for many people.

31. Once in the dugout, the team remained there for the duration of the thunderstorm.

32. Because of our hard work during the campaign, we feel bad about our candidate's loss.

33. As good citizens, we have always cooperated with winning candidates.

34. Politics, according to one very successful politician, has always been the art of the possible.

35. My goal after college remains service in the Peace Corps.

36. Last night after midnight, the weather turned very foul, with lightning, thunder, and heavy rains all around.

37. As a young person, I moved with my family to a small farm in Rhode Island.

38. Soon, however, the isolation of the small farm proved a source of considerable worry for my mother and father.

39. Soon, we migrated across the country to California and a middle-sized city.

40. My physics class seems quite optimistic about the next test.

In Sentence Pattern 2 the intransitive verb links the subject to a noun or adjective that completes the idea of the sentence: "Maria is our pitcher"; "Maria is brilliant." When a **transitive verb** is used, the action expressed by the verb "goes across" to some noun that receives the action. That noun is called the **direct object** and is the receiver of the action expressed in the verb. In the sentence "John watched a game," the action (the verb) is *watched*, and the actor (the subject) is *John*; the receiver of the action (the direct object) is *game*. The direct object can be found by asking the question "What?" after the subject and verb have been found. "John watched what? John watched a game."

SENTENCE PATTERN 3

In Pattern 3 sentences the verb is a transitive verb. It does not link or connect; instead, it identifies an action and transfers that action to a receiver or object of the action (the direct object). The subject–verb combination of the sentence does not complete a thought unless there is an object to receive the action named in the verb. For example, in the sentence "The child hits the ball," the subject–verb combination (*child hits*) does not make a complete statement. A complete statement requires that the child hit *something*.

The direct object is always a noun or a noun equivalent, such as a pronoun:

I broke my glasses. What names the activity? *Broke* is the verb. Who broke? *I* is the subject. I broke what? *Glasses*. Thus, *glasses* is the direct object.

Someone saw us. What names the activity? *Saw*. Who saw? *Someone* saw. Someone saw what? *Us* is the direct object.

We need to draw a contrast between a Pattern 2 sentence and a Pattern 3 sentence. Although both patterns require a complement, in a Pattern 2 sentence such as "The child is a genius," the subject is either renamed or modified by the subjective complement. In the sentence "Someone saw us," it is clear that *someone* and *us* are not the same. *Us* is the receiver of the action *saw* and simply cannot be taken to be the same as the *someone* who saw. In both Pattern 2 and Pattern 3 sentences, the thought of the sentence is not complete without a complement, but in Pattern 3 the subject acts upon the complement, the direct object.

SENTENCE PATTERN 4

Pattern 4 sentences also contain a direct object. But because Pattern 4 sentences use verbs such as *give* or *show*, the sentences need a **second** complement to complete their thought. After a transitive verb such as *shows*, *gives*, or *tells*, the direct object (the receiver of the action) answers the question "What?" and an **indirect object** answers the question "To whom?" or "For whom?" Thus, "She sang a lullaby" is a Pattern 3 sentence, but "She gave the children a gift" is a Pattern 4 sentence.

In the sentence "The parents gave the child a present," you can easily see that two complements are used. The sentence mentions the thing that is given (*present*, the direct object) and the person to whom the direct object is given (*child*, the indirect object). Although the indirect object usually names a person, it can name a nonhuman thing, as in "We gave your *application* a careful reading."

Other verbs that are commonly used this way and therefore produce a Pattern 4 structure are *allow*, *assign*, *ask*, *tell*, *write*, *send*, *pay*, *grant*, and others. Nearly all sentences using such verbs can make essentially the same statement by using a prepositional phrase, usually beginning with the preposition *to* or *for*. When the prepositional phrase is present in the sentence, it is a Pattern 3 sentence.

> The postman brought me a letter. [Pattern 4; *me* is an indirect object.]
> The postman brought a letter to me. [Pattern 3; *me* is the object of a preposition.]
> Mother bought us some candy. [Pattern 4]
> Mother bought some candy for us. [Pattern 3]

SENTENCE PATTERN 5

Pattern 5 sentences regularly use verbs such as *consider*, *call*, *think*, *find*, *make*, *elect*, *appoint*, and *name*. There are two closely related types of Pattern 5 sentences. Each type begins like a Pattern 3 sentence:

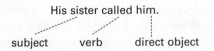

His sister called him.

    subject   verb   direct object

But the nature of the verb *called* allows the use of a second complement answering the question "What?" after *called him*. His sister called him what?

> His sister called him a genius.

The reference of the two nouns following the verb is a key to the difference between this type of sentence and a Pattern 4 sentence. In a Pattern 4 sentence the two noun complements refer to different things, but in a Pattern 5 sentence they refer to the same thing.

> Mother made us some fudge. [Pattern 4: *us* and *fudge* refer to different things.]
> This experience made John an activist. [Pattern 5: *John* and *activist* are the same thing.]

Thus, there are two complements in Pattern 5 sentences. The one closer to the verb is the direct object. The second complement is called the **objective complement**. In the first type of Pattern 5 sentence, the objective complement is a noun that *renames* the direct object. In the second type of Pattern 5 sentence, the objective complement is an adjective that *describes* the direct object.

> His sister called him a genius.
> His sister called him brilliant.

Because the objective complement renames or describes the direct object, we can use a handy test to help us recognize Pattern 5: The insertion of *to be* between the complements will give us an acceptable English wording.

We appointed Jones [to be] our representative.
I thought this action [to be] unnecessary.

Some adjective objective complements are very important to the meaning of the verb. Thus, it is sometimes effective to place these objective complements immediately after the verb and before the direct object:

Usual order: He set the caged animals [D.O.] free [O.C.].
Variation: He set free [O.C.] the caged animals [D.O.].

SUPPLEMENT

One special kind of verb makes it difficult to distinguish between a direct object and the object of a preposition. Here are two examples:

Harry jumped off the box.
Harry took off his raincoat.

The first sentence is Pattern 1. *Off* is a preposition, *box* is the object of the preposition, and the prepositional phrase is used as an adverbial modifier because it tells *where* Harry jumped. The second sentence is Pattern 3. The verb, with its adverbial modifier *off*, is the equivalent of the transitive verb *remove*. *Raincoat* is the direct object.

There is another way to distinguish between the adverbial use and the prepositional use of such a word as *off* in the preceding examples. When the word is a vital adverbial modifier of the verb, it can be used in either of two positions: following the verb or following the direct object.

Harry took off his raincoat.
Harry took his raincoat off.

When the word is a preposition, the alternate position is not possible: "Harry jumped the box off" is not an English sentence. Here are some other examples of verbs with adverbial modifiers. Notice that in each case you can easily find a transitive verb synonym for the combination:

Give up [*relinquish*] her rights.
Leave out [*omit*] the second chapter.
Put out [*extinguish*] the fire.
Make over [*alter*] an old dress.
Make up [*invent*] an excuse.

SUMMARY OF VERBS USED IN DIFFERENT SENTENCE PATTERNS

1. **Verbs that serve a linking function and commonly form Pattern 2 sentences:**
   be, seem, appear, prove, remain, continue, become, turn, grow, work, get, wear, look, smell, taste, feel, sound

2. **Verbs that commonly produce Pattern 4 sentences:**
   allow, assign, ask, tell, write, send, pay, grant

3. **Verbs that commonly produce Pattern 5 sentences:**
   consider, call, think, find, make, elect, appoint, name

English Fundamentals Online

After you have completed the Practice Sheets and Exercises in this lesson, you can find additional help and drill work at **MyWritingLab.com**, in the section on Basic Sentence Patterns; Varying Sentence Structure.

NAME _____   SCORE _____

Directions: Each of these sentences is a Pattern 3 sentence. Circle the subject and underline the verb in each sentence. In the space at the left, copy the word that is the direct object of the verb.

service 1. The company has always provided the best possible service to its customers.

class 2. I have added one more class to my schedule for next term.

machine 3. The operator always runs that machine very carefully.

confidence 4. The team feels great confidence about this week's game.

problems 5. By the end of the evening, Jim will have worked those five difficult problems in the math assignment.

race, 6. Before today, we had never seen a more exciting race.

identity 7. The novel foretold the identity of the killer within the first 100 pages.

nephew 8. The animated characters in that movie for children frightened my young nephew very badly.

pep rally 9. Five hundred people attended last night's pep rally.

_____ 10. Because of our full schedules, none of us have time for many extracurricular activities.

_____ 11. I dropped all my books in the middle of my bedroom floor.

_____ 12. You will find yesterday's lecture notes somewhere in that pile of stuff.

_____ 13. We carried most of those old clothes to the car.

_____ 14. The company has ordered new computers for every member of the office staff.

_____ 15. Everyone in the office will receive a new computer within the next two weeks.

_____ 16. At that point, we will have reached a new level of efficiency.

_____ 17. The company has never replaced all the computers in this office at the same time.

_____ 18. The two of us have not found the key in spite of an intense search of the house.

_____ 19. We will probably call a locksmith a little later in the afternoon.

_____ 20. Neither of us has found any other solution to our problem.

Directions: The following are Pattern 3, 4, or 5 sentences. Identify the italicized complement by writing one of the following abbreviations in the space at the left:

     D.O. [direct object]   I.O. [indirect object]

     O.C. [objective complement]

_____   1. My father has always considered Cousin Mark a very intelligent *person.*

_____   2. The instructor will give your *paper* a very thorough examination.

_____   3. The neighbors found a lost *kitten* behind their garage.

_____   4. The security system in our office detected an *intruder* last night about 11:30 P.M.

_____   5. Vanessa has found a better *solution* to our problem than yours.

_____   6. One of the staff members will contact *you* before the end of business today.

_____   7. The instructor allowed *me* two more days for the submission of my project.

_____   8. My grandfather always told *us* very interesting stories about his adventures as a sailor.

_____   9. The prosecutor has granted that *man* immunity from prosecution in exchange for his testimony.

_____ 10. The manager has made Ellen Thompson our *delegate* to that conference.

_____ 11. By the opening game in the season, the coach will have appointed Marcus Adams *captain* of the team.

_____ 12. The people in this district elected Marie Lopez their *representative* in Congress.

_____ 13. The kind man set the trapped animal *free.*

_____ 14. The compliment from the boss made Sherry very *happy.*

_____ 15. One of my friends has a large *collection* of the songs of early country music stars.

_____ 16. He has shown *me* the collection several times.

_____ 17. The company has rewarded *Alex* with a large increase in his salary.

_____ 18. The company has given *Alex* a large increase in his salary.

_____ 19. The manager considers Alex a very fine *worker.*

_____ 20. Martin took off his wet *jacket* just outside the door.

Exercise 4   *Complements of Transitive Verbs*

NAME _____   SCORE _____

Directions: Identify the italicized complement by writing one of the following abbreviations in the space at the left:

S.C. [subjective complement]   D.O. [direct object]

I.O. [indirect object]   O.C. [objective complement]

Review: Circle the subject and underline the verb in each of the following sentences.

_OC_   1. Everyone in the office thought your work on that project *brilliant*.

_IO_   2. All of the people at the scene showed the *firefighters* great respect.

_DO_   3. All people at the scene showed great *respect* to the firefighters.

_SC_   4. The crowd at the scene was *full* of admiration for the work of the firefighters.

_SC_   5. The work of the firefighters was *admirable* in every way.

?,?,?   _____   6. The three little kids jumped off the high diving *board* into the pool. ✗

_DO_   7. The instructor took his *jacket* off before the beginning of his lecture. ✗

_IO_   8. The teacher showed the young *students* the procedures for leaving the building for a fire drill.

_OC_   9. The committee considered Joe Smith the best *candidate* for that position.

_IO_   10. One of the architects will show *you* the layout of that building before work tomorrow.

_OC_   11. The other debaters considered the premise of my argument *unsound*.

_IO_   12. We taught my little *brother* a new, useful knot.

_DO_   13. He, in turn, helped *us* with his new video game.

_DO_   14. One of my friends has known a *writer* of graphic novels for many years.

_IO_   15. The instructor assigned the *class* a long, complicated reading assignment.

_SC_   16. At the beginning of the work, the assignment seemed impossibly *difficult*.

_SC_   17. After a few pages, however, the concepts became *clear* to us.

_DO_   18. Most of us finished the *work* without much difficulty.

_OC_   19. Only a few members of the class thought the assignment genuinely *hard*.

_IO_   20. The instructor gave *everyone* in the class a very good grade on that assignment.

Directions: Using appropriate forms of the verbs indicated, write 20 original sentences illustrating the following sentence patterns:

Sentences 1–5	Pattern 2	Sentences 11–15	Pattern 4
Sentences 6–10	Pattern 3	Sentences 16–20	Pattern 5

Use the tenses of the verb indicated in parentheses.

1. seem (past) _____

2. wear (past perfect) _____

3. grow (present perfect) _____

4. become (past) _____

5. smell (present) _____

6. grow (present perfect) _____

7. throw (present perfect) _____

8. see (past) _____

9. weave (past perfect) _____

10. take (future perfect) _____

11. give (present perfect) _____

12. tell (past) _____

13. pay (past perfect) _____

14. bring (past) _____

15. write (future perfect) _____

16. think (past perfect) _____

17. consider (present) _____

18. appoint (past) _____

19. make (present perfect) _____

20. elect (past) _____

In this lesson you will examine a few more forms and uses of verbs, including some additional auxiliary verbs. With these forms and those that you have already examined, you will be acquainted with nearly all of the verb forms that the average speaker and writer will ever use.

In Lesson 2 you examined the partial conjugation of three verbs: *earn*, *grow*, and *be*. You may want to refer to that conjugation (pages 9–10) as we discuss a few more points about changes in verb form.

Third-person singular verbs in the present tense end in *s* (or *es*): *earns*, *teaches*, *is*, *has*. Notice that on nouns the *s* (*es*) ending shows a plural form, whereas on verbs it shows a singular form:

dogs, peaches	(plural nouns)
wags, sniffs	(singular verbs)

If you review the conjugation of the verb *be* in Lesson 2, you will notice the verb is completely irregular. Unlike any other verb in the language, it has three forms (*am*, *is*, and *are*) in the present tense and two forms (*was* and *were*) in the past tense.

In general, the tenses are used as follows:

Present:	Action occurring at the present moment.
	He *earns* a good salary.
Past:	Action occurring at a definite time before the present moment.
	Last year he *earned* a good salary.
Future:	Action occurring at some time beyond the present moment.
	Next year he *will earn* a good salary.
Present perfect:	Action continuing up to the present moment.
	So far this year he *has earned* $10,000.
Past perfect:	Action continuing to a fixed moment in the past.
	Before leaving for college, he *had earned* $10,000.
Future perfect:	Action continuing to a fixed moment in the future.
	By next Christmas he *will have earned* $10,000.

In Lesson 21 you will be reminded of a few usage problems involving tenses.

PRINCIPAL PARTS

We noted in Lesson 2 that *earn* is a regular verb and *grow* is an irregular verb. We customarily make use of three distinctive forms, called the **principal parts** of the verb, to show the difference between regular and irregular verbs. The following are the principal parts:

- *Base* or *infinitive*, the "name" of the verb, used in the present tense with *s* (*es*) added in the third-person singular
- *Past*, the form used in the simple past tense
- *Past participle*, the form used in the three perfect tenses

In all regular verbs, the past and the past participle are alike, formed simply by the addition of *ed* to the base form (or only *d* if the base word ends in *e*). Thus, *earn* becomes *earned*. Irregular verbs are more complicated because, for nearly all of them, the past tense and the past participle are not spelled alike. Thus, the past tense of *grow* is *grew*, and the past participle of *grow* is *grown*. Following are the three forms of some irregular verbs illustrating spelling changes and endings:

Base	Past	Past Participle
be	was, were	been
become	became	become
bite	bit	bitten
break	broke	broken
catch	caught	caught
do	did	done
eat	ate	eaten
put	put	put
ring	rang	rung
run	ran	run
see	saw	seen

(You will study more principal parts of verbs and the usage problems associated with them in Lesson 21.) Both regular and irregular verbs add *ing* to their base form to produce the **present participle**. The present participle is often used with auxiliary verbs.

AUXILIARY VERBS

In the sample conjugation in Lesson 2, you observed the use of *will* and *have* as auxiliary verbs in the future tense and the perfect tenses. Another important auxiliary is *be*, used with the present participle (the *ing* form of the main verb) to produce what is called the **progressive form**. As an example of its use, suppose someone asks you what you are doing in your English class. You probably would not reply, "Right now, we *review* parts of speech." Instead, you probably would say, "Right now, we *are reviewing* parts of speech," to show that the action is not fixed in an exact moment of time but is a continuing activity. This very useful type of verb occurs in all six tenses:

We are reviewing.
We were reviewing.
We will be reviewing.
We have been reviewing.
We had been reviewing.
We will have been reviewing.

Another type of auxiliary verb includes *may*, *might*, *must*, *can*, *could*, *would*, and *should*. *May*, *can*, and *might* are used to suggest possibility. *Can* sometimes also suggests capability.

I may go to town tomorrow.   (If certain conditions exist.)
I might go to town tomorrow.   (If certain conditions exist.)
I can go to town tomorrow.   (I am able to go.)

Must indicates an obligation:

I must go to town.

Could is used to indicate ability, possibility, or permission in the past tense:

I could have gone to town.   (If I had wanted to go.)

These words are called **modal auxiliaries**, and they are used the way *will* is used:

I *should study* this weekend.
I *should have studied* last weekend.

Occasionally, *do* acts as a modal auxiliary and combines with the base form of a main verb to make an "emphatic" form: "But I *did* pay that bill last month." In Lesson 6 you will examine the much more common use of the *do* auxiliary in questions and negatives.

Note that each of these modals attaches a slightly different meaning to the verb. A careful writer will study the dictionary for precise meanings and distinctions.

Other variations of some modals and time auxiliaries make use of *to* in the verb phrase:

Mr. Nelson *has to retire* [must retire] early.
You *ought to eat* [should eat] more vegetables.
I *used to be* a secretary.
Jim *was supposed to be* here at 10 o'clock.
I *am to depart* for Miami early in the morning.
I *am going to depart* for Miami early in the morning.
We *meant to leave* much earlier today.

Here are a few other points to remember about auxiliary verbs:

1. *Have*, *be*, and *do* are not used exclusively as auxiliaries; they are three of the most commonly used main verbs:

   I *have* a brown pen. [Main verb]
   I *have* lost my brown pen. [Auxiliary]
   He *is* a good speaker. [Main verb]
   He *is* becoming a good speaker. [Auxiliary]
   He *did* a good job for us. [Main verb]
   Yes, I *did* embellish the story somewhat. [Auxiliary]

2. When the verb unit contains auxiliaries, short adverbial modifiers may separate parts of the whole verb phrase:

> We *have* occasionally *been* sailing.
> He *has*, of course, *been telling* the truth.

3. In a few set expressions following introductory adverbs (usually adverbs of time), the subject is placed within the verb phrase between an auxiliary and the main verb:

> Only lately *have* I *learned* to drive.
> Rarely *do* we *turn on* the television set.

English Fundamentals Online

After you have completed the Practice Sheets and Exercises in this lesson, you can find additional help and drill work at **MyWritingLab.com,** in the section on Basic Sentence Patterns; Varying Sentence Structure.

Auxiliary Verbs; Basic Sentence Patterns

NAME _____ SCORE _____

Directions: Most of these sentences contain at least one auxiliary verb. (Some have two; some have three.) Copy the auxiliary verbs in the first space at the left. In the second space, write **1, 2, 3, 4,** or **5** to identify the sentence pattern. If the sentence does not contain an auxiliary verb, write the base form of the verb in the first space.

_____
_____
1. By tomorrow morning, I will have slept only three hours in the last 24.

_____
_____
2. At the end of the day, the men had been working for two hours on that computer.

_____
_____
3. The team has seemed very tired during the last two practices.

_____
_____
4. Melanie felt well enough for work this afternoon.

_____
_____
5. You will find my car at the very back of the parking lot.

_____
_____
6. They could have left the books on that back table.

_____
_____
7. The Boy Scouts should have showed us the easy way out of that swamp.

_____
_____
8. The instructor has been paying the members of the class high compliments for our work.

_____
9. The manager finds Juan's work excellent.

_____
_____
10. In spite of the late hour, Marcie has not yet arrived on the campus.

_____
_____
11. She should have been meeting us regularly for review.

_____
_____
12. She did feel very bad yesterday afternoon.

_____
_____
13. She has actually run a high fever for the past two days.

_____
_____
14. She probably should have spent the last two days at home.

_____
_____
15. Thus, she could not have given us the flu.

_____
_____
16. The weather forecasters think the prospects for snow excellent.

_____
_____
17. Most of us do not find the forecasters' work very reliable.

_____
_____
18. The personnel office will be giving your application very careful attention.

_____ 19. You may ask me any question from that chapter of the textbook.

_____ 20. By 11:00 A.M. Max should have been taking this package next
_____   door to the post office.

_____ 21. No one in this office has seen Jim since yesterday afternoon.

_____ 22. The class does not find any of the instructor's jokes amusing.

_____ 23. One of Karen's friends is a candidate for a Rhodes Scholarship.

_____ 24. The weather has been sunny for the past three days.

_____ 25. We have not had that much sunshine for the past month.

_____ 26. I will have to walk from home to the campus tomorrow morning.

_____ 27. Matt can take one extra course next term.

_____ 28. Most of the members of the office staff will have been working
_____   here for three years or more by next January.

_____ 29. One of us should have already gone down the street to the
     delicatessen for some sandwiches.

_____ 30. Next week the football team will fly across the country to the
_____   West Coast for a game.

_____ 31. Most of the team members have been anticipating the trip because
_____   of its length and the importance of the game.

_____ 32. Veteran travelers have always considered such a long trip a
_____   moderately unpleasant experience.

_____ 33. Kathryn might lend Andrea the lecture notes from Wednesday's class.

_____ 34. Walt tried, without success, his Aunt Mabel's recipe for apple pie.

_____ 35. In spite of its beautiful shape and color, the pie did not taste at all
_____   good.

_____ 36. No one should be attempting a new recipe without help from an
_____   experienced cook.

_____ 37. Aunt Mabel must have given Walt that recipe on his last visit to her.

_____ 38. Despite the failure of the pie, we all found Walt's interest in
_____   cooking commendable.

_____ 39. Walt's determination will almost surely make his next effort at
_____   baking successful.

_____ 40. His friends should not have been laughing at Walt's first effort as
_____   a baker.

NAME _____   SCORE _____

Directions: In the first space at the left of the sentence, write the base form of the verb. In the second space, write any auxiliary verbs. Some sentences may not have auxiliary verbs. If it is necessary, use a dictionary to find the base form of the verb. **Review:** In the first ten sentences, circle the prepositions and bracket the adverbs.

break
have
1. We have not broken the code for that secret message.
adv.

grow
has
2. The team has grown very tired of that repetitious drill.

enjoy
would have
3. I would have enjoyed a piece of Aunt Emma's delicious cherry pie.

work
will have
4. By the end of the week, my project team will have worked on that phase of the project for ten days.

attend
could
5. Thomas could not attend that meeting because of a prior commitment.
adv.

do
has
6. Anne has not done any more work on that assignment since yesterday afternoon.

go
must have
7. In our haste, we must have gone past that building at least three times.

ring
has
8. That annoying bell has rung at least three times this morning without any reason.

see
will be
9. We will be seeing Barbara and her friend Cathy at the end of the week.

eat
had
10. None of us had eaten such a delicious meal in a long time.

bite
has
11. That dog has never bitten anyone, at least not up until today.

be
should have
12. Uncle James should have been more wary of that salesman's tricky sales pitch.

do
should have
13. Before the day of the exam, everyone in the class should have done a comprehensive review of the materials in the text.

grow
did
14. In spite of its length, I did not grow impatient with that movie because of its terrific plot.

do
did
15. Hugh certainly did a great job on the finish of that cabinet.

Directions: In the space at the left, write one of the following to identify the function of the italicized words:

S.C. [subjective complement]   I.O. [indirect object]

D.O. [direct object]   O.C. [objective complement]

If the italicized word is not a complement, leave the space blank. Circle every auxiliary verb.

O C   1. My little dog has long considered that plastic bone his favorite *toy.*

I O   2. We did show *Richard* that report of the accident.

D̶O̶   3. But we have not shown the report to anyone *else.*

D̶O̶   4. On the sidewalk in front of my house, I found a shiny *coin.*

S̶C̶   5. James has always been one of my best *friends.*

S C   6. That type of assignment has always seemed unnecessarily *complicated* to me.

D O   7. The instructor in that class should not give such complicated *assignments.*

I O   8. The manager has granted the entire *staff* a day off next week.

D̶O̶   9. One of my favorite movies is playing on *television* tonight.

D O   10. I have not watched that *movie* in several years.

D O   11. You should join *me* tonight for that movie.

I O   12. I could show *you* the list of actors in that movie.

O C   13. I have always thought the actors in that movie very *talented.*

S C   14. You can be my *guest* for supper also.

D O   15. Because of the movie, I did not plan *anything* else for tonight.

D O   16. No one in the class could have finished that *test* within the allotted time.

O C   17. We all thought the test unnecessarily *long.*

D O   18. We probably could have displayed all our *knowledge* on that subject in half the time.

SC D̶O̶   19. By the end of the test period, we were all feeling *antagonistic* toward the teacher.

I O   20. One of the members of the class did not give the test paper to the *instructor.*

Any long piece of writing made up exclusively of basic sentences would be too monotonous to read. You should think of the basic sentences not as models for your writing but as elementary units, important because they are the structures from which more effective sentences develop. In this lesson, we look at two alterations of basic sentence patterns:

1. Sentences that use passive verbs
2. Sentences in the form of a question

Lessons 7 through 11 then show how basic sentences can be combined and certain elements can be reduced to subordinate clauses and phrases to produce varied, well-developed sentences.

PASSIVE VOICE

In Lesson 2 you examined a partial conjugation of the verb *earn*. The forms listed there are in the active voice, which means that the subject is the doer of the action. A more complete conjugation would include the passive voice. In the passive voice, the subject is not the *doer* of the action; it is the *receiver* of the action. Thus, the verb is always transitive. Passive verb forms make use of the auxiliary verb *be* combined with the past participle of the verb, as shown in the following illustration of the third-person singular in the six tenses:

> This amount is earned.
> This amount was earned.
> This amount will be earned.
> This amount has been earned.
> This amount had been earned.
> This amount will have been earned.

The present and past tenses of progressive verbs can also be shifted to the passive voice, giving us forms in which *be* is used in two auxiliary capacities in the same verb form:

> These cars *are being sold* at a loss.
> These cars *were being sold* at a loss.

Because only transitive verbs have passive forms, only sentence patterns 3, 4, and 5 can be altered to the passive voice. When the idea of a Pattern 3 sentence in the active voice is expressed with a passive verb, there is no direct object (complement) in the sentence:

Active voice: Children play games.
Passive voice: Games are played [by children].

If the doer of the verb's action is expressed in a sentence using a passive verb, the doer must be the object of the preposition *by*. When a Pattern 4 sentence is altered to form a passive construction, the indirect object that follows the active verb sometimes becomes the subject of the passive verb:

Active voice:	John gave Allen a model plane.
Passive voice:	Allen was given a model plane [by John].

Here the passive verb is followed by a complement, *plane*, which we continue to call a direct object in spite of the fact that it follows a passive verb. It is also possible, in a Pattern 4 sentence, to make the direct object the subject of a passive verb and the indirect object a prepositional phrase, making the sentence read thus:

The model plane was given to Allen (by John).

Notice also how a Pattern 5 sentence can be given a different kind of expression by means of a passive verb:

Active voice:	The parents consider the child a genius.
	The parents consider the child clever.
Passive voice:	The child is considered a genius [by the parents].
	The child is considered clever [by the parents].

In these sentences the direct object becomes the subject, but the passive verb requires a complement (*genius, clever*). Because the complement renames or describes the subject, it is called a subjective complement.

The passive voice serves a real purpose in effective communication: It should be used when the *doer* of the action is unknown or is of secondary interest in the statement. In such a situation, the writer, wishing to focus attention on the *receiver* of the action, places that unit in the emphatic subject position. The passive verb form makes this arrangement possible. Thus, instead of some vague expression, such as "Somebody should wash these windows," we can say, "These windows *should be washed*."

Sometimes the passive voice is described as "weak." Admittedly, some writers do get into the habit of using the passive form when there is little justification for it. In most narrative writing, the doer of the action is logically the subject of the verb. "The fullback crossed the goal line" would certainly be preferred to "The goal line was crossed by the fullback," a version that gives the same information but tends to stop any action suggested by the sentence. The passive voice also lends itself to a kind of muddied, heavy-footed writing that produces prose like this:

It *is* now *rumored* that the secretary of defense *has been informed* that contingent plans *have been made* to. . . .

The writer of such a sentence, however, probably finds that the passive voice effectively hides the identity of the person who is spreading the rumor, who has informed the secretary of defense, and who has made the plans. This use of the passive voice creates an impersonal, bureaucratic language popular in many institutions.

You should practice using passive constructions so you can use this important device when it is called for. Equally important, if a criticism of your writing mentions doubtful uses of the passive voice, you need to be able to recognize passive verbs in order to change them when necessary.

QUESTIONS

In the sentence types you examined in earlier lessons, you noted the normal positioning of the main sentence parts: the subject first, followed by the verb, followed by the complement, if any. In questions, however, other arrangements are possible. As we study these new structures, we must first recognize the fact that there are two kinds of questions:

1. Questions answered by *yes* or *no*
2. Questions answered by information

QUESTIONS ANSWERED BY *YES* OR *NO*

In the following paired sentences, the first sentence is a statement and the second sentence a related question. These sentences demonstrate how the structure of a yes/no question differs from that of a statement.

1. Beth is happy.   Is Beth happy?

2. You were there.   Were you there?

3. You see Ms. Locke often.   Do you see Ms. Locke often?

4. You heard the announcement.   Did you hear the announcement?

Notice from these examples that if the verb is *be* in the present or past tense, the subject and the *be* form (*am*, *are*, *is*, *was*, or *were*) reverse positions. With other one-word verbs in the present or past tense, the proper form of the auxiliary *do* is used, followed by the subject and the base form of the main verb.

If the verb already has an auxiliary, the subject follows the auxiliary verb. If there are two or more auxiliaries, the subject follows the first one.

5. You have seen the movie.   Have you seen the movie?

6. They will arrive later.   Will they arrive later?

7. The house is being painted.   Is the house being painted?

8. He should have been told.   Should he have been told?

When the verb is *have* in the present tense, two versions of the question are possible: the subject–verb reversal and the *do* auxiliary. (See Supplement 1.)

9. You have enough money.   Have you enough money?

10. You have enough money.   Do you have enough money?

QUESTIONS ANSWERED BY INFORMATION

Some questions ask for information rather than for a *yes* or *no* response. These questions make use of words called **interrogatives**, words that stand for unknown persons, things, or descriptive qualities. The most commonly used interrogatives are these:

Pronouns:	*who (whom), which, what*
Adjectives:	*whose, which, what*
Adverbs:	*when, where, why, how*

The interrogative pronoun *who*, which stands for an unknown person or persons, has three forms:

1. *Who*, when it is used as a subject or a subjective complement
2. *Whose*, when it is used as a possessive modifier of a noun
3. *Whom*, when it is used as an object

(In a later lesson you will learn that these three forms of *who* have another important use in subordinate clauses; the choice between *who* and *whom* as a problem of usage is discussed more extensively in Lesson 24.)

In questions using these interrogatives, the normal arrangement of the main sentence parts is retained only when the interrogative is the subject or a modifier of the subject. Here again we use paired statements and related questions to demonstrate these structures:

1. *My brother* [S.] paid the bill. *Who* [S.] paid the bill?

2. *Five cars* [S.] were damaged. *How* many cars [S.] were damaged?

In all other situations the subject–verb position is altered as it is with yes/no questions. The interrogative word, or the unit containing the interrogative word, stands at the beginning of the sentence to signal that a question, not a statement, is forthcoming:

I studied *geometry* [D.O.] last night.
What [D.O.] did you study last night?

You saw *Jim* [D.O.] at the party.
Whom [D.O.] did you see at the party?

She is Mother's *cousin* [S.C.].
Who [S.C.] is she?

We can use Bill's *car* [D.O.].
Whose car [D.O.] can we use?

You spent 15 *dollars* [D.O.].
How much money [D.O.] did you spend?

You [S.] called *Bob* [D.O.] a *friend* [O.C.].
Who [S.] called Bob a friend?

Whom [D.O.] did you call a friend?
What [O.C.] did you call Bob?

When the interrogative unit is the object of a preposition, two arrangements of the question are often possible:

1. The entire prepositional phrase may stand at the beginning.
2. The interrogative may stand at the beginning with the preposition in its usual position.

> The speaker was referring *to the mayor*.
> *To whom* was the speaker referring?
> *Whom* was the speaker referring to?

(See Supplement 2.)

SUPPLEMENT 1

The type of verb also determines the structuring of sentences that are negative rather than positive. The positioning of the negator *not* (or its contraction, *n't*) depends on the presence or absence of an auxiliary verb. Sentences using *be* or *have* must be considered special cases.

1. If the verb is *be* in the present tense or in the past tense, used either as the main verb or as an auxiliary verb, the *not* follows the *be* form:

> I *am not* pleased with the report.
> He *was not* [wasn't] available.
> They *were not* [weren't] invited.

2. With other one-word verbs in the present or past tense, the proper form of the auxiliary *do* is used followed by the negator and the base form of the main verb:

> I *do not* [don't] expect a reward.
> He *does not* [doesn't] attend regularly.
> We *did not* [didn't] respond.

3. If the verb already has an auxiliary, the negator follows the auxiliary. When there are two or more auxiliaries, the *not* follows the first one:

> We *could not* [couldn't] see very well.
> I *may not* have understood him.
> They *will not* [won't] refund my money.
> This cake *ought not* to have been baked so long.

4. When *have* in the present tense is the main verb, two negative forms are possible:

> I *have not* [haven't] enough time to play.
> I *do not* [don't] have enough time to play.

SUPPLEMENT 2

At the informal language level, another version—"*Who* was the speaker referring to?"—is often found, despite the traditional demand for the objective case for the object of a preposition. The formal level of both spoken and written English calls for "*To whom* was the speaker referring?"

English Fundamentals Online

After you have completed the Practice Sheets and Exercises in this lesson, you can find additional help and drill work at **MyWritingLab.com**, in the section on Consistent Verb Tense and Active Voice.

Alterations of Basic Sentence Patterns: Passive Verbs; Questions

NAME _____   SCORE _____

Directions: These sentences follow patterns 3, 4, or 5. In the first space at the left, write the pattern number. In the second space, write the verb form used when the italicized word in the sentence becomes the subject of a passive voice verb.

___4___
will be sent   Tomorrow Jim will send you a *report* on that matter.

___5___   1. The president appointed *Marcia* his new executive assistant.

_____   2. We have given your *proposal* a very thorough examination.

_____   3. The company should find a new *supplier* for that particular part.

_____   4. The union members will probably make *Marlene* their new representative.

_____   5. Surely the members consider *Marlene* a fine replacement for Jim Johnson.

_____   6. Marcia could send the president a *copy* of that report on the performance of our branch office in Pittsburgh.

_____   7. The copy of that report will evaluate the *performance* of that office for the past six months.

_____   8. We thought the *performance* of that office over the past six months excellent.

_____   9. The report, however, shows lower *earnings* by that office over the past six months.

_____   10. Thus, the people in that office must double their *efforts* in the next earnings period.

Directions: This exercise contrasts the structure of a question with the structure of a statement. In the space at the left, copy the word from the question that serves the function indicated in the parentheses in the statement:

S. [subject]	S.C. [subjective complement] D.O. [direct object]
O.C. [objective complement]	O.P. [object of preposition]

_____   1. What color did they paint that outside wall of the garage?
(O.C.)   They painted the outside wall of the garage a bright red. (O.C.)

_____   2. How many students attended last night's pep rally?
(S.)   Two hundred students attended last night's pep rally. (S.)

_____   3. What are those people at the meeting concerned about?
(O.P.)   Those people at the meeting are concerned about traffic safety. (O.P.)

_____   4. Who was the leader of that political party in 2005?
(S.)   William Jackson was the leader of that political party in 2005. (S.)

_____   5. Who will be the leader of that political party next year?
(S.C.)   The leader of that political party next year will be Joan Jenkins. (S.C.)

_____   6. What will I find on page 105 of the textbook?
(D.O.)   I will find an outline of the previous chapter on page 105 of the textbook. (D.O.)

_____   7. What did Jack Barber apply for?
(O.P.)   Jack Barber applied for the sales manager's job. (O.P.)

_____   8. Has the president appointed Jack Barber sales manager?
(O.C.)   The president appointed Jack Barber sales manager. (O.C.)

_____   9. Will the new team captain be Allison Reynolds?
(S.C.)   The new team captain will be Allison Reynolds. (S.C.)

_____   10. Will Allison Reynolds be the new team captain?
(S.)   Allison Reynolds will be the new team captain. (S.)

_____   11. Which applicant is best qualified for that job?
(S.C.)   The last applicant for that job is best qualified. (S.C.)

_____   12. What did you find in your examination of that ledger?
(D.O.)   I found some very strange entries in my examination of that ledger. (D.O.)

_____   13. To whom did you give the money for the field trip?
(O.P.)   I gave the money for the field trip to Mark Rodgers. (O.P.)

_____   14. Did the coach make Larkin the starting quarterback?
(O.C.)   The coach made Larkin the starting quarterback. (O.C.)

_____   15. Will Larkin be the starting quarterback?
(S.C.)   Larkin will be the starting quarterback. (S.C.)

Alterations of Basic Sentence Patterns:
Passive Verbs; Questions

Directions: Each of the following sentences contains a verb in the passive voice. Underline the verb. Rewrite each sentence using an active-voice verb. (You will need to supply a logical subject if the passive verb does not do so.) If your rewrites are done correctly, the first four sentences will follow Pattern 3, the next three will follow Pattern 4, and the last three will follow Pattern 5. **Review:** For each of the sentences printed below, write the base form of the verb at the end of the sentence.

1. Within the first 45 minutes, all the tickets to that concert had been bought by adoring fans.

   _____

2. The disappearance of that money will be carefully investigated by the police.

   _____

3. The sailor's journey was carefully documented by the film maker.

   _____

4. The World Cup finals were watched by hundreds of millions around the world.

   _____

5. Every student was given a copy of the schedule of events for the conference.

   _____

6. All of us should have been shown that new procedure for data entry.

   _____

7. We should have been taught that new procedure for data entry by the IT manager.

   _____

8. My cell phone has been made obsolete by that new model.

   _____

9. By next week our office will be made completely paperless by that new computer system.

   _____

10. The new medicine was proved effective against that disease by that study.

   _____

Directions: The italicized word in each of the following sentences is either a complement or the object of a preposition. In the space at the left, write one of the following abbreviations to indicate the function of the italicized word:

S.C. [subjective complement]   D.O. [direct object]   I.O. [indirect object]

O.C. [objective complement]   O.P. [object of preposition]

_____ 1. Did you find her work on that paper *acceptable?*

_____ 2. Which *city* are you moving to after graduation?

_____ 3. Did you show *everyone* a map to that state park?

_____ 4. Was Justin a *participant* in all the practices last week?

_____ 5. Have you found all the *references* to that event in last week's news reports?

_____ 6. Did you see the *reports* in those two small newspapers?

_____ 7. Can we consider Martin a *volunteer* for the clean-up project next Saturday?

_____ 8. Was our CEO *one* of the leaders in that embezzlement scheme?

_____ 9. Would you call our CEO a *leader* in that embezzlement scheme?

_____ 10. Has the manager given my *report* her most careful attention?

_____ 11. Did you plant those three birch *trees* in the corner of the yard?

_____ 12. Will we show that movie to all three *teams* on that project?

_____ 13. Have you shown *everyone* on that project the movie?

_____ 14. Have you hired more *people* for that massive new undertaking?

_____ 15. Will the new people be sufficiently *skilled* for that work?

_____ 16. Should our office grant every *student* a permit for parking on the campus?

_____ 17. Won't the parking lots be *full* every minute of the day?

_____ 18. Will you take a copy of my report to the professor's *office?*

_____ 19. Is that report the right *length* for that assignment?

_____ 20. Will you tell *me* the teacher's comments on my report?

Check Sheet

You can use Check Sheets in three ways. You can use them as a quick review at the end of each unit; you can use them as another, shorter presentation of the materials in the unit; or you can use them as a quick reference guide to refresh your understanding of a principle as you write papers for English or other classes.

PARTS OF SPEECH

☐ **Nouns**

    ☐ Common nouns are the names of persons, places, things, qualities, or ideas.

    ☐ Proper nouns are the names of specific individuals within a class.

Common	*Proper*
girl	Maria
city	Minneapolis
bat	Omaha Classic
honesty	(no proper form)
economic theory	Marxism

    ☐ Common nouns are not capitalized, but proper nouns are.

    ☐ Nouns are singular if they indicate one in a class, plural if they indicate two or more.

☐ **Pronouns**

    ☐ Pronouns take the place of nouns when reusing the noun would be repetitive.
- *Personal pronouns:* I, you, he, she, it, we, they
- *Demonstrative pronouns:* this, that, these, those
- *Indefinite pronouns:* each, either, neither, one, anyone, and other examples
- *Possessive pronouns:* mine, yours, his, hers, its, ours, theirs

    ☐ Nouns and pronouns answer the question *Who?* or *What?*

☐ **Verbs**

    ☐ Verbs express action, existence, or condition, and they combine with nouns or pronouns used as subjects to make a statement.

        Maria is tired.
        Tom runs.
        Tyrone sees the dog.

    ☐ Verbs answer the question *What happens?* or *What is?*

    ☐ Verbs change form to indicate
- *Person:* first—I, we; second—you; third—he, she, it, they

- *Number:* singular indicates one thing, plural indicates two or more
- *Tense:* time of the action or existence

> *Present:* I run
> *Past:* I ran
> *Future:* I will run
> *Present perfect:* I have run
> *Past perfect:* I had run
> *Future perfect:* I shall have run

☐ Verb forms for the various tenses are developed from the principal parts of the verb: base, past, and past participle.

☐ The sense of verbs may be changed by adding forms of *to be* and an *ing* ending to the verb to create progressive tenses.

☐ The sense of verbs can be changed to indicate condition and possibility by adding modal auxiliaries such as *may*, *might*, *would*, *could*, and *should*.

☐ Transitive verbs change voice from active (*The boy saw the dog.*) to passive (*The dog was seen by the boy.*).

☐ Adjectives

☐ Adjectives modify nouns—that is, adjectives change our sense of the noun by adding a limit, description, or quality to the noun. Adjectives occur in three positions:

> Preceding the noun   The tall girl ran.
> Following a linking verb   The tall girl is happy.
> Directly after the noun   The girl, happy. . . .

☐ Adjectives can show degree or strength by changing their form:
> The girl is happy.
> She is happier than I am.
> She is the happiest girl in our class.

☐ Adjectives answer questions such as *How big? What shape? What color?*

☐ Adverbs

☐ Adverbs change our sense of—modify—verbs, adjectives, other adverbs, or whole sentences:

> The girl walked quickly.
> She walked quite slowly.
> The very young girl walked out of the room.
> Certainly, we'll be there on time.

☐ Adverbs most frequently answer the question *How? When?* or *Where?*

☐ Prepositions

☐ Prepositions establish relationships between a noun (the object of the preposition) and another word in a sentence.

The plane flew into the cloud, under the cloud, behind the cloud.

☐ Sentence Patterns

☐ The parts of speech are combined into sentences that follow five specific patterns. The first two patterns employ intransitive verbs—that is, verbs that transfer no action to an object.

• Pattern 1 (intransitive verb with no complement needed to complete action)

The bird flies.

• Pattern 2 (intransitive linking verb with subjective complement, either a noun or adjective)

The man is a scientist.
The man is brilliant.

The next three patterns employ transitive verbs—that is, verbs that transfer action from the subject to an object.

• Pattern 3 (transitive verb with a direct object receiving the action)
The pilot flies the plane.

Note that some verbs—for example the verb *to fly*—can be intransitive or transitive.

• Pattern 4 (transitive verbs such as *give* and *show*, with a direct object and an indirect object)
The woman showed us two coats.

• Pattern 5 (transitive verb such as *call*, *think*, *find*, and *elect*, with a direct object and an objective complement, either a noun or an adjective)

The teacher called her a genius.
The teacher called her brilliant.

☐ All of these sentence patterns can be enriched with the use of adjective and adverb modifiers and prepositions.

☐ Questions

• Questions answered by *yes* or *no* employ a change in order to indicate the question:

Maria is happy.
Is Maria happy?

• Questions employ interrogatives to request information:

Pronouns: who, whom, which, that
Adjectives: whose, which, what
Adverbs: when, where, why, how

Who is that man?
Whose dog is that?
When will you be home?

Clauses and Phrases

Lessons, Practice Sheets, and Exercises

| Lesson 7 | *Coordination: Compound Sentences* |

To begin to study sentences that build on the simple patterns discussed in the previous lessons, let's examine a student writer's description of a snowstorm. Each sentence is numbered for later reference.

(1) The first really serious snowfall began at dusk and had already spread a treacherous powdering over the roads by the time the homeward-bound crowds reached their peak. (2) As the evening deepened, porch and street lights glowed in tight circles through semi-solid air. (3) The snow did not fall in a mass of fat, jovial flakes; it squatted in a writhing mist of tiny particles and seemed less snow than a dense, animated fog. (4) Through the night the wind rose, worrying the trees as a puppy shakes a slipper. (5) It rushed round the corners of buildings and tumbled over roofs, from which it snatched armfuls of snow to scatter in the streets. (6) Save for the occasional grumble of a sanitation truck sullenly pushing its plow, all sound stopped. (7) Even the wind was more felt than heard. (8) Day did not dawn. (9) The world changed from charcoal gray to lead between six and seven, but the change was one from night to lesser night. (10) The snow still whirled. (11) Drifts had altered the neat symmetry of peaked roofs into irregular mountain ranges ending in sheer cliffs four or five feet above the leeward eaves. (12) The downwind side of every solid object cast a snow shadow that tapered away from a sharp hump until it merged into the surrounding flat pallor. (13) Along the street, windshield wipers, odd bits of chrome, startling blanks of black glass, and isolated headlights decorated large white mounds. (14) Men and women shut off their alarm clocks, stretched, yawned, looked out of their windows, paused in a moment of guilt, and went back to bed. (15) Snow had taken the day for its own, and there was no point in arguing with it.

The 15 sentences of this paragraph are all made up of groups of related words called clauses. A **clause** is a group of words that always contains a subject and a verb in combination. Recalling the scenes, actions, and responses associated with the event, the author has created a series of clauses (subject–verb combinations): the snowfall began, the snowfall had spread a powdering, the homeward-bound crowds reached their peak, the evening deepened, lights glowed, and so on.

Although it may not be apparent when you first read the paragraph, the entire passage is based on short, simple sentences of the patterns studied in the preceding lessons. The writer's problem was to combine or alter these short statements in order to put them into their most pleasing and effective form. Presenting all of them as basic sentences would communicate the author's ideas but in a form that, in addition to being monotonous, would not give proper emphasis to the most important ideas. Only two sentences (8 and 10) are retained as one-subject, one-verb basic sentences. Some of the sentences (3, 9, and 15) combine two basic sentences, giving each clause equal force. Two sentences (1 and 5) join more than one verb to the same subject. Sentence 13 joins four subjects to the same verb, and Sentence 14 has two subjects joined to six verbs.

In the next several lessons, we examine the word groups—independent clauses, subordinate clauses, and phrases—that are the language tools allowing a writer to apply various strategies to produce effective sentences.

COMPOUNDING SENTENCES

A sentence, as you learned in Lesson 1, is a word group containing a subject and a verb. From this definition, and from the one already given for a clause, it would seem that a sentence and a clause are identical. And this is true for one kind of clause, the **independent clause** (also called the *main clause* or *principal clause*). The independent clause can stand by itself as a sentence. Every example sentence and every exercise sentence that you have worked with thus far in this book has been made up of one independent clause. We call a sentence consisting of one independent clause a **simple sentence**.

One means of combining or altering short, simple sentences is called *compounding*, joining grammatically equal parts so they function together. We can join two or more subjects, verbs, complements, or modifiers by using a **coordinating conjunction**. (**Conjunctions** are words that join words, phrases, or clauses; conjunctions that join grammatically equal units are called *coordinating*.) The three common coordinating conjunctions are *and*, *but*, and *or*; other coordinators are *nor*, *for*, *yet*, and *so*. With the use of a coordinating conjunction, we can join two very short sentences and create a longer, more readable sentence.

Dad read the notice. I read the notice.
Dad *and* I read the notice. [Compound subjects]

Margo enjoys golf. Margo enjoys tennis.
Margo enjoys golf *and* tennis. [Compound direct objects]

I studied very hard. I failed the test.
I studied very hard *but* failed the test. [Compound verbs]

I found the lecture interesting. I found the lecture instructive.
I found the lecture interesting *and* instructive. [Compound objective complements]

I can see you during your lunch hour. I can see you after 5 o'clock.
I can see you during your lunch hour *or* after 5 o'clock. [Compound prepositional phrases]

COMPOUND SENTENCES

Compounding is often used with two (sometimes more than two) independent clauses; the result is a common type of sentence called the **compound sentence**. We can create compound sentences in two ways.

CLAUSES JOINED BY A COORDINATING CONJUNCTION

Any of the coordinating conjunctions already mentioned can be used to join two independent clauses. The normal punctuation is a comma before the conjunction:

I had reviewed the material, and I did well on the test.

It is important to distinguish this sentence from a nearly identical version using a compound verb:

I had reviewed the material and did well on the test.

In this version, the sentence is not a compound sentence because there is no separate subject for the second verb. It is a simple sentence with a compound verb and should be written without a comma.

CLAUSES JOINED BY A SEMICOLON

Sometimes the two independent clauses stand side by side with no word tying them together:

No one was in sight; I was alone in the huge auditorium.

Often, the second of the two clauses joined by a semicolon begins with an adverbial unit that serves as a kind of tie between the clauses. This adverbial unit may be:

1. A simple adverb

Currently, we are renting an apartment; *later*, we hope to buy a house.
These were last year's highlights; *now* we must look at plans for next year.

2. A short phrase

I cannot comment on the whole concert; *in fact*, I slept through the last part of it.

3. A conjunctive adverb

Your arguments were well presented; *however*, we feel that the plan is too expensive.

The most common conjunctive adverbs are *therefore, however, nevertheless, consequently, moreover, otherwise, besides, furthermore,* and *accordingly*. These words, often followed by a comma, should be used cautiously; they usually contribute to a heavy, formal tone. To lessen this effect, writers often place them, set off by commas, within the second clause:

Your arguments were well presented; we feel, *however*, that the plan is too expensive.

Because adverbial units like *later* and *therefore* are *not* coordinating conjunctions, the use of a comma to join the two clauses is inappropriate. This error is often called a *comma splice* or a *comma fault*. The important thing to remember is that when independent clauses are joined by a coordinating conjunction, the use of a comma is the custom. When there is no coordinating conjunction, the comma will not suffice; the customary mark is the semicolon. Joining two independent clauses by using only a coordinating conjunction without a comma or by using only a conjunctive adverb with no punctuation creates a problem called a *run-on sentence*. Such sentences are awkward and can create confusion. Following the rules for joining independent clauses will help you to avoid these two problems. We study these punctuation rules thoroughly in Lesson 17.

English Fundamentals **Online**

After you have completed the Practice Sheets and Exercises in this lesson, you can find additional help and drill work at **MyWritingLab.com**, in the section on Basic Sentence Patterns; Combining Sentences; Sentence Structure; Varying Sentence Structure.

NAME _____   SCORE _____

Directions: The following 25 sentences illustrate three types of sentences:

Type 1. The sentence is a simple sentence with a compound verb (i.e., two verbs joined by a coordinating conjunction). Normal punctuation: none

   The people finished their work and headed home.

Type 2. The sentence is a compound sentence (i.e., two independent clauses joined by a coordinating conjunction: *and, but, or, nor, for, yet,* or *so*). Normal punctuation: *comma before the conjunction*

   The people finished their work, and they left for home.

Type 3. The sentence is a compound sentence with no coordinating conjunction joining the independent clauses. (The second clause often contains an adverbial unit such as *now, thus,* or *therefore.*) Normal punctuation: semicolon

   The people finished their work early; therefore they left for the weekend at noon.

In each of the following sentences, a ^ marks the point of punctuation. If the sentence is Type 1, write a **0** in the space at the left. If the sentence is Type 2, write **C** (for comma) in the space. If the sentence is Type 3, write **S** (for semicolon) in the space.

_____   1. The cashier took my money ^ and put it in the cash register.

_____   2. The cashier took my money ^ and he put it in the cash register.

_____   3. The cashier took my money ^ then he put it in the cash register.

_____   4. Two more people walked in the door ^ and I gave them seats at the back of the room.

_____   5. The room was full ^ but the presentation had not begun.

_____   6. The room was full ^ finally, the first speaker walked to the stage.

_____   7. We listened carefully to the speaker ^ but did not learn anything new.

_____   8. The second speaker gave a PowerPoint presentation ^ and we found it quite informative.

_____   9. Not many of us found the third presentation valuable ^ so we left the conference at noon.

_____   10. All the speakers seemed highly skilled ^ yet they could not hold our attention.

_____   11. Parking on the campus is very limited ^ thus I usually walk to class from my dorm.

_____ 12. A new parking garage will be completed by next term ^ so parking will be more readily available.

_____ 13. The new garage will feature a shuttle service ^ for it will be a great distance from the classroom buildings.

_____ 14. The new garage will make life easier for commuter students ^ I, however, will probably still walk to class.

_____ 15. Parking on the campus has always been a problem ^ and will probably continue to be difficult for the rest of my time here.

_____ 16. Alice and Mark studied very hard for today's test ^ they are hoping for high grades.

_____ 17. The test had no tricky questions on it ^ yet no one finished it within the allotted time.

_____ 18. All the questions were long and involved ^ so no one finished on time.

_____ 19. The test questions were long and involved ^ therefore, we hope the teacher will grade on the curve.

_____ 20. Unfortunately, the teacher did not extend the time for the test ^ nor did she grade on the curve.

_____ 21. Next weekend we will drive to the state college ^ and there we will go to a football game.

_____ 22. The game will end about 5:00 P.M. ^ I will then meet my parents for dinner.

_____ 23. I will spend the night at home ^ and enjoy some of my mother's good cooking.

_____ 24. The food in the dining hall is barely acceptable ^ so I always enjoy a home-cooked meal.

_____ 25. Next year I will share an apartment with two other students ^ at that time I will cook my own meals.

Coordination: Compound Sentences

NAME _____   SCORE _____

Directions: The following 25 sentences illustrate three types of sentences:

Type 1. The sentence is a simple sentence with a compound verb (i.e., two verbs joined by a coordinating conjunction). Normal punctuation: none

The people finished their work and headed home.

Type 2. The sentence is a compound sentence (i.e., two independent clauses joined by a coordinating conjunction: *and, but, or, nor, for, yet,* or *so*). Normal punctuation: *comma before the conjunction*

The people finished their work, and they left for home.

Type 3. The sentence is a compound sentence with no coordinating conjunction joining the independent clauses. (The second clause often contains an adverbial unit such as *now, thus,* or *therefore.*) Normal punctuation: semicolon

The people finished their work early; therefore they left for the weekend at noon.

In each of the following sentences, a ^ marks the point of punctuation. If the sentence is Type 1, write a **0** in the space at the left. If the sentence is Type 2, write **C** (for comma) in the space. If the sentence is Type 3, write **S** (for semicolon) in the space.

It is important to establish the relationship between the two clauses of a compound sentence by choosing an appropriate conjunction. In each of the following sentences, a blank space appears where a conjunction might appear. In the blank, write the conjunction needed in the sentence. Type 1 and 2 sentences will require a conjunction. For Type 3 sentences, leave the space blank where no conjunction is needed. An adverbial unit will appear in Type 3 sentences. **Review:** It is vital to recognize subjects and verbs in compound sentences. Circle the subject and underline the verb in each of the following sentences.

_____   1. Al sent a text message to Jenny ^ _____ she was not available to pick up the message.

_____   2. Al sent Jenny a text message ^ _____ she was, however, not available to pick up the message.

_____   3. The three men started work early in the morning ^ _____ the job required a great number of highly technical procedures.

_____   4. Barbara looked everywhere for the lost book ^ _____ did not find it anywhere in her apartment.

_____   5. Finally she looked under the front seat of her car ^ _____ found the book there.

_____   6. Members of the school's marching band will appear at a national competition next month ^ _____ they won the regional competition last week.

_____ 7. Few people are happy about the reduction in municipal services ^ _____ they are not, however, in favor of additional taxes for those services.

_____ 8. None of us is registered for the first aid course ^ _____ does anyone have time for that course.

_____ 9. Those men should either work faster on that project ^ _____ call for more help.

_____ 10. My history assignment was long and complicated ^ _____ therefore I did not finish it until 1:00 A.M. this morning.

_____ 11. My family prepared dinner for 12 people ^ _____ a total of 20 people walked in the door at 6:00 P.M.

_____ 12. The people next door own three dogs ^ _____ they bark constantly during the day.

_____ 13. Students in that class may choose an in-class test ^ _____ they may elect a longer, more difficult take-home test.

_____ 14. Most of the students chose the in-class test ^ _____ take-home tests are almost always long and difficult.

_____ 15. Marcia chose the take-home test ^ _____ she finished the test in a very short time.

_____ 16. There are five people assigned to my group's project ^ _____ two of us usually do most of the work.

_____ 17. That football team must improve its defense ^ _____ the rest of the season will be very difficult.

_____ 18. This morning I could not find any of my notes from biology class ^ _____ could I locate my history textbook.

_____ 19. The managers in my office have very high standards ^ _____ thus they have created a very high-stress work environment.

_____ 20. One of my friends needs a job ^ _____ refuses any stressful work.

_____ 21. Another friend loves high-stress, exciting work ^ _____ he finds any other kind of work extremely boring.

_____ 22. One of my friends is very interested in geology ^ _____ most of my friends, however, find that subject rather uninteresting.

_____ 23. I have not yet started the work on my paper ^ _____ thus I cannot watch that movie at this time.

_____ 24. I cannot watch that movie at this time ^ _____ I would enjoy it at some other time.

_____ 25. I will be working on my paper until late tonight ^ _____ after that project I must study for a botany test.

Directions: Combine the short sentences in each numbered item into one longer compound sentence. Use coordinating conjunctions or conjunctive adverbs that clearly establish the relationship between the two clauses in the new sentence. Supply the proper punctuation for each sentence.

1. The weather is deteriorating rapidly this afternoon. By morning we might be in a snowstorm.

   _____

2. Caldwell and Johnson will try out for the baseball team next week. They will both be a welcome addition to the team.

   _____

3. The instructor in my psychology class assigned a long paper yesterday. Fortunately, the due date is over a month away.

   _____

4. Every person in this office has invested a great deal of time in that project. We have not finished it after all this time and effort.

   _____

5. Because of staff reductions, we cannot finish all our assigned tasks. We will probably find another project on our desks tomorrow.

   _____

6. This office actually needs two additional workers. We cannot keep up with the work without more help.

   _____

7. Perhaps one day the seemingly impossible will happen. We will finish all the work assigned to us.

   _____

8. Many students were late for class today. Bad weather caused a very bad traffic jam.

   _____

9. The weather forecasters predicted a dry, cool day. A heavy rain, however, began about dawn.

   _____

10. Today's baseball game has been postponed. The field is under water from the heavy rain.

    _____

Brief *Writing Assignment:* Write a paragraph of five or six sentences describing the desk or table where you do your college assignments. In the paragraph, use one simple sentence, one compound verb, and two compound sentences.

To this point you have had practice with the simple sentence (one independent clause) and the compound sentence (two or more independent clauses). Basic as these sentences are to your thinking and writing, you need to move beyond these structures in order to make your writing flexible and powerful. Often you can make your statements more precise if you use slightly more complex structures.

"Rain began to fall, and we stopped our ball game" is a perfectly correct sentence. But notice these slightly altered versions of that sentence:

> When rain began to fall, we stopped our ball game.
> After rain began to fall, we stopped our ball game.
> Because rain began to fall, we stopped our ball game.

These three, in addition to lessening the singsong tone that occurs when you join several compound sentences, are more informative. The first two tell the time at which the game was stopped—but *when* and *after* point out slightly different time frames. The third version gives a different relation between the two statements; it tells not the time of, but the reason for, stopping the game.

If, instead of writing the compound sentence "Rain was falling, and we continued our ball game," you write "Although rain was falling, we continued our ball game," you have refined your thinking and your expression. Your readers now interpret the sentence exactly as you want them to; they now know that the ball game was continued in spite of the fact that rain was falling.

The process by which a statement is reduced to a secondary form to show its relation to the main idea is called subordination. The grammatical unit that expresses a secondary idea as it affects a main idea is the subordinate, or dependent, clause, which we define as a subject–verb combination that cannot stand alone as a sentence. A subordinate clause works in a sentence in the same way that a single part of speech—an adverb, an adjective, or a noun—works. Instead of a single word—*quickly, quick, quickness*—used as an adverb, an adjective, or a noun, a group of words is used. A sentence made up of one independent clause and at least one dependent clause is a **complex sentence**.

ADVERB CLAUSE

The **adverb clause** works in exactly the same way a one-word adverb works: It provides information by modifying a verb, an adjective, or another adverb. The most common types of adverb clauses modify verbs. In fact, they answer direct questions about the action: When? (time); Where? (place); Why? (cause); and How? (manner). The role of the adverb clause is shown by the conjunction that introduces the adverb clause. The conjunction—the structural signal of subordination—is not an isolated word standing between the two clauses; it is part of the subordinate clause. In such a sentence as "We left the house after the rain stopped," the unit "the rain stopped" could stand alone as an independent clause. But the clause is made dependent by the inclusion of the conjunction *after*. The dependent clause "after the rain stopped" establishes the time when "we left the house." Thus, the clause works as an adverb of time in the same way that the one-word adverbs work in the following sentences:

We left the house *early.*
We left the house *late.*
We left the house *yesterday.*

Various types of adverb clauses and their most common conjunctions are listed here with examples.

Time (*when, whenever, before, after, since, while, until, as, as soon as*):

The baby cried *when the telephone rang.*
The cat ran out *before Lou could shut the door.*
After the bell rings, no one can enter.
I've known Palmer *since he was in high school.*
You should not whisper *while Dr. Fuller is lecturing.*
You may leave *as soon as your replacement arrives.*

Place (*where, wherever*):

We parted *where the paths separated.*
I will meet you *wherever you want me to.*

Cause [or Reason] (*because, since, as*):

I walk to work every day *because I need the exercise.*
Since she could not pay the fine, she could not drive the car.
As you are the senior member, you should lead the procession.

Purpose (*so that, in order that*):

We left early *so that we could catch the last bus.*
They died *that their nation might live.*
They came to America *in order that they might find freedom.*

Manner (*as, as if, as though*):

Raphael acted *as if the party bored him.*
Please do the work *as you have been instructed.*

Result (*so . . . that, such . . . that*):

Derek arrived so late *that he missed the concert.*
The workmen made such a racket *that I got a headache.*

Condition (*if, unless, provided that, on condition that*). This kind of adverb clause gives a condition under which the main clause is true:

> Sit down and chat *if you are not in a hurry*.
> He will not give his talk *unless we pay his expenses*.
> She will sign the contract *provided that we pay her a bonus*.
> *If I were you*, I would accept the offer.
> *If you had told me earlier*, I could have helped.

There is an alternate arrangement for this kind of conditional clause. In this arrangement, *if* is not used; instead, a subject–verb inversion signals the subordination. Sentences such as the last two preceding examples sometimes take this form:

> *Were I you*, I would accept the offer.
> *Had you told me earlier*, I could have helped.

Concession (*although, though, even if, even though, since*). This clause states a fact in spite of which the main idea is true:

> *Although she is only nine years old*, she plays chess.
> Our car is dependable *even though it is old*.

Comparison (*than, as*). Two distinctive characteristics of the adverb clause of comparison should be noted. First, part or all of the verb, although it is needed grammatically, is usually not expressed. Second, when an action verb is not expressed in the subordinate clause, the appropriate form of the auxiliary *do* is often used even though the *do* does not occur in the main clause:

> Gold is heavier *than iron* [is].
> Your computer is not as new *as mine* [is].
> Her theme was better *than any other student's in the class* [was].
> Ellen earned more bonus points *than her brother* [did].

Modification of Verbs, Adjectives, and Adverbs

Adverb clauses may also modify verbs, adjectives, and adverbs. In this type of clause, the conjunction *that* is sometimes unexpressed.

> Jim slept as late *as possible*. [Modifies the adverb *late*]
> We are sorry *that you must leave early*. [Modifies the adjective *sorry*]
> I am sure *(that) he meant no harm*. [Modifies the adjective *sure*]
> The car is running better *than it did last week*. [Modifies the adverb *better*]

ELLIPTICAL CLAUSE

Ellipsis means *omission, leaving something out*. A clause that leaves some parts implicitly understood or unexpressed is called an **elliptical clause**. There are many types of elliptical clauses. You should be aware of them because they can lend variety to your writing. In the following examples, brackets enclose the parts of the clauses that may be unexpressed. (See

Supplement.) Note that all the types of adverb phrases (time, place, cause, purpose, manner, result, condition, concession, and comparison) may be elliptical.

While [I was] *walking home,* I met Mr. Rodriguez.

When [he is] *in Cleveland,* he stays with us.

Call your office *as soon as* [it is] *possible.*

Adjustments will be made *whenever* [they are] *necessary.*

Mary, *although* [she is] *a talented girl,* is quite lazy.

If [you are] *delayed,* call my secretary.

Your ticket, *unless* [it is] *stamped,* is invalid.

A NOTE ON SENTENCE VARIETY

Although some adverb clauses—those of comparison, for instance—have a fixed position within the sentence, many adverb clauses may be placed before, inside, or following the main clause:

When they deal with the unknown, Greek myths are usually somber.

Greek myths, *when they deal with the unknown,* are usually somber.

Greek myths are usually somber *when they deal with the unknown.*

Notice that no comma is used in the third example above. Usually a comma is not needed when the adverbial clause is the final element of the sentence, as the third example below also illustrates:

Although he did not have authority from Congress, President Theodore Roosevelt ordered construction of the Panama Canal.

President Theodore Roosevelt, *although he did not have authority from Congress,* ordered construction of the Panama Canal.

President Theodore Roosevelt ordered construction of the Panama Canal *although he did not have authority from Congress.*

You should practice various arrangements to relieve the monotony that comes from reliance on too many main-subject-plus-main-verb clauses and sentences.

SUPPLEMENT

Occasionally, an elliptical adverb clause of comparison must be recast because the exact meaning is unclear when parts of the clause are unexpressed. Here are two sentences that are ambiguous in the shortened forms of the clauses:

Mr. Alton will pay you more *than Stan.*

Probable meaning: Mr. Alton will pay you more than [he will pay] Stan.

Possible meaning: Mr. Alton will pay you more than Stan [will pay you].

Parents dislike homework as much *as their offspring.*

Probable meaning: Parents dislike homework as much as their offspring [dislike homework].

Possible meaning: Parents dislike homework as much as [they dislike] their offspring.

Remember to check each sentence for ambiguity and recast any expression that allows for more than one interpretation.

SUMMARY OF ADVERB CLAUSES

1. *Function:* to modify a verb, an adjective, or an adverb

2. *Position:* fixed for some types (She sold more tickets *than I did*); others may be at the beginning, in the interior, or at the end of main clause

3. *Subordinators:* conjunctions, most of which show adverbial relationships such as time (*when, since, while*), cause (*because, as*), and so on

4. *Special structures:*
   a. An adverb clause modifying an adjective subjective complement and subordinated by *that* sometimes has the subordinator *that* unexpressed:

   I'm sure *(that) you are wrong.*

   b. Elliptical clauses:
   Mary is older *than I (am).*
   If (you are) unable to attend, call me.
   While (she was) preparing lunch, Mary cut her finger.

English Fundamentals Online

After you have completed the Practice Sheets and Exercises in this lesson, you can find additional help and drill work at **MyWritingLab.com**, in the section on Combining Sentences; Varying Sentence Structure.

NAME _____   SCORE _____

Directions: Identify each of the italicized adverb clauses by writing one of the following numbers in the space at the left:

1. Time	4. Purpose	7. Condition	10. Modification of an
2. Place	5. Manner	8. Concession	adjective or an adverb
3. Cause	6. Result	9. Comparison	

__1__ 1. *After you left for home*, we all looked carefully for your cell phone.

__2__ 2. We even looked *where the couch stands against the wall.*

_____ 3. We searched the house carefully *because you need your cell phone.*

_____ 4. *Although we searched very thoroughly*, we did not find your cell phone.

_____ 5. We are certainly sorry *that you have lost your phone.*

_____ 6. We searched for the phone *so that we could return it to you.*

_____ 7. We searched for the phone *as if it belonged to us.*

_____ 8. In fact, we searched for so long *that we were late for our first class.*

_____ 9. Perhaps, *although we did not find it here,* you will find your phone at home.

_____ 10. *Unless you find the phone soon*, you should probably buy a new one.

_____ 11. Conditions at the office, *since you first came to work here*, have changed greatly.

_____ 12. *After you came to work here*, a new manager took over the office.

_____ 13. None of the office furniture stands *where it stood two months ago.*

_____ 14. The manager, *because he wanted a new look in the office*, moved all the furniture.

_____ 15. My desk is so far in the back *that I cannot see anyone else in the office.*

_____ 16. The manager separated us *so that we cannot talk to each other.*

_____ 17. He acted *as if we never completed our assignments on time.*

_____ 18. However, we do not now work any faster *than we did earlier.*

_____ 19. The new arrangement, *although we cannot change it*, has made us all very unhappy.

_____ 20. *When a new manager arrives*, perhaps we can change the furniture arrangement again.

_____ 21. It was so cold this morning *that we all stayed home.*

_____ 22. The snow was so deep in the streets *that we could not drive anywhere.*

_____ 23. Most people in town, *because the snow was so deep*, stayed home for the day.

_____ 24. Tomorrow's forecast calls for more snow *than we had today.*

_____ 25. *After the snowplows have cleared the streets*, we can go to work.

_____ 26. *While the snow was falling heavily*, the wind was blowing very hard.

_____ 27. The snow fell *as if it would never stop.*

_____ 28. At my house, the snow drifted higher *than I had ever seen it before.*

_____ 29. My little brother was thrilled *that the bad weather cancelled school for two days.*

_____ 30. *If the weather does not clear up soon*, we might need help from the National Guard.

_____ 31. *When we were in the mountains last summer*, we hiked a beautiful mountain trail.

_____ 32. We used a hand-held GPS *so that we would not lose our way.*

_____ 33. A new GPS is so powerful *that it will never lose the signal from the satellites.*

_____ 34. *Before the GPS came into widespread use*, people relied on compasses for directions.

_____ 35. Once, *while hiking without a compass*, my friend Tom became lost in a dense woods.

_____ 36. He was sure *that he knew the way to a certain campsite.*

_____ 37. Those with him followed him *because he spoke very confidently of his skills.*

_____ 38. In fact, *because he took a wrong turn on the trail*, some people went into a panic.

_____ 39. At noon, he called a halt *so that he could figure out a new way out of the woods.*

_____ 40. Finally, *after walking about a mile*, they came to a road back to town.

NAME _____   SCORE _____

Directions: Each sentence contains one adverb clause. Underline each adverb clause and identify its type by writing one of the following numbers in the space at the left of the sentence:

1. Time	4. Purpose	7. Condition	10. Modification of an
2. Place	5. Manner	8. Concession	adjective or an adverb
3. Cause	6. Result	9. Comparison	

_____   1. The members of that class were very happy that the instructor postponed the test.

_____   2. The man lost his temper because his car got a flat tire.

_____   3. The two boys walked so slowly toward school that they were late for class.

_____   4. Jim is more pessimistic than I am about our team's chances this weekend.

_____   5. The men will meet their boss where the road turns toward the new job site.

_____   6. Mary Ann looked as though she did not understand the directions.

_____   7. Although Roy made his best effort, he could not fix my printer.

_____   8. Two students slipped into the back row after the lecture had begun.

_____   9. Tomorrow for lunch I can meet you wherever you want.

_____   10. Marcia should help us with our project so that we can finish it on time.

_____   11. The dog walked on as though he had not heard my whistle.

_____   12. None of us, because the movie was very interesting, heard the phone ring.

_____   13. Once we had parked the car, the walk to the stadium took 15 minutes.

_____   14. I watched last night's game even though I had three hours of work ahead of me.

_____   15. Had I learned earlier of your arrival, I would have met you at the airport.

_____   16. The two people walked so fast that the rest of us could not keep up.

_____   17. If you're not in a hurry, we should have a cup of coffee together.

_____   18. I followed the directions exactly as you gave them to me.

_____   19. The two men arrived after most of the people had left the party.

_____   20. One of us, because Sam is our friend, should offer some help with that work.

_____ 21. Last night we worked on that project as long as we possibly could.

_____ 22. That old baseball is slightly heavier than the new one.

_____ 23. Since everyone has arrived, we should start the meeting.

_____ 24. You will find that beautiful waterfall where that long trail ends.

_____ 25. The manager started the meeting even though two people had not yet arrived.

_____ 26. Unless Johnson can become a better fielder, he probably will not be a starter.

_____ 27. The road was so icy that several cars slid into the ditch.

_____ 28. Five cars, because the road was very icy, slid off into the ditch.

_____ 29. Even if the two of us work late tonight, we can't finish that project.

_____ 30. Had Cathy thought for just another minute, she would have seen the solution.

_____ 31. I am so annoyed by all that chatter in the back of the theater that I'm moving to another seat.

_____ 32. Those people acted as though they were the only people concerned with the problem.

_____ 33. Many students take the bus because there are no parking spaces available on campus.

_____ 34. As gas prices are extremely high, many people are taking the bus to work.

_____ 35. So that we can find a good location in the amphitheater, we need to arrive very early for the concert.

_____ 36. The weather this past week was colder than I have ever seen it.

_____ 37. If the man had any understanding of the complexity of the project, he would have chosen our firm for its skill and experience.

_____ 38. All the students in the class acted as if they had never seen that type of problem before.

_____ 39. I have known Kevin since we arrived on campus on the first day of our freshman year.

_____ 40. My grade on that test, although it was very difficult, was surprisingly high.

Directions: In the first space at the left, write a subordinating conjunction that logically connects the two clauses in the sentence. In the second space, write one of the following numbers to identify the type of subordinate clause:

1. Time	4. Purpose	7. Condition	10. Modification of an adjective or an adverb
2. Place	5. Manner	8. Concession	
3. Cause	6. Result	9. Comparison	

_____
_____ 1. _____ it is a hot summer day, we should all go to the lake for a swim.

_____
_____ 2. You can find an excellent price on a new television set _____ you shop around for a day.

_____
_____ 3. The men looked at the blueprint _____ they had never seen one before.

_____
_____ 4. I would accept that job offer _____ you must move to another, unfamiliar city.

_____
_____ 5. My papers and projects certainly look better _____ I installed that new printer.

_____
_____ 6. Tomorrow, meet us _____ the road dead-ends at the lake.

_____
_____ 7. That report is so complex _____ I had to read it three times to understand it.

_____
_____ 8. This week's workload at the office is even heavier _____ last week's.

_____
_____ 9. We are delighted _____ you will be able to join us on that trip.

_____
_____ 10. You might need to read that report one more time _____ you can fully understand it.

_____
_____ 11. _____ you might not enjoy the experience, you should take at least one ride on that giant roller coaster.

_____
_____ 12. _____ you can find the time, you should watch that movie just for the hilarious comedy.

_____
_____ 13. You should watch that movie _____ you will find it hilarious.

_____
_____ 14. Janice, _____ she is a terrific athlete, found her first experience on water skis very difficult and embarrassing.

_____
_____ 15. After a twelve-hour day at work, we were so tired _____ we all went straight home.

Directions: Rewrite the following compound sentences as complex sentences using an adverb clause to replace the italicized independent clause. Select a subordinating conjunction that properly establishes the relationship between the two clauses. **Review:** In the sentences below, circle the coordinating conjunctions and conjunctive adverbs.

1. *The announcer read the starting lineups*, and then the umpire called out, "Play ball!"

   (Time)_____

2. *The men tried to finish the job today*, but a heavy snow ended their work early.

   (Concession)_____

3. *The team bus needs to leave early*, or it might be slowed by heavy traffic.

   (Condition) _____

4. *Several members of the class are ill with the flu*; therefore the teacher postponed the test.

   (Cause) _____

5. *You must start work on that paper today*, or you will almost surely not finish it on time.

   (Condition)_____

6. On Monday afternoon we lined up early at the box office; *we wanted to get good seats for the concert.*

   (Purpose) _____

7. Maria gave the officer a perplexed look; *she did not understand the reason for her traffic ticket.*

   (Manner)_____

8. The band played very loudly, and Joan left early with a terrible headache.

   (Result)_____

9. All of the seats on the bus were full, and we could not take any more passengers.

   (Cause) _____

10. All of the seats on the bus were full, but we found room for two additional people in a car.

    (Concession)_____

Brief Writing Assignment: Using the brief paragraph from Lesson 7 as a base, rewrite the paragraph to include three sentences with adverb clauses in them.

Just as a single-word adjective modifies a noun or pronoun, clauses that begin with *who, whom, whose, which,* or *that* can modify nouns or pronouns. A clause that modifies a noun or pronoun is called an **adjective** or **relative clause**. An adjective clause gives information about the noun in the same way that one-word adjectives do. Both one-word adjectives and adjective clauses can be seen as basic sentences that have been worked into a main clause.

> I looked into the sky. The sky was blue.
> I looked into the blue sky.
>
> I looked into the sky. The sky was filled with towering cumulus clouds.
> I looked into the sky, which was filled with towering cumulus clouds.

In Item 1 the sentence "The sky was blue" becomes the one-word adjective *blue* and modifies the noun *sky*. In Item 2 the sentence "The sky was filled with towering cumulus clouds" cannot become a one-word adjective; therefore, the sentence becomes an adjective or relative clause opened by the word *which*. The clause modifies the word *sky* in the sense that it provides us with information about the sky.

ADJECTIVE CLAUSES

Nearly all of the adjective clauses you read, write, or speak use *who, whose, whom, which,* or *that* to tie the adjective clause to the noun it modifies. These words, in spite of the fact that they join one clause to a word in another clause, are not conjunctions. They are pronouns that have a connective or *relating* function; thus they are called **relative pronouns**. (See Supplement.) Relatives can function *within* the adjective clause as subjects, direct objects, or objects of prepositions.

It is helpful to think of an adjective clause as a simple sentence that is incorporated within another sentence. The relative pronoun, by substituting for a noun, refers ("relates") the clause directly to the word being modified. Because the relative pronoun is the word signaling the subordination, the pronoun, sometimes preceded by a preposition, always begins the adjective clause.

Examine the following paired units. Every A unit has two simple sentences; the second repeats a noun from the first sentence. The B sentence shows how the second idea has been reduced to an adjective clause and has become part of the first sentence. Notice that the normal position of an adjective clause is immediately following the noun or the pronoun it modifies.

> A. This is a well-built truck. *The truck* will save you money.
> B. This is a well-built truck *that* will save you money.
> [The clause modifies *truck*. *That* is the subject in the adjective clause.]

A. Alice has a new boyfriend. *The new boyfriend [or He]* sings in a rock group.
B. Alice has a new boyfriend *who* sings in a rock group.
   [*Who* is the subject in the clause that modifies *boyfriend*.]

A. Here is the book. I borrowed *the book [or it]* yesterday.
B. Here is the book *that* I borrowed yesterday.
   [*That* is the direct object in the adjective clause.]

A. The firm hired Chet Brown. The boss had known *Chet Brown [or him]* in Omaha.
B. The firm hired Chet Brown, *whom* the boss had known in Omaha.
   [*Whom* is the direct object in the adjective clause.]

A. May I introduce Dick Hart? I went to college *with Dick Hart [or him]*.
B. May I introduce Dick Hart, with *whom* I went to college?
   [The clause modifies *Dick Hart*. Notice that the preposition *with* stands at the beginning of the clause with its object *whom*. At the informal level of language usage, the preposition in this structure is sometimes found at the end of the clause. See Supplement 2 of Lesson 6 on page 52.]

A. She is a young artist. I admire the young *artist's [or her]* work.
B. She is a young artist *whose* work I admire.
   [*Work* is in this position because, although it is the direct object of *admire*, it cannot be separated from its modifier, the relative adjective *whose*, which must be placed at the beginning of the adjective clause.]

We also use the adverbs *when* and *where* as relatives. *When* and *where* introduce adjective clauses in combinations meaning "time when" and "place where." The following examples show that the subordinator is really the equivalent of an adverbial prepositional phrase. (The B sentences are complex sentences combining the material of the two A sentences.)

A. Beth and I recalled the time. We considered ourselves rebels *at that time*.
B. Beth and I recalled the time *when* we considered ourselves rebels.

A. This is the spot. The explorers came ashore at this spot.
B. This is the spot *where* the explorers came ashore.

These clauses are logically considered adjective clauses because they immediately follow nouns that require identification, and the clauses give the identifying material. If you remember "time-when" and "place-where," you will not confuse this type of adjective clause with other subordinate clauses that may use the same subordinators.

Note: In certain adjective clauses, the relative word is unexpressed; the meaning is instantly clear without it: the food *(that) we eat*, the house *(that) he lived in*, the man *(whom) you saw*, the time *(when) you fell down*, and so on.

RESTRICTIVE AND NONRESTRICTIVE ADJECTIVE CLAUSES

Depending on their role in a sentence, adjective clauses are restrictive or nonrestrictive. A **restrictive clause** provides identification of the noun it modifies. A **nonrestrictive clause** provides information that is not essential for identification. Thus, in the sentence "The man who owns that car just walked up," the man is identified by the clause *who owns that car*. But in the sentence "John Williams, who owns that car, just walked up," the clause *who* *owns that car* does not identify John Williams (he is identified by his name). The clause tells us something additional; it adds information about John Williams.

Restrictive Adjective Clauses

The restrictive adjective clause is not set off by commas because it is essential to the identification of the word being modified.

> The grade *that I received on my report* pleased me.
> Anyone *who saw the accident* should call the police.

Without the modifying clauses (*that I received on my report*; *who saw the accident*), the nouns are not identified. What grade and what anyone are we talking about? But when we add the modifiers, we identify the *particular* grade and the *particular* anyone. In other words, this kind of clause restricts the meaning of a general noun to one specific member of its class.

Nonrestrictive Adjective Clauses

The nonrestrictive adjective clause does require commas. Although the clause supplies additional or incidental information about the word that it modifies, the information is not needed for identifying the noun. (Don't, however, get into the habit of thinking that a nonrestrictive clause is unimportant; unless it has some importance to the meaning of the sentence, it has no right to be in the sentence.) Nonrestrictive modifiers are usually found following proper nouns (*Mount Everest, Philadelphia, Mr. Frank Smith*); nouns already identified (the oldest *boy* in her class, her only *grandchild*); and one-of-a-kind nouns (Alice's *mother*, the *provost* of the college, the *writer* of the editorial).

The following examples contrast restrictive and nonrestrictive adjective clauses. (See Supplement.)

> I visited an old friend *who is retiring soon*. [Restrictive]
> I visited my oldest and closest friend, *who is retiring soon*. [Nonrestrictive]
>
> The man *whose car had been wrecked* asked us for a ride. [Restrictive]
> Mr. Ash, *whose car had been wrecked*, asked us for a ride. [Nonrestrictive]
>
> A small stream *that flows through the property* supplies an occasional trout. [Restrictive]
> Caldwell Creek, *which flows through the property*, supplies an occasional trout. [Nonrestrictive]
>
> She wants to retire to a place *where freezing weather is unknown*. [Restrictive]
> She wants to retire to Panama City, *where freezing weather is unknown*. [Nonrestrictive]

SUPPLEMENT

A few distinctions in the use of *who, which,* and *that* in adjective clauses are generally observed. *Which* refers only to things; *who* refers to people; and *that* refers to things or people. *That* is used only in restrictive clauses; in other words, a "that" adjective clause is not set off by commas. Because *which* is the relative pronoun that must be used in a nonrestrictive clause modifying a thing, there is a convention that *which* should not introduce a restrictive adjective clause. This convention is generally, but by no means always, observed. People tend to use *which* in their writing when *that* would be better.

Certain problems associated with the loose or faulty use of relative pronouns and adjective clauses are discussed in Lesson 23.

SUMMARY OF ADJECTIVE CLAUSES

1. *Function:* to modify a noun or a pronoun

2. *Position:* follows the noun or pronoun that it modifies

3. *Subordinators:*
   a. relative pronouns (*who, whom, which, that*), which function within the adjective clause as subjects, direct objects, or objects of prepositions
   b. relative adjectives (*whose, which*)
   c. relative adverbs (*when, where*)

4. *Special problem:* Adjective clauses vital to the identification of the nouns being modified are restrictive and do not require commas. Clauses not necessary for identification are nonrestrictive and are set off by commas.

English Fundamentals Online

After you have completed the Practice Sheets and Exercises in this lesson, you can find additional help and drill work at **MyWritingLab.com**, in the section on Parts of Speech, Phrases, and Clauses.

NAME _____   SCORE _____

Directions: Each italicized unit is an adjective clause. In the space at the left, copy the word that is the antecedent of the relative pronoun in the clause. Note that some of the adjective clauses occur within an adverbial unit, and others have adverbial clauses within them. Note carefully the occasions when the clause is set off by commas.

someone 1. I need to find someone *who can tutor me in that subject.*

exercises 2. The exercises *the physical therapist gave me* are rather difficult.

gate 3. The gate *which closes off that pasture* was left open yesterday.

Joe Mann 4. Across the mall I spotted Joe Mann, *whom I have not seen for several months.*

Tom Johnson 5. Tom Johnson, *whose lecture notes I borrowed last week,* is an excellent student.

person 6. Please tell me the name of the person *to whom you wrote that letter.*

Senator Matthews 7. I sent that letter to Senator Matthews, *who has represented our state for almost 10 years.*

teacher 8. A teacher *whom I admire very much* will write a letter of recommendation for me.

Allison McGuire 9. That girl across the room is Allison McGuire, *whom you met last week at Linda's house.*

Martha James 10. For my partner on the next project, I will choose Martha James, *whose work in this class has always been excellent.*

sled 11. My little brother is sliding down the hill on a sled *he borrowed from our neighbor.*

Mario Lopez 12. Mario Lopez, *who has been my friend for many years,* is considering a move from here to the coast of Maine.

article 13. Whenever I read an article *that you have recommended,* I learn something amazing about the American political system.

Aunt Autumn 14. Aunt Autumn, *whom I visit whenever I can find time,* bakes incredibly good chocolate chip cookies.

place 15. Once we get to the place in the road *where the pavement ends,* we should probably turn around and go back to town.

shirt 16. I can't see much difference between that shirt, *which costs a small fortune,* and the other shirt for far less money.

photos 17. After we have printed all the photos *we took last weekend,* we need to delete any unwanted pictures from the computer.

town 18. Although I cannot remember the name of the town *we visited last summer,* I have a vivid memory of the ranch just outside of town.

time 19. If your flight will not arrive at the time *when you originally planned,* tell me the new time, and I will meet you at the airport.

bookstore 20. Let's go to that same bookstore, *where we can have coffee and buy a couple of new books.*

Directions: Each sentence contains one adjective clause. Underline the adjective clause and write the word it modifies (the antecedent) in the space at the left.

Jason   1. Jason Schmidt, <u>who maintains our computer system,</u> will be on vacation for the next two weeks.

Jason   2. Jason, <u>whose official title is Manager of Information Technology,</u> is usually called "The IT Guy."

Jason   3. It is Jason <u>whom we call whenever our computers develop problems.</u>

Computers   4. Unfortunately, our computers, <u>which all have been around for several years,</u> have problems on a regular basis.

★ _____ 5. So, whenever we encounter a problem that we cannot solve by re-booting the computer, we call Jason.

computer   6. Sometimes Jason can fix the problem from his own computer, which is in an office in the basement.

solution   7. If that <u>solution, which is easy for Jason,</u> does not work, he pays a personal visit to the computer.

_____ 8. When he arrives in the office for a "house call," Jason, who is always dressed in old blue jeans and a sweatshirt, gives us a bright smile.

_____ 9. Last year a new manager gave Jason a directive that went against everything in Jason's makeup as an IT guy.

_____ 10. The directive read, "Please wear a dress shirt and tie," neither of which was included in Jason's wardrobe.

_____ 11. Jason did not follow the manager's request, which would have choked off his thinking processes and made him ineffective.

_____ 12. Actually, a shirt and tie did not fit the "IT guy" image that Jason carried in his mind.

_____ 13. When Jason was in the college where he learned his computer skills, everyone, including the teachers, dressed very casually.

_____ 14. Finally, since skilled computer technologists are in short supply, the manager withdrew her request, which we had always thought very silly.

_____ 15. So Jason, who is comfortable in his jeans and sweatshirt, comes to the office and fixes our computers.

_____ 16. First, he sits down at the desk and stares at the screen of the computer that has the problem.

_____ 17. Then his fingers fly across the keyboard, and he fixes the problem, which is usually fairly easy for him.

_____ 18. Sometimes the problem is more difficult than he expects, and he must use one of the special discs that he has prepared for emergencies.

_____ 19. The use of a disc always annoys Jason because it undermines his reputation as a wizard, a reputation that he has been building for years.

_____ 20. Everyone in the office loves Jason because he is a cheerful man who always solves our problems.

NAME _____   SCORE _____

Directions: Each of these sentences contains an adjective clause, but necessary commas have been omitted. In the first space at the left, write the antecedent of the relative pronoun in the clause. In the second space at the left, write **N** if the clause is nonrestrictive or **R** if the clause is restrictive. Set off nonrestrictive clauses with commas where needed. **Review:** Underline any adverbial clauses in the sentences in this exercise.

man
R
1. Yesterday I had lunch with a man who went to high school with me.

Richard J.
N
2. Yesterday I had lunch with Richard Johnson who went to high school with me.

man
R
3. The man that you saw at the mall was my chemistry teacher.

Carl Taylor
N
4. In high school chemistry, I had Carl Taylor who ran a very difficult class as my teacher.

Chemistry
R
5. During that year in his class, chemistry proved itself a subject in which I probably would not succeed, or so I thought.

class
N
6. In college I took chemistry again because I needed a chemistry class which was a part of my engineering program.

work
N
7. In my second try at chemistry, I made a good grade because of hard work which I had not done in high school.

students
R
8. In fact, I was so successful that I now regularly tutor students that need help with chemistry.

Mr. Taylor
N
9. My lack of success in high school was not the fault of Mr. Taylor who was actually a very good teacher.

anyone
R
10. My success in college chemistry might serve as an inspiration to anyone who has not succeeded in any class in high school.

man
R
11. Yesterday, when I had a free afternoon, I attended a lecture by a man who is an expert in macroeconomics.

field
R
12. Macroeconomics is a field in which people study the interrelations among major sectors of the economy.

N
13. Since I am only a freshman, I did not understand much of the lecture, which was really at the level of graduate students in economics.

friends
R
14. So at the earliest possible moment, I slipped out of the lecture hall and joined my friends who were waiting for me in the Student Union.

friends
R
15. Those of my friends who are not dedicated students laughed when I told them of my experience.

field
R
16. I, however, was pleased with myself because I had ventured into a field where I knew absolutely nothing and had learned a little bit.

R _____ 17. I'll probably take such a course in the future because everyone needs knowledge of the economic forces that cause booms and depressions.

R _____ 18. For the rest of the afternoon, my friends and I shot a few games of pool and discussed the courses that we might take next term.

N _____ 19. Since I had a major test the next day, I ate supper and went back to my room where I spent the next four hours in review for the test.

R _____ 20. The next day I had good control of the materials I had reviewed, but, as always, there was one unexpected question on the test.

N _____ 21. Yesterday Joan and Tom heard a radio interview with Thomas Perry who is a very successful writer.

R N _____ 22. He specializes in "thrillers" or "mysteries" all of which have intriguing plots and characters.

N _____ 23. James Patterson whose thrillers are much more frightening than Perry's is another of Tom's favorite writers.

N _____ 24. Two of Patterson's books which he wrote very early in his career have been made into movies.

N _____ 25. Because the interview was interesting, Tom decided to buy one of Perry's books which he downloaded to his electronic reader.

R _____ 26. The school's soccer team lost another game yesterday; unfortunately, it was a loss that dropped the team far down in the conference standings.

_____ 27. On Friday the team plays last year's conference champs in a game that may decide whether our team makes the playoffs.

_____ 28. Two of my friends are soccer players whose nerves are already on edge about Friday's game.

_____ 29. Soccer is a sport that is not very popular on campus, so only a few people attend the games.

_____ 30. I have recruited ten people who will attend the game and cheer on our friends.

_____ 31. Please give this package to anyone who answers the door at that office.

_____ 32. Anyone to whom you give that package will deliver it to the right person.

_____ 33. No one here knows the name of the person whose job is the delivery of such packages within that company.

_____ 34. You should find someone who looks trustworthy and hand over the package to that person.

_____ 35. Once we find a person to whom we can entrust that package, our responsibilities will end.

Directions: The two sentences in each item can be combined into one sentence by changing the second sentence into a relative clause. Write the new sentence in the blank. Be sure to punctuate each clause correctly.

1. Last week Tim Wilson visited our campus. Wilson was a friend of ours in high school.

   Last week Tim Wilson, who was a friend of ours in HS, visited our campus

2. Tim is now working as an engineer for an auto racing team. He finished his degree last year.

   _____

3. Tim is a very intelligent man. Many of us sought help from him in high school.

   _____

4. Tim got his job with the team quite by accident. The team is located in Indianapolis.

   _____

5. He was talking on the phone with his uncle. He spoke to his uncle about once a month.

   _____

6. His uncle knew of Tim's impending graduation. He is friends with a well-known race-team owner.

   _____

7. Tim's uncle mentioned him to the owner. His uncle knew of his interest in racing.

   _____

8. The owner was looking for a bright young engineer. Tim fit this description exactly.

   _____

9. The owner interviewed Tim. Tim's credentials greatly impressed the owner.

   _____

10. Shortly thereafter Tim accepted a job with the team. He is extremely happy there.

    _____

Brief Writing Assignment: Write a paragraph of five or six sentences describing your actions as you prepare to write an essay. Write two sentences that contain adverbial clauses and three sentences that contain adjective clauses.

An adverbial clause such as *after the rain stopped* can work to set the time of the main verb just as the single-word adverb *yesterday* does. The adjective clause *whom I knew well* can modify our understanding of a noun in the same way the single-word adjective *tall* does. A noun clause works in a similar way: It does the work of a regular noun.

NOUN CLAUSES

A **noun clause** is a group of words containing a subject–verb combination and a subordinating word. The subordinating words that serve to introduce noun clauses are conjunctions (*that, if, whether*); pronouns (*who, whom, what, which, whoever, whatever, whichever*); adjectives (*whose, which, what*); and adverbs (*when, where, why, how*). Remember that the subordinating word is part of the clause and always stands at or near the beginning of the clause. As an example, consider the following similar sentences:

Marge now understands the answer.

The subject (Marge) acts (understands) on a direct object (the answer). In the same way a noun clause can replace a single word serving as a direct object:

Marge now understands why we were late.

The formula for the sentence is the same:

Marge (subject) now understands (verb) why we were late (direct object).

The only grammatical difference between the two sentences is that the direct object in the second sentence is a clause (a group of words with a subject and a verb) instead of a single word.

Jill now wonders *if her answer was the correct one.*
[Noun clause subordinated by the conjunction *if* and used as a direct object.]

All of us hope *that you'll return soon.*
[Noun clause subordinated by the conjunction *that* and used as a direct object.]

I do not know *who he is.*
[Noun clause subordinated by the pronoun *who* used as the subjective complement within the clause.]

I know *what I would do with the extra money.*
[Noun clause subordinated by the pronoun *what* used as the direct object within the clause.]

Tell me *whom Mary is feuding with now.*
[Noun clause subordinated by the pronoun *whom* used as the object of the preposition *with.*]

You must decide *which car you will use today.*
[Noun clause subordinated by the adjective *which* modifying the direct object *car.*]

Why Morton left school still puzzles his friends.
[Noun clause subordinated by the adverb *why* serving as subject of *puzzles.*]

As you can see from these examples, a noun clause, like a noun, can be a subject, direct object, subjective complement, object of a preposition, or appositive (see page 95). You can understand the uses of the noun clause if you think of it as a clause equivalent to a "something" or a "someone" in one of these noun slots.

Subject (S)

The *girl* opened the window. [Single-word noun as S.]
Whoever came in first opened the window. [Noun clause as S.]

His *story* is very convincing. [Noun as S.]
What he told us is very convincing. [Noun clause as S.]

Subjective Complement (S.C.)

This is his *story.* [Single-word noun as S.C.]
This is *what he told us.* [Noun clause as S.C.]

Direct Object (D.O.)

Mr. Allen announced *his resignation.* [Single-word noun as D.O.]
Mr. Allen announced *that he would resign.* [Noun clause as D.O.]
Can you tell me your *time* of arrival? [Single-word noun as D.O.]
Can you tell me *when you will arrive?* [Noun clause as D.O.]

Object of a Preposition (O.P.)

Give the package to the *man.* [Single-word noun as O.P.]
Give the package to *whoever opens the door.* [Noun clause as O.P.]

Note that the choice between *who/whoever* and *whom/whomever* depends on its use in the clause. This rule creates apparently awkward and sometimes tricky choices:

Give the book to *whomever you see first.* [*whomever* is the object of the verb *see*]
Give the book to *whoever answers the door.* [*whoever* is the subject of the verb *answers*]

(See Supplement 1.)

In noun clauses used as direct objects, the conjunction *that* is often unexpressed because the meaning is usually clear without it.

I know *that you will be happy here.*
[Noun clause subordinated by the conjunction *that.*]

I know *you will be happy here.*
[Noun clause with subordinating word omitted.]

This omission of the subordinating word creates an ellipsis, a construction similar to an elliptical adverbial clause. In adverbial clauses, the subject and part of the verb (the auxiliaries) are omitted. In this construction, only the subordinating word is omitted.

Most of the noun clauses that you read and write will be used as subjects, direct objects (the most common use), subjective complements, or objects of prepositions. However, two rather special uses should be noted, the *delayed* noun clause and the *appositive* noun clause.

DELAYED NOUN CLAUSE

One common use of a noun clause is as a delayed subject. The signal for this construction is the word *it* standing in the subject position, with the meaningful subject being a noun clause following the verb.

> It is unfortunate *that you were delayed.*

Although the sentence begins with *It* and the clause follows the verb, the clause is the real subject. The meaning of the sentence is "That you were delayed is unfortunate."

A related noun clause use puts the word *it* in the direct object slot with a noun clause following as an objective complement. This use, which is encountered less frequently than the delayed subject, gives us a clause that we can call a delayed direct object.

> We think it unlikely *that Jones will be reelected.*

APPOSITIVE NOUN CLAUSE

To understand the other special noun clause, you must know what an appositive is. An **appositive** is a noun unit inserted into a sentence to rename another noun that usually immediately precedes the appositive. A simple example occurs in the following sentence:

> Senator Jackson, a dedicated environmentalist, voted for the amendment.

Because any noun unit can be used as an appositive, noun clauses sometimes function in this position. Some noun clause appositives are separated from the noun they are renaming by at least a comma, sometimes by a heavier mark.

> There still remains one mystery: *how* you found that missing book. [The noun clause renames the preceding noun, *mystery.*]

A rather special type of appositive noun clause, subordinated by *that* and following such nouns as *fact, belief, hope, statement, news,* and *argument,* is usually not set off by any mark of punctuation.

> You cannot deny the fact *that* catcher is your best position.
> Your statement *that* you would answer the question later was diplomatic.

(See Supplement 2.)

SUPPLEMENT 1

You have probably already noticed that the pronouns, adjectives, and adverbs that subordinate noun clauses are essentially the same words that are used in questions (Lesson 6).

The two uses are alike in the important fact that they always stand at the beginning of the clause. The two uses differ in that, as interrogatives, the words bring about the subject–verb inversion, whereas in noun clauses the subject–verb position is the normal one.

> *Whom* will the mayor appoint?
> [This sentence is a direct question; it calls for an answer. *Whom* is the D.O. of the main verb.]
>
> *I* wonder *whom the mayor will appoint.*
> [This sentence is a statement, not a direct question. Notice that a question mark is not required. *Whom* is the D.O. within the noun clause.]

SUPPLEMENT 2

Because an appositive is a renamer, it represents a reduced form of a Pattern 2 sentence in which the subject and a noun subjective complement are joined by a form of *be*. The writer of the sentence "Senator Jackson, a dedicated environmentalist, voted for the amendment" could have written two simple sentences, the second one repeating a noun used in the first:

> Senator Jackson voted for the amendment.
> Senator Jackson [or He] is a dedicated environmentalist.

The adjective clause offers the writer a device for compressing this information into one sentence.

> Senator Jackson, who is a dedicated environmentalist, voted for the amendment.

The appositive represents a further compression.

> Senator Jackson, a dedicated environmentalist, voted for the amendment.

If you think of the appositive as a renamer of the preceding noun (the two nouns could be joined by a form of *be*), you have a handy test to help you recognize any noun clause appositive use.

> There still remains one mystery: *how you found that missing book.*
> [Test: The mystery *is* how you found that missing book.]
>
> You can't deny the fact *that she has real talent.*
> [Test: The fact *is* that she has real talent.]
>
> Your contention *that you should play catcher* has some merit.
> [Test: The contention *is* that you should play catcher.]

If you remember a few points about the form, function, and positioning of adjective and noun clauses, you should have little difficulty in distinguishing between them. Although certain kinds of noun clauses in apposition may, at first glance, look like adjective clauses, a few simple tests clearly show the difference.

> The news *that you brought us* is welcome. [Adjective clause]
> The news *that Bob has recovered* is welcome. [Noun clause]

If you remember that an adjective clause is a describer and that an appositive noun clause is a renamer, you can see that in the first sentence the clause describes—in fact, identifies—the noun *news*, but it does not tell us what the news is. In the second sentence the clause does more: It tells us what the news is. Remember the *be* test. "The news is *that you brought us* . . ." does not make sense, but "The news is *that Bob has recovered* . . ." does; therefore, the second clause is a noun clause in apposition.

Another test that can be applied to these two types of sentences is based on the fact that in adjective clauses, but not in noun clauses, *which* can be substituted for *that*. "The news *which* you brought us . . ." is acceptable English; the clause, in this case, is an adjective clause. But because we can't say "The news *which* Bob has recovered . . ." the clause is a noun clause; it cannot be an adjective clause.

SUMMARY OF NOUN CLAUSES

1. *Function:* to work as a noun within a clause

2. *Positions:* subject (or delayed subject), renaming subjective complement, direct object (or delayed direct object), object of preposition, or appositive

3. *Subordinators:*
   a. conjunctions: *that, if, whether*
   b. pronouns: *who, whom, which, what,* and . . . *ever* forms, standing for unknown persons or things
   c. adjectives: *whose, which, what*
   d. adverbs: *when, where, why, how*

4. *Special problem:* Some noun appositive clauses closely resemble adjective clauses. They differ in that, in addition to describing the noun, the appositive clause renames the noun:

   The remark *that Jim made* (adjective clause) was unwise.

   The remark *that Mr. Smith cannot be trusted* (appositive noun clause) was unwise.

English Fundamentals Online

After you have completed the Practice Sheets and Exercises in this lesson, you can find additional help and drill work at **MyWritingLab.com**, in the section on Parts of Speech, Phrases, and Clauses.

NAME _____   SCORE _____

Directions: Identify the function of each noun clause by writing one of the following abbreviations in the space at the left:

S. [subject or delayed subject]   S.C. [subjective complement]

D.O. [direct object or   O.P. [object of preposition]
    delayed direct object]   Ap. [appositive]

_DO_   1. The weather forecasters predicted *that today would be bright and sunny.*

_S_   2. *What you heard about the new agenda for the meeting* is correct.

_S_   3. *Whoever answers the phone* can direct your call to me.

_S_   4. *Whomever you see at the front desk* can direct you to my office.

_S_   5. It's wonderful *that you can come for a visit.*

_OP_   6. We should be delighted by *whoever is qualified for that difficult job.*

_OP_   7. We should be delighted by *whomever we can find for that difficult job.*

_SC_   8. The important news is *that the bus is leaving for the game two hours ahead of schedule.*

_Ap_   9. The men were pleasantly surprised by the news *that they will receive a raise.*

_S_   10. *That they will receive a raise* surprised the men.

_S_   11. In these economic times, it is amazing *that the men will receive a raise.*

_DO_   12. Yesterday the coach announced *that Mike Johnson will start as pitcher in the first game.*

_DO_   13. We all know *that Mike will do a great job on the mound.*

_S_   14. In this case, *whatever choice you make* will be fine.

_DO_   15. The class did not know *why the test had been postponed.*

~~DO~~ _DO_   16. I often wonder *if my choice of majors is a good one for me.*

_OP_   17. Make that idea clear to *whoever is still in the classroom.*

_OP_   18. Please make that announcement to *whomever you see in the classroom.*

_Ap_   19. Make the news *that the test has been postponed* clear to everyone in the classroom.

_S_   20. It is lucky for me *that the test has been postponed.*

Directions: Each of the following sentences contains a noun clause. Put brackets around the noun clause and identify its function in the sentence by writing one of the following abbreviations in the space at the left of the sentence:

S. [subject or delayed subject]　　　　S.C. [subjective complement]

D.O. [direct object or delayed　　　　O.P. [object of preposition]
　　　direct object]　　　　　　　　　A.P. [appositive]

_____ 1. The fact that James is a good choice for that job became clear immediately.

_____ 2. It is quite clear that James is a good choice for that job.

_____ 3. All of the office workers wondered where Les has been this morning.

_____ 4. How we can work out a solution to this problem is not clear yet.

_____ 5. The boss has not decided which computer system is best for our purposes.

_____ 6. You will certainly be successful in whichever job you choose.

_____ 7. I believe you will enjoy that novel.

_____ 8. Send a copy of that article to whomever you think will be interested in it.

_____ 9. I found it unfortunate that I could not attend that seminar.

_____ 10. It was unfortunate that I could not attend that seminar.

_____ 11. Please ask whoever has it for a copy of that article.

_____ 12. The coach was amazed by the fact that 97 people came for the initial tryouts.

_____ 13. That all those people were interested in soccer was amazing to everyone.

_____ 14. It seems wrong that the coach can only keep 35 players for the soccer team.

_____ 15. That wild story is what he told us as an excuse for his absence.

_____ 16. We will never know what the real reason for his absence was.

_____ 17. Perhaps it was a mistake that I considered him a good source of notes for that test.

_____ 18. This request is meant for whichever of those two people parked in my driveway.

_____ 19. Can you tell me when Jason left for home this morning?

_____ 20. Please tell me whose bright idea this project was.

Subordination: Noun Clauses

Directions: Each of the following sentences contains a noun clause. Some noun clauses occur within other subordinate clauses. Others have such clauses within them. Put brackets around each noun clause and identify its function by writing one of the following abbreviations in the space at the left of the sentence:

S. [subject or delayed subject]   S.C. [subjective complement]

D.O. [direct object or delayed direct   O.P. [object of preposition]
object]   A.P. [appositive]

Note that some of the sentences are quite similar in wording but not in structure. These changes in structure should demonstrate that it is not difficult to achieve variety in your writing. **Review:** Underline and identify any other subordinate clauses in these sentences.

DO 1. I was surprised when I saw that you had bought a new car.

DO 2. Do you know where Jan found the funny hat she wore to the game yesterday?

DS 3. It always amazes me that people know only a few facts about the city where they live.

AP 4. The fact that 25 people came to my party was delightful.

SC 5. This silly song is what she sang in the karaoke contest last Saturday night.

OP 6. Give this note to whomever you see at the desk when you open the door of the office.

AP 7. You will surely be pleased by the fact that you bought that brand of mountain bike.

DO 8. At this time, the counselor cannot determine whether you will be a junior or a senior at the end of this term.

DO 9. No one knows where Jean and Martha will be living during the summer term.

DS 10. It seems unlikely that I will find a job for this summer.

DO 11. When you find out which classmate is the one who has your textbook, give him a call.

DO 12. I wonder why he called you when he was looking for a ride.

DO 13. All of us here at the office hope that you will feel better soon.

S 14. What became of all that money collected by his office remains a mystery to this day.

DO 15. We all wonder if we can find time for the final work on the project the corporate office assigned to us.

SKIP 16. Can you tell me something that will help me understand why my printer is not working?

Ap 17. The fact that the printer is out of black ink may be part of the explanation.

SS 18. What really annoys me is the constant changes in my schedule at work.

SC 19. The really annoying thing is that my schedule at work changes constantly.

DO 20. If you can tell me why I did not make an A on my paper, I will feel much better about the world.

_____ 21. I could see by your bouncy personality that you'd enjoy bungee jumping.

_____ 22. Although I knew that I would miss your arrival, I hurried to the airport as fast as I possibly could.

_____ 23. Senator Gordon believes that the last version of the bill, which went to the President this morning, is a very good piece of legislation.

_____ 24. The manager is looking for whoever can solve the problem that keeps our shipping department perpetually 3 days behind in its work.

_____ 25. Now we all know whom the memo that came yesterday morning was intended for.

_____ 26. What we don't understand is the widespread distribution of the memo.

_____ 27. The very heavy clouds overhead are what made us cancel outdoor band practice for today.

_____ 28. Let me tell you to what great expense we have gone so that we could solve that problem.

_____ 29. When it became clear that we could not solve that problem, we called you.

_____ 30. One mystery still lingers on: how we got into this situation in the first place.

_____ 31. We do hope that we can find a solution that will prevent this problem in the future.

_____ 32. The fact that your team of troubleshooters came so quickly is very encouraging.

_____ 33. That your team of troubleshooters came so quickly is very encouraging.

_____ 34. It is very encouraging that your team of troubleshooters came so quickly.

_____ 35. An easy solution to that problem is what we all secretly hope for.

_____ 36. From the time that the team members arrived until they had discovered what the problem was could not have been more than 3 hours.

_____ 37. The boss has decided that one of us should go to a seminar for training in the maintenance of that system.

_____ 38. If one of us learns how that system works, we can probably avoid these problems in the future.

_____ 39. We all owe that group a debt of gratitude because they so easily fixed what was wrong with that system.

Directions: Combine the following pairs of word groups into a single sentence by joining the second to the first as a noun clause.

1. (Something) seemed strange. Margie walked to class today instead of driving.

   _____

2. Please give this message to (someone). Whomever you find at the front desk.

   _____

3. (Something) is not clear in those instructions. When to tighten the bolts on the bottom of the chair.

   _____

4. That idea caught everyone by surprise. (The idea was) that you would sell your car and ride a bike to class.

   _____

5. Few of the people in the office know (something). Why that project has been postponed.

   _____

6. Obviously, there's only one solution to our problem. We need to buy a new lawnmower so we can cut the grass in the yard efficiently.

   _____

7. Ginny found it wonderful. We called and invited her to join us for dinner.

   _____

8. The team does not know (something) yet. Where the regional playoffs will be played.

   _____

9. The mechanic explained (something). Why Allison needs to change the oil in her car regularly.

   _____

10. Senator Ramirez told the caucus (something). He had voted for that bill every time it came to the floor.

    _____

Brief Writing Assignment: Write a paragraph of five or six sentences discussing your thoughts and attitudes before you begin working on a writing assignment. Use three noun clauses and one adjective clause in the sentences.

NAME _____   SCORE _____

Directions: The italicized material in each item is a subordinate clause. In the first space at the left, write one of the following to identify the clause:

Adv. [adverb clause]   Adj. [adjective clause]   N. [noun clause]

In the second space, write one of the following to identify the use within the clause of the word printed in bold-face type:

S. [subject]   I.O. [indirect object]   O.C. [objective complement]

D.O. [direct object]   S.C. [subjective complement]   O.P. [object of preposition]

Adv
OP
1. *When you come to the **end** of the road*, you will see a large house on the top of the hill.

Adj
SC
2. The fact *that the test is **difficult*** means a full night of study for me.

DO
3. I will give you the information *that* you *need* once I receive the e-mail containing it.

IO
4. Tomorrow I will introduce you to Harold Jameson, *who can give **you** some help with your problem.*

OP
5. *If we do not find the deed to that piece of **property***, we will retain an attorney to conduct a search.

OC
6. I believe *that the ride down the river made Jim a true **believer*** in the power of the river.

OC
7. Anyone *who found that ride down the river **unexciting*** must be a person with nerves of steel.

DO
8. *After we had reached the **end** of that exciting ride*, we were all soaking wet and very cold.

DO
9. Those men will finish that job by tomorrow afternoon *unless the weather keeps them from the **job**.*

DO
10. *That bad weather might prevent the **conclusion** of the project* never entered our minds.

_____
_____
11. At the meeting, I did not see some of the people *who might have shown **us** other solutions to that problem.*

_____
_____
12. The idea *that **Jim** would one day write a best-selling novel* never would have occurred to us back in college.

_____
_____
13. I think *we should find an alternate route through that area because of the **congestion*** in those small towns.

_____
DO
14. *After I had read 5 **articles** on that subject*, I still did not understand that subject very well.

_____
_____
15. One of the people *who* worked with us on that volunteer project has signed up for a day's work again next Saturday.

_____ 16. It is obvious to many people *that a new approach to our experimental study*
_____ *would probably make the project more **successful***.

_____ 17. Please show us *where we can find some people **trained** in that highly*
_____ *specialized field*.

_____ 18. The fact *that Jim asked **us** for help with his paper surprised all of us*.
_____

_____ 19. Jim has always been one of those people *who would rather do their **work***
_____ *independently*.

_____ 20. It was a big moment for all of us *when Jim finally asked us for **help** on that*
_____ *paper*.

_____ 21. After all that study, I realized *that I had become **one** of the few people on this*
_____ *campus with a thorough knowledge of that subject*.

_____ 22. *Although we have no **idea** of the importance of that scientist's discovery,* its
_____ uses will become evident in the near future.

_____ 23. *Once the **expedition** arrived at the top of the mountain,* the guide planted a
_____ flag at the summit.

_____ 24. The women on the soccer team want a coach *who will recruit **players** to carry*
_____ *on the team's winning tradition*.

_____ 25. At first, no one could remember Jackson, *whose personality is a little **bland***.

_____ 26. Please tell me the name of the person ***whom** you saw in that car*.
_____

_____ 27. The workers will move to that next room *when **they** have finished the carpet*
_____ *in this room*.

_____ 28. Will you show the changes in these plans to the man *who is the **foreman** on*
_____ *that job?*

_____ 29. *Unless you work very hard on that **paper** tonight,* you probably will not finish
_____ it in time for class tomorrow.

_____ 30. *Where the lost **book** is at this particular moment* remains a mystery to all of
_____ us.

Directions: In each pair of word groups, use the first group as the main clause and resolve the second into it as an adverb, adjective, or noun clause. Write the new sentence in the space below each item. Identify the subordinate clause you have created by writing one of the following in the space at the left.

       Adv. [adverb]   Adj. [adjective clause]   N. [noun clause]

In some sentences the suggested subordinating word is included in brackets with the item. Be sure to add punctuation where needed.

_____ 1. I will probably take my car to the shop this week. [since, because] The air conditioning system is not working correctly.

_____

_____ 2. I followed the directions for the assembly of those shelves exactly. Exactly as they were written.

_____

_____ 3. *Something* is not believable. The fact that only one person reported a sighting of the UFO.

_____

_____ 4. Can you tell me *something*? When the next door neighbors will be back from their vacation.

_____

_____ 5. Give the check to the woman. [whom] You will see behind the desk just inside the door.

_____

_____ 6. Can you show me the person? [whose] The person's coat was hanging next to mine on the coat rack.

_____

_____ 7. It seems unlikely that *something*. All five of us will be able to enroll in the same class.

_____

_____ 8. The party will start without us. [unless] We can avoid that traffic jam on the East-West Connector.

_____

_____ 9. This morning I actually saw the dog. [that] The dog steals my newspaper from my driveway every morning.

_____

_____ 10. The shop owners on Main Street don't know *something*. [when] The paving of the street in front of their shops will be finished.

_____

_____ 11. The workers set up the power tools and went to work. Once they finally arrived at the job site.

_____

_____ 12. You should show us the general area. [where] You lost your class ring.

_____

_____ 13. Charlie will help you with the format for documentation of that paper. [if] You call him before the last minute.

_____

_____ 14. Jim pointed out *something*. [where] He last saw his lost puppy.

_____

_____ 15. *Something* seems a little odd to me. [That] we cannot find any more sources for that report.

_____

_____ 15. We all thought it wonderful that *something*. The first big snow of winter had fallen.

_____

_____ 16. I would like to introduce you to Alex Mendez. He is the president of one of the local banks.

_____

_____ 17. We should be able to see the waterfall. [once] We reach the crest of this hill.

_____

_____ 18. Robin Stanley is the girl. [who, that] She is standing over there by the window.

_____

_____ 19. My good grade on that test does not surprise me. [because] I studied hard for three nights in a row before the test.

_____

_____ 20. The fact made everyone in the office very happy. The fact was that the long, boring staff meeting was finally over.

_____

A **phrase** is a group of related words that does *not* contain a subject and a verb in combination. Like the subordinate clause, the phrase is used in a sentence as a single part of speech. Many of the sentences that you have studied so far have contained a prepositional phrase, which consists of a preposition, a noun or a pronoun used as its object, and any modifiers of the object. Most prepositional phrases are used as adjectives or adverbs:

> Most *of my friends* live *in the East*.
>
> [The first phrase is used as an adjective to modify the pronoun *most*; the second is used as an adverb to modify the verb *live*.]

Much less commonly, a prepositional phrase is used as a noun:

> *Before lunch* is the best time for the meeting.
>
> [The phrase is the subject of the verb *is*.]
>
> She waved to us from *across the room*.
>
> [The phrase is the object of the preposition *from*.]

Another important kind of phrase makes use of a verbal. A **verbal** is a word formed from a verb but used as a different part of speech. There are three kinds of verbals: the gerund, the infinitive, and the participle.

GERUNDS

A **gerund** is a noun formed by adding *ing* either to the base of the verb (*studying*) or to an auxiliary (*having studied, being studied, having been studied*). You might think of the gerund phrase as the equivalent of a noun. It can appear in any place in a sentence where a noun might appear: subject, direct object, renaming subjective complement, object of preposition, or (rarely) appositive.

> *Studying* demands most of my time. [Subject]
>
> I usually enjoy *studying*. [Direct object]
>
> My main activity is *studying*. [Renaming subjective complement]
>
> You won't pass the course without *studying*. [Object of preposition]
>
> Might I suggest to you another activity: *studying*? [Appositive]

These single-word gerund uses are uncomplicated. "He enjoys *studying*" and "He enjoys football" are alike in their structure; the only difference is that in one the direct object is a word formed from a verb and in the other it is a regular noun. Because they are formed from verbs and are thus "verbal nouns," gerunds can have a direct object or a subjective complement. The following examples will help clarify this important point.

> He enjoys *walking in the snow*.
>
> [The gerund has no complement. Compare "He walks in the snow."]

She enjoys *building model airplanes.*

[*Airplanes* is the direct object of the gerund *building*. Compare "She builds model airplanes."]

He enjoys *being helpful.* He enjoyed *being elected treasurer.*

[*Helpful* is the subjective complement of the gerund *being; treasurer* is the subjective complement of the passive gerund *being elected*. Compare "He is helpful" and "He was elected treasurer."]

She enjoyed *telling us the good news.*

[*Us* is the indirect object and *news* is the direct object of the gerund *telling*. Compare "She told us the good news."]

He enjoyed *making our vacation pleasant.*

[*Vacation* is the direct object of the gerund *making*, and *pleasant* is the objective complement of *vacation*. Compare "He made our vacation pleasant."]

A gerund phrase may contain a noun or pronoun that precedes the gerund to show the actor performing the action named by the gerund.

The group considered **your** *making those comments* a helpful addition to the discussion.

The group considered **Bob's** *making those comments* a helpful addition to the discussion.

Because *making those comments* is a gerund or verbal noun, the noun or pronoun showing who made the comments is in the possessive case. Contrast the use of a simple noun in these sentences:

The group considered her comments a helpful addition to the discussion.

The group considered Bob's comments a useful addition to the discussion.

In other words, the subject of a gerund phrase should be in the possessive case.

INFINITIVES

An **infinitive** is a verbal consisting of the base of the verb, usually preceded by *to* (*to* is called the sign of the infinitive). The infinitive uses auxiliaries to show tense and voice: *to study, to have studied, to be studying, to have been studying, to be studied, to have been studied*. An **infinitive phrase** consists of an infinitive plus its modifiers and/or complements. Infinitive units are used as nouns, as adjectives, and as adverbs:

To attend the party without an invitation would be tactless.

[The infinitive phrase is used as the subject of the sentence. Within the phrase, *party* is the direct object.]

It would be tactless *to attend the party without an invitation.*

[In this pattern, the infinitive phrase is called a delayed subject; hence it serves a noun use. The signal word is *it*; although *it* stands in subject position, the infinitive phrase is the meaningful subject. Sometimes the *it* is in the direct object slot with the delayed infinitive phrase following an objective complement: I would consider it tactless *to attend the party without an invitation*. Compare a similar noun clause use in Lesson 10.]

I wanted *to give Charles another chance.*

[The infinitive phrase is the direct object of *wanted*. Within the phrase, *Charles* is the indirect object and *chance* the direct object of the infinitive. Compare "I gave Charles another chance."]

My plan is *to become an active precinct worker.*

[The infinitive phrase is used as a noun; it is a subjective complement that renames the subject *plan*. Within the phrase, *worker* is the subjective complement of the infinitive. Compare "I became an active precinct worker."]

The test *to be taken next Friday* is an important one.
[The infinitive phrase is used as an adjective modifying *test*.]

I am happy *to meet you*.
[The infinitive phrase is used as an adverb modifying the adjective *happy*.]

To be sure of a good seat, you should arrive early.
[The infinitive phrase is used as an adverb modifying *should arrive*.]

Infinitive phrases sometimes include their own subjects. Notice that when a pronoun is used as the subject of an infinitive, the pronoun is in the objective case (see Lesson 24).

We wanted *her to resign*.
We know *him to be a good referee*.

In a rather common sentence type, the subject of an infinitive is preceded by *for*, which in this case is considered part of the phrase.

For us to leave now would be impolite.
It's silly *for you to feel neglected*.

The infinitive without *to* may form a phrase that is used as the direct object of such verbs as *let*, *help*, *make*, *see*, *hear*, and *watch*:

The teacher let *us leave early*.
Martha watched *her son score the winning touchdown*.

The infinitive without *to* is also sometimes used as the object of a preposition, such as *except*, *but*, and *besides*:

He could do nothing except *resign gracefully*.
He did everything but *write the paper for me*.

SUPPLEMENT 1

In Lesson 6, you learned that an interrogative unit in a direct question stands at the beginning of the sentence. Notice how this positioning can affect the internal makeup of a gerund phrase or an infinitive phrase:

How many new members did we succeed in enrolling?
[*Enrolling* is the gerund form of a transitive verb and therefore requires a direct object—in this case, *members*.]

Which car did you finally decide *to buy*?
[*Car* is the direct object of the infinitive *to buy*.]

SUPPLEMENT 2

When the gerund is preceded by a pronoun, the pronoun should be in the possessive case.

The audience *enjoyed her dancing in the first act*.
[Compare "The audience enjoyed her dance in the first act."]

We appreciated *your helping the class with that project.*
[Compare "We appreciated your help with that project."]

SUMMARY OF GERUND AND INFINITIVE PHRASES

Gerund Phrases

1. Forms: *studying, having studied, being studied, having been studied*

2. Function: as a noun within the larger unit

3. Positions: subject, renaming subjective complement, direct object, object of preposition.

Infinitive Phrases

1. Forms: *to study, to have studied, to be studying, to have been studying, to be studied, to have been studied.* Some infinitive phrases have subjects (We wanted her *to run for office*) in the objective case.

2. Function: as adjective (Here are the letters *to be mailed today*), as adverb (I am happy *to meet you*), or as noun (*To leave* now would be unwise).

3. Positions: subject (or delayed subject), direct object (or delayed direct object), renaming subjective complement, and (rarely) object of preposition.

4. Special structures:
   a. *For* sometimes introduces an infinitive phrase that has a subject.

      For you to criticize his work would be presumptuous.

   b. A phrase with a subject but without the marker *to* is often used as a direct object following one of these verbs: *let, help, make, see, hear, watch.*

      Mother let *us mix the cookie dough.*
      Ms. Jones heard *the man threaten the cashier.*

   c. The infinitive without *to* is used as the object of the prepositions *except, but, besides.*

      He could do nothing but *leave quietly.*

English Fundamentals Online

After you have completed the Practice Sheets and Exercises in this lesson, you can find additional help and drill work at **MyWritingLab.com**, in the section on Gerund and Infinitive Phrases.

NAME _____   SCORE _____ *in*

Directions: In the space at the left, copy the abbreviation that identifies the use in the sentence of the italicized gerund phrase:

S. [subject]   S.C. [subjective complement]
D.O. [direct object]   O.P. [object of preposition]

DO   1. Mark briefly considered *studying architecture* as a major.

S   2. Then *working in aeronautical engineering* caught his fancy for a time.

DO   3. In two year's time, he thought about *majoring in four or five different subjects.*

SC   4. For most students, one of college's important rituals is *considering several majors.*

S   5. Finally, *choosing a major* became an important goal for Mark.

OP   6. He helped himself in the selection process by *talking at length with his parents.*

DO   7. His college advisor suggested *taking an aptitude and interest test.*

SC   8. The biggest help in the decision was *working as an engineer's assistant for a summer.*

OP   9. He became fascinated by the complexities of *constructing bridges and large buildings.*

S   10. *Deciding on civil engineering as a major* was very satisfying to Mark.

S   11. *Postponing decisions* is a firmly entrenched habit for some people.

OP   12. Others specialize in *making decisions in great haste.*

OP   13. Occasionally, people get themselves in difficulty by *deciding too quickly.*

OP   14. One of my cousins made a hasty decision about *buying a car.*

S   15. *Seeing one commercial on television* was enough for her.

S   16. *Driving the car around the block* clinched the sale for her.

DO   17. After the sale, she began *evaluating the qualities of the car.*

OP   18. She determined the actual fuel mileage by *measuring fuel consumption against the actual mileage in everyday driving.*

SC   19. The disappointing discovery was *the car's burning of large quantities of fuel in the course of her daily driving.*

S   20. *Uncovering several other deficiencies in the car* made my cousin regret her decision.

Directions: Each sentence contains one italicized infinitive phrase. Some phrases contain subjects. In the space at the left, write the abbreviation that identifies the use of the phrase in the sentence:

      N. [noun]   Adj. [adjective]   Adv. [adverb]

N   1. At that point, we could do nothing but *turn toward home.*

N   2. Janice and Joan helped *us finish that report.*

N   3. It certainly seems strange *for you to be afraid of the dark.*

_____ 4. *To be sure of a good grade on that test,* I will study for several hours tonight.

_____ 5. The instructor wants *us to turn in our papers tomorrow.*

_____ 6. I was delighted *to find my lost textbook in that stack of old books.*

_____ 7. The stretching exercises *to be done before each practice* take about 20 minutes.

_____ 8. The plan for tomorrow is *to allow about an hour for the final touches on that paper.*

_____ 9. The instructor wanted *to give us a second chance on that difficult test.*

_____ 10. It would be a wonderful thing *to take a full day off from work.*

_____ 11. I would think it wonderful *to take a full day off from work.*

_____ 12. *To leave the house without my wallet and driver's license* was a careless mistake.

_____ 13. It was a careless mistake *to leave the house without my wallet and driver's license.*

_____ 14. Fortunately, the technician was able *to recover most of the data on my hard drive.*

_____ 15. *To determine the next step in the process,* read the directions very carefully.

_____ 16. The step *for you to take next* is carefully explained in those instructions.

_____ 17. The instructor wanted *Ron to work independently on that project.*

_____ 18. That medicine will make *you feel better in just a short time.*

_____ 19. We could not do anything but *watch as the car slid slowly down the icy road.*

_____ 20. The runners were very happy *to see the end of that long trail.*

Exercise 11   *Gerund and Infinitive Phrases*

NAME _____ SCORE _____

Directions: Each sentence contains one gerund phrase. Underline the gerund phrase and identify its use in the sentence by writing one of the following abbreviations in the space at the left of the sentence:

     S. [subject]   S.C. [subjective complement]

     D.O. [direct object]   O.P. [object of preposition]

Review: In sentences 1–10, circle the prepositional phrases.

_____ 1. Working on campus has been a good solution for my financial problems.

_____ 2. A good solution for my financial problems has been working at an on-campus job.

_____ 3. So far in this term, I have enjoyed working at my job on campus.

_____ 4. I have provided myself with some extra spending money by working at my on-campus job.

_____ 5. Using financial aid and scholarships has paid my major expenses such as tuition.

_____ 6. Last summer, Mike Johnson found waiting on tables at a restaurant a good source of income.

_____ 7. His first job at the restaurant was seating people as they came in the door.

_____ 8. Then he moved to delivering the food to the proper tables.

_____ 9. Clearing the tables was also part of that second job.

_____ 10. Finally, as a member of the wait staff, he began earning tips from the patrons.

_____ 11. Earning tips is a large portion of a server's income in a restaurant.

_____ 12. The word "Tips" was probably formed by creating an acronym from the phrase *To Insure Prompt Service.*

_____ 13. Using the first letter of each word in a phrase creates an acronym.

_____ 14. By learning a simple memorization system, Tom was able to take orders from his parties without an order pad.

_____ 15. Identifying each customer by hair color or an article of clothing allowed Tom to remember each person's order.

_____ 16. Arranging each individual order in his mind by time—appetizer, salad, entree, and dessert—helped Tom with the items within an order.

_____ 17. Tom so impressed his customers by taking orders without a written record that his tips increased by 50%.

_____ 18. This skill of using his memory was considered a magic trick by the other servers.

_____ 19. The others began pressuring Tom for his secrets.

_____ 20. Finally, Tom helped his fellow workers by teaching them his system.

Directions: Each sentence contains an infinitive phrase. Underline the phrase. In the space at the left, identify the use of the phrase in the sentence by writing one of the following abbreviations:

N/s [subject or delayed subject]	Adj. [adjective]
N/sc [subjective complement]	Adv. [adverb]
N/d [direct object]	
N/op [object of preposition]	

Review: In sentences 1–10, circle the main verb.

_____ 1. Cathy Robinson was extremely happy to receive a promotion last month.

_____ 2. My plan for future success in that class is to be much more attentive to the lectures.

_____ 3. To predict precisely his time for the 400-meter race was, for Larson, a great accomplishment.

_____ 4. The entire class wanted desperately to postpone that test.

_____ 5. After all that work, I could do nothing but turn in my paper and hope for the best.

_____ 6. The workouts to be followed for that week are very strenuous.

_____ 7. Alicia was very unhappy to be asked that particular question on the oral quiz.

_____ 8. It seemed very silly to enter that race without any prior preparation.

_____ 9. We all thought it foolish for Manny to enter that race without any prior training.

_____ 10. Many marathons and ultra-distance races now require an entrant to submit a qualifying time from previous races.

_____ 11. My opening strategy for this job was to work very hard for the first two weeks.

_____ 12. After that first burst, I hoped to slow down a little.

_____ 13. Since the first day, however, I have done nothing but work very, very hard.

_____ 14. In spite of the hard work, I have found the job to be very satisfying.

_____ 15. Perhaps the boss will let us go home early on Friday afternoon.

_____ 16. We will find it a difficult task to finish our project before Friday.

_____ 17. It will be a difficult task to finish our project before Friday.

_____ 18. Even though we did not finish our project, the boss allowed us to take Friday afternoon off.

_____ 19. When we return on Monday, we should find it easy to finish the project.

_____ 20. But by Monday afternoon, we will be asked to start another difficult project.

Directions: Combine the two sentences into one sentence by resolving one sentence into a gerund phrase or an infinitive phrase to replace the italicized word(s) in the other sentence.

1. Alice is working hard on that important science project.
   Alice enjoys *something*.

   _____

2. I stayed awake during that spectacular thunderstorm.
   Doing something was very easy for me.

   _____

3. I stayed awake during that spectacular thunderstorm.
   It was very easy for me *to do something*.

   _____

4. My first priority for tonight is to study for tomorrow's test.
   My first priority for tonight is *doing something*.

   _____

5. When I arrived at home after exams, my greatest need was *something*.
   I needed to catch up on my sleep.

   _____

6. *Something* was difficult before I organized and outlined my notes.
   It was difficult to study for that exam.

   _____

7. Maria left work suddenly without even *doing something*.
   Maria did not even lock up her desk.

   _____

8. I don't like to do *something*.
   I don't like checking myself out at the grocery store.

   _____

9. *Doing something* is a great pleasure for me.
   I hike that trail to the top of the mountain.

   _____

10. In some cities in this country, it is possible to *do something*.
    You can get a traffic ticket because a camera took a picture of your car.

    _____

Brief Writing Assignment: In a paragraph of six or seven sentences, tell how you wrote your most successful writing assignment. Use two gerund phrases and two infinitive phrases.

A participle is an adjective formed from a verb by adding *ing* or *ed* to the base form of the verb (*studying, studied*) or to an auxiliary (*having studied, being studied, having been studied*). (Note that many verbs have irregular past participles. See pages 224–226 for lists of such verbs.) By itself, a participle works exactly as any one-word adjective works:

> The *injured* bird clung to the *swaying* branch.
>
> [The past participle *injured* modifies the noun *bird*; the present participle *swaying* modifies the noun *branch*.]

Often, however, the participle is combined with other words to form a **participial phrase** that modifies a noun.

> The taxi driver, *being a war veteran*, signed the petition.
>
> [The participial phrase modifies the noun *taxi driver*. Within the phrase, *veteran* is a subjective complement.]
>
> *Calling the man a hero*, the mayor gave him an award.
>
> [The participial phrase modifies the noun *mayor*. Within the phrase, *man* is a direct object and *hero* is an objective complement.]

PARTICIPIAL PHRASES

The similarity between an adjective clause and a participial phrase is obvious:

1. A clown grabbed the microphone. The clown [*or* He] was wearing a painted mask.
   [Two independent clauses.]

   a. A clown *who was wearing a painted mask* grabbed the microphone.
   [Adjective clause. *Mask* is a direct object of the verb.]
   b. A clown *wearing a painted mask* grabbed the microphone.
   [Participial phrase. *Mask* is a direct object of the participle.]

2. Jo's parents left the concert early. They found the music uncomfortably loud.
   [Two independent clauses.]

   a. Jo's parents, *who found the music uncomfortably loud*, left the concert early.
   [Adjective clause. *Music* is a direct object and *loud* an objective complement.]
   b. Jo's parents, *finding the music uncomfortably loud*, left the concert early.
   [Participial phrase. *Music* is a direct object and *loud* an objective complement.]

These two examples point out another similarity: Like the adjective clause, the participial phrase can be either restrictive or nonrestrictive. The phrase in the first example identifies the clown; it is restrictive and is not set off by commas. The phrase in the second example is not needed to identify parents; it requires commas because it is nonrestrictive.

Like adjective clauses, participial phrases must be very close to the noun they modify. An adjective clause must follow the noun it modifies. A restrictive (identifying) participial phrase normally follows the noun it modifies, as in the example, "A man wearing a black mask. . . ." Unlike a nonrestrictive adjective clause, however, a nonrestrictive participial phrase can move into another position in the sentence. Observe the positions of the participial phrase in the following sentences:

> Steve, having passed the test with flying colors, decided to celebrate.
>
> Having passed the test with flying colors, Steve decided to celebrate.

Occasionally, the participial phrase can be moved to the end of the clause:

> Steve decided to celebrate, having passed the test with flying colors.

Because a participle is an adjective formed from a verb and thus suggests an action, the participial phrase can be used to relieve the monotony of a series of short, independent clauses:

> Pam wanted desperately to hear the rock concert, but she was temporarily short of funds, and she knew that her cousin Alice had an extra ticket, and so she decided to call her. [Four independent clauses]
>
> Wanting desperately to hear the rock concert but being temporarily short of funds, Pam decided to call her cousin Alice, knowing that she had an extra ticket. [One independent clause and three participial phrases]
>
> Jensen stood at home plate. He waggled his bat. He eyed the pitcher coldly. He took a mighty swing at the first pitch. He hit the ball out of the park. [Five independent clauses]
>
> Standing at home plate, waggling his bat, and eyeing the pitcher coldly, Jensen took a mighty swing at the first pitch, hitting the ball out of the park. [One independent clause and four participial phrases]

ABSOLUTE PHRASES

The **absolute phrase** is a special kind of phrase using a participle, but it is unlike a standard participial phrase in two important ways:

1. The absolute phrase contains both a noun (or a pronoun) and a participle, which almost always follows the noun.

2. The absolute phrase does not directly modify a noun or pronoun in the main clause; rather, the absolute phrase modifies the entire main clause.

The absolute phrase is a versatile structure capable of many variations and widely used in modern writing to point out subtle relationships underlying the ideas within a sentence:

> *All things being equal*, Mary should easily win the race.
>
> *The storm having passed*, the ball game resumed.
>
> The police recovered eight of the paintings, *three of them badly damaged*.
>
> The mob reached the palace gates, *the leader (being) a burly, red-haired sailor*.
>
> [Occasionally an absolute phrase having a noun and a complement appears with the participle unexpressed.]

A special kind of phrase using *with* to introduce the absolute phrase can add subtle modifying and narrative coloring to a sentence:

With the band playing and the crowd applauding furiously, Jim Kinman was obviously uncomfortable as he stood on the stage.

They held the funeral on the second day, *with the town coming to look at Miss Emily beneath a mass of bought flowers, with the crayon face of her father musing profoundly above the bier.* . . . (William Faulkner)

But we can't possibly have a garden party *with a dead man just outside the front gate.* (Katherine Mansfield)

The face was a curious mixture of sensibility, *with some elements very hard and others very pretty*—perhaps it was in the mouth. (Katherine Anne Porter)

Notice that the *with* in this construction is quite unlike *with* in its common prepositional use:

The acquitted woman left the courtroom *with her* lawyer.

[*with* used as a preposition]

The acquitted woman left the courtroom *with her head held high.*

[*with* used to introduce the absolute phrase]

SUMMARY OF PARTICIPIAL AND ABSOLUTE PHRASES

Participial Phrases

1. Forms: *studying, studied, having studied, being studied, having been studied, having been studying*

2. Function: to modify a noun or pronoun. Those that identify the noun or pronoun are restrictive and require no punctuation; others are nonrestrictive and are set off by commas.

3. Position: if restrictive, always following the word it modifies. Nonrestrictive phrases may stand after the noun, at the beginning of the sentence, and occasionally at the end of the sentence.

Absolute Phrases

1. Form: a noun or pronoun followed by a participle

   His last crop a huge success, Grandfather sold the farm.

2. Function: adds to the meaning of the entire sentence but does not modify a word or fill a noun slot

3. Position: at the beginning, in the interior, or at the end of the larger unit; usually set off by commas

4. Special structures:
   a. The participle *being* is sometimes unexpressed.

      Its chairman [being] a retired military person, the committee is well disciplined.

   b. The phrase sometimes begins with the word *with*.

      With its supply of ammunition exhausted, the garrison surrendered.

English Fundamentals Online

After you have completed the Practice Sheets and Exercises in this lesson, you can find additional help and drill work at **MyWritingLab.com**, in the section on Parts of Speech, Phrases, and Clauses.

Participial and Absolute Phrases

NAME _____   SCORE _____

Directions: The italicized unit in each sentence is either a participial phrase or an absolute phrase. If the unit is a participial phrase, write in the space at the left the noun or pronoun the phrase modifies. If the unit is an absolute phrase, leave the space at the left blank.

man   PP   1. *Walking slowly down the street,* the man looked closely at all the shop windows.

sun   PP   2. From the deck, we watched the sun *rising slowly above the mountains.*

_____ AP   3. The men, *with all their work for the day completed,* drove quickly back to town.

_____ AP   4. *All those facts having been considered,* I would still choose the larger of the two trucks.

I   PP   5. *Having considered all the facts,* I chose the larger of the two trucks.

man   PP   6. Yesterday we watched a man *trying desperately to pedal his bicycle up that steep hill.*

_____ AP   7. The band marched down the street in perfect formation, *the leader moving a baton in time to the music.*

players   PP   8. The players sat in the dugout, *waiting for the lightning storm to pass.*

those   PP   9. The speaker asked for help from those *standing in the back of the room.*

Louisa   PP 10. Louisa, *having called all three of her roommates for a ride,* took the bus back to her apartment.

_____ AP 11. *With clouds building up on the horizon,* we decided to move the photo session indoors.

intruder PP 12. The intruder, *having been seen by at least three people,* ran out of the house and down the street.

_____ AP 13. We began to work seriously on the paper, *the last two members of the group having finally arrived.*

_____ 14. Finally, the speaker, *her annoyance quite visible,* began her lecture.

speaker PP 15. Finally the speaker, *grimacing with annoyance,* began her lecture.

person   PP 16. If you can find the person *running the projector,* ask him to correct the focus.

David   PP 17. The committee decided that David, *having long experience in that field of study,* should help us choose a textbook.

someone PP 18. To find someone *trained in that particular art* will be a very difficult task.

picture PP 19. No one I questioned about the picture *missing from the wall in the stairwell* could give me any information.

photo   PP 20. The Maxwell photo, *missing from the wall in the stairwell,* cannot be found anywhere.

_____ 21. *With no information about the photo forthcoming*, we have no choice but to find something else to fill the space.

_____ 22. We will need to replace the photo in the stairwell, *missing now for almost two weeks.*

_____ 23. Perhaps someone *wishing to fill that blank space on the wall* will donate another portrait.

_____ 24. We have chosen a new portrait for the wall in the stairwell, *all hope of recovering the other portrait having been abandoned.*

_____ 25. We see another weather system *moving in from the Great Plains,* this one bringing high winds and more snow.

_____ 26. *The earlier system having dumped six inches of snow in the city,* we have only now begun to dig our way out of the drifts.

_____ 27. The earlier system, *having dumped at least six inches of snow in the city*, has brought everything to a standstill.

_____ 28. Now, *with another snowstorm looming on the horizon,* everyone in town is planning to stay home for a few days.

_____ 29. It is clear that another snowstorm, *arriving so soon after the last one*, will create immense problems in the city.

_____ 30. I am sitting beside my front window, *looking forward to summer vacation.*

_____ 31. *With all the work done on my classes and at my job,* I'm burned out and in need of a change.

_____ 32. In my mind's eye, I see myself *sitting on a deserted beach.*

_____ 33. Instead, I might enjoy a cross-country trip with my friends *riding beside me in a luxury touring car.*

_____ 34. Sailing the Caribbean, *my friends helping as the crew*, might be an enjoyable holiday.

_____ 35. *Sitting here near the window*, however, I realize that those trips are only daydreams.

_____ 36. I will need, *considering the state of my finances*, a major reorganization to bring any of the trips to reality.

_____ 37. First, *my bank balance being rather low,* I will need to earn some additional money.

_____ 38. Then, *keeping in mind that I'd like to take my friends with me*, I'll need to work out a plan with them.

_____ 39. Finally, *with everyone in agreement,* we will follow through with reservations and other arrangements.

_____ 40. On second thought, *seeing all the complications that are involved,* I'll probably visit my grandmother for a few days and then go to work.

Participial and Absolute Phrases

NAME _____ SCORE _____

Directions: Each of the following sentences contains either a participial phrase or an absolute phrase. Put brackets around the phrase. If the phrase is a participial phrase, copy in the space at the left the noun or pronoun the phrase modifies. If the phrase is an absolute phrase, leave the space blank. **Review:** Circle the subject and the main verb(s) in sentences 1–10.

_____ AP _____ 1. With no one available to help him, Marcus was forced to begin preparations for lunch by himself.

_____ PP _____ 2. First he prepared the table, spreading a tablecloth and setting 15 places on the long, rectangular table.

_____ AP _____ 3. Then, the table having been set, he entered the walk-in cooler and brought out 5 pounds of ground beef.

_____ PP _____ 4. Taking the ground beef to the table, he took out the hamburger press and made 15 patties.

_____ AP _____ 5. The hamburger patties having been made, he set them aside for the moment.

_____ PP _____ 6. Marcus then looked on the canned goods shelf, locating 3 large cans of baked beans.

_____ PP _____ 7. Then, deciding that the beans needed some additional flavor, he chopped up some onions and put them on the grill.

_____ PP _____ 8. He also put a pound of bacon on the grill, frying the strips of bacon along with the onions.

_____ AP _____ 9. The onions and bacon having browned, he put the beans in a large pot and set them on the stove.

_____ PP _____ 10. Waiting for the beans in the pot to come to a boil, he stirred in the bacon and onions to add some flavor to the beans.

_____ AP _____ 11. The beans having come to a boil, he turned down the heat under the pot and left it to simmer.

_____ PP _____ 12. Seeing that those two menu items were prepared, he turned his attention to a salad.

_____ PP _____ 13. Taking three heads of lettuce and several tomatoes from the cooler, he proceeded to chop them up for the salad.

_____ PP _____ 14. He opened several different bottles of salad dressing, placing them carefully on the counter beside the salad.

_____ PP _____ 15. Having made all those preparations, Marcus put the hamburger patties on the grill.

_____ AP _____ 16. The hamburgers cooking and the other preparations completed, Marcus called his friends to come and help him serve the meal.

_____ PP _____ 17. Two of his friends, walking into the dining hall, asked him what other preparations needed to be done.

_____ PP _____ 18. Pleased to have help at last, Marcus asked them to bring the tea and other drinks to the end of the counter.

_____ PP _____ 19. Then Marcus turned to the hamburgers, using his spatula to place each patty on a bun.

_____ PP _____ 20. Moving the beans from the stove to the counter, his two friends prepared to serve the meal.

_____ _____ 21. When everything was prepared and in place, the doors opened and the 15 men filed into the hall, expressing their thanks for the warm meal.

_____ _____ 22. The fact is that, even with all his studies completed, Jackson will not have time to go to the game with us.

_____ PP _____ 23. Keeping those pertinent facts in mind, we need to give careful consideration to our decision.

_____ _____ 24. The excited fans ran down on the field, the band playing the school fight song and the cheerleaders screaming at the top of their lungs.

_____ _____ 25. One of the first people I saw when I came out of the jetway was my little sister, standing at the gate with a wide smile on her face.

_____ PP _____ 26. Standing at the gate was my little sister, a huge smile covering her face.

_____ AP _____ 27. The two dogs, each one gripping an end of the blanket in its teeth, tore the blanket into two long strips.

_____ PP _____ 28. The two dogs, gripping the ends of the blanket in their teeth, tore it into long shreds.

_____ _____ 29. While the two dogs tore the blanket to shreds, the man stood by, screaming at the dogs to stop.

_____ _____ 30. Alerted by the shouts of the man, the owners of the dogs ran out and grabbed them.

_____ AP _____ 31. The blanket was in tatters, but the two men controlled the dogs, dragging them back into their yards.

_____ PP _____ 32. When the weather warms up this spring, we should hike into the mountains, taking our camping gear with us.

_____ _____ 33. With the weather warming up this spring, a hike into the mountains would be a wonderful experience.

_____ _____ 34. I already own a backpack, but I need to buy new hiking boots, my old pair being totally worn out.

_____ _____ 35. Taking our gear with us, we can camp beside that beautiful lake.

_____ _____ 36. If we spend a few days beside the lake during spring break, we can then return to class with our minds totally refreshed.

_____ _____ 37. Loving horses as much as she does, it seems only right that Ashley should try to go out on the rodeo circuit.

_____ _____ 38. Opportunities for women on the circuit being rather limited, she would only be able to become a barrel racer.

_____ _____ 39. Given her strength and courage, her real goal is the calf-roping event.

_____ _____ 40. Unfortunately, the rodeo circuit being dominated by men, Ashley will not be permitted to enter the calf-roping competition.

_____ _____ 41. That event being out of the question for her, she has sold her horse and will become a professional snow-boarder.

Exercise 12A   *Verbal Phrases; Complements in Phrases*

NAME _____   SCORE _____

Directions: In the first space at the left, write one of the following letters to identify the italicized verbal phrase:

G. [gerund phrase]   I. [infinitive phrase]

P. [participial phrase]   A. [absolute phrase]

In the second space at the left, write one of the following abbreviations to identify the complement printed in bold type within the phrase:

S.C. [subjective complement]   I.O. [indirect object]

D.O. [direct object]   O.C. [objective complement]

O.P. [object of preposition]

_____   1. The city council has voted to give the **city hall** a new stone facade.
_____

_____   2. Janice wants to paint her classic Mustang metallic **black**.
_____

_____   3. I worked very hard at finding that last **source** for my research paper.
_____

_____   4. Jerry's summer job will be running a **milling machine** in a local factory.
_____

_____   5. We all believe that being a **partner** in that law firm will require incredible
_____   amounts of work.

_____   6. Having given the **valet** your car keys, you should stand under that awning out
_____   of the rain.

_____   7. To be the **captain** of the baseball team is both an exciting challenge and a
_____   great honor.

_____   8. With the road made **impassable** by a rock slide, we had no choice but to
_____   take a long detour.

_____   9. Seeing that huge **snake** coiled in the path, we stopped and walked around it
_____   in a wide circle.

_____   10. With that huge snake blocking our **path**, we stopped and retraced our steps
_____   to the last fork in the trail.

_____   11. Please ask Jaime to tell **me** the combination to the safe, as I will need some
_____   cash for the trip.

_____   12. The weather patterns being very **stable** right now, the flight should arrive in
_____   Peoria in time for dinner.

_____   13. Having made those graphs different bright **colors**, we demonstrated quite
_____   clearly the impact of the economy on our sales.

_____   14. Having created a new set of **pie charts** helped greatly in that demonstration.
_____

_____   15. Jim Walker, the man showing those **people** his new orchids, serves as president
_____   of the local orchid society.

_____ 16. We can't possibly start the meeting with all those people still telling **each**
_____   **other** stories in the back of the room.

_____ 17. Finding the feedback over the loudspeaker system impossibly **noisy**, we
_____   sent a technician to the control room.

_____ 18. Correction of the problem at this time being **impossible**, the chair adjourned
_____   the meeting.

_____ 19. Making several **attempts** at repair, the technician instead made matters with
_____   the sound system even worse.

_____ 20. It is not possible for the technician to tell **us** when repairs can be completed.
_____

_____ 21. Making the system **workable** again seems an impossible task for this
_____   technician.

_____ 22. When you get to the place where the road dead-ends, making a left **turn**
_____   will bring you to the little country store within 5 minutes.

_____ 23. To make a right **turn** at that point would probably be a mistake.
_____

_____ 24. With a right turn at that point creating serious **confusion**, make a left turn
_____   where the road dead-ends.

_____ 25. A right turn at that point will lead to your becoming seriously **lost**.
_____

_____ 26. To make a right **turn** at that point will lead you to an interstate highway,
_____   which does not have an exit for about 15 miles.

_____ 27. Giving these **directions** close attention, you can make a left turn and find
_____   yourself at the country store within a few minutes.

_____ 28. Then, the store owner having sold **you** a glass of sweet tea, another left turn
_____   will lead you right back here to me.

_____ 29. Once we have finished the estimates for that job, we can let ourselves enjoy
_____   a job well **done** and leave work for the day.

_____ 30. Everyone finds creating **estimates** for such a complicated job a very difficult
_____   task.

_____ 31. Every detail having great **importance**, the estimates require enormous focus
_____   and concentration.

_____ 32. Any mistake in an estimate can cause the company to lose large **amounts** of
_____   money.

_____ 33. Having handed the **boss** a carefully constructed estimate, all of us left work
_____   about 3:00 P.M.

_____ 34. Most of the staff, with that work finished, left the **office** for a nearby
_____   restaurant and an early dinner.

_____ 35. Since we had been working late every night for a week, I found leaving
_____   work early very **refreshing**.

Directions: Combine the two short sentences into one by converting the second sentence into a verbal phrase.

1. The two women left early for the airport.
   They wanted to have ample time for processing through security. (infinitive phrase)

   _____

2. Albert worked at his computer for an hour.
   He was trying to find information about a company that had offered him a job. (participial phrase)

   _____

3. The hike exhausted all of us.
   The hike over that 6-mile trail to the waterfall. (gerund phrase)

   _____

4. The instructor dismissed the class.
   There were no more questions from the students. (absolute phrase)

   _____

5. The crowd in the stadium stood at attention.
   The pop star sang the national anthem. (absolute phrase)

   _____

6. I left the dinner before the speeches.
   I had already heard everything the speakers would say. (participial phrase)

   _____

7. The work made the man tired and sore.
   He worked for three hours on that mess in the storeroom. (gerund phrase)

   _____

8. There was nothing left for Jim to do.
   He waited for the next shipment from the warehouse. (infinitive phrase)

   _____

9. We picked up our chairs and left the beach.
   The sun had sunk beneath the horizon. (absolute phrase)

   _____

10. The brilliant student wrote out the solution to the problem.
    He walked slowly to the blackboard. (participial phrase)

    _____

Brief Writing Assignment: In a paragraph of five or six sentences, tell the story of a recent exciting experience. Use two participial phrases and two absolute phrases in the sentences.

Check Sheet

☐ Sentences, also known as *independent clauses*, can be joined to make writing more effective.

☐ Compound Sentences

☐ Two independent clauses joined by a comma and a coordinating conjunction (*and, but, or, nor, for, yet, so*) or by a semicolon create a compound sentence.

> The two men left work at noon, and the three women left at 12:30 P.M.
> The two men left work at noon; then the three women left at 12:30 P.M.

Punctuation note: Omitting the comma before the coordinating conjunction creates an error called a *run-on sentence*; omitting the coordinating conjunction creates an error called a *comma splice*.

☐ Each coordinating conjunction establishes a different relationship (time, cause, etc.) between the two clauses. Considerable care must be exercised to select the proper coordinating conjunction. The relationships between clauses joined with a semicolon are often established by using conjunctive adverbs such as *therefore* and *however*. Note that compound verbs—that is, a subject with two verbs—require no punctuation.

> John picked up the book and left the room.

☐ Complex Sentences

☐ Sentences formed by subordinating one clause and including it with a second sentence create a complex sentence.

☐ Adverbial Clauses

☐ Adverbial clauses are word groups opened with subordinating conjunctions such as *when, since, after, although, if, unless, because*, and others. The clauses perform the same functions as one-word adverbs that modify verbs.

> The men left town early.
> After the rain stopped, the men left town.
> The men, after the rain stopped, left town.
> The men left town after the rain stopped.

The clause stands as an opening element, an interrupting element between subject and verb, or as the final element of a sentence.

Punctuation note: When an adverbial clause stands as the opening element of a sentence, it is joined to the main clause with a comma. That same clause, when it stands between the subject and verb, is set off with commas. The adverbial clause requires no punctuation when it stands as the final element of the sentence.

☐ Adjective or Relative Clauses

☐ Just as adjectives modify (change the reader's conception of) nouns,

> the red rose
> the changeable weather

clauses that begin with *who, whose, whom, which,* and *that* can also modify nouns. The words opening these clauses are called relative pronouns. Most adjective clauses stand immediately after the noun they modify; occasionally, a preposition or even a prepositional phrase intervenes between the noun and the modifying clause, but the position of the clause must clearly establish the relationship between the clause and the noun (called the *antecedent*) it modifies.

> The man *who won the award* will be here soon.
> The man *whose brilliant discovery* won the prize will soon be here.
> The man to *whom we will give the prize* will appear soon.
> The man *whom I pointed out* is the winner of the prize.
> The man of the hour, about *whom you have heard so much,* just walked into the room.

☐ Some adjective clauses identify the noun modified by the clause. All of the clauses in the examples above identify the noun. Such clauses, called *restrictive relative* or *adjective clauses*, are not set off with commas. Adjective clauses that modify but do not identify are called *nonrestrictive relatives* and *are* set off by commas.

> The person *who owns that car* should move it from my driveway.
> June Williams, who owns that car, should move it from my driveway.

☐ Remember certain distinctions in using *who, which,* and *that. Who* refers only to people; *which* refers only to things. *That* is used only in restrictive clauses, and there is a convention (though not a hard-and-fast rule) that *which* is never used to open a restrictive clause.

☐ The adverbs *when* and *where* are sometimes used as though they are relative pronouns. In sentences such as

> I carefully searched the place in which I had dropped my wallet.

we sometimes say

> I carefully searched the place where I had dropped my wallet.

In the same way, *when* can be used as a replacement for *in which.*

> Jan recalled the very minute when she met Tom.

☐ Noun Clauses

☐ In the same way that adjective clauses can replace one-word adjectives, word groups containing a subject–verb combination and a subordinating word can do the work of a noun. These structures, called *noun clauses*, can do whatever simple nouns can do in a sentence: They can be the subject, subjective complement, direct object, object of a preposition, and an appositive.

Whoever answered the phone (S.) asked *what we wanted from the store.* (D.O.)
The next question was *how we intended to pay for it.* (S.C.)
The person then gave the phone to *whoever was standing next to her.* (O.P.)
He objected to the fact *that we were taking so much time.* (Ap.)

The subordinating words can be conjunctions, adjectives, or adverbs.

Jill wonders *if* Mom and Dad are coming. (conjunction)
Jill wonders *when* they will arrive. (adverb)
Jill wonders *which* car they be driving. (adjective)
Jill wonders *what* they will do tomorrow. (pronoun)

☐ Gerunds, Infinitives, and Verbal Phrases

☐ Word groups that employ a form of a verb and associated words can be used as noun replacements and perform most of the functions that ordinary nouns perform in a sentence.

☐ Gerund Phrases

☐ Gerunds are formed by adding *ing* to a verb's base form or to an auxiliary.

flying, having flown, having been flown

☐ Gerunds can stand alone in sentences:

Running is good exercise. Barb enjoys *running.*

☐ Gerunds can also be joined with other words to create gerund phrases.

Running three miles can be exhausting.
Maria enjoys *operating that video camera.*

These phrases can serve any purpose in a sentence that a simple noun serves: subject, subjective complement, direct object, or object of a preposition.

☐ Infinitive Phrases

☐ An infinitive is a verbal formed from the base of the verb and the word *to*. Infinitives change tense and voice by adding auxiliaries. Modifiers and complements are added to infinitives to create infinitive phrases. Infinitives and infinitive phrases serve as nouns, adjectives, and adverbs.

To find that source was a difficult task. (subject)
It was a difficult task *to find that source.* (delayed subject)
My next step is *to find that source.* (subjective complement)
Jill wanted desperately *to find that source.* (direct object)
My plan *to find that source* did not work. (adjective)
To find that source, you should check on the Internet. (adverb)

☐ Infinitive phrases sometimes contain their own subjects.

> The instructor asked *Mary to find that source.*

☐ Infinitive phrases can open with *for* and the subject of the infinitive.

> *For us to find that source* was an almost impossible task.

☐ Infinitive phrases without the word *to* can serve as the direct object of verbs such as *let*, *help*, *make*, *see*, *hear*, and *watch*.

> Anne let *Mary find that source first.*

☐ Infinitive phrases without *to* can serve as the object of a preposition such as *except*, *but*, and *besides*.

> There is nothing left for me to do *but find that source.*

☐ Participial Phrases

☐ A participle is a verbal adjective formed by adding *ing* or *ed* to the base of a verb or to an auxiliary. Participles can be used as simple adjectives.

> The *exhausted* man faced another *exhausting* climb.

☐ Participles can be joined by other words to form a participial phrase that modifies a noun.

> *Exhausted from the first long climb*, the girl stopped to rest on a ledge.
> *Exhausting every ounce of energy*, the girl finally reached the summit.

☐ Participial phrases, like adjective clauses, can be either restrictive or nonrestrictive. Usually, restrictive phrases follow the noun being modified.

> The girl *just reaching the summit* is my sister.

The nonrestrictive phrase can appear in three positions in the sentence, but it must always be clearly related to the noun it modifies.

> *Having reached the summit at last*, the girl raised her hands in triumph.
> The girl, *having reached the summit at last*, raised her hands in triumph.
> The girl raised her hands in triumph, *having reached the summit at last.*

Note that, in the third version, no confusion is created by moving the phrase to the end of the sentence because the closest noun cannot sensibly be modified by the phrase. In another sentence,

> The girl shook hands with Jim, having reached the summit at last.

it is possible to make the phrase modify the word *Jim*, so the phrase must not be moved to the end of the sentence if the phrase modifies the word *girl*.

☐ **Absolute Phrases**

☐ Phrases composed of a noun plus a participle sometimes modify the sentence as a whole without being closely related to any noun in the rest of the sentence. In fact, the phrase should not include a noun that appears in the rest of the sentence. The absolute phrase, although it is not a sentence, is in that one sense independent of the rest of the sentence.

> *The job having been completed*, the workers left for the day.
> The workers left for the day, *the job having been completed*.

☐ An absolute phrase can be opened by the word *with*.

> *With the hard part of the work already finished*, the workers began to relax.

Sentence Building

Lessons, Practice Sheets, and Exercises

To be complete, a sentence must

1. Contain a subject and a verb.
2. Be able to stand alone as an independent unit.

A group of words without both a subject and a verb cannot be a complete sentence. A group of words containing both a subject and a verb but opening with a subordinating conjunction cannot be a complete sentence. The subordinating conjunction makes the clause dependent instead of independent.

SENTENCE FRAGMENTS

A group of words that does not have a subject and a verb and cannot stand alone is called an incomplete sentence, or **sentence fragment**. Sometimes a sentence fragment is punctuated as if it were a sentence. This mistake of punctuation is called a **period fault**. Sentence fragments almost always fit one of the following patterns:

1. A subordinate clause standing as a sentence. (But remember that *and*, *but*, *or*, *nor*, *for*, *yet*, and *so* do not subordinate. A clause introduced by one of these words may stand as a sentence.)

   Fragments: The clerk finally let us see the contract. *Although she clearly hated to reveal its contents.*

   Bob tried to start the old lawn mower. *Which never seemed to work properly for him.*

2. A verbal phrase punctuated as a sentence:

   Fragments: The delegates agreed on a compromise wage scale. *Realizing that the strike could not go on indefinitely.*

   Nell had ordered her tickets a month ago. *To be sure of getting good seats.*

137

3. A noun followed by a phrase or a subordinate clause but lacking a main verb:

> **Fragments:**　The committee should include Ms. Jones. *A tireless worker with many constructive ideas.*
>
> The mayor asked Bentley to take the job. *Bentley being the only available person with field experience.*
>
> The coach thinks our prospects are good. *A chance, perhaps, to win back the conference championship.*
>
> That injury will require special therapy. *The kind that will slowly rebuild the muscles in the shoulder.*

You should learn to avoid using fragments in your writing. Usually a close reading of anything you have written will reveal sentence fragments so that you can correct them. You can improve your skill at identifying fragments by using the following strategy: When you check what you have written, read the sentences in a paragraph in reverse order. Start with your last sentence and work back to your first. This process, which breaks the tie between a fragment and the sentence that it depends on, makes any grammatically incomplete sentence stand out.

CORRECTING SENTENCE FRAGMENTS

When you have discovered a fragment in your writing, any one of several possible corrections is easy to make.

- You can attach the fragment to the preceding sentence by doing away with the fragment's capital letter and supplying the right punctuation.
- You can change the fragment to a subordinate clause and attach it to the appropriate main clause by means of the right connective.
- You can change the fragment to an independent clause or a complete sentence by supplying a subject or a verb or both.
- You can change the fragment to an appositive or some other appropriate phrase.

Consider the following corrected sentences:

> The clerk finally let us see the contract, *although she clearly hated to reveal its contents.*
>
> Bob tried to start the old lawn mower, *which never seemed to work properly for him.*
>
> The delegates agreed on a compromise wage scale *because they realized that the strike could not go on indefinitely.*
>
> *To be sure of getting good seats,* Nell had ordered her tickets a month ago.
>
> The committee should include Ms. Jones, *a tireless worker with many constructive ideas.*
>
> *Bentley being the only available person with field experience,* the mayor asked him to take the job.
>
> The coach thinks our prospects are good; *we have a chance, perhaps, to win back the conference championship.*
>
> That injury will require special therapy. *It must be the kind that slowly rebuilds the muscles in the shoulder.*

There are a few types of word groups that are not considered fragments. Although they lack a complete subject–verb combination, these types of word groups are accepted as legitimate language patterns. They are

1. **Commands:** in which the subject *you* is understood:

> Please be seated. Put your name on a slip of paper. Pass the papers to the left aisle. [See Lesson 21, Supplement.]

2. **Exclamations:**

> What excitement! Only two minutes to go! Good Heavens, not a fumble? How terrible!

3. **Bits of dialogue:**

> "New car?" she asked. "Had it long?"
> "Picked it up last week," he replied.

4. **Occasional transitions between units of thought:**

> On with the story.
> And now to conclude.

You have very likely observed in your reading that experienced writers sometimes use sentence fragments, especially in narrative and descriptive writing. But these writers are skilled workers who know how to use fragments to achieve particular stylistic effects. You should first master the fundamental forms of the sentence. Once you have learned to write clear, correct sentences without faltering, there will be plenty of time for experimenting.

English Fundamentals Online

After you have completed the Practice Sheets and Exercises in this lesson, you can find additional help and drill work at **MyWritingLab.com**, in the section on Completeness: Run-Ons; Completeness: Dealing with Sentence Fragments.

NAME _____   SCORE _____

Directions: Study the following word groups for completeness. In the space at the left, write **S** if the word group is a complete sentence or a grammatically acceptable fragment. Write **F** if the word group is a fragment. **Review:** Underline and identify any adverbial and adjective clauses in sentences 1–10.

_____ 1. Although the people who are coming to fix the heating system haven't arrived yet.

_____ 2. Running down the street as fast as possible and coming to a stop in front of the store.

_____ 3. James, who recently submitted an entry in a screen play contest and has not received any notification about the results.

_____ 4. Richard, running down the street as fast as possible and coming to a stop in front of the store, went inside and asked for help from the sales clerk.

_____ 5. We need to start work on that project although the people who are coming to fix the heating system haven't arrived yet.

_____ 6. James, who recently submitted an entry in a screenplay contest, hasn't received any notification about the results.

_____ 7. And now, let's return to our regularly scheduled programming.

_____ 8. And now, back to our regularly scheduled programming.

_____ 9. Please take your seats and open your textbooks to page 105.

_____ 10. No one taking that test on that difficult chapter in the textbook and finishing within the allotted time.

_____ 11. Taking the test on that difficult chapter in the textbook and finishing within the allotted time seemed impossible for everyone.

_____ 12. With everyone in the room sitting quietly and concentrating on the speaker.

_____ 13. Everyone in the room sat quietly and concentrated on the speaker while the lawn mowers roared by just outside the windows.

_____ 14. While she still had the strength to walk after that long workout, Carol went to her car and drove slowly home.

_____ 15. Yesterday we met Mr. Carson, a man who has much experience in engineering and little experience in manufacturing products similar to ours.

_____ 16. When you have the time, come to my office and show me the sketches of the new building.

_____ 17. Someone who has that information about the new highway and can show us the exact location as it goes through the south part of the county.

_____ 18. Kelli Kirkland, a woman who can certainly help us as we make plans to locate that shopping center somewhere along the new highway.

_____ 19. As we make plans to locate that shopping center somewhere along the new highway, Kelli Kirkland is certainly someone who can help us.

_____ 20. Go online and purchase tickets now to assure yourself of getting good seats for the concert when it takes place in two months.

_____ 21. Whenever you can find time to look up Joan's telephone number and send it to me by e-mail.

_____ 22. Joan, whom I haven't seen in about 6 months, not since the last big football game last season.

_____ 23. Send me Joan's telephone number or her e-mail address so that I can get in touch with her again after all these months.

_____ 24. Joan is one of those people who seems to know everything about every one of her friends and everything about what is going on in town.

_____ 25. Mr. Marks, a man I met through friends and have lost contact with since he moved to Denver.

_____ 26. Since meeting Mr. Marks, I have changed jobs twice and moved to a new city, where I work for a large law firm.

_____ 27. Changing jobs twice and moving to a new city, probably the main reason I have lost contact with many of my old friends.

_____ 28. Because the men could not find the pipe that carried water from the house to the barn and from there into the stable.

_____ 29. The stableman had difficulty watering the horses because the plumber could not repair the pipe leading from the house to the barn and from there to the stable.

_____ 30. We all helped walk the horses from the stable to a water trough near the house, thus solving the problem without repairing the pipe.

_____ 31. Walking the horses from the stable through the barn to the water trough near the house while the plumber tried in vain to repair the pipe solved the problem.

_____ 32. We spoke yesterday to Al Johnson, a man with whom my father once did business when we lived across the state.

_____ 33. And then, for no apparent reason, bells ringing and sirens sounding throughout the building to signal some kind of emergency.

_____ 34. Hearing the bells ring and the sirens sound, we all walked out to the sidewalk until we were told to return to our work.

_____ 35. Now, tell us the story of how the team managed to win that game in the last two minutes and thus secure the championship for the season.

_____ 36. When you see Bob, please tell him that amazing story so that he will know how the team won the conference championship.

_____ 37. Needing to be absolutely certain that the last paper for the term could be handed in on time.

_____ 38. The need to turn that last paper in on time became a driving force in our lives during that week.

_____ 39. The paper, which was long and very detailed, presenting many problems during the writing.

_____ 40. That paper, which was long and very detailed, presented us with many problems during both the research and the writing.

NAME _____   SCORE _____

Directions: Each numbered unit contains a complete sentence and a sentence fragment. Rewrite each item to eliminate the fragment by joining the fragment to the complete sentence or making the fragment a complete sentence in itself. The suggested form for the correction is in parentheses.

1. Jackson finally got a hit in the fourth game. Although he had already had 13 at-bats. (Adverbial clause of concession)

   _____

2. Ginny had re-written her paper twice. Wanting it to be perfect. (Participial phrase)

   _____

3. That raise should go to Alicia. A highly skilled, hard-working individual. (Relative clause)

   _____

4. The prize goes to Jan. A clever creative writer who always tells a good story. (Appositive)

   _____

5. The two students struggled for 30 minutes with that tricky problem. Without coming anywhere close to a solution. (Compound sentence with *but*)

   _____

6. The committee members want to add one more member. Someone with skills in the graphic arts. (Compound sentence with a semicolon)

   _____

7. We took the longer route to that town. A beautiful drive along a scenic river. (Two complete sentences)

   _____

8. Look! A beautiful horse. Galloping across that pasture. (Participial phrase)

   _____

9. One of us needs to put the new battery in the car. Who understands which cable goes where. (Relative clause)

   _____

10. You should taste that peppermint milkshake. An unusual tangy, sweet taste. (Two complete sentences)

   _____

11. We tried (something new) for our workout today. Training with very heavy weights. (Gerund phrase)

_____

12. We are working very hard right now. In order that we might be in peak condition for the start of the season. (Infinitive phrase)

_____

13. One that looks flashy and is fun to drive. I wish I had a different car. (Appositive phrase)

_____

14. Yesterday I met the new staff member. Cathy Smith, who holds a degree in mechanical engineering. (Appositive plus relative clause)

_____

15. Yesterday I met Cathy Smith. A skilled mechanical engineer. (Relative clause)

_____

16. Yesterday I met Cathy Smith. A skilled mechanical engineer. (Two complete sentences)

_____

17. My car sitting in my driveway with a flat tire. I need a ride to work. (Adverbial clause of reason)

_____

18. We need to find a gas station. The gas gauge already reading below "empty." (Absolute phrase)

_____

19. We need to pull into a gas station. Whenever you see one. (Adverbial clause of time)

_____

20. I am relieved to see it. That gas station we desperately needed to find.

_____

Brief Writing Assignment: Write a paragraph of six to eight sentences explaining what you will do on a day-to-day basis in your chosen career. Intentionally include three sentence fragments in the paragraph. After you have written the fragments, show how to correct them.

Correcting Sentence Fragments

NAME _____   SCORE _____

Directions: Each numbered unit consists of a complete sentence and a fragment or a complete sentence. In the space provided, eliminate the fragment by using the techniques suggested in the text (pages 138–139) as specified in each item:

   a. Attach the fragment to the sentence.
   b. Change the fragment to a subordinate clause.
   c. Change the fragment to an independent clause.
   d. Change the fragment to an appropriate verbal phrase or an appositive.

1. For summer Judy has secured what she calls a "dirty job." Grooms horses and shovels out their stalls.

   c. _____

   d. _____

2. When you see Joe, who is an old friend of mine and one of the nicest men I know. Please tell Joe that I will call him soon.

   a. _____

   b. _____

3. The wind speed dropping a few knots. We were able to raise the sails and make port.

   c. _____

   d. _____

4. Running downhill to the edge of the river. The two runners fell headlong into the cold water.

   a. _____

   b. _____

5. Samantha has agreed to become the treasurer for the band. A student of accounting with an eye for fine details.

   c. _____

   d. _____

6. Running this machine with all its intricate controls, which Tom has not quite mastered. This work is tiring and nerve-wracking.

   a. _____

   d. _____

7. The work in the factory is exhausting. Consisting of lifting tool boxes onto a dolly and rolling them to the end of the loading dock.

   a. _____

   d. _____

8. Our state senator has decided not to run for re-election. A brilliant man who always maintained high ethical standards.

   c. _____

   d. _____

9. I lost my cell phone yesterday. A very annoying and costly loss.

   a. _____

   c. _____

10. The baseball game has been postponed until Friday. With the rain having made the field unplayable.

    c. _____

    d. _____

11. The men arrived at the camp tired and hungry. Having been lost for almost two hours.

    a. _____

    c. _____

12. We have hired a new estimator. An engineer named Joan Hackley.

    b. _____

    d. _____

13. Charlie has bought a car that he does not like. And he is a man who knows a great deal about cars.

    a. _____

    c. _____

14. Two days of steady rain have raised the water level in the creek. Probably as high as I have seen it in years.

    b. _____

    c. _____

15. The last rays of the sun are stretched out over the waters of the lake. A sight that is extremely beautiful.

    c. _____

    d. _____

The English language applies modifying words, phrases, and subordinate clauses to the words they modify by their position in the sentence; therefore, it is important for you to be precise in your positioning of such modifiers in your sentences. Ordinarily the main parts—the subjects, the verbs, the complements—cause no problems. Modifying words and phrases and subordinate clauses can be problematic if they are not located carefully. Here we consider five possible trouble spots in the placing of modifiers.

1. Although we sometimes use a rather loose placement for some common adverbs, such as *only*, *nearly*, *almost*, and *hardly*, we can write precise sentences only when such adverbs are placed close to the words they modify:

   Loose: This job will only take five minutes.
   Better: This job will take only five minutes.

   Loose: Jill nearly saw 90 movies last year.
   Better: Jill saw nearly 90 movies last year.

2. Words and phrases that attach themselves to the wrong word can confuse the reader:

   Loose: I wish every person in this class could know the man I'm going to talk about *personally*.
   Better: I wish every person in this class could know *personally* the man I'm going to talk about.

   Loose: It was reported that the Italian premier had died *on the 8 o'clock newscast*.
   Better: *On the 8 o'clock newscast*, it was reported that the Italian premier had died.

   Loose: The police department will be notified of all reported obscene phone calls *by the telephone company*.
   Better: The police department will be notified *by the telephone company* of all reported obscene phone calls.

3. The **squinting modifier** is one that is placed between two units, either of which it could modify:

   Loose: Students who can already type *normally* are put into an advanced class.
   Better: Students who can already type are *normally* put into an advanced class.

   Loose: He said *after the dinner* a presentation would be given.
   Better: He said a presentation would be given *after the dinner*.

4. The **split infinitive** results from the placing of an adverbial modifier between the *to* and the verb stem of an infinitive. Although greatly overemphasized by some as an error, the split infinitive, particularly with a modifier consisting of more than one word, is usually avoided by careful writers:

> **Loose:** Dad likes to *once in a while* plan and cook a dinner.
>
> **Better:** *Once in a while*, Dad likes to plan and cook a dinner.

5. The conjunctions *both . . . and, not only . . . but also, either . . . or*, and *neither . . . nor* are used in pairs and are called **correlatives**. Because they point out the equal relationship between units, they should be placed immediately before the parallel units that they connect:

> **Loose:** We sent invitations *both* to Webster *and* Jenkins.
>
> **Better:** We sent invitations to *both* Webster *and* Jenkins.
>
> [The parallel words are *Webster* and *Jenkins*.]

> **Loose:** This woman *not only* can get along with young people *but also* with their parents.
>
> **Better:** This woman can get along *not only* with young people *but also* with their parents.

> **Loose:** You must *either* promise me that you will come *or* send a substitute.
>
> **Better:** You must promise me that you will *either* come *or* send a substitute.

DANGLING MODIFIERS

The relationship between a word being modified and the modifying phrase should be clear. Any modifying phrase that does not attach itself clearly to the word it is supposed to modify is called a **dangling modifier**. A dangling modifier can create a confusing sentence. Participial phrases are especially apt to float free in a sentence.

> *Stepping into the boat*, my camera fell into the water.

This sentence contains a participial phrase and a main clause, but the phrase does not actually modify any word in the main clause. The sentence is made up of two thoughts that can be expressed as

> I stepped into the boat.
> My camera fell into the water.

We can make the two sentences into a compound sentence:

> I stepped into the boat, and my camera fell into the water.

Or we can make the first clause an introductory adverbial element:

> As I stepped into the boat, my camera fell into the water.

But we cannot convert the first sentence into a participial phrase because the only noun the phrase could modify is *camera*, and the camera did not step into the boat. The sentence, if read literally, becomes nonsense. We could rework the sentence by changing the subject of the second clause in a way that allows the participial phrase to modify the new subject:

> Stepping into the boat, I dropped my camera into the water.

Because the person who dropped the camera and the person who is stepping into the boat are the same, *I*, the sentence is now correct.

Gerund Phrases and Infinitive Phrases

Gerund phrases and infinitive phrases can also cause problems when they are randomly inserted into sentences:

> *After studying all morning*, a nap was Mary's only goal for the afternoon.

The intended meaning of the sentence is clear, but the literal meaning is that the nap studied all morning; the phrase attaches itself to the first available noun—in this case, a noun that produces a nonsense statement.

> *To qualify for that job*, good typing skills are a necessity.

Again, the intended meaning is clear, but the literal meaning is nonsense. Good typing skills are not qualifying for that job; a person with good typing skills is qualifying for that job. Remember the phrase that contains the verbal must have a word to refer to, and that word must be close enough to the phrase so that the reader does not associate the phrase with the wrong word.

CORRECTING DANGLING MODIFIERS

The easiest way to correct a dangling modifier is to supply the word that the phrase should modify and to place the phrase next to that word. Another way is to change the dangling phrase to a subordinate clause with a subject and verb expressed.

1. Participial phrase at the beginning of a sentence

Dangling Modifier:	*Burned to a crisp,* I could not eat the toast. [The sentence sounds as if *I* were burned to a crisp. The word that the phrase modifies is *toast,* but this word is too far from the phrase to be associated with it.]
Precise:	*Burned to a crisp,* the toast could not be eaten. I could not eat the toast because it was burned to a crisp.

2. Gerund following a preposition

Dangling Modifier:	*Before making a final decision,* other cars should be driven. [Are the other cars making the decision? That is not what is meant, but that is what the sentence says.]
Precise:	*Before making a decision,* drive other cars. *Before you make a decision,* you should drive other cars.

3. Elliptical "time" clauses usually introduced by *when* or *while*.

> **Dangling Modifier:** When ten years old, my father sold the farm and moved to Dallas.
> [The father in this sentence was not ten years old when he sold the farm, but that meaning is the literal sense of the sentence.]
>
> **Precise:** When I was ten years old, my father sold the farm, and we moved to Dallas.
>
> **Dangling Modifier:** While weeding my garden, a blacksnake startled me.
> [The snake was not weeding the garden, but that meaning is the literal sense of the sentence.]
>
> **Precise:** While weeding my garden, I was startled by a blacksnake.
> While I was weeding my garden, a blacksnake startled me.

4. Introductory infinitive phrase naming a specific action

> **Dangling Modifier:** To obtain the rebate, the sales receipt must be sent in to the company.
> [The sales receipt is not asking for the rebate. But the literal sense of the sentence makes just that statement.]
>
> **Precise:** To obtain the rebate you must send the sales receipt to the company.
> If you want to obtain the rebate, send the sales receipt to the company.

Note that in sentences with dangling modifiers, the meaning can often be deduced by the reader. It is important, however, to develop the habit of precision in your writing.

English Fundamentals Online

> After you have completed the Practice Sheets and Exercises in this lesson, you can find additional help and drill work at **MyWritingLab.com**, in the sections on Misplaced Modifiers; Dangling Modifiers.

NAME _____   SCORE _____

Directions: From each of the following pairs of sentences, select the one that is more clear and write its letter in the space at the left of the item.

_A_ 1. a. My uncle Joe has a large collection of model cars stored in his basement, which he constructed as a boy.
    b. My uncle Joe has a large collection of model cars which he constructed as a boy stored in his basement.

_B_ 2. a. Tom likes to occasionally take his dog for a long walk in the woods.
    b. Occasionally, Tom likes to take his dog for a long walk in the woods.

_B_ 3. a. Students who allot an hour for reading a chapter in the textbook regularly should have no trouble finishing this shorter chapter.
    b. Students who regularly allot an hour for reading a chapter in the textbook should have no trouble finishing this shorter chapter.

_A_ 4. a. Jen not only works well with groups but also works alone with great success.
    b. Jen works not only well with groups but also works alone with great success.

_A_ 5. a. Cathy has read nearly the entire first half of that long novel.
    b. Cathy has nearly read almost the entire first half of that long novel.

_B_ 6. a. I almost found $20 in the pages of an old book that once belonged to my father.
    b. I found almost $20 in the pages of an old book that once belonged to my father.

_A_ 7. a. To immediately watch that game on your computer, you need to install a special download.
    b. To watch that game immediately on your computer, you need to install a special download.

_B_ 8. a. The newscaster reported that our basketball team won this afternoon's game on the six o'clock news.
    b. The newscaster on the six o'clock news reported that our basketball team won this afternoon's game.

_A_ 9. a. Earlier today, our assistant went to both the office supply store and the bookstore to pick up items we need.
    b. Earlier today, our assistant both went to the office supply store and the bookstore to pick up some items we need.

_B_ 10. a. Yesterday, I nearly talked to every member of my study group about that assignment.
    b. Yesterday, I talked to nearly every member of my study group about that assignment.

Directions: In the space at the left of each item, write either **a** or **b** to indicate the logical placement of the modifier shown in parentheses.

_____ 1. (either) The staff members **a** were **b** surprised or delighted by the manager's announcement of the raise in pay for everyone.

_____ 2. (when the opportunity arises) **a** Jason is always happy to **b** discuss films he has enjoyed recently.

_____ 3. (in the trunk of her car) **a** Annie always carries her ropes and other equipment for rock climbing **b**.

_____ 4. (only) We **a** need **b** to fill the car with gas before we can leave for the weekend.

_____ 5. (from the top of the stairs to the bottom) **a** I watched in frustration as the stack of books tumbled **b**.

_____ 6. (from inside the house) Jim watched **a** as the two dogs dug up the flower bed **b**.

_____ 7. (not) But **a** everyone does **b** agree that we should purchase that expensive plasma television for the players' lounge.

_____ 8. (under the car) **a** Jan watched with annoyance as her daughter's ball rolled away from her **b**.

_____ 9. (in the local newspaper) It was reported **a** that one of our neighbors found $1,000 **b**.

_____ 10. (almost) During her workout, Stacie **a** lifted **b**150 pounds in a bench press.

_____ 11. (regularly) Students who **a** speak a foreign language are **b** put into a second year class.

_____ 12. (neither) The students in this class **a** should **b** come late to any class nor miss any class altogether.

_____ 13. (both) My mother **a** invited **b** James and Robert to dinner on Thursday night.

_____ 14. (as the sun sets) **a** I like to **b** sit on my porch and watch the birds come to the feeder.

_____ 15. (not only) Janine wants to **a** go **b** to Europe but also Mexico after she graduates.

Exercise 14   *Misplaced Modifiers*

Directions: Each of the following sentences contains a poorly positioned word or phrase. Rewrite enough of the sentence to show where the phrase should fit into the sentence. Add or omit words as needed.

1. Last night I watched the lights of an airplane as it flew across the sky standing in my backyard.

   _____

2. The tree that fell across my driveway nearly was 40 feet tall.

   _____

3. All the members of that organization are not interested in local political problems.

   _____

4. All of us in the organization decided to complain to the commission at the meeting yesterday.

   _____

5. After the rest of us drove away, Howard nearly waited for 15 minutes before he left the parking lot.

   _____

6. My little sister read two short novels written by Louisa May Alcott at the insistence of her mother.

   _____

7. My grandmother has stored all the sweaters she ever knitted in a cedar chest in her bedroom.

   _____

8. Last week, I both sent an invitation to Sue and to Mary.

   _____

9. Those who ride mountain bikes regularly are assigned to the intermediate instructional class.

   _____

10. My brothers and I were able to last week go to a very enjoyable concert.

   _____

Directions: In the space at the left, write **a** or **b** to indicate the logical placement of the modifier within the parentheses. Note that in some items both choices are logical; be prepared to explain the precise meaning of your choices.

_____ 1. (either) On weekends, the weather is **a** always **b** rainy or cold, or so it seems.

_____ 2. (only) The manager **a** chose to buy **b** a week's supply of paper instead of a month's supply.

_____ 3. (almost) Rhonda **a** ran **b** 5 miles last Saturday morning during the cold and rain.

_____ 4. (immediately) It seems like a good idea to **a** repair that slow leak in my tire **b**.

_____ 5. (on the morning news) **a** I heard an interesting story about a man who built an innovative kind of house **b**.

_____ 6. (regularly) People who work out **a** are **b** placed in the advanced classes for physical fitness.

_____ 7. (both) The company **a** needs **b** to cut costs and to improve the quality of its products.

_____ 8. (either) **a** You must **b** give me a solution to that problem or find me some people who can help us out.

_____ 9. (not only) That man **a** can **b** make a terrific speech but also write inspirational poetry.

_____ 10. (both) The boss **a** sent that message **b** to Jose and to Candace.

_____ 11. (deliberately) It seems that Alex **a** chose to **b** change the program that controls the thermostats in the building to make it cooler inside.

_____ 12. (nearly) In preparation for that test, I **a** read **b** 10 articles and 5 chapters in the textbook.

_____ 13. (personally) **a** I admire that man's work, but I admire his actions in life **b** even more.

_____ 14. (only) **a** Jim can **b** provide us with a solution to that problem; no one else understands the situation.

_____ 15. (not only) Janice **a** can create **b** an impressive presentation but also write very effective proposals.

NAME _____   SCORE _____

Directions: One sentence of each pair contains a dangling modifier. In the space at the left, write the letter that identifies the correct sentence. Be prepared to explain why the incorrect sentence contains a dangling modifier. **Review:** Underline and identify any infinitive and participial phrases in the first ten sentences.

_B_ 1. a. To find the best route through the mountains, accurate maps must be consulted.
  b. To find the best route through the mountains, you must consult accurate maps.

_B_ 2. a. Looking at the horizon in the distance, the sea seemed almost endless.
  b. Looking at the horizon in the distance, I thought the sea seemed almost endless.

_A_ 3. a. If you are running late for the meeting, please call me on my cell phone.
  b. Running late to the meeting, a call to my cell phone would be appreciated.

_A_ 4. a. When I met the professor after class, he suggested a brief conference over a cup of coffee.
  b. Meeting the professor after class, he suggested a brief conference over a cup of coffee.

_A_ 5. a. We could not read the directions, covered with mud and dirt, to help us find the cabin.
  b. Covered with mud and dirt, we could not read the directions to help us find the cabin.

_B_ 6. a. Approaching the coast, the smell of salty sea air became quite noticeable.
  b. As we approached the coast, we noticed the smell of salty sea air.

_B_ 7. a. At the age of five, my parents sold our house on the East Coast and we moved to Kansas.
  b. When I was five, my parents sold our house on the East Coast and we moved to Kansas.

_B_ 8. a. Covered with mud, Andrea found her book in the driveway.
  b. Andrea found her book, covered with mud, in the driveway.

_B_ 9. a. Opening the heavy door into the library, my books fell out on the floor with a great crashing sound.
  b. As I opened the heavy door into the library, my books fell out on the floor with a great crashing sound.

_A_ 10. a. After looking everywhere in the house, I found my wallet in the glove compartment of my pickup.
  b. After looking everywhere in the house, my wallet appeared in the glove compartment of my pickup.

_B_   11. a. While walking down that trail, a bolt of lightning struck a tree just ahead of Alan.
         b. While Alan was walking down the trail, a bolt of lightning struck a tree just ahead of him.

_A_   12. a. Since moving to Seattle, I have found the extremely rainy conditions a little depressing.
         b. Since moving to Seattle, the extremely rainy conditions have been a little depressing for me.

_A_   13. a. To take that course in computer graphics, you must first complete two prerequisite courses.
         b. To take that course in computer graphics, two prerequisite courses must be completed.

_B_   14. a. The apartment manager needs to refund your security deposit when leaving for the summer.
         b. The apartment manager needs to refund your security deposit when you leave for the summer.

_B_   15. a. To protect that crystal vase, it needs to be wrapped in bubble wrap and cushioned with Styrofoam.
         b. To protect that crystal vase, you need to wrap it in bubble wrap and cushion it with Styrofoam.

_A_   16. a. When reading the evening weather report, the meteorologist made two silly mistakes.
         b. When reading the evening weather report, two silly mistakes were made by the meteorologist.

_A_   17. a. As we tried to find that new restaurant, we were confused by a series of one-way streets.
         b. Trying to find that new restaurant, a series of one-way streets confused us.

_B_   18. a. Having watched the weather forecast closely, tomorrow will probably not be a good day for hiking that trail.
         b. Having watched the weather forecast closely, we determined that tomorrow will not be a good day for hiking that trail.

_A_   19. a. Cathy fed some scraps to her dog waiting hungrily beneath the dining room table.
         b. Waiting hungrily beneath the dining room table, Cathy fed some scraps to her dog.

_B_   20. a. To ride that roller coaster safely, both the seat belt and the safety bar must be employed.
         b. To ride that roller coaster safely, you must employ both the seat belt and the safety bar.

NAME _____   SCORE _____

Directions: Rewrite each of the following sentences twice:
   a. Change the dangling modifier to a complete clause with a subject and a verb.
   b. Retain the phrase but begin the main clause with a word it can logically modify.

1. Looking everywhere in the library, no books necessary for my paper were on the shelves.

   a. _____

   b. _____

2. Before buying that used car, its history should be checked through a computerized service.

   a. _____

   b. _____

3. To become a success in business, skill and luck are important.

   a. _____

   b. _____

4. While going to the movies last night, someone borrowed my biology textbook and did not return it.

   a. _____

   b. _____

5. To find directions to that address in Rapid City, a computerized map service such as MapQuest will be a big help.

   a. _____

   b. _____

6. Changing the oil on her antique Ford, some oil dripped onto Melanie's face.

   a. _____

   b. _____

7. Spraining my ankle severely, the trainer gave me an ice pack to put on it.

   a. _____

   b. _____

8. Having already picked two quarts of blueberries, this morning can already be called successful.

   a. _____

   b. _____

9. Before submitting that paper to your professor, the spelling needs to be checked with your computer.

   a. _____

   b. _____

10. To be sure every word in the essay is correct, homophones need to be checked after the computer has checked the spelling.

    a. _____

    b. _____

11. Having worked the first part of the equation incorrectly, the rest of Jim's work on the problem was also incorrect.

    a. _____

    b. _____

12. To find your way through the house when the electricity is off, a good flashlight is needed.

    a. _____

    b. _____

13. Jogging through the neighborhood this morning, a dog inside a fenced yard barked and growled at me.

    a. _____

    b. _____

14. Having worked for several hours at the computer, Maria's neck became quite stiff.

    a. _____

    b. _____

15. Being very tall and athletic, people encouraged Heather to become a volleyball player.

    a. _____

    b. _____

Brief Writing Assignment: Write a paragraph of eight or nine sentences describing a perfect day in your life ten years from now. Use at least four adverbs, correctly placed, and write two sentences that contain dangling modifiers. Then rewrite the sentences to eliminate the dangling modifiers.

Beginning writers sometimes string together too many short sentences, or they tie clauses together with conjunctions—*and*, *but*, *or*—that fail to establish precise relations between the clauses.

Poor:	Sally usually attends each concert. She missed this one. She went to the airport to meet her cousin Ellen. Ellen was arriving from Atlanta.
	I rode around town for three days, but I couldn't find a place to stay, and then I located this apartment, and so I am comfortable.

If you use the methods of creating and combining sentences that we have studied, you will make your writing more precise, more economical, and more meaningful:

Improved:	Although Sally usually attends each concert, she missed this one because she went to the airport to meet her cousin Ellen, who was arriving from Atlanta.
	After riding around town for three days without finding a place to stay, I finally located this apartment, where I am comfortable.

Get into the habit of trying different methods of subordinating material. Notice in the following sentences how an idea can be expressed in a variety of ways:

Two Sentences:	The small car was inexpensive to drive. It had only four cylinders.
Compound Verb:	The small car had only four cylinders and was inexpensive to drive.
Compound Sentence:	The small car was inexpensive to drive, for it had only four cylinders.
Adverbial Clause:	Because the small car had only four cylinders, it was inexpensive to drive.
Adjective Clause:	The small car, which had only four cylinders, was inexpensive to drive.
Participial Phrase:	The small car, having only four cylinders, was inexpensive to drive.
	Having only four cylinders, the small car was inexpensive to drive.
	The small car was inexpensive to drive, having only four cylinders.
Absolute Phrase:	The small car having only four cylinders, it was inexpensive to drive.
Prepositional Phrase:	The small car with only four cylinders was inexpensive to drive.
Appositive:	The small car, a four-cylinder model, was inexpensive to drive.
Adjective Modifier:	The small four-cylinder car was inexpensive to drive.

The use of subordination produces more than a pleasing sound in writing. It makes a crucial contribution to meaning by eliminating uncertainty about what is most important in a message. Consider the following string of simple sentences:

The management and union representatives announced an agreement. A strike had been threatened but was averted. The employees of Grantex Company reported for work today. They were relieved.

There is no way of knowing from these sentences which fact is most significant: The agreement? The avoidance of a strike? The workers' reporting for work? Their relief? Rewritten with proper subordination, the news reveals what the writer believes is most significant:

> The relieved employees of Grantex Company reported for work today after the management and union representatives announced an agreement that averted a threatened strike.

The only independent clause in the sentence concerns the workers' return to work. That is the important message. A writer more interested in strikes and their effect on the general economy might report the event in this way:

> The strike threatened at Grantex Company was averted when the management and union representatives announced an agreement, after which the relieved employees reported for work today.

A NOTE ON SENTENCE VARIETY

Preceding lessons have demonstrated how subordinate clauses and phrases, by compressing material, help the writer avoid tiresome strings of independent clauses. You have also seen that certain subordinate units—adverbial clauses and participial phrases in particular—can be put in several places within the sentence, thus helping prevent monotony in your sentences.

Another unit useful for achieving compression and variety is the appositive. (See Lesson 10.) As noun renamers, appositives closely resemble—they might be called the final reduction of—Pattern 2 clause and phrase modifiers of nouns:

> Ted could explain the trick to us. Ted [or He] is an amateur magician. [two independent clauses]
> Ted, *who is an amateur magician*, could explain the trick to us. [adjective clause]
> Ted, *being an amateur magician*, could explain the trick to us. [participial phrase]
> Ted, *an amateur magician*, could explain the trick to us. [appositive]

Although the usual position of an appositive is immediately following the noun it renames, many appositives, like many nonrestrictive participial phrases, can precede the main noun (in which case they are called *pre-positional appositives*); sometimes they are effectively placed at the end of the clause:

> Lawyer Somers, *a master of wit and guile*, cajoles and browbeats in the courtroom.
> *A master of wit and guile*, Lawyer Somers cajoles and browbeats in the courtroom.
> Lawyer Somers cajoles and browbeats in the courtroom, *a master of wit and guile*.

As a final example of language tools for renaming and modifying nouns, study this tightly constructed sentence:

> One of the five largest towns in Roman England, home of King Arthur's legendary Round Table, seat of Alfred the Great, whose statue looks down its main street, early capital of England, and victim of Cromwell's destructive forces, Winchester is an enchanting cathedral city in which layer after layer of history is visibly present.
>
> Elisabeth Lambert Ortiz, "Exploring Winchester," *Gourmet*,
> March 1978, p. 21

This sentence is made up of one independent clause, which includes an adjective clause, and five pre-positional appositives, the third of which contains an adjective clause. The statements underlying this sentence might be charted as follows:

[Winchester was] one of the five largest towns in Roman England.

[Winchester was] the home of King Arthur's legendary Round Table.

[Winchester was] the seat of Alfred the Great.

[Alfred the Great's] statue looks down its main street.

[Winchester was] the early capital of England.

[Winchester was] the victim of Cromwell's destructive forces.

Winchester is an enchanting cathedral city.

[In this city] layer after layer of history is visibly present.

We see here that eight statements—enough to make up a paragraph of clear but unrelieved simple sentences—have been shortened into one complex sentence. The layering of appositives and adjective clauses produces compression, sentence variety, and proper emphasis.

English Fundamentals Online

After you have completed the Practice Sheets and Exercises in this lesson, you can find additional help and drill work at **MyWritingLab.com**, in the sections on Parts of Speech, Phrases and Clauses; Combining Sentences; Varying Sentence Patterns.

NAME _____ SCORE _____

Directions: Each of the following numbered units consists of either two independent clauses in the form of a compound sentence or two sentences. One of the structures is italicized. In the second version (b) of the item, the italicized structure has been reduced to a subordinate clause or phrase. In the space at the left of each item, write one of the following numbers to identify the type of clause or phrase:

1. Adverb clause   4. Gerund phrase   7. Infinitive phrase
2. Adjective clause   5. Absolute phrase
3. Participial phrase   6. Appositive

_____ 1. a. *The store opened at 8:00 A.M.* The shoppers rushed in to take advantage of the sale.
   b. *When the store opened at 8:00 A.M.*, the shoppers rushed in to take advantage of the sale.

_____ 2. a. *The store opened at 8:00 A.M.* The shoppers rushed in to take advantage of the sale.
   b. *The store having opened at 8:00 A.M.*, the shoppers rushed in to take advantage of the sale.

_____ 3. a. My sister was awake at 7:00 A.M. this morning. *She is usually a late sleeper*.
   b. My sister, *who is usually a late sleeper*, was awake at 7:00 A.M. this morning.

_____ 4. a. My sister was awake at 7:00 A.M. this morning. *She is usually a late sleeper*
   b. My sister, *usually a late sleeper*, was awake at 7:00 A.M. this morning.

_____ 5. a. *You must bubble in your student ID number in the proper blanks*, or your test cannot be scored by computer.
   b. *Unless you bubble in your student ID number in the proper blanks*, your test cannot be scored by computer.

_____ 6. a. *My dad has used that tractor for years,* but it still performs perfectly.
   b. *Although my dad has used that tractor for years*, it still performs perfectly.

_____ 7. a. *My dad has used that tractor for years,* but it still performs perfectly.
   b. That tractor, *which my dad has used for years*, still performs perfectly.

_____ 8. a. *Cover that table with several coats of polyurethane*, and it will resist scratches and other damage.
   b. *Covering that table with several coats of polyurethane* will make it resistant to scratches and other damage.

_____ 9. a. Cover that table with several coats of polyurethane, and *it will resist scratches and other damage*.
   b. *To make that table resistant to scratches and other damage*, cover it with several coats of polyurethane.

_____ 10. a. *Marcus saw the deer walk slowly into the clearing*. He took several shots of it with his camera.
   b. *When Marcus saw the deer walk slowly into the clearing*, he took several shots of it with his camera.

_____ 11. a. *Marcus saw the deer walk slowly into the clearing.* He took several shots of it with his camera.

b. *Seeing the deer walk slowly into the clearing*, Marcus took several shots of it with his camera.

_____ 12. a. *The last flight for Boston has already left,* and all those people in the waiting room will need rooms for the night.

b. *The last flight for Boston having already left,* all those people in the waiting room will need rooms for the night.

_____ 13. a. *The last flight for Boston has already left,* and all those people in the waiting room will need rooms for the night.

b. *Because the last flight for Boston has already left,* all those people in the waiting room will need rooms for the night.

_____ 14. a. *Study chapters 6 and 7 in the text*, and you will pass tomorrow's test.

b. *If you study chapters 6 and 7 in the text*, you will pass tomorrow's test.

_____ 15. a. *Study chapters 6 and 7 in the text*, and you will pass tomorrow's test.

b. *Studying chapters 6 and 7 in the text* will enable you to pass tomorrow's test.

_____ 16. a. Study chapters 6 and 7 in the text, and *you will pass tomorrow's test.*

b. Study chapters 6 and 7 in the text *to pass tomorrow's test.*

_____ 17. a. *We left the game a few minutes early,* and we were able to avoid most of the traffic.

b. *Leaving the game a few minutes early* enabled us to avoid most of the traffic.

_____ 18. a. *The election was clearly lost*, and the unhappy politician made her concession speech about midnight.

b. *With the election clearly lost*, the unhappy politician made her concession speech about midnight.

_____ 19. a. *The last guest has finally left for home*, so we can begin to clean up the mess in the dining room.

b. *With the last guest having finally left for home*, we can begin to clean up the mess in the dining room.

_____ 20. a. *The last guest has finally left for home*, so we can begin to clean up the mess in the dining room.

b. *Since the last guest has finally left for home*, we can begin to clean up the mess in the dining room.

NAME _____   SCORE _____

Directions: Preceding lessons have demonstrated various types of noun modification. When two sentences employ the same noun or pronoun, one sentence can be reduced to a modifying phrase or clause. In the following pairs of sentences, the word printed in bold-faced type in the first sentence is the noun or pronoun to be modified. Combine the sentences by reducing the second sentence to the kind of unit indicated by the following letters:

   a. Adjective clause   c. Participial phrase preceding the noun

   b. Participial phrase following the noun   d. Appositive

Review: Form items 1–5 into compound sentences. Use either coordinating conjunctions or semicolons with conjunctive adverbs.

1. My brother recently bought a new **car**. It is equipped with an on-board navigation system.

   a. _____

   b. _____

2. Alina is going to see her **brother**. He is a research scientist at a university out west.

   a. _____

   d. _____

3. A **stranger** entered the room. She was dressed in a black overcoat.

   a. _____

   b. _____

   c. _____

4. Today we had lunch with **Tom Reynolds.** He is the manager of the Cleveland office.

   a. _____

   d. _____

5. **Tomas's aunt** is a computer consultant. She travels frequently throughout the country.

   a. _____

   b. _____

   c. _____

6. The lost **puppy** was found about midnight. He was sleeping on a neighbor's porch.

   a. _____

   b. _____

   c. _____

7. **Jack** stayed home last night. He was exhausted from studying for finals.

   a. _____

   b. _____

   c. _____

8. **Ida** stayed home last weekend. She wanted to study for final exams.

   a. _____

   b. _____

   c. _____

9. Most **people** went to the football game. They needed a break from their studies.

   b. _____

   c. _____

10. **Exam week** has finally ended. It was a difficult experience for most of us.

   a. _____

   d. _____

11. The boss handed Jim an important **letter**. It contained good news about a new account.

   a. _____

   b. _____

12. One **building** needs extensive repairs. It has not been maintained for years.

   a. _____

   b. _____

   c. _____

13. One **building** needs extensive repairs. It is an important part of the town's history.

   a. _____

   d. _____

14. **Jean** was extremely happy. She had just completed her first major mountain bike race.

   a. _____

   b. _____

   c. _____

15. **Terry** nervously climbed the steps to the platform. She had never dived from this height before.

   a. _____

   b. _____

   c. _____

Brief Writing Assignment: In a six-sentence paragraph discuss two of your most highly developed skills. Write one compound sentence and sentences containing one adverbial clause, one adjective clause, and one noun clause.

There are two other situations in which the underlying logic of the sentence requires the writer to select carefully the structure and position of the sentence units.

PARALLEL STRUCTURE

When two or more parts of a sentence are similar in function, they should be expressed in the same grammatical construction; in other words, they should be **parallel**. The principle of parallelism implies that, in a series, nouns should be balanced with nouns, adjectives with adjectives, prepositional phrases with prepositional phrases, clauses with clauses, and so forth. The following sentence owes much of its clarity and effectiveness to its careful parallel arrangement: Two adjective clauses are joined with *and*, two adverbs with *but*, and three noun direct objects with *and*.

> Anyone who studies world affairs *and* who remembers our last three wars will realize, sadly *but* inevitably, that another conflict will endanger the economic strength of our nation, the complacency of our political institutions, *and* the moral fiber of our people.

Anyone | who studies world affairs *and*
who remembers our last three wars will realize, | sadly *but*
inevitably,
that another conflict will endanger | the economic strength of our nation,
the complacency of our political institutions,
and the moral fiber of our people.

Two types of errors, the *false series* and the *and who* construction, work to destroy parallelism by using coordinate conjunctions to join grammatical units that are not alike.

1. The false or shifted series

Weak: Most people play golf for exercise, pleasure, and so they can meet others.
[The *and* ties an adverb clause to two nouns.]

Better: Most people play golf for exercise, for pleasure, and for social contacts.

Weak: Our new teacher was young, tall, slender, and with red hair.
[The *and* suggests that it will be followed by a fourth adjective, not a prepositional phrase.]

Better: Our new teacher was young, tall, slender, and red-haired.

Weak: Mr. Little's speech was tiresome, inaccurate, and should have been omitted.

Better: Mr. Little's speech was tiresome, inaccurate, and unnecessary.

2. The *and who* or *and which* construction

Weak:	Their son is an athlete with great talent *and who* will soon be well known.
Better:	Their son is an athlete who has great talent and who will soon be well known.
	Their son is a greatly talented athlete who will soon be well known.
	[Here the unbalanced modification is avoided.]

Weak:	I am taking Physics 388, a difficult course *and which* demands much time.
Better:	I am taking Physics 388, which is a difficult course and demands much time.
	I am taking Physics 388, which is difficult and demands much time.

COMPARISONS

When you write sentences that make comparisons or contrasts, you must observe certain forms if your writing is to be clear and precise.

1. Be sure that you compare only those things that are capable of being compared:

Faulty:	The storage capacity of this computer is much greater than our old one.
	[*One* refers to computer; thus, two unlike things, storage capacity and the computer, are being compared.]
Improved:	The storage capacity of this computer is much greater than *the storage capacity of* our old one.
	The storage capacity of this computer is much greater than *that of* our old one.

Faulty:	The influence of the political leader is more ephemeral than the artist.
	[Here, *influence*, an abstract quality, is being compared to a person, the artist.]
Improved:	The influence of the political leader is more ephemeral than *the influence of* the artist.
	The influence of the political leader is more ephemeral than *that of* the artist.
	The political leader's influence is more ephemeral than *the artist's*.

2. When you use the comparative form of an adjective in a comparison, use *any other* when it is necessary to exclude the subject of the comparison from the group:

Faulty:	Wilson, the first-string center, is heavier than any man on the team.
	[In this version the writer is comparing Wilson to the members of a group that includes Wilson.]
Improved:	Wilson, the first-string center, is heavier than *any other* man on the team.

3. When your sentence contains a double comparison, be sure to include all the words necessary to make the idiom complete and be sure that the second comparative phrase does not, because of its position, create problems of agreement or number.

Faulty:	As our new baseball coach, the college has selected Jaime Ruiz, one of the best, if not the best, coaches in our conference.
Improved:	As our new baseball coach, the college has selected Jaime Ruiz, one of the best coaches, if not the best coach, in our conference.

The wordiness of this version can be solved by moving the phrase *if not the best coach* to the end of the sentence.

> As our new baseball coach, the college has selected Jaime Ruiz, one of the best coaches in our conference, if not the best (coach).

Double comparisons may create sentences that sound awkward even though they form the comparison correctly and completely. You may want to recast the sentence to make it read more smoothly.

1. Try forming two sentences:

> He is now as tall as his mother. He may, indeed, be taller than she.
> She is one of the best runners in the club. She may even be the best runner in the club.

2. Try writing two independent clauses:

> He is now as tall as his mother, and he may be even taller than she is.
> She is one of the best runners in the club, and she may be the best runner in the club.

(See Supplement for more details on sentences used to compare and contrast.)

SUPPLEMENT

In addition to requiring the structural units already mentioned, comparison-contrast sentences place a few constraints on the form of the adjective or adverb.

1. When your comparison is limited to two things, use the comparative degree:

> Both Jane and Laura sing well, but Jane has the *better* voice.
> Which takes *more* time, your studies or your job?

2. Use the superlative for more than two things:

> January is the *worst* month of the year.

You learned in Lesson 2 that there are two ways of forming the comparative and superlative degrees. In general, *er* and *est* are used with short words, and *more* and *most* with longer words.

> When I was *younger*, I was *more apprehensive* about thunder and lightning than I am now.
> This atlas is the *newest* and the *most comprehensive* in this country.
> Maria works *faster* than I and also *more accurately*.

Remember that in present-day standard English, *er* or *est* is not combined with *more* or *most* in the same word. We don't say, for example, *more pleasanter*, *most loveliest*, or *more faster*.

English Fundamentals Online

After you have completed the Practice Sheets and Exercises in this lesson, you can find additional help and drill work at **MyWritingLab.com**, in the section on Parallel Structure.

NAME _____   SCORE _____

Directions: In the space at the left of each pair of sentences, copy the letter identifying the sentence that is logically structured. Be prepared to point out in class the faulty parallelism in the sentences you rejected. **Review:** On this page underline any participial and gerund phrases.

___A___ 1. a. Bringing up the rear was Jones, puffing and sweating, and trying desperately not to be the last to cross the finish line.
            b. Bringing up the rear was Jones, puffing and sweating, and he tried desperately not to be the last to cross the finish line.

___B___ 2. a. Several people in the office believe that the boss's daughter is more a hindrance than helpful.
            b. Several people in the office believe that the boss's daughter is more a hindrance than a help.

___A___ 3. a. We learned that a good stable should be dry, airy, and filled with good light.
            b. We learned that a good stable should be dry, airy, and having plenty of good light.

___A___ 4. a. Next year I am going to start fresh and make an all-out effort to keep myself organized.
            b. Next year I am going to start fresh and making an all-out effort to keep myself organized.

___B___ 5. a. As an accomplished public speaker, he speaks clearly, directly, and with effectiveness.
            b. As an accomplished public speaker, he speaks clearly, directly and effectively.

___A___ 6. a. My brother acted as he did out of true affection and generosity.
            b. My brother acted as he did out of true affection and because he is generous.

___A___ 7. a. The sorority president is tall and fairly slender, has long black hair, and has a radiant smile.
            b. The sorority president is tall and fairly slender, with long black hair and smiling radiantly.

_____ 8. a. We looked for a leader who has great courage and will take a stand on important issues.
            b. We looked for a leader with great courage and who will take a stand on important issues.

_____ 9. a. Far away we saw a runner struggling to cross the river, and he fell as he climbed the bank.
            b. Far away we saw a runner struggle to cross the river and falling as he climbed the bank.

_____ 10. a. Janet is a person with limited experience in that field and little ability to learn quickly on the job.
            b. Janet is a person who has limited experience in that field and with little ability to learn quickly on the job.

Directions: From each of the following pairs of sentences, select the one you prefer and write its letter in the space at the left. Be prepared to justify your choice.

_____ 1. a. Recreational facilities here in this small town are not much different from any small town.
   b. Recreational facilities here in this small town are not much different from those in any other small town.

_____ 2. a. I find her writing as interesting, if not more interesting, than most other women writers.
   b. I find her writing as interesting as the writing of most other women writers, if not more interesting.

_____ 3. a. Old man Larkins is reputed to have more money than any resident of the county.
   b. Old man Larkins is reputed to have more money than any other resident of the county.

_____ 4. a. Jim's work is certainly better than his competitors.
   b. Jim's work is certainly better than his competitors'.

_____ 5. a. Armando, sheltered in school work all his life, found the competition in the business world much harder to manage than did his brother, Jose.
   b. Armando, sheltered in school work all his life, found the competition in the business world much harder to manage than his brother, Jose.

_____ 6. a. His friends often teased him about his nose, which they said looked like a hawk.
   b. His friends often teased him about his nose, which they said looked like a hawk's beak.

_____ 7. a. Is Mike the tallest of your two brothers?
   b. Is Mike the taller of your two brothers?

_____ 8. a. Of all my friends, Janice has the most varied talents.
   b. Of any of my friends, Janice has the most varied talents.

_____ 9. a. I believe that wages for working construction are better here than those paid in the East.
   b. I believe that wages for working construction are better here than the East.

_____ 10. a. Jenny is one of the happiest, if not the happiest girl, in that class.
   b. Jenny is, if not the happiest girl, at least one of the happiest girls in that class.

Exercise 16   *Parallel Structure; Comparisons*

NAME *Rachel Schmitt*   SCORE _____

Directions: Rewrite each sentence to correct the faulty parallelism.

1. I always thought of Camp Wellmore more as a resort than as if it were a place where I could work.

   I always thought of camp more as a resort than a workplace

2. Ryan is looking for an affordable car but which would still look good at the country club.

   an affordable, nice looking car

3. The new novel has an interesting story, colorfully written, and I can identify with the characters.

   interesting story, colorful writing, relatable identifiable characters

4. The class reunion had a good program: a good band, a great singer, and the master of ceremonies was a great comedian.

   good band, great singer, & a comical comedic master of ceremonies

5. To be a good golfer, Marsha needs to groove her swing, hit through the ball, and with great concentration.

   groove, hit, and concentrate.

6. John Ormond is one man whose power of persuasion is great and has widely known ability as an organizer.

   who has great power of persuasion & organizational skills

7. This company needs people who think innovatively and always working to develop new products.

   think & work

8. Our job here in security is the safety of the crowd and to protect the rock stars from autograph seekers.

   is to protect the crowd's safety & rock stars from autograph seekers

9. My problem with that test came more from lacking time than from the fact that I did not understand the material.

   more from lack of time than lack of material

10. The president of that toy company looks like a typical teenager wearing old jeans and with hair down in her eyes.

    wearing long jeans & having messy hair

173

Directions: Rewrite each sentence to correct the faulty comparison.

1. I did not know that working in business was so much harder than college.

   so much harder than ~~completing~~ college

   other

2. My sister is the smartest of any/girl in her school.

   smartest girl in her school

3. That movie is one of the dullest, if not the dullest movie, I've seen in years.

   _____

4. Who is tallest, you or Martha?

   _____

5. The goalie is short and stocky ~~and~~ with legs like a gorilla. *'s*

   _____

6. Sam likes rock music just as much as his mother. *does ~~rock music~~*

   _____

7. Yesterday's temperature here was much lower than the interior of the state.

   _____

8. The local bicycle shop has a better mechanic than any shop in this area.

   _____

9. Using a computer to balance your checkbook is as complicated, if not more complicated, than a calculator.

   _____

10. Her accuracy record is equal, and in many cases better than, the other secretaries.

    _____

Brief Writing Assignment: Write a paragraph of seven sentences telling the story of a kindness someone did for you recently. Somewhere in the seven sentences, create two parallel structures and two comparisons.

Check Sheet

SENTENCE BUILDING

☐ **Completeness**

☐ To be a complete sentence, a word group must
1. Contain a subject and a verb.
2. Be independent rather than subordinate.

☐ Sentences tend to be incomplete for three reasons:
1. They are actually subordinate clauses.

   Although we never tried to drive that car again

   This clause must be attached to a main clause because the word *although* is a subordinating conjunction.

2. They are verbal phrases.

   Running down the street with a large kite suspended overhead

   To be sure of an early arrival

   Participles and infinitives cannot stand alone; they must function in or be attached to a main clause.

3. They are an incomplete construction made up of a noun and a phrase or subordinate clause.

   A man of good reputation who needs no introduction to this group because he has performed so many vital services to the city where he has lived for so many years...

   No matter how long the word group continues, no matter how many phrases and subordinate clauses it contains, it can't be a sentence unless it has a subject and a verb.

☐ Correcting fragments is relatively easy once they are detected:
- Attach the fragment to the previous sentence or to the following sentence as the sense of the sentence allows.
- Change the fragment to a subordinate clause with an appropriate subordinating word and attach it to a main clause.
- Change the fragment to an independent clause by supplying either a subject or verb or both as the sense of the sentence demands.

☐ Some expressions that lack a subject–verb combination are not considered fragments:
- Commands (The subject *you* is not voiced in such expressions.)

   Step right up. Take a ticket. Go to your seat.

- Exclamations

    Wow! Triplets? What a surprise!

- Bits of dialog (Note that much of our day-to-day, informal conversation is couched in sentence fragments.)

    "Running late?" she asked. "Better hurry. Only a few seats left."

- Short transitional expressions

    Now for the last step. On to the next stop.

☐ Traps

☐ *Misplaced Modifiers*

We often place modifiers rather loosely in sentences in our conversation and informal writing, but in more formal writing and when precise expression is important, modifying words, phrases, and clauses must be located carefully.

1. Putting adverbs such as *only*, *nearly*, *almost*, and *hardly* in the wrong place can change the meaning of the sentence. Put modifying words, phrases, and clauses as close as possible to the word they modify.

    James nearly found $100 on the beach yesterday.

    technically means that James almost found, but did not find, money on the beach. Someone found the money ahead of James, or James walked past it without seeing it.

    James found nearly $100 on the beach.

    means that he found money on the beach, probably between $90 and $99. Changing the position of the adverb changes the meaning of the sentence.

2. Putting modifying words and phrases where they can attach themselves to the wrong word can confuse the reader.

    We heard that a forest fire burned thousands of acres of land on the evening news.

    literally means that the acreage burned on the news—that is, while the reporters watched—or perhaps the burning occurred in the newsroom. In either case, the reader can be confused. The intended meaning is that we heard the report on the news.

3. Putting modifiers where they can apply equally to two words can confuse the reader. In the sentence

    Students who can solve this problem easily can succeed in my logic course.

    the meaning might be

    Students who can easily solve this problem can succeed . . .

    or it might mean

    Students who can solve this problem can easily succeed . . .

    Position the modifier so that it can apply to only one word.

4. Place modifying words and phrases outside an infinitive, not between *to* and the verb stem.

> My brother likes to once in a while visit the zoo.

is a clear but awkward statement.

> Once in a while, my brother likes to visit the zoo.

is a much smoother expression.

5. Place the correlatives such as *both … and* and *not only … but also* immediately before the parallel units they connect

	We sent tickets to both Janice and Joan.
not	We sent tickets both to Janice and Joan.
and certainly not	We both sent tickets to Janice and Joan.

☐ Dangling Modifiers

Any phrase that does not attach itself clearly to the word it modifies is called a *dangling modifier*. Connect participial, gerund, and infinitive phrases as closely as possible to the words they modify. In the sentence

> Coming into town, the stately trees shaded both sides of the road.

the literal meaning of the structure has the trees coming into town and shading both sides of the road. The participial phrase modifies the noun following it closely in the sentence. Unless the trees are coming into town—perhaps on a truck—make the sentence read

> As we came into town, the stately trees shaded both sides of the road.

> or Coming into town, we saw the stately trees shading both sides of the road.

Be sure that gerund and infinitive phrases, especially those that serve as opening elements of the sentence, can attach themselves logically to the next noun in the sentence.

> To work as a truck driver, a commercial driver's license is required.

Logically, the commercial driver's license is not going to work as a truck driver; while the meaning is probably clear, it is better to say

> To work as a truck driver, you need a commercial driver's license.

or, more formally,

> To work as a truck driver, one needs a commercial driver's license.

☐ Parallel Structures

Two or more parts of sentences that are similar in function should be similar in grammatical construction—that is, parallel. Nouns should be balanced with nouns, verbs with verbs, and so on.

- Avoid the false or shifted series.

> He took that job for its challenges, its high pay, and *because it allowed him to travel.*

- Avoid the *and who, and which* construction.

> That is a job that offers challenges, high pay, *and which allows Hank to travel extensively.*

☐ *Comparisons*

    ☐ Be sure that comparisons and contrasts are made at the same level.

       Her car's engine is more powerful *than my car*.

    Engines cannot logically be compared to cars.

    In using the comparative form of an adjective in a comparison, use *any other* to exclude the subject of the comparison from the group.

       Our state university is bigger than any university in the state.

    If "our state university" is in the state, it must be compared to *any **other** university* in the state.

    In making double comparisons, include all the words necessary to make the expression complete.

       Alicia is easily as smart as Robert, if not smarter.

       Alicia is easily as smart as, if not smarter *than*, Robert.

    ☐ Use the comparative degree of the adjective or adverb when two items are compared.

       Alicia is *smarter* than Robert.

    ☐ Use the superlative degree when three or more items are involved.

       Alicia is the *smartest* person in the entire class.

☐ *Subordination*

Use compound verbs and sentences and subordinate clauses and phrases to create varied sentences.

    • Two simple sentences: The gun fired. The runners broke from the starting blocks.

    Compound verb: (not a possible construction because the two sentences have different subjects)

    Compound sentence: The gun fired, and the runners broke from the starting blocks.

    Adverbial clause: When the gun fired, the runners broke from the starting blocks.

    Participial phrase: (not a possible construction)

    Absolute phrase: With the gun having fired, the runners broke from the starting blocks.

    • Other constructions are possible when the subjects of the sentences are the same:

       I raised the flag. I unlocked the gate.

    Compound verb: I raised the flag and unlocked the gate.

    Compound sentence: I raised the flag; then I unlocked the gate.

    Participial phrase: Having raised the flag, I unlocked the gate.

Punctuation

Lessons, Practice Sheets, and Exercises

Lesson 17 — *Commas to Separate*

As your writing grows more precise and more powerful, you will need to use commas to separate certain parts of sentences so that your work cannot be misunderstood. Five rules cover the occasions when commas are used to separate parts of a sentence.

THE FIVE RULES FOR COMMAS TO SEPARATE

1. Use commas before *and*, *but*, *or*, *nor*, *yet*, *for*, and *so* when they join the clauses of a compound sentence:

> I placed the typed sheet on his desk, and he read it slowly.
> His face turned red, but he did not say a word.
> I knew he was angry, for he rose and stomped out of the room. [Note that no comma is used before the conjunction in a compound predicate.]

At this point, you might reread Lesson 7. Remember that a semicolon rather than a comma is usually required in a compound sentence when no coordinating conjunction is present.

2. Use a comma between the items of a series.

> The land looked brown, parched, lifeless, and ominous. [four adjectives]
> Volunteers may be students, office workers, housewives, or retirees. [four nouns]
> The dog charged through the door, down the steps, and into the garage. [three phrases]
> He understands what he must do, when he must do it, and why he must do it. [three subordinate clauses]
> Larry brought the wood, Mark built the fire, and I got the steaks ready. [three independent clauses]

A series is composed of three or more words, phrases, or clauses of equal grammatical rank. A series usually takes the form of *a*, *b*, *and* *c*; sometimes it may be *a*, *b*, *or* *c*. Although commas may be used to separate a series of short clauses, the punctuation must change if the clauses have commas within them.

> Larry, who has a pickup truck, brought the wood, Mark, who was once a Boy Scout, built the fire, and I got the steaks ready.

Obviously commas do not effectively separate the independent clauses in this sentence, so we need to use a mark with greater strength—in this case, the semicolon.

> Larry, who has a pickup truck, brought the wood; Mark, who was once a Boy Scout, built the fire; and I got the steaks ready.

In journalism, writers often omit the comma before the final conjunction. It is easier to remember the rule if you develop a consistent pattern of using the comma before the final conjunction.

3. Use a comma between coordinate adjectives preceding a noun.

> the harsh, cold wind

When applied to adjectives, the word **coordinate** indicates that two adjectives modify a single noun with equal force. We usually separate coordinate adjectives with a comma. Sometimes it is difficult to know whether or not two adjectives are equal. Consider the following:

> the harsh cold wind
> the difficult final exam

Two tests will help you to decide if the adjectives are equal.

First, if you can use the word *and* instead of a comma between the two words and still produce a correct statement, the adjectives are equal, and a comma should be used to separate them. *The harsh and cold wind* makes perfect sense in English, demonstrating that the adjectives are equal in force and need a comma. But you would never say *the difficult and final exam*; thus, the adjectives are not coordinate, and the comma is not needed.

Second, if the adjectives sound natural in reversed position, they are equal and can be separated by a comma if the word *and* is not used. The phrase *the cold, harsh wind* is just as readable as *the harsh, cold wind*, again demonstrating that the adjectives are equal.

When you use more than two adjectives before a noun, you should use the *and* test, checking the adjectives by pairs—the first with the second, the second with the third, and so on—to determine the need for commas. It may help you to know that we usually do not use commas before adjectives denoting size or age. And remember that you never use a comma between the last adjective and the noun.

Observe how use of these tests determines punctuation in the following examples:

> a neat, courteous little boy
> a hot, steamy summer day

Because we don't say "a neat and courteous and little boy," we would place a comma between *neat* and *courteous*, but not between *courteous* and *little*. We could say *a hot, steamy summer day* or *a steamy, hot summer day*, but not *a hot and steamy and summer day*.

4. Use a comma after most introductory modifiers. The following specific applications of this rule will help you use it correctly.

a. Put commas after introductory adverbial clauses:

> *When the sky clears*, we'll resume the game.
>
> *If we can prove that the signature was forged*, we will win the case.
>
> *Before sophomores will be admitted to courses numbered 300 or above*, they must have official permission.
>
> *Before I answer you*, I want to ask another question.
>
> *When he arrived*, he seemed happy.

b. Put commas after introductory verbal-phrase modifiers:

> *Having climbed the steep trail up Cougar Mountain*, Bob decided to take some pictures.
>
> *To get the best view of the valley*, he walked to the edge of the cliff.
>
> *After opening his backpack*, he searched for his new telephoto lens.

c. Put a comma after an introductory absolute element, such as a phrase, an adverb modifying the whole sentence, a mild exclamation, and *yes* and *no*.

> *In fact*, there was no way to keep the front door closed.
>
> *Certainly*, I'll be glad to help you.
>
> *Well*, what are we to do now?
>
> *No*, we are not in danger.

d. Ordinarily, do not put a comma after a single prepositional phrase at the beginning of a sentence. If the opening element contains two or more phrases, use a comma to separate the phrases from the main clause. A long introductory prepositional phrase is not followed by a comma when the subject and verb are reversed.

> *After a heavy dinner* we usually went for a short walk.
>
> *In early summer* many birds nested there.
>
> *In spite of the very heavy wind and the pelting hailstones*, the third race was completed.
>
> *In the name of justice*, please help these people.
>
> *After school, or during the evening*, teachers were expected to find time for grading papers and preparing lessons.
>
> *Between the dusty night table and the unmade bed* were all the magazines that I wanted to read.

5. Use a comma between any two words that might be mistakenly read together:

> *Before*, he had been industrious and sober. [not *before he had been*]
>
> *Once inside*, the dog scampered all over the furniture. [not *inside the dog*]
>
> *While we were eating*, the table collapsed. [not *eating the table*]
>
> *After we had washed*, Mother prepared breakfast. [not *washed Mother*]
>
> *Ever since*, he has been afraid of deep water. [not *ever since he has been*]
>
> *Shortly after ten*, thirty new recruits appeared. [not *shortly after ten thirty*]

English Fundamentals **Online**

After you have completed the Practice Sheets and Exercises in this lesson, you can find additional help and drill work at **MyWritingLab.com**, in the section on Commas.

Commas to Separate

NAME _____ SCORE _____

Directions: Each of the following sentences is missing two commas. Add the commas where they are necessary. Then, in the space at the left, write the numbers of the rules that apply to the commas you added:

1. before a coordinating conjunction
2. in a series
3. between coordinate adjectives
4. after an introductory modifier
5. to prevent misreading

_____   1. We looked at the sleek, beautiful new cars in the showroom, and then we
_____   walked out to the used cars to find something we could afford.

_____   2. When she had finished her current project, Julie went to the store to buy a
_____   stapler, a paper cutter and a three-hole punch and then came back to the office.

_____   3. As the sun set over the mountain came a string of pack mules, three men on
_____   horseback and two dogs; the men dismounted and joined us for supper.

_____   4. At noon the men put down their hammers saws, and drills and then they sat
_____   down in the shade to eat lunch.

_____   5. The handsome well-dressed news anchor lost his place on the teleprompter
_____   and read three strange-sounding incomprehensible lines before he found his
               place again.

_____   6. When we finally found the folder that had fallen out of the car we realized
_____   that the papers the pictures, and the other important notes had blown away in
               the wind.

_____   7. Because the man and the woman were late for the game they had to sit on the
_____   very top row of the stadium so they could hardly see the players from that
               height.

_____   8. Earlier we had seen John at the basketball game but we could not locate him
_____   at the end of the game to invite him to go out for pizza.

3, 1   9. The tall, thin trunk of the pine tree was bent over by the wind, and the men had
_____   to straighten it and brace it upright with pieces of wood.

_____   10. So then tell us all why you think it is a good idea to leave school and take a
_____   job exercising race horses, grooming them and cleaning out their stalls.

_____   11. Walking slowly through the bookstore picking up books at random, and looking
_____   at them briefly the woman finally selected a romance novel and paid for it.

_____   12. As the child watched the tigers leaped through the burning ring, and the restless
_____   impatient lions crouched atop their perches.

_____   13. Although the number of choices overwhelmed him Walter finally settled on
_____   a mid-priced well-known sound system for his car.

_____   14. Walking slowly as he warmed up then jogging slowly for about a mile, and
_____   finally running as fast as he could, Tim finished the steep challenging course
               with ease.

183

_____ 15. Once we had come into the clearing we saw a bear cub sitting in front of our
_____ tent so we tried to frighten him away by screaming at him.

_____ 16. Once we saw a coyote out on that trail; he seemed menacing but he vanished
_____ before we even got close to him.

_____ 17. The tall handsome calf roper smiled at the girl from the next booth and soon
_____ they were engaged in an animated conversation.

_____ 18. Smiling at us from the door Grandma ushered us into the house and offered
_____ us some of her enticing delicious chocolate cookies.

_____ 19. At dawn of the next day the weather had cleared and we were able to hoist
_____ the sails and run down the coast to our next stop.

_____ 20. After the test most of the class members walked down the street to the deli,
_____ where they all had hot delicious sandwiches for lunch.

_____ 21. The crew members laid out the job site drove stakes to mark the boundaries
_____ of the house, and then brought in a small efficient backhoe to dig the foundations.

_____ 22. Once I had established the outline for my paper I was able to write long effective
_____ paragraphs based on the information I had collected.

_____ 23. Standing on the observation platform of the skyscraper and looking east we
_____ were able to see the mountains rising from the plain in their hazy majestic
beauty.

_____ 24. Jim caught several trout Harry cleaned them, and I broiled them over the open
_____ fire and, on the shore of the lake, we ate a meal fit for a king.

_____ 25. While walking the dog found an old bone and he brought it into the living
_____ room at home.

_____ 26. As he got out of the car the tall, strong and handsome movie actor tripped on
_____ the curb and fell headlong onto the sidewalk.

_____ 27. The narrow shaky bridge across the gorge frightened all of us but, after gathering
_____ our courage, we all walked slowly to the other side.

_____ 28. After we had stowed our gear hoisted the sails, and cast off the dock lines we
_____ sailed bravely out of the harbor and onto the open sea.

_____ 29. In the afternoon of the next day after John's visit we decided to mow the yard,
_____ trim the hedges and rake up all the leaves and branches.

_____ 30. At the mall down the street we met Barbara, Jim and Mark and went to lunch with
_____ them; afterward, we went to a movie that starred one of our favorite actors.

NAME _____ SCORE _____

Directions: The following passage is missing commas that should be used to separate certain words, phrases, or clauses. Insert commas where they are needed. Then, underneath each comma you insert, write the number of the rule that governs the use of that comma.

1. before a coordinating conjunction in a compound sentence
2. in a series
3. between coordinate adjectives
4. after an introductory modifier
5. to prevent misreading

   The first computers were huge collections of tubes, wires, and awkward switches. Called main-frame computers, these first machines were made from vacuum tubes about as big as a bread box, and the collection of them filled up a room the size of an average school classroom. When they were running, they generated an intense radiating heat. If the heat was not controlled, the tubes blew out, and they had to be replaced. In addition to this sensitivity to heat the tubes went completely irreparably haywire whenever they came in contact with the slightest speck of dust. To control the heat and dust the computers were enclosed in an air-tight air-conditioned room made with glass walls. With potential trouble approaching from every direction these main-frame computers needed the attention of highly trained protective technicians dressed in white coats. Protected by these guardians in the white coats the computers were not readily available to anyone else. The technicians in the white coats standing guard ordinary workers were kept at a distance from the machines and they usually had to deal with the technicians in order to get any computer time. As scientists and technicians refined the operation of the main-frame computer other scientists worked to produce a smaller less fragile machine. The first step in this process was the invention of a small inexpensive device, called a transistor, which controlled the flow of electricity. When transistors are hooked together they form integrated circuits or microchips. These microchips can contain complicated enormous circuits on a piece of silicon no bigger than a person's thumbnail. With these microchips having become available scientists constructed microprocessors and thus they opened the way for the development of small shock-resistant desktop and laptop computers. When scientists learned to miniaturize the workings of a computer, they opened the way for all of us to become computer experts and they gave all of us the power once reserved for the technicians in the white coats.

Directions: Under each rule, write two sentences of your own to illustrate the punctuation designated. The purpose of the exercise is to practice correct comma usage.

1. Comma used before a coordinating conjunction in a compound sentence

   a. _____

   _____

   b. _____

   _____

2. Commas used in a series (one series of single words and one series of phrases)

   a. _____

   _____

   b. _____

   _____

3. Comma used after an introductory modifier (one adverb clause and one verbal phrase)

   a. _____

   _____

   b. _____

   _____

4. Comma used between coordinate adjectives

   a. _____

   _____

   b. _____

   _____

5. Commas used to prevent misreading

   a. _____

   _____

   b. _____

   _____

Exercise 17A   *Commas and Semicolons to Separate*

NAME _____   SCORE _____

Directions: The following sentences contain numbered spots where punctuation might be needed. In the correspondingly numbered spaces at the left, write **C** if a comma is needed, **S** if a semicolon is needed, or **0** if no punctuation is needed. **Review:** In sentences 1–10, underline all adverbial clauses.

1. _____   (1) "When you have nothing to say don't say anything and you won't get
                                                                    1   2

2. _____   yourself into trouble," said my wise old grandmother.

3. _____   (2) Racing swiftly to the fence Garnett turned, leaped high and snared the ball
                                                      3   4

4. _____   in the webbing of her glove.

5. _____   (3) Because he had a few spare minutes before lunch Jim checked the library
                                                                            5

6. _____   shelves he was delighted to find a book he had been trying to locate.
                              6

7. _____   (4) Inside the room was lit by a single small bulb I was barely able to make my way
                        7   8

8. _____   through the tangle of furniture to the phone.

9. _____   (5) The father grinned broadly and hugged the small, tired girl but she continued
                                                      9   10

10. _____   to sob softly into her handkerchief.

11. _____   (6) She has a fine collection of beautiful antique cars a 1937 Cord and a 1955
                                                                    11   12

12. _____   Chevy Nomad station wagon are the showpieces of the entire group.

13. _____   (7) While the flustered young man was trying to answer an expensively dressed
                                                                            13   14

14. _____   older woman interrupted with another question.

15. _____   (8) "Senator, we need to know why you voted against that bill," said an irate
                                                            15

16. _____   citizen" it would have provided the city with badly needed jobs."
                              16

17. _____   (9) Three beautiful, well-dressed children sat quietly in the airport lounge and
                                                                                              17

18. _____   read magazines while waiting for their flight.
                              18

19. __C__ (10) Down below the boat had a large stateroom complete with sauna and television

           19   20

20. __S__ the owner, however, always slept in a hammock on the foredeck.

21. _____ (11) The reputation of the new bank president is excellent people say he is intelligent,

                                                               21

22. _____ hard-working and scrupulously honest.

                           22

23. _____ (12) A few minutes later the three girls left the campus and began their trip to

                                           23   24

24. _____ New York.

25. _____ (13) If our money lasts the living room and sun porch will be enlarged, and

                                         25   26

26. _____ completely redecorated in bright cheerful pastel colors.

27. _____ (14) Although I studied French grammar and French conversation in middle

28. _____ school, high school, and college, my accent is atrocious.

                                27   28

29. __C__ (15) Joan tried to comfort the lost puppy and Jim soon found its distraught weeping

                                         29   30

30. __C__ owner.

31. _____ (16) A graceful, gray and white sea gull soared past us, banked suddenly and floated

                                         31   32

32. _____ off on the wind.

33. __C__ (17) Looking down from the mountain for the first time I knew I wanted to buy the

                                                 33

34. _____ property for the view was magnificent.

                                34

35. __SC__ (18) We'll not need the forklift today the three of us can turn the rock roll it down

                                         35   36

36. __C__ the hill, and set it in place.

37. __C__ (19) Shortly before midnight a cranky old neighborhood grouch called me and

                                     37   38

38. _____ complained about my barking dogs.

39. _____ (20) Standing in front of the house painters and carpenters argued over the

         use of the   39

40. _____ ladders and the other workmen laughed out loud at their childishness.

                                40

Brief Writing Assignment: In a paragraph of seven sentences, express your gratitude for the kindness you discussed in Lesson 16. Employ and properly punctuate a compound sentence, a pair of coordinate adjectives, and an introductory participial phrase.

Just as there are times when you need to use commas to separate items, there are times when you need to use commas to enclose items. Use commas to enclose **interrupters**—those words, phrases, or clauses that interrupt the normal word order of a sentence.

COMMON INTERRUPTERS

The most common types of interrupters are discussed below.

1. Nonrestrictive adjective clauses and phrases

> The coach's Awards Banquet speech, *which was one of her best*, should be published. [nonrestrictive adjective clause]
>
> Jan's mother, *holding a winning ticket*, went to the desk. [nonrestrictive participial phrase]
>
> Professor Angela Charles, *at the far end of the head table*, summoned a waiter. [nonrestrictive prepositional phrase]

Clauses and phrases not essential to identify a noun are set off by commas. (See Lesson 9 to review restrictive and nonrestrictive clauses and phrases.) Note that, in some cases, the meaning of the sentence depends on whether a clause is taken as restrictive or nonrestrictive.

> My brother-in-law *who lives in Akron* is a chemist.
>
> [The writer has more than one brother-in-law. The restrictive clause is needed to distinguish this brother-in-law from other brothers-in-law.]
>
> My brother-in-law, *who lives in Akron*, is a chemist.
>
> [The writer is telling us that he or she has only one brother-in-law. Identification is not explicit.]

2. Most appositives

> One comedian, *the one with the blonde hair*, was booed.
>
> The major, *a veteran of three wars*, accepted the award.
>
> Mr. Tate, *our head counselor*, will speak.
>
> Our head counselor, *Mr. Tate*, will speak.

As you learned in Lesson 10, the most common type of appositive immediately follows the noun or pronoun that it renames. Appositives like these are called *loose* or *nonrestrictive appositives* and are set off. Sometimes, however, an appositive functions in the same way that a restrictive adjective clause functions: It identifies a preceding noun that, without the appositive, could refer to any member of a class. An appositive of this sort is not set off:

> my brother Jack
>
> the poet Keats

the apostle Paul

the preposition *to*

3. Absolute phrases

Today being a holiday, I plan to loaf and relax.

Her replacement having arrived early, Bea had time to shop.

He sat there in silence, *his eyes closed in sleep.*

He stood in the doorway, *his wet coat dripping water on the rug*, and waited for some sign of recognition.

An absolute phrase, which consists of a noun or a pronoun and a verbal (see Lesson 12), modifies the sentence as a whole, not any special part of it. Because the phrase is not restricted to any special part of the sentence, the phrase should be set off.

4. Parenthetical expressions

The text, *moreover*, had not been carefully proofread.

You will find, *for example*, that the format is not attractive.

The meal, *to tell the truth*, was quite unappetizing.

His appearance, *I must admit*, would startle anyone.

These are words, phrases, or clauses that break into the sentence to explain, to emphasize, to qualify, or to point the direction of the thought, and they should be set off.

5. Words used in direct address

"Remember, *Jimmy*, that we like your work," he said.

"*Henry*," said the teacher, "you made an A on your paper."

"I believe, *sir*, that you have been misinformed," she replied.

"And now, *dear friends and neighbors*, let's eat," said MP. Jamison.

6. Expressions designating the speaker in direct quotations

"With your permission," *Tom replied*, "I'll go home for the day."

"That will have to do," *said Mrs. Garcia*, "until we think of something better."

Other punctuation marks may be used instead of the comma if the sentence justifies their use.

"How shall I tell him?" asked Mary timidly. [question mark after question]

"Silence!" he shouted. "Get to work at once!" [exclamation point]

"Two of the buildings are in beautiful shape," replied the inspector; "however, the library needs a new roof." [semicolon required to avoid a comma fault between independent clauses]

7. Negative insertions used for emphasis, units out of their position, and tag questions (short interrogative clauses combined with statements)

> Our plane was an old propeller model, *not the jet we had expected*.
> *Tired and footsore*, the hikers finally reached camp.
> The hikers finally reached camp, *tired and footsore*.
> Her answer was a good one, *don't you think?*
> You remember, *don't you*, Dr. Wade's eloquent speech?

8. Degrees, titles, and the like when they follow names

> Helen Lyle, *Ph.D.*, gave the opening address.
> The new ambassador is Peter Jones, *Esq.*

9. In dates and addresses

> On July 14, *1904*, in a little cottage at 316 High Street, *Mayville, Illinois*, the wedding took place.

When a year follows a month, rather than a day of the month, the year is usually not set off. No comma is needed before a ZIP code number:

> As of March 1995 his mailing address was 1675 East Union Street, Seattle, WA 98122.

English Fundamentals Online

After you have completed the Practice Sheets and Exercises in this lesson, you can find additional help and drill work at **MyWritingLab.com**, in the section on Commas.

NAME _____   SCORE _____

Directions: Insert commas where they are needed in the following sentences. Then, in the space at the left, write one of the following numbers to indicate the rule that governs the use of the comma or commas in the sentence:

    1. a nonrestrictive clause or phrase   4. a parenthetical element

    2. an appositive →noun/participle   5. the speaker in dialogue

    3. a noun in direct address   6. an absolute phrase

_____ 1. With no one at the airport to meet us we took a taxi to our hotel.

_____ 2. My friend who earned a master's degree last fall has taken a job in Paris.

__5__ 3. "I wish" said Karen "that someone in that class would help me study for this test."

__2__ 4. Joe Johnson, an avid photographer is going to a seminar on nature photography next week.

__3__ 5. "I hope, John, that you will take off from work this afternoon and work on your paper," said the instructor.

__4__ 6. That business venture was, to say the least, extraordinarily profitable.

__1__ 7. Rob Smith, walking into the room and taking off his jacket, took a seat at the end of the table.

__2__ 8. The weather forecast for this weekend, a cold front accompanied by heavy rain, means that we will not be outside very much.

__3__ 9. "Richard, can you help me rearrange the chairs in the back of the room?" asked the kindergarten teacher.

__4__ 10. The woman speaking to our class this morning, I'm sure you know, is a foremost civil engineer.

__5__ 11. Mark said, "Our speaker this morning is a man who needs no introduction, so I will turn the program over to him."

__6__ 12. The group stood up, walked to the door, and left the room, the important decisions for that meeting having been made.

__1__ 13. The man walking into the hotel lobby is Kent Williams, who is a reporter from a local television station.

__2__ 14. The man walking into the hotel lobby is Kent Williams, a reporter from a local television station.

_____ 15. Kent Williams, walking through the door at this moment, is a reporter from a local television station.

Directions: Each of the following sentences contains an adjective clause or a participial phrase. Underline each clause or phrase and insert commas where they are needed. Then, in the space at the left, write **R** if the clause or phrase is restrictive; write **N** if it is nonrestrictive.

_R_   1. Can you tell me the name of the street <u>where Mr. Roberts has his office?</u>

_R_   2. The restaurant on the other side of town that <u>has such good Italian food</u> is called, simply, Mario's Italian Restaurant.

_R_   3. I would like to meet the two people <u>who wrote this report.</u>

_____ 4. I would like to meet Lisa Concepcion and Marcus Roberts who wrote this report.

_____ 5. The two names that appear on the cover of the report are Lisa Concepcion and Marcus Roberts.

_____ 6. The people whose names appear on the cover are Lisa Concepcion and Marcus Roberts.

_____ 7. Do you know the name of the person whom the company president named CFO?

_____ 8. Lexington Street which runs north and south at this end of town turns into an east-west street after it crosses the freeway.

_____ 9. The tall man striding purposefully into the room will be our instructor for this term.

_____ 10. Mr. Black who is striding purposefully into the room at this moment will be our instructor for this term.

_____ 11. His degree and his experience in the field which are both quite impressive make him a logical choice to teach the class.

_____ 12. One of my friends who took a class from Mr. Black last term found his work very impressive.

_____ 13. Mr. Black's work last term certainly impressed Ron Steinberg who took this class from him last term.

_____ 14. Ron whom you met at my house last week was quite impressed with Mr. Black.

_____ 15. The day when my history paper is due is sometime at the end of the month.

_____ 16. Tuesday, March 30 when my history paper is due is still three weeks away.

_____ 17. Lauren is a woman whose pleasing personality wins many friends.

_____ 18. Lauren whose pleasing personality impresses many people is a good friend of mine.

_____ 19. Marshall's new house shielded from the north winds by a hill stays warm even on the coldest days.

_____ 20. At a time when you have about an hour to spare I'll tell you the story of our disastrous ski trip.

Exercise 18   *Commas to Enclose*

NAME _____   SCORE _____

Directions: Insert commas where they are necessary in the following sentences. Then, underneath each comma write one of the following numbers to indicate the rule that governs the use of the commas:

1. a nonrestrictive clause or phrase
2. an appositive
3. a noun in direct address
4. a parenthetical element
5. the speaker in dialog
6. an absolute phrase

Sometimes parents tell children fanciful stories fairy tales that are supposed to teach the children some kind of lesson. These stories called by psychologists "cautionary tales" are often designed to make children aware of possible danger. One of these stories "Little Red Riding Hood" is a frightening story about a little girl and her encounter with a wolf. Little Red Riding Hood whose real name is never recorded anywhere lived in a small village near a deep woods. The girl got her nickname from a very special red hat which she wore every day all the time. The hat was knitted by the little girl's grandmother who loved the little girl more than anything else in the world. One day the grandmother a kind and wonderfully loving woman became sick and was unable to cook for herself. With the grandmother ill Red Riding Hood's mother decided to cook a meal and have the little girl deliver it. The mother called to the little girl "Red please take this soup and this fine sandwich to your grandmother."

"I am delighted to take this meal to my sweet grandmother" the little girl replied. The little girl always a dutiful daughter gathered up the lunch and prepared to walk to her grandmother's house.

The mother said "Red you must go straight to your grandmother's house and take care not to walk into the woods."

The little girl walking carefully along the edge of the woods to her grandmother's house met a big, bad wolf.

"Hello little girl" said the wolf. "Where are you taking that wonderful, tasty lunch?"

"I'm taking it to my grandmother who lives just a little bit farther down this path" replied the girl.

The wolf said "Take that path to your right; it is a shortcut to your grandmother's house."

The girl set off down the path, and the wolf anticipating a wonderful meal hurried ahead to the grandmother's house. The wolf a ravenous beast devoured the grandmother and waited for the little girl to arrive. Some versions of the story the goriest versions say that the wolf ate both the grandmother and the girl; others say that both were rescued.

The moral of the story as anyone can see is the same for both endings: Follow your mother's directions, and stay away from talking animals with large, sharp teeth.

Directions: Insert commas where they are needed in the following sentences. Then, in the space at the left of each sentence, write one of the following numbers to indicate the rule that governs the punctuation of the sentence:

1. a nonrestrictive clause or phrase
2. an appositive
3. a noun in direct address
4. a parenthetical element
5. the speaker in dialogue
6. an absolute phrase
7. negative insertions, etc.
8. degrees, titles, etc.
9. dates and addresses

_____ 1. That course which meets on Tuesdays and Thursdays does not fit into my schedule.

_____ 2. Patrick and Richard who are both very good students recommended that course to me.

_____ 3. Perhaps I can take that course next term a term in which my schedule will be a little more flexible.

_____ 4. Yesterday I met Paul Anderson the new manager of my department at the bank.

_____ 5. I think I'm sure you will agree that he will be a fine addition to the company.

_____ 6. I would like incidentally to borrow that copy of the financial report.

_____ 7. Next week our law practice will add a new lawyer John Baldwin J.D.

_____ 8. On April 2nd 2008 the school will celebrate the 200th anniversary of its founding by a group of local citizens.

_____ 9. Please send that package to my brother, whose address is 4972 Riverfront Parkway Chillicothe OH 56203.

_____ 10. Larry said "We need to work an extra hour tonight so that we can get that report finished."

_____ 11. We adjourned the department meeting at 5:00 P.M. all the business on the agenda having been completed.

_____ 12. My friend Walter who works as a media specialist in the library has traced his family tree back to the time of the Revolutionary War.

_____ 13. Walter a librarian by profession studies genealogies as a hobby.

_____ 14. Actually Walter prefers to be known as a media specialist rather than as a librarian.

_____ 15. "The word 'librarian'" Walter says "sounds a little stuffy and old-fashioned."

_____ 16. I don't believe he is correct in that opinion do you?

_____ 17. I mailed my order to 35 East 54th Street New York NY 10022.

_____ 18. How is it possible that the man can continue his lecture with half the people in the audience sound asleep?

_____ 19. The paddlers exhausted from fighting the rapids finally found a calm spot and a small, sandy beach where they could rest.

_____ 20. "I don't know" said Mary plaintively "how I can possibly finish this long paper by tomorrow morning."

NAME _____   SCORE _____

Directions: Insert commas where they are needed. Then, in the space at the left, write the number of commas you used in each sentence.

_____   1. Walking slowly down the street through the center of town which has been restored so that it looks as it did 100 years ago Raul stopped in front of a store window went into the store and bought a book about the history of the town.

_____   2. Yesterday when I went downtown I visited Jim Marshal a local contractor who grew up in this area and he said "The town especially the restored part of downtown is experiencing a wonderful boom in business which of course helps everyone living in the area."

_____   3. The older lovingly restored brick buildings lining Main Street are beautiful examples of the work that Marshal and others have done and they stand as monuments to the efforts of the city's leaders as fine a group of citizens as anyone could hope to meet.

_____   4. "Jim" I said "I know you are proud of that restoration project" and he told me that the project which took almost 3 years is the best thing he's ever done in his work as a contractor and then showed me plans for additional work on another major street near the same area.

_____   5. Everyone visiting the downtown area says "The downtown area has become a beautiful restful place the kind of place where people can enjoy walking and more importantly can enjoy shopping without feeling rushed or pressured by noise and traffic."

_____   6. After all the work has been completed the town's citizens will have a downtown area they can be proud of and they will have preserved many of the town's historical buildings which might have been destroyed the citizens having not intervened.

_____   7. When I left Jim and his staff of architects and engineers all highly trained people went back to their desks and their computers and they began to plan additional ways to save older sections of the town by restoring buildings that had been left to deteriorate.

_____   8. Whenever you see an older building especially one that has been carefully restored stop for a moment to look at it closely because that warm old brick building might have been replaced by a stark cold concrete and glass structure.

_____   9. Once many years ago my grandfather owned an old barn that had beautiful oak siding which had weathered to a soft creamy gray color so with the barn no longer needed he took down the siding and used it to cover his house which up to that time had been covered in ugly asphalt shingles.

_____   10. Re-using a natural substance such as wood to replace a manufactured product I'm sure you'll agree will almost always improve the appearance of any building and such a replacement should be done whenever it is possible.

_____ 11. The three people came to work late they didn't do anything constructive and they left early so the manager who is usually a very patient person discharged them and she gave them their last pay as they walked out the door of the shop.

_____ 12. At 10:00 A.M. on Monday morning last week we went to our first accounting class for this semester and there we met our instructor Arnold Mill Ph.D. a man who has had many years of experience in the practice of accounting.

_____ 13. "Try these cookies" said my sister; "I made them from Grandma's old recipe which has been handed down for generations in our family and people have always liked them so much that they called them 'Grandma's Famous Cookies.'"

_____ 14. The three little boys ran through the old man's yard frightened his dog and knocked over two of his rose bushes so the old man his feelings hurt by their actions waited for them to come back and then he squirted them with his hose.

_____ 15. Although my address is 1462 Robinson Drive Kansas City KS 61329 I am having my mail forwarded to my father's house in Bend Oregon because I am as everyone knows currently traveling in Spain and I will not be home for another 2 months.

_____ 16. Yesterday in our environmental science class Eric Lawson a noted meteorologist spoke about global warming which is a subject that causes great debate among scientists and politicians.

_____ 17. My sister and I when we were out shopping yesterday went to a garden supply store and we brought home two dogwood trees several bags of potting soil and a new shovel which we will use to dig the holes for the trees.

_____ 18. "With everything working out as I plan" said Andy "my GPA for this term should be much higher than it has been in the past for I have attended every class taken careful notes studied every day and reviewed thoroughly before each test."

_____ 19. After we had used the new software for a few days we realized that it needed to be changed to suit our complicated highly technical financial requirements so we called in Arthur Patton an outside computer consultant so that he could change the code.

_____ 20. Everyone in this class and that means every single person needs to purchase the new edition of our textbook not the earlier edition because the earlier edition which is still on the shelves has page numbers quite different from the page numbers found in the new edition.

NAME _____   SCORE _____

Directions: The following sentences contain 40 numbered spots, some with punctuation and some without. In the correspondingly numbered spots at the left, write **C** if the punctuation is correct or **W** if the punctuation is incorrect. **Review:** In the sentences below, underline the appositives and put brackets around the relative clauses.

1. _____   (1) Will had a successful game today; he threw out two runners caught a foul ball,
                  ¹   ²

2. _____   and hit a double.

3. _____   (2) Jim Robinson who has had little experience with carpentry work, came
                  ³

4. _____   out to the job and helped us today.
                  ⁴

5. _____   (3) Jim Robinson obviously a man without much experience in carpentry, came to
                  ⁵

6. _____   the job site today and he helped us by cleaning up the site.
                  ⁶

7. _____   (4) The job site having been completely cleaned we all left for home thanking Jim
                  ⁷   ⁸

8. _____   for all his help during the day.

9. _____   (5) All of us workers are indebted to Jim, for quite clearly, he made a major
                  ⁹   ¹⁰

10. _____   contribution to our work.

11. _____ (6) As the two men drove down the road they saw two stately, beautiful pheasants
                  ¹¹   ¹²

12. _____   walking along the side of the road.

13. _____ (7) While we were walking along the road came a group of motorcycle riders
                  ¹³   ¹⁴

14. _____   probably about 20 of them, and they all waved to us as they passed by.

15. _____ (8) "Robbie please take these checks to the bank and deposit them in the company
                  ¹⁵

16. _____   account," said Ms. Adams to her executive assistant.
                  ¹⁶

17. _____ (9) The weather forecasters, whom we have come to trust without question missed
                  ¹⁷

18. _____   their prediction badly when they said that it would not rain today.
                  ¹⁸

19. _____ (10) "I wonder why the forecasters predicted clear skies today; when I am huddled
                                                                    19

20. _____   here under this awning while the rain comes pelting down" said Marta.
                                                                    20

21. _____ (11) With the rain pelting down as she huddled under an awning, Marta
                                        21   22

22. _____   complained good-naturedly about the quality of weather forecasting.

23. _____ (12) Yesterday I watched Joe Simmons my new neighbor, as he washed his car,
                              23   24

24. _____   mowed the grass, and trimmed the hedges on two sides of his yard.

25. _____ (13) "Wow, Joe," I called out to him, "you've already done a long, tough day's work,
                              25   26

26. _____   and it's only a little after noon."

27. _____ (14) That tedious complicated repair job which Mark had postponed until the last
                              27   28

28. _____   minute, left him tired and frustrated.

29. _____ (15) When Joanie heard the good news she went immediately to her computer;
                                        29   30

30. _____   there she e-mailed all her friends about the job offer she had just received.

31. _____ (16) At about ten twenty people pulled their cars into the parking lot, then they
                              31   32

32. _____   walked slowly into the restaurant.

33. _____ (17) Soon, with all the work on that renovation completed the crew will move on to
                                                              33

34. _____   another job, which is already one week behind schedule.
                              34

35. _____ (18) The engineers had run several tests on the engine, and made some minor
                                                              35

36. _____   adjustments, then they pronounced the whole project completed.
                              36

37. _____ (19) Kathleen Wilson, standing near the back of the room, searched in vain for a
                              37

38. _____   place to sit before the movie began.
                              38

39. _____ (20) Having been ordered three weeks ago the new computers are long overdue,
                                        39   40

40. _____   and our work has begun to slow down disastrously.

Brief Writing Assignment: Write a paragraph of seven sentences discussing two academic goals you have set for yourself for next year. Employ one nonrestrictive clause, one quotation, and one parenthetical element. Punctuate all the sentences correctly.

This lesson covers a number of tricky punctuation marks.

APOSTROPHE

The apostrophe (') has three uses:

1. To form the possessive of nouns and indefinite pronouns
2. To mark the omitted material in contractions
3. To form certain plurals, such as those of letters and abbreviations

Forming Possessives

Any noun, whether singular or plural, that does not end in *s* shows ownership by adding an apostrophe and *s*:

> a boy's hat [the hat belongs to the boy], the horse's tail, Carol's car, men's shoes, children's toys

Plural nouns that end in *s* form possessives by adding an apostrophe after the *s*:

> boys' hats, horses' tails, the Smiths' home, ladies' dresses

Singular nouns ending in *s* or *z* form the possessive by adding *'s*.

> the countess's castle, Frances's reply, Mr. Gomez's report

On rare occasions, if the pronunciation of the word with the additional *s*-sound would be awkward, it is permissible to form the possessive with an apostrophe alone.

> for goodness' sake

For the sake of uniformity, the exercises on possessives will ask that you use the *'s* after singular nouns ending in *s*.

The indefinite pronouns, but not the personal pronouns, form the possessive with the aid of the apostrophe:

> somebody's sweater, anyone's opinion, anybody's game [But note the possessive forms of pronouns: his, hers, its, theirs, ours, yours, whose.]

Compound words and word groups form the possessive by adding an apostrophe and *s* to the last word of the group:

> My sister-in-law's last visit was in December.
> Did you get anyone else's opinion of your paper?

Note that establishing ownership of two or more items requires careful attention. For individual ownership, add an apostrophe and *s* at the end of both owners.

Oliver Stone's and Alfred Hitchcock's movies [indicating that each made certain movies]

For joint ownership of two or more items, add an apostrophe and *s* at the end of the second owner's name:

Rogers and Hammerstein's musicals [indicating that they wrote musicals as joint projects]

Omitted Material

The apostrophe is used to stand for the omitted material in contractions:

doesn't [does not], won't [will not], she's [she is, she has], o'clock [of the clock], rock 'n' roll [rock and roll]

You must learn to distinguish carefully between the following pairs of contractions and possessives:

Contraction	Possessive
it's [it is, it has]	its
there's [there is, there has]	theirs
they're [they are]	their
who's [who is, who has]	whose
you're [you are]	your

Unusual Plurals

Use an apostrophe to form the plural of letters and words that are treated as words.

the three *R*'s; mostly *A*'s and *B*'s; too many *and*'s; no *if*'s, *and*'s, or *but*'s about it

Although some authorities no longer require the formation of the plural of numbers and symbols with an apostrophe, there are times when the lack of an apostrophe creates confusion. Thus, it seems logical to retain the apostrophe for the sake of clarity.

Btu's, CPA's, 1980's, scores in the 80's and 90's

Many writers need to be reminded regularly of an important related fact: An apostrophe is never used in forming the plural of either a common or a proper noun.

There are two Kathys in the class. Two grandmas attended.

COLON

The colon (:) is a formal mark announcing an explanation, an appositive, a list, or a quotation to follow.

"My friends: Tonight I want to discuss. . . ."
Last year Hank took up a new hobby: drag racing.

You should bring to class the following items: index cards, permanent markers, and notebook paper.

The sign reads: "Bridge ices in winter."

The colon is used in formal papers to begin a quotation of four lines or more. The text of the quotation is indented one inch from the left and runs to the right margin. It is not set off by quotation marks.

In cases where the colon sets off a quotation, the identifying tag should appear in the independent clause.

Colons are also used as a mark of separation in certain special constructions:

Hours, minutes, and seconds
    1:14:10 P.M.

Biblical chapters and verses
    I Kings 2:1

Titles and subtitles
    Conversations: Famous Women Speak Out

The colon is also used after the salutation in a business letter and after the words *To, From,* and *Subject* in the heading of a memorandum.

    MEMORANDUM
    To:
    From:
    Subject:

Note that after a colon it is permissible to have an initial capital letter if the text following the colon is a complete sentence. Do not use a colon to separate a verb from its complement or a preposition from its object.

Faulty: All hikers must bring: a flashlight, a small ax, and a waterproof tarpaulin.

Faulty: The things a hiker must bring are: a flashlight, a small ax, and a waterproof tarpaulin.

Faulty: The hiker's equipment should consist of: a flashlight, a small ax, and a waterproof tarpaulin.

DASH

The dash (—) is used to show an abrupt change in thought in the sentence. It must be used sparingly and never as a substitute for other marks.

Superior students—notice that I said *superior*—will not have to take the test.

New surroundings, new friends, a challenging new job—all these helped Eugene overcome his grief.

HYPHEN

The hyphen (-) is used to divide a word at the end of a line and to join words to form various types of compounds. Divide a word between syllables only. With words having a prefix or a suffix, divide the word after the prefix and before the suffix. Avoid dividing a word so that a single letter ends or begins a line. (Consult your dictionary for problems of syllabic division.)

> mathe-matics *not* mathem-atics
> inter-collegiate *not* intercol-legiate
> govern-ess *not* gov-erness
> enough *not* e-nough
> many *not* man-y

It is important to note that the use of word processing programs by newspaper and magazine publishers has created a situation where words seem to be divided at random wherever the end of the line occurs. In academic writing, however, it is a good idea to continue the practice of dividing words by the rules stated here.

Use hyphens to join the parts of compound modifiers preceding nouns.

> Observe his well-kept lawn. His lawn is well kept.
> We deplore your devil-may-care attitude.

This use of a hyphen sometimes determines an exact meaning:

> a roll of 20-dollar bills; a roll of 20 dollar bills
> all-American boys; all American boys

Use hyphens with compound numbers from twenty-one to ninety-nine and with fractions:

> Twenty-two people claimed the one-third share of the reward money but received only one-eighth.

Use hyphens, particularly with prefixes and suffixes, to avoid awkward combinations of letters or to distinguish between two meanings of a word:

> anti-intellectual
> pre-Aztec
> her doll-like face
> re-cover a couch [not recover the money]

PARENTHESES

Parentheses are very similar to dashes in that they allow the insertion of an additional thought or explanation in a sentence. Dashes tend to emphasize an interruption; parentheses place less important information in a sentence. Nevertheless, parentheses tend to interrupt the flow of a sentence and should (like dashes) be used sparingly.

> I showed Robert my favorite poem (Robert Frost's *Two Tramps in Mud Time*), but he said that he does not like any poetry.
> His dislike for poetry goes back to the fifth grade (his teacher asked him to read a difficult poem aloud) when he had an embarrassing experience in class.
> His dislike for poetry goes back to the fifth grade when he had an embarrassing experience in class. (His teacher asked him to read a difficult poem aloud.)

Note the differences in capitalization and punctuation in the second and third example sentences:

When a complete sentence in parentheses occurs inside a sentence, do not use capitals or a period. When the complete sentence in parentheses stands outside the sentence, use capitals and a period.

QUOTATION MARKS

Quotation marks should be used to enclose quoted material and words you may use in some special way. Use double quotation marks (" ") to enclose the exact words of a quoted speech. Quotation marks always come in pairs. The marks show the beginning and the end of a speech, whether it is part of a sentence, one sentence, or several sentences. If a speech is interrupted by material showing who said it, quotation marks set off the quoted material from the explanatory material. Use quotation marks where the directly quoted material begins and where it ends or is interrupted. Indirect quotations are *not* set off by quotation marks:

"I admit," said Ralph, "that I was mistaken."
[Note that the explanatory material is set off from the direct quotation.]
Peg answered, "I didn't attend. I wasn't in town." [More than one sentence.]
Peg answered that she hadn't attended because she hadn't been in town.
[This is an indirect quotation. Words not directly quoted should not be enclosed in quotation marks.]

Use double quotation marks to set off the subdivisions of books, names of songs, and titles of units of less than book length, such as short stories, short poems, essays, and articles:

The second chapter of *Moby Dick* is entitled "The Carpet-Bag."
Eva Peron sings "Don't Cry for Me, Argentina" in the musical *Evita*.
Our anthology includes "Threes," a poem from Sandburg's *Smoke and Steel*.
The first article I read for my research paper was William Calvin's "The Great Climate Flip-flop" in the *Atlantic Monthly*.

Titles of books, magazines, long poems, newspapers, motion pictures, and radio and television series are not set in double quotation marks. In printed material, these items are set in italic type (*type like this*). Other special uses of italics are for foreign words and phrases and for names of ships, planes, and spacecraft. In handwritten or word-processed papers, underlining (underline like this) is the equivalent of italics in printed material.

Double quotation marks are also used to set off slang words used in serious writing. Sometimes double quotation marks are used to set off words when they are referred to as words:

The witness had only recently been released from the "slammer."
Words like "seize" and "siege" are often misspelled.

Usage is divided on these applications of quotation marks. The two words in the second example would almost certainly appear in italics in printed material. Student writers of handwritten material should either underline such words or set them off by quotation marks, the first method being the more common practice.

Double Quotation Marks with Other Punctuation

Follow this usage in the placing of quotation marks in relation to other marks:

1. Commas and periods always go inside quotation marks.
2. Semicolons and colons always go outside quotation marks.
3. Question marks and exclamation points go inside if they belong to the quoted part, outside if they do not.

> "Come in," said my uncle, "and take off your coats." [comma and period]
>
> Mr. Lowe said, "I heartily endorse this candidate"; unfortunately most of the audience thought he said *hardly* instead of *heartily*. [semicolon outside]
>
> "Heavens!" he exclaimed. "Is this the best you can do?" [exclamation point and question mark]
>
> Mother asked, "Where were you last night?" [no double punctuation]
>
> Did she say, "I came home early"? [question mark belongs to the whole sentence, not to the quoted part]
>
> Did Mother ask, "Where were you last night?" [note that there is only one question mark after a double question like this]

Single Quotation Marks

Use single quotation marks to enclose a speech within a speech:

> "I wonder what he meant," said Betty, "when he said, 'There are wheels within wheels.'"

You may not write many sentences like this one, but just the same, you should note that when you have quotes within quotes, the period comes inside both the single and double quotation marks.

English Fundamentals Online

After you have completed the Practice Sheets and Exercises in this lesson, you can find additional help and drill work at **MyWritingLab.com**, in the sections on Apostrophes; Quotation Marks; Semicolons, Colons, Dashes, and Parentheses.

NAME _____   SCORE _____

Directions: In the space at the left of each sentence, write **C** if the punctuation in the sentence is correct and **W** if it is incorrect. Within the incorrect sentences, correct the faulty punctuation by adding, removing, or changing marks and adding, where needed, an additional **s** after an apostrophe. **Review:** In the sentences on this page, underline any infinitive phrases.

_____C_____ 1. They'll need another's opinion on that presentation; its content and data aren't familiar to most of us.

_____ 2. "Did she say, 'Your works not finished yet'? asked Diane.

_____ 3. We're not sure–no ones ever really sure–how fast that weather system will move once its crossed the Mississippi River.

_____ 4. Mark responded that she's given contradictory statements about that task, so hes not sure which parts are your's and which parts are his.

_____ 5. The list of guests at the conference is impressive; the companys president, two past CFOs, and two well-known politicians.

_____ 6. Its going to be difficult to find Arlenes replacement; her skills with computers–not to mention her easygoing personality–will be hard to duplicate.

_____ 7. "My grades were all As and Bs last term, said Mary, "so Ill need to work very hard to match that record."

_____ 8. The boss said, Tomorrows our day to finish that report; there'll be no *ifs, ands,* or *buts* about it.

_____ 9. That huge heater blasts out too many Btu's for this room, so its always too warm for comfort in here.

_____ 10. That's my cousins brother-in-laws sister, but its impossible to tell if shes really related to me.

_____ 11. Our jackets look the same, but, since mine's at home, thats your's on the table.

_____ 12. "Two things hurt my performance on that test, failing to study beforehand and working too slowly on the first twenty five questions, said Mike.

_____ 13. I think she said, 'Meet me at the restaurant at 8:30 tonight,' said Allen, "but Im not really sure which restaurant shed selected."

_____ 14. At five oclock you'll need to check the length of the lines' outside; perhaps well need to open a second ticket-window.

_____ 15. If its true that the paper is due tomorrow, I've less than twenty-four hours time to do my research and write the papers final draft.

Directions: Sentences 1–5 are indirect quotations. In the space provided, rewrite each sentence as a direct quotation. Sentences 6–10 are direct quotations. Rewrite each as an indirect quotation. In certain cases, you will need to alter some verb forms, some pronouns, and the punctuation.

1. Harry said that he would arrive about five o'clock tomorrow afternoon, unless he gets caught up in rush-hour traffic.

   _____

2. The office manager claims that he will need to hire three additional people if we take on that new client.

   _____

3. My brother said to me that he would need to gain about 15 pounds of hard muscle before football practice starts in August.

   _____

4. Mrs. Carlson asked us if we would be willing to help her move some furniture on Saturday morning.

   _____

5. Did the dispatcher say that all the trains are running behind schedule today?

   _____

6. The officer told us, "It will be almost an hour before that tree can be removed from the road."

   _____

7. The technician tells me, "Your computer will need an increase in its RAM before it can handle that new program."

   _____

8. The coach told me, "Your fielding is excellent, but you need to improve your ability to hit with men on base."

   _____

9. The tourists asked, "Can you tell us where that famous waterfall is located?"

   _____

10. "Can you tell me when the repairs on my car will be completed?" Sam asked the mechanic.

    _____

NAME _____   SCORE _____

Directions: The following exercise is a formal business letter addressed to an individual whose name you know. No punctuation (except end marks) has been inserted. Insert punctuation marks where they are needed. Note that, contrary to formal practice, the letter contains a few contractions so that you may practice recognizing and punctuating them correctly.

John Smith
9555 Peterson Rd
Seattle WA 90132
555-678-4100

Ms Linda Jackson
Jackson Moving and Storage Inc
4122 Constable Rd
Van Buren WA 90044

Dear Ms Jackson

Your advertisement in the magazine *Fine Places to Live* November 2010 attracted my attention because it contained the following lines

We value your business.

We know you value your possessions.

We at Jackson Moving value your possessions as much as you do.

We will move the contents of your home and deliver them on time in perfect condition at the price quoted by our representative.

We guarantee your satisfaction with our work.

In the past five years time I have moved three times two of those coast to coast. On each move the moving companies performance was far less than satisfactory. Those companies lost or damaged 12 count them 12 valuable antiques or paintings. In addition to those losses no company stayed with it's estimated price in fact the estimates were not even close to the final price. Needless to say my opinion of the moving industry is not very high.

However your ads statements give me hope yes Im still an optimist that this time the results will be better and Ive found a company that will deliver what its promised. Next month Im moving to Atlanta and Ill need a moving company. If youre able to meet the standard I see in the lines quoted above please have a representative call me at the number listed above.

Yours truly

John Smith

Directions: The following brief memorandum contains no punctuation (except end marks). Add punctuation marks where they are needed. Note that again some contractions are employed that might not be used in a strictly formal memorandum.

<u>MEMORANDUM</u>
To Jim Anderson Estimator
From Linda Jackson President
Subject Potential Customer

John Smiths letter attached here presents a challenge to our company. Smiths past experience with moving companies work has left a bad taste in his mouth. Hes dissatisfied with our competitors work as he experienced it in previous moves. Please call him as soon as possible to meet him and give him a price for moving his household goods to Atlanta. Youll need to be especially careful to identify Smiths antiques and paintings for special treatment. Apparently loss or damage to these valuable items was a particular sore spot for him in his past experiences. Hell appreciate Im sure your careful attention but you always pay careful attention to a customers needs so I neednt worry about satisfying him.

Thanks for giving this matter your most professional attention.

Brief Writing Assignment: Assume the identity of Jim Anderson from the previous memorandum. Write a response of six sentences in the form used above in which you include a colon followed by a quote, a dash to show an abrupt change of thought, and a quotation within a quotation in which you use both single and double quotation marks.

This lesson discusses end marks and summarizes all the punctuation rules presented in this book.

PERIOD

The **period** is used after a complete declarative sentence and after ordinary abbreviations. Its use as end punctuation after sentences needs no examples. Its use after abbreviations is a little more complicated.

Personal Titles

A period is used in the following abbreviations: *Mr.*, *Mrs.*, *Ms.*, *Messrs.*, *Mmes.*, and *Dr.* These abbreviations appear before the name. Periods are also used for *Jr.*, *Sr.*, *Esq.*, *D.D.*, *Ph.D.*, and so forth, which are used after names. Miss does not require a period. *Ms.*, used instead of *Miss* or *Mrs.* when marital status is not indicated, is usually considered an abbreviation and uses a period, although some dictionaries have entries for it either with or without a period.

Latin-Based Terms

The following initials and abbreviations, used only in documentation pages and tabulations but not in ordinary writing, require periods: *e.g.* (for example), *etc.* (and so forth), *i.e.* (that is), *p.*, *pp.* (page, pages), and *vol.* (volume). A.D., B.C., B.C.E., C.E., A.M., and P.M. (usually set in small caps in printed material) are used only with figures and where necessary for clarity. Note: A.D. and C.E. should precede the year (A.D. 37); B.C. and B.C.E., however, should follow the year (31 B.C.).

For personal titles and Latin-based terms, usage seems to be mixed. Dictionaries often list the terms without punctuation: MD, PhD, LLD, AD, and others, but rules in grammar texts and in punctuation sections of dictionaries continue to list the titles with punctuation. Until the issue resolves itself, it is probably best to stay with the older forms, i.e., to use periods.

Addresses

The following abbreviations require periods and are acceptable in addresses but should be spelled out in ordinary writing: *St.* (Street), *Ave.* (Avenue), *Blvd.* (Boulevard), *Dr.* (Drive), *Rd.* (Road), *Co.* (Company), and *Inc.* (Incorporated). The two-letter capitalized symbols authorized by the U.S. Postal Service (*MA*, *MN*, *TX*, *WV*) do not require periods.

Poor:	Last Mon. P.M. I visited my two older bros., who live in N.Y. Chas. works for a mfg. co. there. Thos. attends NYU, preparing himself for a gov't. job. He's coming home for Xmas.
Right:	Last Monday afternoon I visited my two older brothers, who live in New York. Charles works for a manufacturing company there. Thomas attends New York University, preparing himself for a government job. He's coming home for Christmas.

Acronyms and Measurements

In modern usage, the "alphabet" name forms, or acronyms, of various governmental or intergovernmental agencies, social or professional organizations, and units of measurement used in scientific contexts are usually not followed by periods: *ACLU, CARE, CBS, CIA, NAACP, NCAA, NATO, PTA, SEC, UNESCO, Btu* (British thermal unit), *mpg, mph, rpm.* New acronyms and abbreviated forms spring into existence with regularity. The following examples are some that have gained common acceptance fairly recently: *AIDS* (acquired immune deficiency syndrome), *CAT scan* (computerized axial tomography), *CD* (certificate of deposit), *CEO* (chief executive officer), *COLA* (cost-of-living adjustment), *CPR* (cardiopulmonary resuscitation), *DWI* (driving while intoxicated), *IRA* (individual retirement account), *MIA* (missing in action), *MRI* (magnetic resonance imaging), *OPEC* (Organization of Petroleum Exporting Countries), *PC* (personal computer), *STOL* (short takeoff and landing), *DVD* (digital video disc). Refer to your dictionary when in doubt about the meaning of an abbreviated form or the possibility of using periods. Be prepared to find apparent inconsistencies and divided usage.

QUESTION MARK

The **question mark** is used after a *direct question*, which is an utterance that calls for an answer. (See Lesson 6.) A question mark is not used after an *indirect question*, which is a statement giving the substance of a question but not the words that would be used in a direct question.

Direct:	Who goes there? Is that you? When do we eat? How much do I owe you? "Who goes there?" he demanded. [in dialogue]
Indirect:	She asked me how old I was. I wondered why she would ask such a question. [Note that these are statements, not direct questions.]

Refer to page 206 to review the use of question marks with quotation marks.

EXCLAMATION POINT

The **exclamation point** is used sparingly in modern writing and should be reserved for statements of strong feeling. Mild exclamations, such as *oh, goodness, well, yes,* and *no,* are followed by commas, not exclamation points. Be sure to place the exclamation mark after the exclamation itself.

"Help! I'm slipping!" he shouted. [Note the period after *shouted*.]

"Stop that!" she screamed. [Do not put the exclamation point after *screamed*.]

"Well, it was exciting, wasn't it?" "Oh, I had a pleasant time."

SUMMARY OF PUNCTUATION RULES

This summary covers the indispensable punctuation rules for anything you write. Colons, commas, periods, and even question marks and exclamation points do have other uses for special occasions or effects, but these occasional applications rarely cause problems for most writers.

Commas to Separate: Five Rules

1. Compound sentences
2. Items in a series
3. Coordinate adjectives
4. Introductory modifiers
5. Words that may be misread together

Colon: Two Rules

1. Use a colon to announce a list, an explanation, or a long quotation.
   a. If the text following a colon is a complete sentence, use an initial capital letter.
   b. Do not use a colon to separate a verb from its complement or a preposition from its object.
2. Use a colon to separate hours, minutes, and seconds; biblical chapters and verses; titles and subtitles.

Apostrophe: Two Rules

1. With possessives
2. With contractions

Period: Two Rules

1. After declarative sentences
2. After most abbreviations

Commas to Enclose: Eight Rules

1. Nonrestrictive clauses and phrases
2. Appositives
3. Absolute phrases
4. Parenthetical expressions
5. Words in direct address
6. The speaker in dialog
7. Negative insertions
8. Dates, addresses, degrees, and titles

Semicolon: Two Rules

1. In compound sentences without a conjunction joining the independent clauses
2. To separate items in a series when commas occur within items

Quotation Marks: Three Rules

1. Enclose direct quotations
2. Set off titles
3. Set off words used in some special way

Question Mark: One Rule

1. After direct questions

English Fundamentals Online

After you have completed the Practice Sheets and Exercises in this lesson, you can find additional help and drill work at **MyWritingLab.com**, in the section on End Marks.

NAME _____   SCORE _____

Directions: In the space at the left, write **C** if the sentence is correct, **W** if it is incorrect. Within the incorrect sentences, correct the faulty punctuation.

_____ 1. Once inside the police searched the house for signs of a robbery once they finished the house was no longer officially a crime scene.

_____ 2. "Have you ever seen a longer home run!" asked Jaime? "That was the longest I've ever seen."

_____ 3. With our minds filled with Jims complex directions we soon became confused, and found ourselves on the wrong end of Main Street.

_____ 4. In the statistics of football YAC stands for "yards after catch; but in the animal world a yak is a Tibetan ox.

_____ 5. "Do you know anyone who understands how this G.P.S. works,' asked Allison, "I keep getting lost when I try to use it."

_____ 6. The instructions clearly say we should bring only the following items when we come to take the test: two #2 pencils and one sheet of scratch paper.

_____ 7. "Only one question remains in my mind: how you got so many answers correct when you say you were only guessing," said Max.

_____ 8. "I know we need to turn onto Maple Street which should be coming up soon– whoops, we just passed it. said Ray"

_____ 9. It is strange that we use an apostrophe to show possession with nouns; but there is no apostrophe in the possessives his and its.

_____ 10. "Someone needs to tell me where we are going to dinner?" said Brett, 'If its expensive, I think Ill stay home.'

_____ 11. "Does anyone know where we are going to dinner?" asked Brett. "If it's expensive, I think I'll stay home."

_____ 12. AL is the postal abbreviation for the state of Alabama; and the letters Al are the chemical symbol for the element aluminum.

_____ 13. Mrs Johnson has a very well kept garden it is beautiful, and produces bumper crops of tomatoes green beans and squash.

_____ 14. Somehow the word gift has become a verb, as in the expression, I gifted her my favorite song, but she deleted it almost immediately.

_____ 15. In our ordinary correspondence and writing, we spell out the word "Avenue," but we abbreviate it "Ave." when we use it in an address.

Directions: The following sentences contain errors in punctuation. Add, delete, or change punctuation wherever an error occurs.

1. Besides Crawford who is certainly qualified to do the job we cant find anyone who possesses both the skill and intelligence needed to finish that project.

2. Theres no reason is there why we couldn't leave my car here and take your's to the out of town convention, so that we can save some money on gas.

3. For that white water rafting trip; Joan invited Barbara whos very experienced Rosa who is an excellent swimmer and a strong paddler, and Kelli who unfortunately has little experience on any rivers, but has a great sense of adventure.

4. For the meeting in the branch office we were expected to bring: a laptop computer, several highlight pens and a loose leaf notebook for inserting handouts from the speakers.

5. A huge muscular dog barking and growling threateningly confronted the two would be burglars as they crept down the alleyway; so they turned and ran away as quickly as they could.

6. Drs Keller and Jameson noted scholars in their own right led the panel discussion, after the experts presentations on the effects of the use of mixed fuel vehicles on the price of corn and soybeans.

7. The little kids were impressed didnt you think by the football players appearance on the program even if they didnt wear their uniforms?

8. I sent you a note regarding your attendance at the upcoming meeting on the changes were considering in the by laws of the organization– ah, I can tell, by the look on your face that youve already read it and probably don't agree with some of the changes, that have been proposed.

9. When do you anticipate or can't you even guess that the part ordered for the air-conditioning system will arrive and your crew can come out and make the much needed repairs so that our students can once again sit comfortably in their classroom's.

10. Its been some time now, since the boys called from the intersection and told us that theyd had some car trouble, you don't suppose do you that something else has gone wrong and theyre delayed even longer.

NAME _____　　SCORE _____

Directions: The following sentences contain 40 numbered spots between words. The punctuation for each numbered spot is either incorrect or missing. Correct the punctuation by supplying a comma, a semicolon, a question mark, or a period in the space above the number. If no punctuation is needed, write **N** in the spot above the number. **Review:** In this exercise underline the noun clauses.

1. Because the weather report calls for snow and ice I think we should
   ₁

   put blankets, a thermos of hot coffee, and tire chains in the car, don't you.
   ₂

2. With the weather report calling for snow and ice we should be prepared
   ₃　　　　　　　　　　　　　　　　₄

   and put our foul-weather equipment in the car.

3. The men always prepared for emergency conditions, put some special
   ₅

   equipment in the trunk of the car before they left on their trip.
   ₆

4. Dark threatening clouds soon covered the sky and a heavy snow had
   ₇　　　　　　　　　　　　　　　　₈

   begun to fall long before the men stopped for lunch.

5. Jim Thompson who had lived for several years in Alaska, said "I think at lunch
   ₉　　　　　　　　　　　　　　　　　　　　　₁₀

   we should put the chains on the tires to keep the car from sliding on the ice."

6. The men took the advice of Jim Thompson a longtime resident of
   ₁₁

   Alaska and traveled safely to their destination.
   ₁₂

7. The next day the men attended a long boring series of meetings and conferences
   ₁₃　　　　　　　　　　　　　　　　　　　　　　　　　　　₁₄

   they actually wished that the bad weather had forced them to stay home.

8. Can you tell me please, where the next conference will be held and
   ₁₅　　　　　　　　　　　　　　　　　　₁₆

   whether I will be expected to attend?

9. I plan if the next conference doesn't look more interesting than the last to
   ₁₇　　　　　　　　　　　　　　　　　　　　　　　　　　₁₈

   take a few days of vacation and miss all the excitement.

10. I wish that people who plan workshops and conferences would apply
    19
    some creativity and imagination to their work and make presentations that
    20
    are a little bit out of the ordinary.

11. "Stop and wait here," said the police officer, "there is a fallen tree blocking
    21
    the road and it will take the crew about an hour to clear the way."
    22

12. After we had stopped the officer came over to the car to chat with us for
    23
    a few minutes and said "The crews do their best, but in this weather they
    24
    can't keep up with their work."

13. "I think" said Roger, "that there is a direct correlation between our need
    25
    to hurry and the number of obstacles that appear in our way."
    26

14. "Well" said Morgan, "there's nothing we can do to speed up that crew so
    27   28
    we might as well relax and enjoy ourselves."

15. Because it was not anyone's fault that the tree fell and blocked the road the
    29
    people in the car simply sat and waited while listening to music on the
    30
    CD player.

16. Listening to music on the CD player was a pleasant way to pass the time,
    and before they grew bored the police officer blew his whistle and waved
    31   32
    them on down the road.

17. In rural areas during the winter it is not uncommon for ice storms and high
    33   34
    winds to knock trees down and block the roads.

18. In summer time is available for the crews to do some tree-trimming and
    35
    brush-clearing but the crews never have enough time to take care of all
    36
    the potential problems.

19. In winter the crews are on call 24 hours a day, and they often work very
    37
    long hours after a severe storm has passed through the area.
    38

20. We are, in fact quite fortunate that there are men and women willing to
    39   40
    dedicate themselves to such difficult work.

The following passage contains no internal punctuation and may lack quotation marks where they are needed. Insert punctuation marks where they are needed and be prepared to cite the rule for the use of any mark you insert.

Thomas A. Edison

Thomas Edison was one of the most successful prolific inventors in United States history. Edison born in Milan Ohio in 1847 was slow to learn to talk but once he learned he asked questions constantly about the way things worked. A very curious child his constant barrage of questions caused his first grade teacher to lose patience with him and therefore his mother withdrew him from school and taught him at home. Edison was also partially deaf, probably because of a childhood attack of scarlet fever. When the railroad came to Ohio it by passed Milan and the town went into a depression. Therefore the family moved to Port Huron Michigan. It was there that Edison discovered his talent for business. He wrote a newspaper about local events and sold it on the train that ran from Port Huron to Detroit. He found his first career as the result of a heroic deed. A young boy Jimmie MacKenzie fell in front of a run-away train and Edison leaped onto the track and saved him. Jimmies grateful father J U MacKenzie taught Edison to operate a telegraph machine. The telegraph was a communication device that sent messages through the use of Morse Code a system that spelled out words by using dots and dashes. He worked for years for Western Union an early telegraph company. Edison worked for Western Union in Canada and in Lexington Kentucky. There he worked the night shift so he would have ample time for reading and conducting various experiments. One story from this period says that Edison was fired from that job because he spilled sulphuric acid which leaked through the floor from the second story onto his boss s desk. His interest in the telegraph led him to invent and patent improvements to that device. Later his work took him to Menlo Park New Jersey. His first major invention was a primitive form of the phonograph probably the first device for recording and playing back sound. The general public thought this device worked by some kind of magic, and people began to call him The Wizard of Menlo Park. His long list of inventions also includes the Kinetoscope, an early version of a motion picture projector. He also developed an early version of the X ray machine and made a contribution to the development of the telephone. Early in his life as an inventor and businessman he opened the first research laboratory where he employed scientists and engineers and stocked every item that his work in the lab could possibly use. His major accomplishments however were in the field of electricity. Many people had attempted to construct a workable light bulb but they all gave up when the filament in the bulb burned for only a sort period of time. Edison a very persistent man is said to have tried 3000 kinds of light bulb before he discovered one filament that actually worked. Although this quotation is probably made up, he is quoted as saying We never failed we simply discovered 3000 ways not to make a light bulb. With the development of a commercially workable light bulb Edison was able to move on to the distribution of electricity through wiring systems that carried electric power to homes and businesses. He later founded the company called General Electric. These two inventions the light bulb and the distribution system totally remade business social and personal life. People no longer had to regulate their lives by the onset of daylight and darkness. Reading and working at night became possible. Night shifts in factories became a way of increasing production. Students who are behind in their work at college can do what is called pulling an all nighter thus they wait until the last minute to write papers and study for tests.

Brief Writing Assignment: In a paragraph of seven sentences, discuss the ways in which your life would be different if there were no electrical system to deliver power to your home. State your complete address, and employ three acronyms and one question mark.

Check Sheet

PUNCTUATION

There are 15 rules for the use of commas, two for semicolons, and more for using apostrophes, colons, dashes, hyphens, quotation marks, periods, and question marks, but for practical purposes you should focus on a more limited list of rules.

☐ Commas

1. Use commas to separate the independent clauses of a compound sentence when a coordinating conjunction is present. [Note that a semicolon can replace the comma and coordinating conjunction. This use is the only common use of the semicolon.]

   Maria opened her books, and she began to study.
   Maria opened her books; then she began to study.

2. Use commas to separate items in a series.

   We saw Thomas, Richard, and Harrison at the movie.

3. Use a comma between coordinate adjectives.

   We finally completed that long, difficult project.

4. Use a comma to set off introductory verbal phrases and subordinate clauses.

   Jumping into the chair, the cat curled up and went to sleep.

5. Use a comma to set off two or more prepositional phrases at the beginning of a sentence. Single phrases and, when the subject and verb are reversed, longer phrases at the beginning of a sentence are usually not set off with a comma.

6. Use a comma to prevent misreading. Misreading often occurs if an introductory element is not punctuated correctly, but some short prepositional phrases cause problems in certain contexts.

   Once inside, the dog and cat slept soundly before the fire.

   The comma is essential to maintain the sense of the sentence.

7. Most sentence interrupters, with the exception of restrictive appositives, restrictive participial phrases, and restrictive adjective clauses, are set off by commas.

   Note that with few exceptions, participial phrases are not set off with commas when they are the final element of the sentence.

   Thus we can establish a rule of thumb: Opening elements are set off with one comma, interrupting elements are set off by two, and final elements connect to the sentence without punctuation. Some have called this generalization the rule of one, two, and zero.

8. Set off both the speaker in dialogue and any person addressed in the text.

221

☐ **End Marks**

   ☐ End marks are fairly simple: Periods end sentences. Question marks end questions.

☐ **Exclamation Points**

   ☐ Exclamation points are used sparingly, and most often in dialogue. It is better to create emphasis through the use of word choice and emphatic sentence structure than through exclamation points.

☐ **Apostrophe**

   ☐ Use apostrophes to create possessives and to indicate contractions. Apostrophes are used for clarity's sake in creating unusual plurals. In other cases, do not use apostrophes to create plurals.

☐ **Dashes, Hyphens, and Quotation Marks**

   ☐ Dashes, hyphens, and quotation marks have special functions, and their use should be checked against the rules in this text.

Usage

Lessons, Practice Sheets, and Exercises

Lesson 21 — *Using Verbs Correctly: Principal Parts; Tense*

In Lesson 2 you learned that some verbs are regular and others are irregular. Regular verbs add an *ed* ending in the past tense (*earn, earned*), but irregular verbs change their form (*grow, grew*). Since verb forms change to indicate changes in tense and voice, it is necessary to pay close attention to the forms of all verbs. We will now review certain places where incorrect forms sometimes appear because of confusion in the use of the principal parts (the base, past tense, and past participle) of verbs. (See Supplement.)

VERB FORMS

To gain assurance in your use of verbs, you must remember how the past tense and the past participle are used. The **past tense** is always a single-word verb; it is never used with an auxiliary:

> I *ate* my lunch. [Not: I *have ate* my lunch.]

The **past participle**, when it is used as a verb, is *never* a single word; it is used with the auxiliary *have* (in the correct tense) to form the perfect tenses or the auxiliary *be* (in the correct tense) to form the passive voice:

> I *have done* the work. [Not: I *done* the work.]
> The work *was done*. [Not: The work *was did*.]

(The past participle is, of course, used as a single word when it is a modifier of a noun: the *broken* toy, the *worried* parents, some *known* criminals.)

Four groups of verbs often cause confusion. Each group contains verbs that have similar trouble spots. The basic solution for the problem in each group is to master the principal parts of the verbs. The principal parts are listed in this lesson in the customary order: base form, past tense, and past participle (P.P.).

Past Tense Versus Past Participle

Sometimes errors occur because the past tense of a verb is confused with the past participle of the verb.

223

	Verb	Past Tense	P.P.
Later they *became* [not *become*] more friendly.	become	became	become
They *began* [not *begun*] to laugh at us.	begin	began	begun
He had never *broken* [not *broke*] the law.	break	broke	broken
I should have *chosen* [not *chose*] a larger car.	choose	chose	chosen
Yesterday the child *came* [not *come*] home.	come	came	come
I *did* [not *done*] what she told me to do.	do	did	done
He *drank* [not *drunk*] some water.	drink	drank	drunk
I had *driven* [not *drove*] all day.	drive	drove	driven
The lamp had *fallen* [not *fell*] over.	fall	fell	fallen
The bird has *flown* [not *flew*] away.	fly	flew	flown
Small puddles have *frozen* [not *froze*] on the sidewalks.	freeze	froze	frozen
Dad has *given* [not *gave*] me a car.	give	gave	given
Theresa has *gone* [not *went*] to school.	go	went	gone
I've never *ridden* [not *rode*] a horse.	ride	rode	ridden
We ran out when the fire alarm *rang* [not *rung*].	ring	rang	rung
Lenny has *run* [not *ran*] in two marathons.	run	ran	run
I *saw* [not *seen*] your nephew yesterday.	see	saw	seen
It must have *sunk* [not *sank*] in deep water.	sink	sank	sunk
She should have *spoken* [not *spoke*] louder.	speak	spoke	spoken
The car had been *stolen* [not *stole*].	steal	stole	stolen
The witness was *sworn* [not *swore*] in.	swear	swore	sworn
John has *swum* [not *swam*] across the lake.	swim	swam	swum
Someone had *torn* [not *tore*] the dollar bill.	tear	tore	torn
You should have *worn* [not *wore*] a hat.	wear	wore	worn
I have already *written* [not *wrote*] my essay.	write	wrote	written

Regular Versus Irregular

Sometimes errors occur because an irregular verb is thought to be regular.

	Verb	Past Tense	P.P.
The wind *blew* [not *blowed*] steadily all day.	blow	blew	blown
John *brought* [not *bringed*] Mary some flowers.	bring	brought	brought
This house was *built* [not *builded*] in 1795.	build	built	built
Barbara *caught* [not *catched*] two trout.	catch	caught	caught
Slowly they *crept* [not *creeped*] up the stairs.	creep	crept	crept
He *dealt* [not *dealed*] me a good hand.	deal	dealt	dealt
The men quickly *dug* [not *digged*] a pit.	dig	dug	dug
She *drew* [not *drawed*] a caricature of me.	draw	drew	drawn
All the men *grew* [not *growed*] long beards.	grow	grew	grown
Ben *hung* [not *hanged*] his cap on the hook.	hang	hung	hung
I *knew* [not *knowed*] him at college.	know	knew	known
I have never *lent* [not *lended*] him money.	lend	lent	lent
We *sought* [not *seeked*] shelter from the rain.	seek	sought	sought
The sun *shone* [not *shined*] all day yesterday.	shine	shone	shone
The prince *slew* [not *slayed*] the fierce dragon.	slay	slew	slain
I soon *spent* [not *spended*] the money.	spend	spent	spent
Ms. Andrews *taught* [not *teached*] us algebra.	teach	taught	taught
Lou *threw* [not *throwed*] the receipt away.	throw	threw	thrown
The old man *wept* [not *weeped*] piteously.	weep	wept	wept

Obsolete or Dialectal Forms

A third type of error results from the use of an obsolete or dialectal form of the verb, a form not considered standard now:

	Verb	*Past Tense*	*P.P.*
I *am* [not *be*] working regularly.	be*	was, were	been*
I *have been* [not *been*] working regularly.			
The child *burst* [not *bursted*] out crying.	burst	burst	burst
I've *bought* [not *boughten*] a car.	buy	bought	bought
I *climbed* [not *clumb*] a tree for a better view.	climb	climbed	climbed
The women *clung* [not *clang*] to the raft.	cling	clung	clung
The dog *dragged* [not *drug*] the old shoe home.	drag	dragged	dragged
The boy was nearly *drowned* [not *drownded*].	drown	drowned	drowned
At the picnic I *ate* [not *et*] too many hot dogs.	eat	ate	eaten
Betty *flung* [not *flang*] the stick away.	fling	flung	flung
You *paid* [not *payed*] too much for it.	pay	paid	paid
It had been *shaken* [not *shooken*] to pieces.	shake	shook	shaken
He had never *skinned* [not *skun*] an animal.	skin	skinned	skinned
A bee *stung* [not *stang*] me as I stood there.	sting	stung	stung
The girl *swung* [not *swang*] at the ball.	swing	swung	swung
I wonder who could have *taken* [not *tooken*] it.	take	took	taken

Confusing Verb Forms

A fourth type of verb error results from a confusion of forms of certain verbs that look or sound almost alike but are actually quite different in meaning, such as *lie*, *lay*; *sit*, *set*; and *rise*, *raise*. Note that three of these troublesome verbs—*lay*, *set*, and *raise*—in their ordinary uses take an object. The other three—*lie*, *sit*, *rise*—do not take an object.

	Verb	*Past Tense*	*P.P.*
Please *lay* your books [D.O.] on the table.	lay	laid	laid
Mary *laid* several logs [D.O.] on the fire.			
The men have *laid* some boards [D.O.] over the puddle.			
Our cat often *lies* [not *lays*] on the couch.	lie	lay	lain
Yesterday our cat *lay* [not *laid*] on the couch.			
Our cat has *lain* [not *laid*] on the couch all morning.			
She *sets* the plate [D.O.] in front of me.	set	set	set
An hour ago Tom *set* out some food [D.O.] for the birds.			
I had *set* the timer [D.O.] for ten minutes.			
I usually *sit* in that chair.	sit	sat	sat
Yesterday he *sat* in my chair.			
I have *sat* at my desk all morning.			

---

*As you learned in Lesson 2, the irregular verb *be* has three forms (*am, are, is*) in the present tense and two forms (*was, were*) in the past tense.

At her command they *raise* the flag [D.O.].	raise	raised	raised
The boy quickly *raised* his hand [D.O.].			
He had *raised* the price [D.O.] of his old car.			

He *rises* when we enter the room.	rise	rose	risen
Everyone *rose* as the speaker entered the room.			
The water has *risen* a foot since midnight.			

Exceptions

The rules and illustrations given here are an adequate guide in most situations. They show the importance of knowing the principal parts of these verbs. Note, however, that there are a few exceptions, such as the intransitive uses of *set*:

A *setting* [not *sitting*] hen *sets*. [Of course, a hen, like a rooster, may be said to *sit* when that is what is meant.]

The sun *sets* in the west.

Cement or dye *sets*.

A jacket *sets* (*fits*) well.

With a few verbs, special meanings demand different principal parts. For example, the past tense and the past participle of *shine*, when the verb is used as a transitive verb, are *shined*:

This morning I *shined* [not *shone*] my shoes.

The verb *hang* with the meaning "to execute by suspending by the neck until dead" uses *hanged*, not *hung*, for the past tense and the past participle. When in doubt, always refer to your dictionary.

SEQUENCE OF TENSES

In Lesson 2 you studied a partial conjugation showing the forms of three sample verbs as they occur in six tenses. In Lesson 5 you were told the basic uses of the six tenses. Although most student writers usually have little difficulty in establishing and maintaining logical time relationships in their sentences, a few situations sometimes cause confusion.

Subordinate Clauses

The tense in a subordinate clause is normally the same as that in the main clause unless a different time for the subordinate statement is clearly indicated.

We think that Mary studies hard all the time.

We think that Mary studied hard for the last test.

We think that Mary will study hard for the next test.

We think that Mary has studied hard for all her tests.

We think that Mary had studied hard before last week's test.

We thought that Mary studied hard all the time.

We thought that Mary studied hard in the past.
We thought that Mary would study hard for the next test.
We thought that Mary has studied hard all year.
We thought that Mary had studied hard last semester.

Universally True Statements

The present tense is used for a statement that is universally true.

The dietitian reminded us that whipped cream *is* (not *was*) fattening.
I wonder who first discovered that oysters *are* (not *were*) edible.

Shifting Tenses

In narrative writing a shift from past tense to present tense or from present to past should be avoided.

The library *was* silent except for an occasional whisper, when suddenly a side door *opened* [not *opens*] and a disheveled young man *dashed* [not *dashes*] in and *started* [not *starts*] yelling, "Man the lifeboats!" After the librarians *managed* to restore order . . .

Present Perfect Tense

The perfect form of an infinitive should not be used when the controlling verb is in the present perfect tense with a modal auxiliary.

Correct: I would have liked to see that performance.
Incorrect: I would have liked to have seen that performance.

In the indicative mood, there is rarely any confusion over the correct form of the infinitive.

Correct: I have wanted to run that marathon for years.

SUPPLEMENT

When a sentence makes a statement or asks a question, the verb is said to be in the **indicative mood** or **mode** (see Lesson 2). Two other moods indicate a different purpose in the sentence.

Imperative Mood
When a sentence gives a direction or command, the verb is in the **imperative mood.** The imperative of all regular verbs simply uses the base form of the verb without a subject.

Please *give* me the ball.
Take out your pen and paper.

Even the verb *to be*, irregular in most formations, uses the base to form the imperative.

Be careful; the steps are slippery.
Please *be* on time; the bus will depart promptly.

Subjunctive Mood

The present subjunctive uses the base form of the verb, regardless of the subject.

The catalog recommends that she *study* accounting in the first semester.

The past subjunctive takes the same form as the past tense of the verb. (The auxiliary *be* is always *were* regardless of the number or person of the subject.)

I wish I *were* at home today.

The past perfect subjunctive has the same form as the past perfect.

I wish I *had gone* home earlier.

We also use the subjunctive in these special ways:

1. In clauses beginning with *that* when they follow words such as *ask, suggest, require, recommend,* and *demand.*

   The policy requires that we *submit* our requests in writing.
   The manager insisted that we *be* present for the ceremony.

2. In clauses beginning with *if* when the clause makes a statement that is clearly and unmistakably contrary to fact.

   If I *were* able to sing, I would try out for the Met.
   If he were young again, he would live life differently.

English Fundamentals Online

After you have completed the Practice Sheets and Exercises in this lesson, you can find additional help and drill work at **MyWritingLab.com**, in the sections on Tense; Consistent Verb Tense and Active Voice; Regular and Irregular Verbs.

NAME _____ SCORE _____

Directions: In the space at the left, write the correct form of the verb shown in the parentheses. Do not use any *ing* forms.

_____ 1. "My alarm clock did not (ring)," said Martin, "so I (drag) myself
_____   out of bed about an hour late."

_____ 2. Jackson (set) his books down on that table when he walked in last
_____   night, but now they are nowhere to be (see).

_____ 3. The men (lay) almost 300 blocks yesterday; that number (be) a
_____   new record for that group.

_____ 4. "You should not have (lay) your jacket on that chair," said Mark;
_____   "instead, you should have (hang) it in the hall closet."

_____ 5. The dog has (lay) there in the sun all morning; he didn't even
_____   move when Jan (drive) in the driveway.

_____ 6. Later in the afternoon the clouds overhead (become) very thick;
_____   the wind has (blow) quite hard since about noon.

_____ 7. Mr. Thompson has (draw) on his many years of experience to solve
_____   that problem; the rest of us had (drown) ourselves in the tiny details.

_____ 8. Look! Someone has (tear) a page from this book; now we will
_____   never (know) how the mystery ended.

_____ 9. Have you ever (swim) all the way across the river? It (be) nearly a
_____   mile across at this point.

_____ 10. Lately, John and I have (grow) interested in American history;
_____   before, I had not (pay) much attention to the past.

_____ 11. "At the picnic I (eat) three hot dogs and a piece of cake," said Al;
_____   "I have (eat) enough to last till tomorrow morning."

_____ 12. The batter (swing) at the ball and drove it to deep short, but the
_____   shortstop made a fine play and (throw) the batter out by one step.

_____ 13. We have (begin) work on that next paper, but we both think we
_____   should have (choose) less obscure topics.

_____ 14. "I have not (bring) enough money with me to the game," said
_____   Cheryl; "I (lend) Mary twenty dollars before I left the house."

_____ 15. The pitcher has already (throw) 94 pitches, and he's only in the fourth
_____   inning; I'm afraid he will have (spend) himself before too long.

_____ 16. We have (sit) in this room listening to that man for 2 hours, and
_____   no one has (catch) more than 3 or 4 understandable sentences.

_____ 17. Have you (set) the oven timer for those cookies? The last time we
_____   baked, the cookies (burst) into flames before we could save them.

_____ 18. Those boys should have (seek) shelter some time ago, for that last
_____   stroke of lightning (strike) very close to them.

_____ 19. For Old Settlers Day, all the men have (grow) beards and (break) out their old plaid flannel shirts.

_____ 20. Hal's new fishing rod has (fall) overboard and (sink) in deep water, never to be seen again.

_____ 21. Dad has (build) a small porch outside his bedroom; he usually (sit) there early in the morning drinking his coffee.

_____ 22. Robert (buy) a number of landscape timbers and (lay) them end to end around the garden

_____ 23. The puppy (creep) up behind the man and had (steal) his sandwich before he had a chance to stop the theft.

_____ 24. Once the boat had (get) past the boundaries of the harbor, the waves (fling) the boat violently from side to side in the water.

_____ 25. If you had (teach) Jane how to parallel park, she would not have (has) to drive around the parking lot before finding a place.

_____ 26. The school has (build) its reputation on the success of its sports teams and its academics, but lately the teams have not (be) very successful.

_____ 27. Jeremy has (buy) a new car, but he has only (drive) it a few hundred miles since he brought it home.

_____ 28. "I have not (take) a vacation in two years," said Ben; "I think it's time I (take) some time off."

_____ 29. The instructor's sharp words (sting) us all badly; we hope that he will have (begin) to feel better before the next class.

_____ 30. John (shake) up his schedule for next term; all his classes will (meet) in the early morning.

_____ 31. The shortstop (skin) both her elbows when she made that diving stop, but she (feel) good about getting the runner at first.

_____ 32. Fred (burst) noisily into the room, but then (slink) quietly to his seat when he realized that he was late.

_____ 33. We should have (find) shelter an hour ago; I am almost (freeze) by the cold wind and the rain.

_____ 34. Cathy should have (deal) with that paper earlier in the week because now she has (run) out of time to work on it.

_____ 35. Jones has (come) into the game too late to salvage a win; the other team's lead has (grow) to five runs.

_____ 36. I had (shook) my clock several times and was ready to throw it against the wall, but it finally (begin) to work correctly again.

_____ 37. Although I had (shine) all that brass until it nearly blinded me, the Drill instructor has not (give) me permission to move to the next task.

_____ 38. Although the sun (shine) all day yesterday, the field did not (become) playable until late this afternoon.

_____ 39. The hero (slay) all the dragons and other monsters, so she (be) able to save civilization, at least temporarily.

_____ 40. Tom (lie) down for a nap, but the cat (leap) up on the bed and kept him awake.

Directions: Each sentence contains two italicized verbs. If the principal part or tense of the verb is correct, write **C** in the corresponding space at the left. If the verb form is incorrect, write the correct form in the space at the left.

_____ 1. All that paper you *threw* away yesterday has spilled out of the
_____ trash can and is *laying* on the floor.

_____ 2. "*Set* your work aside for a few minutes, and let's *sit* down for a
_____ cup of coffee," said Melissa.

_____ 3. The worker had *got* very tired, so he *stoled* away for a few
_____ minutes of rest.

_____ 4. If we can't *rise* the height of that door jamb three inches, the new
_____ door can't be *slud* into the opening.

_____ 5. "The challenges *be* great," said the coach, "but I'm sure we can
_____ *raise* to the occasion."

_____ 6. The tires on Jan's car are nearly *wore* out, so she will *buy* new
_____ ones before her trip.

_____ 7. "I *payed* a high price for that jacket, so I'm surprised that it has
_____ *worn* out so soon," said Jane.

_____ 8. That tree in the front yard has *growed* about a foot since last year;
_____ soon it will have *catched* up with the older trees.

_____ 9. Jack *lain* his briefcase on the desk and *walks* down the hall to get
_____ a cup of coffee.

_____ 10. I have been *sitting* here for 20 minutes, but the doctor has not
_____ *shone* up to talk to me.

_____ 11. The dog *sleeped* soundly on the bed for almost an hour, then he
_____ *run* outside and spent an hour chasing squirrels.

_____ 12. That book has *laid* on the seat of Carl's car for several days, so today
_____ he took it inside and *sat* it on the coffee table in the living room.

_____ 13. My grandfather *rises* very early in the morning, so after lunch he
_____ *lays* down for a short nap.

_____ 14. Al has been *satting* at his desk all morning working on that paper,
_____ so a few minutes ago he leaped up and *run* down the stairs and outside.

_____ 15. "I have *lived* here through five winters now, but this past winter
_____ *been* worse than any of the others."

_____ 16. "I *lay* my keys in the same place every day," said Martha, "but this
_____ morning they are not *laying* where I left them yesterday evening."

_____ 17. Someone has *tooken* Jim's seat in that back row; he always *sets* in
_____ that same seat for this class.

_____ 18. "I *blowed* out all the candles on my birthday cake," said Art, "but
_____ my wish has not *came* true yet."

_____ 19. Bob *bringed* Allison some beautiful roses, but she still has not
_____ *forgave* him for standing her up last Friday night.

_____ 20. The men *builded* a beautiful deck on that house, but the new
_____ owners have never even *standed* out there to watch the sunset.

_____ 21. Johnson *went* to the library yesterday, and tomorrow he *comes*
_____ back again to finish his research in those dusty old magazines.

_____ 22. Jan *done* all that work yesterday raking up the leaves, but today
_____ even more leaves have *blowed* into the yard.

_____ 23. Everyone thought that Becky *had studied* hard for yesterday's test,
_____ but she actually *had been reading* a romance novel the whole time.

_____ 24. Once the men *had finished* painting that fence, they *move* their location
_____ to the side of the garage, which has not been painted for five years.

_____ 25. Once the men *finish* painting that fence, they *will move* their location
_____ to the side of the garage, which has not been painted for five years.

_____ 26. The technician *reminded* us that those units *are* as reliable as any
_____ ever built.

_____ 27. I would have liked *to have seen* Jerry's face when his old girl
_____ friend *walks* into the restaurant.

_____ 28. The bitter cold outside *made* my whole body shudder when I *walk*
_____ outside without my jacket.

_____ 29. When Diane *seen* those men walking up the driveway, she
_____ *knowed* immediately that one was her cousin from Milwaukee.

_____ 30. The noise from the lawnmower outside the classroom *drownded*
_____ out the voice of the instructor as he *gives* his lecture.

_____ 31. Evan seems to have *et* too much of that candy; his face is white
_____ and his hands *are shaking*.

_____ 32. The girl *swang* her axe and *splitted* the log exactly into two
_____ pieces.

_____ 33. After Frank *had dug* in the hard clay for about an hour, he *finded*
_____ the place where the pipe was leaking.

_____ 34. The first time Gail *worn* that beautiful new jacket, she *torn* the
_____ sleeve on a sharp nail.

_____ 35. The exhausted boy slowly *clumb* the stairs and *falled* into bed; he
_____ was asleep almost as soon as his head hit the pillow.

_____ 36. Harry *hanged* that hose on the big hook in the shop, and then
_____ he *organizes* all the tools on the workbench.

_____ 37. Once Karen had *wrote* the last page of her paper, she *prints* two
_____ copies of it and filed one away for safekeeping.

_____ 38. "I *been* very happy with that car because it has not *given* me any
_____ trouble in the three years I've owned it," said Luis.

_____ 39. Before Laura pulled on her hiking boots, she *shaked* them, and a
_____ huge spider *falled* out of one of them.

_____ 40. "I *skint* my knees when I slipped and *went* down on the
_____ sidewalk," said Max as he limped into the house.

Using Verbs Correctly: Principal Parts; Tense

NAME _____ SCORE _____

Directions: In the space at the left of each sentence, write the correct form of the verb shown in parentheses. Do not use any *ing* forms.

_____ 1. Once we (come) into town, we saw the new buildings where they
_____   (stand) in the formerly vacant lots.

_____ 2. Most people (believe) that eating three servings of vegetables (be)
_____   good for their health.

_____ 3. In yesterday's speech, the lecturer (lay) the groundwork for his
_____   argument that today's politicians (be) ultimately the responsibility
         of the voters.

_____ 4. At the sound of the gun, the runners (break) from the starting line;
_____   then they sprinted to the first turn and (move) out of sight.

_____ 5. As though they had been (give) a cue, the entire team (sing)
_____   "Happy Birthday" when the coach walked into the room.

_____ 6. I would not have (choose) to wear that hat to a formal party, but
_____   then I rarely ever (wear) a hat under any circumstance.

_____ 7. "Where have you (be)?" asked Wendy when we walked up. "I
_____   almost (leave) because I thought you weren't coming."

_____ 8. Now, who would have (take) my books? I (put) them right here
_____   on this table just a few minutes ago.

_____ 9. When Warren (swing) the newspaper at the wasp, he missed the
_____   wasp but (give) his little brother a sharp smack on the shoulder.

_____ 10. The crowd (burst) into laughter when the two clowns, falling all
_____   over each other, seized the mike and (begin) to sing a serious song.

_____ 11. "One of us should have (think) to bring sandwiches," said one
_____   hiker to the other; "we're going to be hungry long before we have
         (find) that little store."

_____ 12. The bear (shake) that slender tree very hard, and the sack of food
_____   (fall) to the ground at his feet.

_____ 13. Although she had not (do) the entire assignment, Terri thought
_____   she should have (earn) partial credit for her efforts.

_____ 14. When the bell (ring), all the students raced out of their classrooms
_____   and (run) to the cafeteria.

_____ 15. "I've (drink) almost two full pints of water," said Sam, "but I've
_____   never (feel) so thirsty."

Directions: Each sentence has two italicized verb units. If the principal part or tense of the verb is the proper form for serious writing, write **C** in the corresponding space at the left. If the verb is incorrect, write the correct form in the space. **Review:** Underline the auxiliary verbs in the sentences on this page.

1. The child *swum* to the end of the pool, *climbed* up the diving tower, and jumped back into the pool.
2. Surely, you should have *knew* that Texas *was* the largest of the 48 contiguous states.
3. "I've never *saw* anything as silly as this letter," said the editor as he *flang* the letter into the trash can.
4. The sun has *shined* every day for a week, but my dogwood tree has not *bursted* into bloom.
5. "Your class *begun* 30 minutes ago, and here you are, still *lying* in bed," Rob's roommate said.
6. My friend Joe had just walked up to the park bench and *set* down when a little boy ran by and *stealed* his newspaper.
7. Anyone can see that your report was hastily *wrote* and that you *should have spent* more time on it.
8. After we *had gone* about a mile, we saw the church that marked the street where we *were supposed* to turn.
9. "That project *been* a disaster since the first day," said the boss; "I think we *should lay* it aside for a while and go on to something new."
10. The men *been trying* all day to find the leak in the roof, but so far they *have* not *had* any success.
11. "I *finded* your lost glove out in left field, probably exactly where you *leaved* it yesterday," said the coach.
12. Although Paul *had wore* that jacket only once, he *hanged* it in the back of his closet and tried to forget that he had bought it.
13. His friends *set* down around the dining room table and waited while Larry *shone* his shoes for the dance.
14. Martha ran downstairs, *opens* the front door, and moved to the sidewall; then she stopped and *drunk* some water before she started her run.
15. The dog often *lays* right in the doorway, and yesterday I stumbled over him and almost *falled* when I came into the house.
16. Nan has never *rode* on a Jet Ski before today, but, after a few minutes of practice, she *looks* like a professional.
17. "*Set* down at the table," said Grannie, "and have some cookies and milk; my cookies *be* famous in our family."
18. We have raised the flag and *hung* the banners; we *must be* ready for the big celebration.
19. Mark *payed* a steep price for that car, so I hope he *will enjoy* driving it.
20. The pitcher *throwed* his best fastball, but the batter *drived* it into the upper deck for a home run.

Brief Writing Assignment: Write a paragraph of five sentences describing the making of your favorite sandwich. Write the paragraph in the first person (I); use only past tense verbs in the sentences.

Examine the following conjugation. Note that in the present tense, the third-person singular (*he*, *she*, *it*) verb form differs from the third-person plural (*they*) verb form.

I earn	We earn
You earn	You earn
He, She, It *earns*	They *earn*

We refer to this change as a change in number. As noted in Lesson 2, **singular number** refers to only *one* thing; **plural number** refers to *more than one* thing. Notice how verbs and nouns differ in this respect: The *s* ending on nouns is a plural marker, but on verbs it designates the singular form.

The following examples show how the number of the subject (one or more than one) affects the form of the verb. (See Supplement.) The verbs *have*, *do*, and *be* are important because they have auxiliary uses as well as main-verb uses. *Be* is an exceptional verb; it changes form in the past tense as well as in the present tense.

Singular	*Plural*
She *walks* slowly.	They *walk* slowly.
Mother *seems* pleased.	My parents *seem* pleased.
Mary *has* a new dress.	All of the girls *have* new dresses.
He *has traveled* widely.	They *have traveled* widely.
She *does* her work easily.	They *do* their work easily.
Does he *have* enough time?	*Do* they *have* enough time?
He *is* a friend of mine.	They *are* friends of mine.
My brother *is coming* home.	My brothers *are coming* home.
His camera *was taken* from him.	Their cameras *were taken* from them.

VERB AGREES IN NUMBER

The relation of verb form to subject follows an important principle of usage: The verb always agrees in number with its subject. Although the principle is simple, some of the situations in which it applies are not. You will avoid some common writing errors if you keep in mind the following seven extensions of the principle. The first is probably the most important.

1. The number of the verb is not affected by material that comes between the verb and the subject.

> Immediate *settlement* of these problems *is* [not *are*] vital. [The subject is *settlement*. Problems, being here the object of the preposition *of*, cannot be a subject.]
>
> The *cost* of replacing the asbestos shingles with cedar shakes *was* [not *were*] considerable.
>
> *Tact*, as well as patience, *is* [not *are*] required.

235

Mr. Sheldon, together with several other division heads, *has* [not *have*] left.

Each of the plans *has* [not *have*] its good points.

Is [not *Are*] *either* of the contestants ready?

Determine the *real* subject of the verb; watch out for intervening words that might mislead you. The number of the verb is not altered when other nouns are attached to the subject by means of prepositions such as *in addition to*, *together with*, *as well as*, *with*, and *along with*. Remember that indefinite pronoun subjects like *either*, *neither*, *each*, *one*, *everyone*, *no one*, and *somebody* take singular verbs. *None* may take either a singular or a plural verb, depending on whether the writer wishes to emphasize "not one" or "no members" of the group.

None of us *is* [or *are*] perfect.

2. A verb agrees with its subject even when the subject follows the verb.

On the wall *hangs* a *portrait* of his father. [*portrait hangs*]
On the wall *hang portraits* of his parents. [*portraits hang*]
He handed us a piece of paper on which *was scribbled* a *warning*. [*warning was scribbled*]
There *was* barely enough *time* remaining.
There *were* only ten *minutes* remaining.
There *seems* to be one *problem* remaining.
There *seem* to be a few *problems* remaining.
Here *is* a free *ticket* to the game.
Here *are* some free *tickets* to the game.

Be especially careful to find the real subject in sentences starting with *there* or *here*.

3. Compound subjects joined by *and* take a plural verb.

A little *boy* and his *dog were* playing in the yard.
On the platform *were* a *table* and four *chairs*.

But the verb should be singular if the subjects joined by *and* are thought of as a single thing, or if the subjects are considered separately, as when they are modified by *every* or *each*:

Plain *vinegar* and *oil is* all the dressing my salad needs. [one thing]
Every *man* and every *woman is* asked to help. [considered separately]

4. Singular subjects joined by *or* or *nor* take singular verbs.

Either a *check* or a money *order is* required.
Neither the *manager* nor his *assistant has* arrived yet.
Was Mr. *Phelps* or his *son* put on the committee?

In some sentences of this pattern, especially in questions like the last example, a plural verb is sometimes used, both in casual conversation and in writing. In serious and formal writing, the singular verb is considered appropriate. If the subjects joined by *or* or *nor* differ in number, the verb agrees with the subject nearer to it:

Neither the *mother* nor the two *boys were* able to identify him.
Either the *players* or the *coach is* responsible for the defeat.

5. Plural nouns of amount, distance, and so on, when they are used as singular units of measurement, take singular verbs.

> A hundred *dollars was* once paid for a single tulip bulb.'
> Thirty *miles seems* like a long walk to me.
> Seven *years* in school *was* the length of the degree program.

6. A collective noun is considered singular when the group is regarded as a unit; it is plural when the individuals of the group are referred to.

> The *audience is* very enthusiastic tonight.
> The *audience are* returning to their seats. [Notice pronoun *their.*]
> The *band is* playing a rousing march.
> Now the *band are* putting away their instruments. [Again note *their.*]
> *Most* of the book *is* blatant propaganda.
> *Most* of her novels *are* now out of print.
> The *rest* of the fortune *was* soon gone.
> The *rest* of his debts *were* left unpaid.
> The *number* of bank failures *is* increasing.
> A *number* of these bank failures *are* being investigated.

Words like *number, all, rest, part, some, more, most, half* are singular or plural, depending on the meaning intended. A word of this type is often accompanied by a modifier or referred to by a pronoun, either of which gives a clue to the number intended. When the word *number* is a subject, it is considered singular if it is preceded by *the* and plural if it is preceded by *a*.

7. When the subject is a relative pronoun, the antecedent of the pronoun determines the number (and person) of the verb. (See Lesson 23, page 243.)

> He told a joke *that was* pointless. [*joke was*]
> He told several jokes *that were* pointless. [*jokes were*]
> I paid the expenses of the trip, *which were* minimal. [*expenses were*]
> Jack is one of those boys *who enjoy* fierce competition. [*boys enjoy*]

The last example, sometimes called the "one of those . . . who" sentence, is particularly troublesome. Often a singular verb is used. If we recast the sentence to read "Of those boys who enjoy fierce competition, Jack is one," however, it becomes clear that the logical antecedent of *who* is the plural noun *boys*. However, usage is divided. And notice that a singular verb must be used when the pattern is altered slightly:

> Jack is the only *one* of my friends *who enjoys* fierce competition.

Because a relative pronoun subject nearly always has an antecedent that is third-person singular or third-person plural, we are accustomed to pronoun–verb combinations like these:

> A boy *who is* . . .
> Boys *who are* . . .
> A woman *who knows* . . .
> Women *who know* . . .

But in those occasional sentences in which a relative pronoun subject has an antecedent that is in the first or second person, meticulously correct usage calls for subject–verb combinations like the following:

> I, *who am* in charge here, should pay the bill. [*I . . . am*]
> They should ask me, *who know* all the answers. [*I . . . know*]
> You, *who are* in charge here, should pay the bill. [*You . . . are*]
> They should ask you, *who know* all the answers. [*you . . . know*]

SUPPLEMENT

One particular error of subject–verb agreement warrants special attention. The third-person singular present tense form of the verb *do* is *does*. The plural form is *do*. The misuse of the negative contraction *don't* (instead of *doesn't*) with a third-person singular subject is quite often encountered in spoken English. Many people, justly or unjustly, look on the it-don't misuse as an important marker of grossly substandard English. Such forms as the following should be avoided in all spoken and written English:

Faulty:	My father *don't* like broccoli.
Faulty:	It really *don't* matter.
Faulty:	Jack Johnson *don't* live here now.
Faulty:	One of her teachers *don't* like her.
Faulty:	This fudge tastes good, *don't* it?
Faulty:	The fact that the bill is overdue *don't* bother him.

SUMMARY OF CORRECT VERB USE

1. The principal parts of a verb are the present, the past, and the past participle. Avoid confusing the principal parts of irregular verbs (*run, ran, run*; *eat, ate, eaten*; *fly, flew, flown*) with those of regular verbs (*study, studied, studied*). Be especially careful with the often confused principal parts of *lie* and *lay*, *sit* and *set*.

2. Singular verbs are used with singular subjects; plural verbs are used with plural subjects.
   a. Nouns intervening between the subject and the verb do not determine the number of the verb. (Resistance to the actions of these government agencies *is* [not *are*] growing.)
   b. Singular subjects joined by *and* normally take plural verbs. Singular subjects joined by *or* or *nor* normally take singular verbs.
   c. Some nouns and pronouns (collective nouns, and words like *number, all, half*, etc.) are singular in some meanings, plural in others.

English Fundamentals Online

After you have completed the Practice Sheets and Exercises in this lesson, you can find additional help and drill work at **MyWritingLab.com**, in the section on Subject–Verb Agreement.

Using Verbs Correctly: Subject–Verb Agreement

NAME _____ SCORE _____

Directions: These sentences are examples of structures that can lead to subject–verb agreement. In the space at the left, copy the word in parentheses that provides correct subject–verb agreement.

sit   1. In the back of my shop (sits, sit) my two power saws, both of which I use almost every day.

were   2. I have seen four movies this summer that (was, were) filled with scenes of incredible action.

was   3. Almost half of my block (was, were) without power for two hours last night.

were   4. Over half of my neighbors (was, were) without power for two hours last night.

oppose   5. A large majority of my fellow students (opposes, oppose) the increase in the student activities fee.

oppose   6. Most of us in the student body (opposes, oppose) the increase in the student activities fee.

repeats   7. Most of the information in the newspaper (repeats, repeat) what I heard on television last night.

were   8. Half of the writers mentioned in my history class (was, were) already familiar to me.

are   9. There (is, are) a few people in the crowd who have never heard this speaker before today.

_____ 10. Either Tom or Jim (is, are) coming tomorrow to help us with moving the furniture into the new room.

fills   11. A group of fifty people (fills, fill) that small room for presentations of the musical.

_____ 12. Neither Joe's sister nor his two brothers (is, are) able to attend today's banquet and awards ceremony.

_____ 13. In addition to the original five people, two men and three women (has, have) signed up to help with the adventure race.

_____ 14. A glass of milk and two blueberry muffins (is, are) one of my favorite combinations for breakfast.

_____ 15. On the wall in the coach's office (hangs, hang) pictures of past state championship teams.

_____ 16. The coaching staff (is, are) meeting with their respective position players for work on specific situations.

_____ 17. The coaching staff (seems, seem) pleased with the team's overall performance in last Saturday's game.

_____ 18. The two boys and their mother (is, are) coming to tonight's meeting about art classes for the summer months.

_____ 19. On the platform (was, were) the speaker and two of the company executives; behind them, a huge video screen hung from the ceiling.

_____ 20. Either my sister or my brothers (is, are) coming to help us with the moving.

Directions: If you find an error in subject–verb agreement, write the correct verb form in the space at the left of the sentence. If the sentence is correct, write **C** in the space.

_____ 1. Our team leader, who is fairly wealthy, always takes us team members out for dinner after the last day of work on a project.

_____ 2. Neither Al nor his two helpers has been able to find the problem with our air conditioning unit.

_____ 3. There are a rather large group of people outside the door of the senator's office.

_____ 4. The two quarterbacks and Coach Nelson has been meeting for the last 45 minutes.

_____ 5. Either Bart or Carl usually work on that kind of problem in our computer system, which is old and very temperamental.

_____ 6. Five years of school are the amount of time required to finish many engineering programs.

_____ 7. After that last set, which was the last of the night, the band are putting away their instruments and packing up the other equipment.

_____ 8. The members of the band, which has been in operation for several years, also works as officers in the local bank.

_____ 9. George's family run a huge farm outside of town; the farm has been in the family for several generations.

_____ 10. Joellen is one of those women who seems to have a boundless supply of energy, especially for anything athletic.

_____ 11. Of the people who started college with me, Kelly is the only one of my friends who has already finished his degree.

_____ 12. Lawrence, out of all the people in our office, are the only one who seems to have a firm grasp of basic accounting.

_____ 13. Bill said, "I, who am responsible for the work on this project, should make the final presentation to the executive committee."

_____ 14. The men who is walking into the room now will give the award for the most valuable player to Bryan, our team captain for the past two years.

_____ 15. Jackson, along with Jeff his understudy, have the lead in the play that opens next week in our community theater.

_____ 16. Milk or cream is the only thing my father ever puts in his coffee; he says that sugar spoils the taste of a good cup of coffee.

_____ 17. "It take all kinds of people to make up the world," said my grandmother, "and I try to put up with all of them I meet."

_____ 18. As long as we watch them from the deck, neither the two fawns nor the doe seem to be afraid of us.

_____ 19. When I consider all the time and effort I put into that job, a hundred dollars seem to be a small payment.

_____ 20. In retrospect, the comment that Julie made seem both pointless and a little cruel.

NAME _____ SCORE _____

Directions: If you find an error in subject–verb agreement, write the correct form of the verb in the space at the left of the sentence. Circle the subject of each verb you correct. If a sentence is correct, write **C** in the corresponding space. **Review:** Write the base of the main verb of the sentence for items 1–10 in the space at the end of each sentence.

_____was_____ 1. The solution to the problem posed to the class by the three professors were long and extremely complex.

_____Are_____ 2. Is Ms. Johnson and the other coaches coming to the meeting to discuss changes in the rules for academic eligibility?

_____provide_____ 3. Either that book or those two pamphlets provides information about the future of solar power in providing electric power to rural communities.

_____was_____ 4. Every boy and every girl in the youth soccer league were told to remind the sponsors of Saturday's work day.

_____are_____ 5. Incredibly, there is no records at the courthouse of the sale of those pieces of property by the creek.

_____C_____ 6. In the backyard of that house down the street two young boys and their dog are playing with a large rubber ball.

_____C_____ 7. The dog next door, or perhaps it was one of those two dogs living across the street, has dug up the roses in our back yard.

_____needs_____ 8. One of you men, and it doesn't matter which one, need to take charge of this project and see that it gets finished this week.

_____are_____ 9. A number of the students in the class is unhappy because the next test has been moved up by two days.

_____grows_____ 10. The number of unhappy students in that class grow larger every time changes are made in the schedule.

_____C_____ 11. Has Mr. White or his daughter taken that painting to an appraiser to determine its value?

_____do_____ 12. Oil and water does not mix easily, and my brother and his former girl friend were very similar: they did not get along well at all.

_____has_____ 13. The rest of the lost money have been discovered in an old trunk in the attic in a second, more thorough search by the police.

_____have_____ 14. Some of the participants has not yet arrived, so perhaps we should delay the start of the meeting.

_____were_____ 15. I do not think that any of the books and other items that was lost by the movers will ever be recovered.

_____were_____ 16. Few of the people who was standing in the crowd that day will forget the impact of that speech on our nation's history.

_____C_____ 17. Here are two second-hand lawnmowers, either of which are light enough for your daughter to operate.

_____C_____ 18. Every single one of our scouts have filed glowing reports on Stockbridge, the goalie at South Central High School.

_____C_____ 19. The exciting possibilities open to anyone who is willing to take some risks are almost too numerous to count.

_____have_____ 20. "The plans submitted by each of you has good points, so we should combine the two plans into one so as to achieve success," said Robert.

_____had_____ 21. "Each of you have submitted plans that have good points, so we will combine the two plans to insure our success," said Robert.

_____ 22. "The check that you has sent us did not cover all the costs of the items you bought," said the letter; "send us the balance as soon as possible."

_____ 23. When you was here in town last week, we enjoyed our visit with you very much, so I hope we can see each other again soon.

_____ 24. Neither Mr. Phillips nor his two sons have filed their applications for membership in the club; one of us needs to call them.

_____ 25. Five hours seem far too short for a drive of that distance, but I believe we can make the trip in seven hours.

_____ 26. The club intends to support that project at the library; all the members are in agreement about its importance.

_____ 27. The audience are returning to their seats very slowly, so we should delay opening the curtain for the second act.

_____ 28. Most of the team members has already arrived; two more will arrive this afternoon on a later flight.

_____ 29. Half of the money collected at the meetings yesterday have been designated for the soccer team; the other half has yet to be allotted.

_____ 30. Of the people who has signed up for the conference this weekend, Joan is the only one who has put down a deposit for a room.

_____ 31. My brother don't think he will be able to meet us for lunch because he is working on a high priority project for his company.

_____ 32. All the men who intends to try out for a club lacrosse team should meet the organizers at noon tomorrow in the recreation center.

_____ 33. Everyone who intend to sign up for that field trip to the new aquarium should plan to pay the fee by Monday morning.

_____ 34. Every man and every woman who is interested in that issue should plan to attend the town council meeting on Tuesday night.

_____ 35. It really don't matter whether we are tired or not; we need to finish the last mile of this hike before the rain starts.

_____ 36. The two girls and their mother has started on their trip; they will be gone about two weeks.

_____ 37. Most of his novels was detailed, intricately plotted murder mysteries, but one is a comic story about two little kids and a dog.

_____ 38. Most of the gravel in the driveway have run down to the bottom because of the recent heavy rains.

_____ 39. Many of those who have been members of the club for a long time know that public service projects are a very important part of its life.

_____ 40. Uncle Joe often tells stories that seems long and pointless, but we respect him too much to complain.

Brief Writing Assignment: In a paragraph seven sentences long, describe your first hour on campus. Use only past and perfect tenses, and be sure that all subjects and verbs are in correct agreement.

As you learned in Lesson 1, a pronoun is a word that substitutes for a noun or another pronoun. The word for which a pronoun stands is called the pronoun's **antecedent**:

> I called *Harry,* but *he* didn't answer. [*He* substitutes for *Harry. Harry* is the antecedent of *he.*]
>
> My *cap and scarf* were where I had left *them.* [The antecedent of *them* is the plural unit *cap and scarf.*]
>
> *I* will wash *my* car tomorrow.
>
> *One* of my friends is painting *his* house.
>
> *Three* of my friends are painting *their* houses.

To use pronouns effectively and without confusing your reader, you must follow two basic principles:

1. Establish a clear, easily identified relationship between a pronoun and its antecedent.
2. Make the pronoun and its antecedent agree in person, number, and gender.

Let us examine these requirements more fully.

ROLE OF ANTECEDENTS

Personal pronouns should have definite antecedents and should be placed as near their antecedents as possible. Your readers should know exactly what a pronoun stands for. They should not be made to look through several sentences for a pronoun's antecedent, nor should they be asked to manufacture an antecedent for a pronoun. When you discover in your writing a pronoun with no clear and unmistakable antecedent, your revision, as many of the following examples demonstrate, will often require rewriting to remove the faulty pronoun from your sentence.

Faulty:	A strange car followed us closely, and *he* kept blinking his lights at us.
Improved:	A strange car followed us closely, and the driver kept blinking his lights at us.

Faulty:	Although Jenny was a real sports fan, her brother never became interested in *them.*
Improved:	Although Jenny really liked sports, her brother never became interested in them.

Faulty:	Mike is an excellent typist although he never took a course in *it.*
Improved:	Mike is an excellent typist although he never took a course in typing.

The indefinite *you* or *they* is quite common in speech and in chatty, informal writing, but one should avoid using either in serious writing:

Faulty:	In Alaska *they* catch huge king crabs.
Improved:	In Alaska huge king crabs are caught. [Often the best way to correct an indefinite *they* or *you* sentence is to use a passive verb.]

Faulty:	Before the reform measures were passed, *you* had few rights.
Improved:	Before the reform measures were passed, people had few rights.
	Before the reform measures were passed, one had few rights.

Faulty:	At the hotel *they* gave me a registration form.
Improved:	A clerk at the hotel gave me a registration form.
	At the hotel I was given a registration form.

A pronoun should not appear to refer equally well to either of two antecedents:

| **Faulty:** | Frank told Bill that *he* needed a haircut. [Which one needed a haircut?] |
| **Improved:** | "You need a haircut," said Frank to Bill. [In sentences of this type, the direct quotation is sometimes the only possible correction.] |

Avoid the Indefinite *It*

The "it says" or "it said" introduction to statements, although common in informal language, is objectionable in serious writing because the *it* has no antecedent. (See Supplement.)

| **Faulty:** | *It* says in the directions that the powder will dissolve in hot water. |
| **Improved:** | The directions say that the powder will dissolve in hot water. |

| **Faulty:** | *It* said on the morning news program that a bad storm is coming. |
| **Improved:** | According to the morning news program, a bad storm is coming. |

Avoid Unclear References

Avoid vague or ambiguous reference of relative and demonstrative pronouns.

| **Faulty:** | Only 20 people attended the lecture, *which* was due to poor publicity. |
| **Improved:** | Because of poor publicity, only 20 people attended the lecture. |

| **Faulty:** | Good writers usually have large vocabularies, and *this* is why I get poor grades on my papers. |
| **Improved:** | I get poor grades on my papers because my vocabulary is inadequate; good writers usually have large vocabularies. |

Special Cases: *Which, This, That*

Sometimes the antecedent of the pronouns *which*, *this*, and *that* is an idea rather than the expressed noun. In a sentence such as "The children giggled, *which* annoyed the teacher" or "The children giggled, and *this* annoyed the teacher," what annoyed the teacher is not the *children* but "the giggling of the children" or "the fact that the children giggled." This kind of reference to a preceding idea rather than to an expressed noun is unobjectionable provided that the meaning is instantly and unmistakably clear. But you should avoid sentences like those shown below. In the first example, readers would be hard-pressed to discover exactly what the *which* means, and in the second, they must decide whether the antecedent is the preceding idea or the noun immediately preceding the *which*:

Faulty:	Hathaway's application was rejected because he spells poorly, *which* is very important in an application letter.
Improved:	Hathaway's application was rejected because he spells poorly; correct spelling is very important in an application letter.
Faulty:	The defense attorney did not object to the judge's concluding remark, *which* surprised me.
Improved:	I was surprised that the defense attorney did not object to the judge's concluding remark.

PRONOUN AGREEMENT

Personal pronouns have separate forms for the three cases, subjective, objective, and possessive. These forms change for each person and number. The chart below displays these forms:

	Subjective	*Objective*	*Possessive*
First Person	I, we	me, us	mine, my
Second Person	you	you	yours, your
Third Person	he/she/it, they	him/her/it, them	his/hers/its, ours

Note the second form in the possessive precedes the noun and functions as an adjective. These forms are sometimes called pronominal adjectives. Thus we say

Pronouns	*Pronominal Adjectives*
That book is *mine*.	That is *my* book.
That book is *yours*.	That is *your* book.
That book is *hers*.	That is *her* book.

The rule for pronouns and pronominal adjectives is quite simple: They agree with their antecedents in person, number, and gender.

> Dad says that *he* is sure that *his* new friend will visit *him* soon.
> Dad and Mother say that *they* are sure that *their* new friend will visit *them* soon.

This principle of logical pronoun agreement is not as simple as these two examples might suggest. Recent language practices have given rise to two situations for which it is impossible to make rules that apply in every instance. Student writers must, first, be aware of certain changing ideas about pronoun usage; they must then prepare themselves to make decisions among the choices available.

Indefinite Pronouns

The first of these two troublesome situations relates to some of the indefinite pronouns: *one, everyone, someone, no one, anyone, anybody, everybody, somebody, nobody, each, either,* and *neither.* These words have generally been felt to be singular; hence, pronouns and pronominal adjectives referring to them have customarily been singular and, unless the antecedent specifies otherwise, masculine. Singular pronouns have also been used in formal writing and speaking to refer to noun antecedents modified by singular qualifiers such as *each* and *every*. The following examples illustrate the traditional, formal practice:

> Everybody has *his* faults and *his* virtues.
>
> Each of the sons is doing what *he* thinks is best.
>
> England expects every man to do *his* duty.
>
> No one succeeds in this firm if Dobbins doesn't like *him*.

The principal difficulty with this usage is that these indefinites, although regarded by strict grammarians as singular in form, carry with them a group or plural sense, with the result that people are often unsure whether pronouns referring to them should be singular or plural. Despite traditional pronouncements, every day we hear sentences of the "Everyone-will-do-*their*-best" type. Beginning writers, however, would do well to follow the established practice until they feel relatively secure about recognizing the occasional sentence in which a singular pronoun referring to an indefinite produces a strained or unnatural effect even though it agrees in form with its antecedent.

Gender Issues

Closely related to this troublesome matter of pronoun agreement is the second problem, gender. What reference words should be used to refer to such a word as *student*? Obviously there are both female students and male students. Plural nouns present no problem; *they*, *their*, and *them* refer to both masculine and feminine. Singular nouns take *she*, *hers*, *her* and *he*, *his*, *him*, but no pronoun refers to third-person singular words that contain either male or female members.

Here again, as with the reference to third-person singular indefinites, the traditional practice has been to use masculine singular pronouns. More than one hundred years ago, Henry James wrote the following sentence: "We must grant the artist his subject, his idea, his *donné*; our criticism is applied only to what he makes of it." In James's day, that sentence was undoubtedly looked upon as unexceptionable; the pronouns followed what was then standard practice. But attitudes have changed. These days, if that sentence got past the eyes of an editor and appeared on the printed page, its implication that artists are exclusively male would make the sentence unacceptably discriminatory to many readers.

Reliance on the *he or she* pronoun forms is an increasingly popular solution to some of these worrisome problems of pronoun reference. The *he or she* forms agree in number with the third-person singular indefinites, and the use of these forms obviates any possible charge of gender preference. However, excessive use of *he or she*, *his or her*, and *him or her* is undesirable. (Notice the cumbersome result, for instance, if a *he or she* form is substituted for all four of the third-person singular masculine pronouns in the Henry James sentence.)

Here is an important point to remember: When you are worried about a third-person singular masculine pronoun you have written, either because its reference to an indefinite antecedent does not sound quite right to you or because it shows an undesirable gender preference, you can remove the awkwardness, in nearly every instance that arises, by changing the antecedent to a plural noun, to which you then refer by using *they*, *their*, and *them*.

By way of summary, study these four versions of a sentence as they relate to the two problems just discussed:

Every member of the graduating class, if *he* wishes, may have *his* diploma mailed to *him* after August 15. [This usage reflects traditional practice that is still quite widely followed. The objection to it is that the reference words are exclusively masculine.]

Every member of the graduating class, if *he or she* wishes, may have *his or her* diploma mailed to *him or her* after August 15. [The singular reference is satisfactory, but the avoidance of masculine reference has resulted in clumsy wordiness.]

Every member of the graduating class, if *they* wish, may have *their* diplomas mailed to *them* after August 15. [This version, particularly if used in spoken English, would probably not offend many people, but the lack of proper number agreement between the pronouns and the antecedent would rule out its appearance in edited material.]

Members of the graduating class, if they wish, may have their diplomas mailed to them after August 15. [In this version the pronouns are logical and correct in both number and gender.]

A few other matters of pronoun reference, mercifully quite uncomplicated, should be called to your attention. If a pronoun refers to a compound unit or to a noun that may be either singular or plural, the pronoun agrees in number with the antecedent. (See Lesson 22, Rule 6.)

Wilson and his wife arrived in *their* new car.

Neither Jill nor Martha has finished *her* term paper.

The rest of the lecture had somehow lost *its* point.

The rest of the workers will receive *their* money soon.

The 8 o'clock class has *its* test tomorrow.

The 10 o'clock class finished writing *their* themes.

Beware of *You*

An antecedent in the third person should not be referred to by the second person *you*. This misuse develops when writers, forgetting that they have established the third person in the sentence, shift the structure and begin to talk directly to the reader:

Faulty:	In a large university a *freshman* can feel lost if *you* have grown up in a small town.
Improved:	In a large university a freshman can feel lost if he or she has grown up in a small town.
Faulty:	If a *person* really wants to become an expert golfer, *you* must practice every day.
Improved:	If a person really wants to become an expert golfer, *she or he* must practice every day.

SUPPLEMENT

At this point, you should be reminded that *it* without an antecedent has some uses that are completely acceptable in both formal and informal English. One of these is in the delayed subject or object pattern. (See Lesson 10.) Another is its use as a kind of filler word in expressions having to do with weather, time, distance, and so forth.

It is fortunate that you had a spare tire.

I find *it* difficult to believe Ted's story.

It is cold today; *it* snowed last night.

It is 12 o'clock; *it* is almost time for lunch.

How far is *it* to Phoenix?

English Fundamentals Online

After you have completed the Practice Sheets and Exercises in this lesson, you can find additional help and drill work at **MyWritingLab.com**, in the sections on Pronoun Reference; Pronoun Agreement.

NAME _____ SCORE _____

Directions: One sentence in each of the following pairs is correct, the other contains at least one pronoun that is vaguely or incorrectly used. In the space at the left, write the letter that identifies the correct sentence. In the other sentence, circle the pronoun or pronouns that have vague or incorrect reference.

_____ 1. a. My sister works out faithfully almost every day, and this is because she lost some weight recently and wants to keep it off.
  b. My sister works out faithfully almost every day because she recently lost some weight and wants to keep it off.

_____ 2. a. The two students at the back of the room were whispering and giggling, and the noise annoyed the instructor and the other students at the front of the room.
  b. The two students at the back of the room were whispering and giggling, which annoyed the instructor and the students at the front of the room.

_____ 3. a. The Department of Transportation is doing its best to finish work on that access ramp so that drivers can enjoy a faster ride to their destinations.
  b. The Department of Transportation is doing their best to finish work on that access ramp so that everyone can enjoy a faster ride to their destinations.

_____ 4. a. All the members of the campus newspaper staff will have to work their very hardest to get this edition out on time.
  b. Every member of the campus newspaper staff will have to work their very hardest to get it out on time.

_____ 5. a. In the southern part of the country, raising oranges and other citrus fruit is commercially successful because the climate is well suited to it.
  b. In the southern part of the country, raising oranges and other citrus fruit is commercially successful because the climate is well suited to those crops.

_____ 6. a. Walt told Matt, "I need to do some extensive training and lose some weight before the start of baseball practice."
  b. Walt told Matt that he needed to do some extensive training and lose some weight before the start of baseball practice.

_____ 7. a. A car turned into the driveway, and he left the lights on when he got out of it and walked up to the house.
  b. A car turned into the driveway, and the driver left the lights on when he got out of the car and walked up to the house.

_____ 8. a. A very small crowd showed up for the soccer game because this week is exam week and the weather is cold and rainy.
  b. A very small crowd showed up for the soccer game, probably because it is exam week and the weather is cold and rainy.

_____ 9. a. The announcer on the morning news said that a line of severe squalls is approaching the city, so drivers need to exercise caution out on the streets.
  b. It said on the morning news that a line of severe squalls is approaching the city, which means we need to exercise caution out on the streets.

_____ 10. a. Does anyone in this room remember their first day on campus when it was all confusing and a little frightening?

   b. Does anyone in this room remember his or her first day on campus when everything was confusing and a little frightening?

_____ 11. a. On the screen of my computer it said that it is no longer protected against viruses and other threats to its data.

   b. A message on the screen of my computer said that the computer is no longer protected against viruses and other threats to the data in the computer.

_____ 12. a. Al recently ordered two novels from an online distributor, and they are shipping them today.

   b. Al recently ordered two novels from an online distributor, and the company is shipping the books today.

_____ 13. a. Guides told me that people are catching large fish near that small island off the point on the north end of the lake.

   b. They say that they are catching large fish near that small island off the point on the north end of the lake.

_____ 14. a. When I went to register for my classes for next term, the clerk told me I needed a signature from one of the departments, so I could not register that day.

   b. When I went to register for my classes for next term, they told me I needed a signature from one of the departments, and they said I could not register that day.

_____ 15. a. John had a flat tire this morning on his way to the campus, which made him late for one of his classes.

   b. John's car had a flat tire on the way to the campus this morning, and so he was late for one of his classes.

_____ 16. a. Every student at the college has their own strengths and weaknesses, and each has his own particular interests.

   b. All students at the college have their own strengths and weaknesses, and they all have their own particular interests.

_____ 17. a. "It is 1:30 P.M. and it is well past lunch time. Has everyone been out to get their lunch yet?" asked the manager.

   b. "It is 1:30 P.M. and it is well past lunch time. Have you all been out to get your lunch yet?" asked the manager.

_____ 18. a. If anyone tries to access the Internet this morning, you'll find that our system is down and you won't be able to use it.

   b. If you try to access the Internet this morning, you will find that our system is down and you won't be able to search the Web.

_____ 19. a. It is difficult for people to advance in this company if they do not have the approval and support of George Walsh.

   b. It is difficult for anyone to advance in this firm if they do not have the approval and support of George Walsh.

_____ 20. a. It says in this article on job availability that in the future you might find that jobs such as accountant and radiologist will be outsourced to other countries.

   b. This article on job availability says that in the future jobs such as accountant and radiologist might be outsourced to other countries.

NAME _____   SCORE _____

Directions: In the space at the left, copy the correct pronoun or pronoun–verb combination given in the parentheses. Circle the antecedent of the pronoun.

_____ 1. At the end of the sports banquet, the coaches will hand each player (his or her, their) letter and a jacket.

_____ 2. Each of the men leaving the factory at the end of the shift punched (his, their) identification number into the time clock to show that he had left.

_____ 3. The nominating committee will decide this afternoon whom (it wants, they want) to nominate for membership for this year.

_____ 4. Every one of the people in my class (insists, insist) that he or she studied very hard for today's test.

_____ 5. "Not one of my students (has, have) been able to solve that problem; it's much too complicated for any of them to solve," gloated the instructor.

_____ 6. "You may borrow one of the ATV's," said the farmer, "but you need to return (it, them) by noon tomorrow."

_____ 7. "If anyone has an A average at the end of the term," said the professor, "I will exempt (him or her, them) from taking the final exam."

_____ 8. The people who came into my office this morning certainly used great imagination in making up (his, their) story.

_____ 9. All of the candidates for that job studied engineering when (he was, they were) in college.

_____ 10. The members of the Executive Committee will be wise if (it selects, they select) Mark Hudson as the new vice president.

_____ 11. In that large clothing store, every customer can find items to suit (his or her, their) taste and budget.

_____ 12. The counselor said that each of us (needs, need) to select a major early in this term.

_____ 13. All of the citizens in this township (has, have) to make a decision about their choices for township council.

_____ 14. Every man in this office (tries, try) his best to meet the boss's deadlines, but sometimes they are impossibly short.

_____ 15. All of us in this office (tries, try) to meet the boss's deadlines, but sometimes they are impossibly short.

Directions: Each sentence contains a problem related to the use of a pronoun. Rewrite enough of the sentence to eliminate the problems.

1. Meg told her sister that she needs to buy a new textbook for biology class.

   _____

2. Drivers who take wrong turns downtown expect that they will give you directions if you stop and ask.

   _____

3. A blue car came up behind us on the road, and he flashed his lights at us to suggest we move over.

   _____

4. It said on the weather report this morning that showers will follow us as you go across the state for the tournament.

   _____

5. Only a few people showed up for the work project this morning, which was probably due to the bad weather the night before.

   _____

6. Everyone has their eyes focused on the pitcher, and they all wonder why he can't throw strikes.

   _____

7. They say that you have to be careful driving through that small town because they might give you a speeding ticket.

   _____

8. I have trouble running fast because of my short legs, which is why I never enter any events that require you to run.

   _____

9. At the registration for today's meeting, they gave everyone a ticket so you could get a free lunch at noon.

   _____

10. Everyone should bring their notebooks to tomorrow's session, and you should be ready to take notes on this important subject.

    _____

Brief Writing Assignment: Using only second-person pronouns, write a five-sentence paragraph explaining why a friend should go with you to the next volleyball game. Work carefully to produce proper reference and agreement for all pronouns.

In Lesson 23, the chart on page 245 classifies the personal pronouns on the basis of person, number, and gender. The three forms that are listed there for each person—first, second, and third, singular and plural—illustrate the three cases nouns and pronouns fall into: nominative, possessive, and objective. *I* and *they* are nominative, *my* and *their* are possessive, and *me* and *them* are objective, for example.

The way you use these pronouns in everyday language, in sentences such as "Two of *my* books have disappeared; *they* cost *me* 20 dollars, and *I* must find *them*," demonstrates that the case form you choose depends on how the word is used within the sentence. In this lesson we examine instances where the wrong choice of pronoun form is possible.

The only words in modern English that retain distinctions between nominative and objective case forms are the first- and third-person personal pronouns and the relative pronouns *who* and *whoever*. In nouns, the nominative and objective forms are identical, and the correct use of the one distinctive form, the possessive, requires essentially only a knowledge of how the apostrophe is used. (See Lesson 19.)

Here are the pronouns arranged according to their case forms. The first eight are the personal pronouns; notice that the only distinctive form of *you* and *it* is the possessive. The last three pronouns, which we examine separately from the personal pronouns, are used only in questions and in subordinate clauses. (See Supplement for a discussion of *which* in the possessive case.)

Nominative	Possessive	Objective
I	my, mine	me
you	your, yours	you
he	his, his	him
she	her, hers	her
it	its, its	it
we	our, ours	us
you	your, yours	you
they	their, theirs	them
which		which
who	whose	whom
whoever	whosever	whomever

PERSONAL PRONOUNS IN THE POSSESSIVE CASE

The **possessive case** is used to show possession. Note that the first form in each of the listings of the possessives (*my* and all the rest) is actually an adjective formed from the possessive pronoun and is properly called a *pronominal adjective*. Pronominal adjectives modify nouns in the same way as any other adjective, but they also follow the rules of reference and agreement that govern pronouns.

253

This is *your* seat; *mine* is in the next row.

Jane preferred *my* cookies; some of *hers* were burned.

Their product is good, but the public prefers *ours*.

Indefinite Pronouns

The indefinite pronouns use an apostrophe to form the possessive case: *everybody's* duty, *one's* lifetime, *everyone's* hopes, someone *else's* car. But the personal pronouns do not.

These seats are *ours* [not *our's*]. *Yours* [not *Your's*] are in the next row.

Learn to distinguish carefully between the following possessives and contractions that are pronounced alike: *its* (possessive), *it's* (it is, it has); *theirs* (possessive), *there's* (there is, there has); *their* (possessive), *they're* (they are); *whose* (possessive), *who's* (who is, who has); *your* (possessive), *you're* (you are):

It's obvious that the car has outlived *its* usefulness.

There's new evidence that *they're* changing *their* tactics.

Possessive Pronouns with Gerunds

Formal usage prefers the possessive form of pronouns (occasionally of nouns also) preceding gerunds in constructions like the following:

He was unhappy about *my* [not *me*] voting for the bill.

Her report led to *our* [not *us*] buying additional stock.

Chad boasted about his *son's* [not *son*] having won the scholarship.

It is important to note that a very similar construction employing a participle uses the objective case, not the possessive.

We watched *him* walking down the street.

PERSONAL PRONOUNS IN THE NOMINATIVE AND OBJECTIVE CASES

The rules governing the uses of the other two cases are simple. A pronoun is in the **nominative case** when it is used

1. As a subject: *They* suspected that *he* was lying.
2. As a subjective complement: This is *she* speaking.
3. As an appositive of a nominative noun: *We* editors help young writers.

A pronoun is in the **objective case** when it is used

1. As an object of a verb or verbal: Ted told *her* the news. We enjoyed meeting *them*.
2. As an object of a preposition: Everyone except *me* had left the room.
3. As the subject of an infinitive: The police officer ordered *me* to halt.
4. As an appositive of an objective noun: Three of *us* truck drivers stopped to help.

We need not examine in detail every one of these applications. As people become more adept at using the English language, they learn that such usages as "*Them* arrived late" and "I spoke to *she*" do not conform to the system of the language. Instead, we should examine the trouble spots where confusion may arise.

When you use the nominative and objective personal pronouns, exercise care in the following situations.

A Pronoun as Part of a Compound Unit

When the pronoun follows *and* (sometimes *or*) as part of a compound unit, determine its use in the sentence and choose the appropriate case form. The temptation here is usually to use the nominative, although the last example in the following list shows a trouble spot where the objective case is sometimes misused. If you test these troublesome constructions by using the pronoun by itself, you will often discover which form is the correct one:

The man gave Sue and *me* some candy. [Not: Sue and *I*. Both words are indirect objects. Apply the test. Notice how strange "The man gave . . . *I* some candy" sounds.]

Send your check to either my lawyer or *me*. [Not: to . . . *I*.]

Have you seen Bob or *her* lately? [Direct objects require the objective case.]

Just between you and *me*, the lecture was a bore. [Never say "between you and *I*." Both pronouns are objects of the preposition *between*. If this set phrase is a problem for you, find the correct form by reversing the pronouns: You would never say "between *I* and you."]

Ms. Estes took *him* and *me* to school.
[Not *he* and *I* or *him* and *I*. Both pronouns are direct objects.]

Will my sister and *I* be invited? [Not *me*. The subject is *sister* and *I*.]

Comparisons After "As" and "Than"

In comparisons after *as* and *than*, when the pronoun is the subject of an understood verb, use the nominative form:

He is taller than *I* [*am*]. I am older than *he* [*is*].
Can you talk as fast as *she* [*can talk*]?
No one knew more about art than *he* [*did*].

Sentences like these nearly always call for nominative case subjects. Occasionally the meaning of a sentence may demand an objective pronoun. Both of the following sentences are correct; notice the difference in meaning:

You trust Mr. Alton more than *I*. [Meaning ". . . more than I (trust Mr. Alton)".]
You trust Mr. Alton more than *me*. [Meaning ". . . more than (you trust) me."]

"It is" Expressions

Ordinarily, use the nominative form for the subjective complement. The specific problem here concerns such expressions as *It's me, It is I, It was they*, or *It was them*. Many people say *It's me*, but they would hesitate to say *It was her, It was him*, or *It was them*, instead of *It was she*, *It was he*, or *It was they*. However, this problem does not arise often in the writing of students. The following are examples of correct formal usage:

> It is *I*.
> It could have been *he*.
> Was it *she*?
> Was it *they* who called?

"We" Versus "Us" and "I" Versus "Me"

An appositive should be in the same case as the word that it refers to. Notice particularly the first three examples that follow. This usage employing *we* and *us* as an appositive modifier preceding a noun is a real trouble spot:

> *We* boys were hired. [The unit *We boys* is the subject and requires the nominative.]
> Two of *us* boys were hired. [The object of a preposition requires the objective case.]
> Mr. Elder hired *us* boys. [Not *we boys* for a direct object.]
> Two boys—you and *I*—will be hired. [In apposition with the subject.]
> Mr. Elder will hire two boys—you and *me*. [In apposition with the object.]

PROBLEMS WITH *WHO* AND *WHOM*

The only other pronouns in standard modern English that have distinctive nominative, possessive, and objective forms are *who/whose/whom* and *whoever/whosever/whomever*. (See Supplement.) The rules that apply to the personal pronouns apply to these words as well: In the subject position *who/whoever* should be used; in the direct object position *whom/whomever* should be used; and so forth. (These pronouns, it should be noted, are never used as appositives.)

The special problem in the application of the case rules to these words comes from their use as interrogatives and as subordinating words. As you learned in Lessons 6, 9, and 10, these words, because they serve as signal words, always stand at the beginning of their clauses.

To locate the grammatical function of the pronoun within its clause, you must examine the clause to determine the normal subject–verb–complement positioning.

Direct Object or Object of a Preposition

In formal usage, *whom* is required when it is a direct object or the object of a preposition, even though it stands ahead of its subject and verb:

> *Whom* did Mr. Long hire?
> [If you are troubled by this sort of construction, try substituting a personal pronoun and placing it after the verb, where it normally comes: "Did Mr. Long hire *him*?" You would never say "Did Mr. Long hire *he*?" The transitive verb *hire* requires a direct object pronoun in the objective case.]
> He is a boy *whom* everyone can like. [*Whom* is the object of *can like*.]
> Wilson was the man *whom* everybody trusted. [Everybody trusted *whom*.]
> She is the girl *whom* Mother wants me to marry. [object of the verbal *to marry*]
> *Whom* was she speaking to just then? [To *whom* was she speaking?]

Beginning a Subordinate Clause

When *who(m)* or *who(m)ever* begins a subordinate clause that follows a verb or a preposition, the use of the pronoun *within its own clause* determines its case form:

We do not know *who* broke the window.

[*Who* is the subject of *broke*, not the direct object of *do know*.]

No one knows *who* the intruder was.

[*Who* is the subjective complement in the noun clause.]

We do not know *whom* the police have arrested.

[The objective form *whom* is used because it is the direct object of *have arrested*. The direct object of *do know* is the whole noun clause.]

I will sell the car to *whoever* offers the best price.

[The whole clause, *whoever offers the best price*, is the object of the preposition *to*. *Whoever* is the subject of *offers*. The subject of a verb must be in the nominative case.]

After a Parenthetical Insertion

When the pronoun subject is followed by a parenthetical insertion like *do you think*, *I suspect*, *everyone believes*, or *we know*, the nominative case form must be used:

Who do you think *has* the best chance of winning?

[*Who* is the subject of *has*. The *do you think* is a parenthetical insertion.]

Jenkins is the one *who* I suspect *will make* the best impression.

[Determine the verb that goes with the pronoun. If you are puzzled by this type of sentence, try reading it this way: "Jenkins is the one *who will make* the best impression—I suspect."]

But if the pronoun is not the subject of the verb, the objective form should be used:

He is an achiever *whom* I suspect you will eventually envy.

[*Whom* is the direct object of *will envy*.]

SUPPLEMENT

The chart on page 253 shows that the pronoun *which* has no possessive case form, a situation that brings about a minor problem of word choice. As you learned when you studied the adjective clause, *who(m)* normally refers to persons and *which* to things. But *whose* may be used in an adjective clause as the possessive form of *which* to refer to a nonhuman antecedent:

It is a disease *whose* long-term effects are minor.

If *whose* is not used in such a sentence, the "of which" form must be used, producing a perfectly correct but cumbersome sentence:

It is a disease the long-term effects *of which* are minor.

SUMMARY OF CORRECT PRONOUN USE

1. A pronoun should have a clearly identified antecedent with which it agrees in person, number, and gender.

2. Be aware of the special problem of pronoun reference to third-person singular antecedents that include both masculine and feminine members—pronouns like *everybody* and *someone* and nouns like *person, student, employee*, and so on. *Note*: Using a plural rather than a singular antecedent is one obvious way of avoiding this problem.

3. Use nominative forms of pronouns for subjects, subjective complements, and appositives that rename nominative nouns. Use objective forms of pronouns for objects of verbs or prepositions, subjects of infinitives, and appositives that rename objective nouns.

4. Be aware of a particular pronoun problem when a personal pronoun is tied to a noun or another pronoun by *and* or *or*:

   Mickey and I [not *Mickey and me*] were sent to the principal's office.

   Mr. Case sent *Mickey and me* [not *Mickey and I*] to the principal's office.

   And so, neighbors, please vote for *Ms. Stone and me* [not *Ms. Stone and I*].

5. Remember that the case of *who* is determined by its use in its own clause. It may be a direct object that precedes the subject [*Whom* has your wife invited?] or a subject immediately following a verb or a preposition [We wonder *who* will win. Our dog is friendly with *whoever* pets it.].

English Fundamentals Online

After you have completed the Practice Sheets and Exercises in this lesson, you can find additional help and drill work at **MyWritingLab.com**, in the section on Pronoun Case.

NAME _____   SCORE _____

Directions: Each italicized pronoun in these sentences is correctly used. In the space at the left, write one of the following numbers to identify the use of the pronoun.

1. subject
2. subjective complement
3. appositive modifier of nomina- tive noun

4. direct or indirect object
5. object of preposition
6. appositive modifier of objective noun

_____ 1. Grandmother always sent my sister and *me* beautiful birthday cards.

_____ 2. *We* volunteers support Senator Walters' campaign.

_____ 3. All of *us* volunteers support Senator Walters' campaign.

_____ 4. Martha hinted broadly that she could have handled the situation better than *I*.

_____ 5. Pioneer Day trophies will be given to *whoever* has the longest beard, the red- dest beard, and the most unusual beard.

_____ 6. Just between you and *me*, I suspect that many coworkers were happy to see him leave.

_____ 7. Joe Parker, Jim's 75-year-old grandfather, is a man *who*, his friends all report, is an extremely careful driver.

_____ 8. A young man assisted Mother and *me* across the busy street.

_____ 9. Marybeth is very timid; it couldn't have been *she* who sent that letter to the editor.

_____ 10. *Whom* do you suppose we overlooked when we sent out the ballots?

_____ 11. *Who* do you suppose was overlooked when we sent out the ballots?

_____ 12. Not one of *us* camp counselors can read music.

_____ 13. We all wondered *who* Linda's escort was.

_____ 14. Sophisticated people like you and *me* know better, of course.

_____ 15. The thief, *whoever* he was, obviously knew his way about the museum.

__2__ 16. The lucky prizewinners were Luke, Stanton, and *I*.

__5__ 17. The lucky prizewinners included Luke, Stanton, and *me*.

__5__ 18. Ms. Stubbs thought that the subcommittee should consist of her sister, her cousin, and *her*.

__4__ 19. We haven't been told *whom* the mayor is considering for the post.

__1__ 20. We haven't been told *who* is being consider for the post.

Directions: In the space at the left, copy the correct pronoun from within the parentheses.

_____ 1. Larry adamantly refused to tell the judge (who, whom) his companions had been.

_____ 2. The coach asked three of (we, us) tallest boys to carry the flags in the parade.

_____ 3. (You, Your) arriving on time for that meeting is very important in the eyes of the boss.

_____ 4. The captain told the coach that the hardest working players are Robbie, Joe, and (I, me).

_____ 5. Can you prove that the lost article is really (yours, your's)?

_____ 6. The public needs to be protected against car salesmen as unscrupulous as (he, him) and his partner.

_____ 7. The defeated candidate promised to cooperate with (whoever, whomever) is elected.

_____ 8. The defeated candidate promised to cooperate with (whoever, whomever) the voters elect.

_____ 9. Sensible people like you and (I, me) would never take a chance on such a wild scheme as this one.

_____ 10. It is (nobodys, nobody's) fault but your own.

_____ 11. I admit that (we, us) men were not interested in the lecture.

_____ 12. I admit that some of (we, us) men were not interested in the lecture.

_____ 13. I predict real trouble for the person (whose, who's) car is parked in the boss's reserved spot.

_____ 14. The coach said that girls as tall as Edie and (I, me) should try out for basketball.

_____ 15. Jenkins is the only person I've ever met (who, whom) I instantly trusted.

_____ 16. "I'll bet you ten dollars I can correctly predict (who, whom) the next heavyweight champion will be," boasted Lenny.

_____ 17. Nine sophomores and juniors, including my best friend and (I, me), make up the team.

_____ 18. If you aren't the person who set off the alarm, (who, whom) do you think it could have been?

_____ 19. On one of our trips to New York Aunt Lou took my sister and (I, me) to the Museum of Modern Art.

_____ 20. My old neighbor will tell endless stories about his fishing skills to (whoever, whomever) will listen to him.

Using Pronouns Correctly: Case

NAME _____   SCORE _____

Directions: If you find an incorrectly used pronoun, underline it and write the correct form in the space at the left. If a sentence is correct, leave the space blank. **Review:** In the first 10 items, circle the adjectives and put brackets around the adverbs.

_____ 1. As usual, the kitchen cleanup work was left to my sister and me.

_____ 2. Leonard boasted that none of us other fellows had worked as hard as him.

_____ 3. The old hermit would get out his shotgun and threaten whomever dared to walk across his property.

_____ 4. The small umbrella kept the doorman dry but not my escort or me.

_____ 5. Who do you suppose asked if she could go to the concert with you and I?

_____ 6. My sister Helen, who is ten years older than me, usually baby-sat with us younger children.

_____ 7. Regardless of who actually gave out the misinformation, all of us sales people must share the blame.

_____ 8. I hope you don't object to me turning off this lamp; it's shining in my eyes.

_____ 9. Here are the names of a few candidates whom I hope you will vote for next Tuesday.

_____ 10. This responsibility, Mr. Chairman, should be everybody's, not solely your's.

_____ 11. The news had been leaked to only three of us people in the office—Mr. Fisher, his secretary, and me.

_____ 12. Not one of us guests knew whom the masked man in the clown suit was.

_____ 13. Among those selected to serve were my office mate, a new man from the accounting department, and I.

_____ 14. The strained relations between Professor Watkins and I began at the very first meeting of the committee.

_____ 15. The bank president hired a bodyguard whom, we later learned, had once been awarded a medal for bravery.

_____ 16. While our car was in the repair shop, Mrs. Langley occasionally would let my wife or me use her's.

_____ 17. Senator Williams is one leader who's support in the campaign we desperately need.

_____ 18. Who do you think Jean will invite to her party?

_____ 19. Who do you think will be invited to Jean's party?

_____ 20. I told Lucas that I'd get a second opinion, if I were he.

_____ 21. All the girls at camp except Jennie and I were good swimmers.

_____ 22. Someone should have told one of we ushers that the main door was still locked.

_____ 23. Will your parents object to your dropping out of school for one semester?

_____ 24. "Who do you suggest that I vote for?" Valerie asked her father.

_____ 25. "Vote for whomever you think is the best candidate," her father replied.

_____ 26. "The record shows that the message was received by the office receptionist, not me," said the witness.

_____ 27. The bill will pass handily in the Senate, but it's fate in the House is uncertain.

_____ 28. My father-in-law is vacationing in Mexico; it couldn't have been he whom you saw at the auction.

_____ 29. Seated at the head table will be the club officers, the honored guests, and us hospitality committee members.

_____ 30. Jim admitted that there had been a mix-up in the ball handling between he and the quarterback.

_____ 31. Who is the main office sending to Toledo as your replacement?

_____ 32. Whom do you think your replacement in Toledo will be?

_____ 33. Everyone else's essays seemed much longer than those submitted by my roommate and me.

_____ 34. Mrs. Benham says that she worries about her father, whom she thinks is too old to be jogging and lifting weights.

_____ 35. None of us secretaries have been told who the new personnel director will be.

_____ 36. Don't worry about Martin; experienced woodsmen like he and his partner will surely find their way back to camp.

_____ 37. The new contract is popular with nearly everyone except we part-time hourly workers.

_____ 38. "Who's the classmate whose attendance record is better than your's?" Mr. Swift asked his daughter.

_____ 39. Every summer my uncle gave my cousin and me jobs on his farm.

_____ 40. The new office manager, whoever he is, will inherit some really troublesome problems.

NAME _____   SCORE _____

Directions: Circle the incorrect pronouns in each sentence. Then, in the space provided, rewrite enough of the sentence to show how you would correct problems with case and reference. No sentence contains more than two poorly used pronouns.

1. Ask James if he knows who's backpack is lying on the floor; Jane says it's not her's.

   _____

2. The receptionist told Mr. Robinson that you had to show a picture ID before they let him see the doctor.

   _____

3. Send this message to whomever you think has our report, and tell them to send it to us immediately.

   _____

4. Mary asked Gina if her sister had brought the notes from that last lecture in biology, the notes from the class that she missed.

   _____

5. It says on the news that you need to avoid Cross Street this morning because traffic will be especially heavy on that street.

   _____

6. "Choose whoever you want as a lab partner," said the lab assistant; "the choice is completely your's."

   _____

7. The boss asked we three programmers who we would choose as the head of the team for that new project.

   _____

8. My cousin says she will teach we three how to wakeboard if we are interested in it.

   _____

9. Every student needs their own computer, and the school should include them in the cost of tuition.

   _____

10. Al Hartley, whom most of you think should be our next COO, has better credentials for it than anyone else who has applied.

   _____

11. Joan is too short to reach those books, but Jim, whom is much taller than her, reached them easily.

_____

12. The dean told all we sophomores that you had to register early to be sure to get the classes that you need for this next term.

_____

13. My brothers, who you met at the last baseball game, bought my sister and I tickets for that great concert that's coming next month.

_____

14. The hostess poured everyone a cup of coffee, but they drank it immediately and asked for another cup.

_____

15. Will me turning in my part of that project late anger the others in the group, who have already finished it by now?

_____

16. You driving home during that snowstorm frightened all we family members, who worried intensely until you arrived at home.

_____

17. Every person who we tested passed with flying colors, but it makes us wonder if the test was valid.

_____

18. The snow is falling heavily, which, I guess, will keep most of our students from getting themself to the campus.

_____

19. It said on the news that the President is coming to town next week, so all we drivers need to plan to avoid his route from the airport.

_____

20. The boss is counting on us finishing that report so that he can take it with him when they go to the conference on Friday.

_____

Brief Writing Assignment: In a paragraph of six or seven sentences, narrate the story of a younger friend taking the driving test for a driver's license. Use the name of the friend and the evaluator just once; then use appropriate pronouns for the rest of the story. Take care to establish proper case, reference, and agreement for all the pronouns.

In Lesson 2, you learned that an adjective is a word that describes or limits a noun or a pronoun. You also learned that an adverb modifies a verb, an adjective, or another adverb. Many adverbs end in *ly*, such as *happily*, *beautifully*, and *extremely*. But some adjectives—*lovely*, *likely*, *deadly*, *neighborly*, and *homely*, for instance—also end in *ly*. Some adverbs do not end in *ly*, and these happen to be among the most frequently used words in speech and writing: *after, always, before, far, forever, here, not, now, often, quite, rather, soon, then, there, too, very*. Some words can be used either as adjectives or as adverbs, as the following examples show:

Adverbs	Adjectives
He came *close*.	That was a *close* call.
She talks too *fast*.	She's a *fast* thinker.
Hit it *hard*.	That was a *hard* blow.
She usually arrives *late*.	She arrived at a *late* hour.
He went *straight* to bed.	I can't draw a *straight* line.

Some adverbs have two forms, one without and one with the *ly*: *cheap, cheaply; close, closely; deep, deeply; hard, hardly; high, highly; late, lately; loud, loudly; quick, quickly; right, rightly; slow, slowly*. In some of these pairs the words are interchangeable; in most they are not. The idiomatic use of adverbs is a rather complex matter; no rules can be made that govern every situation. We can, however, make a few generalizations that reflect present-day practice.

1. The shorter form of a few of these—*late*, *hard*, and *near*, for example—fills most adverbial functions because the corresponding *ly* forms have acquired special meanings:

We must not stay *late*.	I have not seen him *lately* [recently].
I studied *hard* last night.	I *hardly* [scarcely] know him.
Winter is drawing *near*.	I *nearly* [almost] missed the last flight.

2. The *ly* form tends toward the formal, with the short form lending itself to more casual, informal speech and writing:

Informal	Formal
It fell *close* to the target.	You must watch him *closely*.
The child swung *high* over the water.	She was *highly* respected.
Drive *slow*!	Please drive more *slowly*.
Must you sing so *loud*?	He *loudly* denied the charges.
We searched far and *wide*.	She is *widely* known as an artist.

3. Because the short form seems more direct and forceful, it is often used in imperative sentences:

Hold *firm* to this railing.

"Come *quick*," yelled the officer.

4. The short form is often the one used when combined with an adjective to make a compound modifier preceding a noun:

a *wide*-ranging species	The species ranges *widely.*
a *slow*-moving truck	The truck moved *slowly.*

TYPICAL ADVERB/ADJECTIVE TROUBLE SPOTS

For the sake of simplifying the problem of the right use of adverbs and adjectives, we will point out the three main trouble spots here.

Misusing an Adjective for an Adverb

A word is an adverb if it modifies a verb, an adjective, or another adverb. The words that usually cause trouble here are *good, bad, well; sure, surely; real, really; most, almost; awful, awfully;* and *some, somewhat*:

Chip played *well* [not *good*] in the last game. [Modifies the verb *played.*]

This paint adheres *well* [not *good*] to concrete. [Modifies the verb *adheres.*]

Almost [not *Most*] every student has a job. [Modifies the adjective *every.*]

Today my shoulder is *really* [or *very*—not *real*] sore. [Modifies the adjective *sore.*]

He was driving *really* [or *very*—not *real*] fast. [Modifies the adverb *fast.*]

This rain has been falling *steadily* [not *steady*] for a week.

The champion should win his first match *easily* [not *easy*].

You'll improve if you practice *regularly* [not *regular*].

She wants that prize very *badly* [not *bad*].

Misusing Adverbs for Adjectives as Subjective Complements

The most common verb to take the subjective complement is *be*; fortunately, mistakes with this verb are nearly impossible. A few other verbs—like *appear, become, go, grow, prove, remain, seem, stay,* and *turn,* when they are used in a sense close to that of *be*—take subjective complements. This complement must be an adjective, not an adverb.

The house *seems empty.* [House *is* empty.]

Their plans *became apparent.* [Plans *were* apparent.]

The work *proved* very *hard.* [Work *was* hard.]

The adjective subjective complement is also used with another group of verbs, the so-called verbs of the senses. These are *feel, look, smell, sound,* and *taste*:

You shouldn't feel *bad* about this. [Not *badly.*]

His cough sounds *bad* this morning. [Not *badly.*]

At first our prospects looked *bad.* [Not *badly.*]

Doesn't the air smell *sweet* today? [Not *sweetly.*]

The verb *feel* is involved in two special problems. In the first place, it is often used with both *good* and *well.* These two words have different meanings; one is not a substitute for the other. When used with the verb *feel, well* is an adjective meaning "in good health." The adjective *good*, when used with *feel*, means "filled with a sense of vigor and excitement." Of course, both *well* and *good* have other meanings when used with other verbs. In the second place, the expression "I feel badly" is used so widely, especially in spoken English, that it can hardly be considered an error in usage. Many careful writers, however, prefer the adjective here, with the result that "feel bad" is usually found in written English.

Misusing a Comparative or a Superlative Form of a Modifier

Most adverbs are compared in the same way as adjectives. (For a discussion of the comparison of adjectives, see Lesson 2.) Some common adverbs cannot be compared, such as *here*, *now*, *then*, *when*, and *before*. As you learned in Lesson 16, we use the comparative degree (*taller, better, more intelligent, more rapidly*) in a comparison limited to two things. We use the superlative degree (*tallest, best, most intelligent, most rapidly*) for more than two things.

Two other problems, both of minor importance, are involved in comparisons. First, we do not combine the two forms (*more + er, most + est*) in forming the comparative and superlative degrees:

> Later the landlord became *friendlier* [not *more friendlier*].
> Please drive *slower* [not *more slower*].
> Please drive *more slowly* [not *more slower*].

Second, some purists object to the comparison of the so-called absolute qualities, such as *unique* ("being the only one"), *perfect*, *round*, *exact*, and so forth. They argue that, instead of such uses as *most perfect, straighter, more unique*, the intended meaning is *most nearly perfect, more nearly straight, more nearly unique*. General usage, however, has pretty well established both forms.

PROBLEMS WITH PREPOSITIONS

Three reminders should be made about the use of prepositions. One problem is the selection of the exact preposition for the meaning intended.

Idioms Using Prepositions

Many words, especially verbs and adjectives, give their full meaning only when modified by a prepositional phrase. In most cases, the meaning of the preposition dictates a logical idiom: to sit *on* a couch, to walk *with* a friend, to lean *against* a fence, and so on. For some more abstract concepts, however, the acceptable preposition may seem to have been selected arbitrarily. Here are a few examples of different meanings of different prepositions:

> agree *to* a proposal, *with* a person, *on* a price, *in* principle
> argue *about* a matter, *with* a person, *for* or *against* a proposition
> compare *to* to show likenesses, *with* to show differences [sometimes similarities]
> correspond *to* a thing, *with* a person
> differ *from* an unlike thing, *with* a person
> live *at* an address, *in* a house or city, *on* a street, *with* other people

Note: Good modern dictionaries provide information about and examples of the correct usage of prepositions.

Unnecessary Prepositions

Although at colloquial levels of language we sometimes find unnecessary prepositions used, examples like the following are improved in serious contexts if written without the words in brackets:

> I met [up with] your uncle yesterday.
>
> We keep our dog inside [of] the house.
>
> Our cat, however, sleeps outside [of] the house.
>
> The package fell off [of] the speeding truck.

Note that care must be taken to check the meanings of expressions that contain what might appear to be extra prepositions, such as "meet up with." The expression is colloquial but occurs regularly in speech and informal writing. The expression carries with it a connotation of a meeting that is both unplanned and brief. The expression "meet with" suggests a rather formal, almost businesslike meeting. In many cases, adding or dropping a preposition can change the meaning of a phrase significantly. Careful writers will play close attention to these changes in meaning and check a collegiate dictionary to be certain of meaning.

Avoid especially the needless preposition at the end of a sentence or the repeated preposition in adjective clauses and in direct or indirect questions:

> Where is your older brother *at*?
>
> He is one of the few people *to* whom I usually feel superior *to*.
>
> To what do you attribute your luck at poker *to*?
>
> [Use one *to* or the other, but not both.]

Repeated Prepositions in Compound Units

When two words of a compound unit require the same preposition to be idiomatically correct, the preposition need not be stated with the first unit:

> **Correct:**   We were both *repelled* and *fascinated by* the snake charmer's act.

But when the two units require different prepositions, both must be expressed:

> **Incomplete:**   The child shows an *interest* and a *talent for* music. [interest . . . for (?)]
>
> **Correct:**   The child shows an *interest in* and a *talent for* music.
>
> **Incomplete:**   I am sure that Ms. Lewis would both *contribute* and *gain from* a summer workshop. [contribute . . . from (?)]
>
> **Correct:**   I am sure that Ms. Lewis would both *contribute to* and *gain from* a summer workshop.

English Fundamentals Online

After you have completed the Practice Sheets and Exercises in this lesson, you can find additional help and drill work at **MyWritingLab.com**, in the section on Adjectives, Adverbs, and Modifiers.

Using Modifiers and Prepositions Correctly

NAME _____ SCORE _____

Directions: In the first space at the left, write the word (or words) that the italicized word modifies. In the second space, write *Adj.* if the italicized word is an adjective or *Adv.* if it is an adverb. Circle any incorrect prepositions.

_____ 1. Lydia accepted her prize and *quickly* left the stage.
_____

_____ 2. We shall expect a *quick* answer from you.
_____

_____ 3. "Come *quick!*" she shouted. "The roof is on fire!"
_____

_____ 4. Certainly you could have found a *better* spot for our picnic.
_____

_____ 5. The car sounds *better* now that I have had the engine tuned.
_____

_____ 6. The car runs *better* now that I have had the engine tuned.
_____

_____ 7. His behavior could hardly be called *gentlemanly*.
_____

_____ 8. We were surprised at his *unfriendly* manner.
_____

_____ 9. The invaders began a *fast* retreat from the coast.
_____

_____ 10. My little brother certainly is growing *fast*.
_____

_____ 11. The rising waters are growing more *dangerous* by the hour.
_____

_____ 12. Jerry followed the nurse's instructions *well*.
_____

_____ 13. Jerry has been ill, but he is now feeling *well*.
_____

_____ 14. Jerry felt *good* when he received the favorable report.
_____

_____ 15. Would this purple necktie look *good* with my green jacket?
_____

Directions: In the space at the left, copy the correct form given in the parentheses. **Review:** Underline the subjects and bracket the verbs of the first 10 sentences.

_____   1. The man looked at me and said, "Sir, I'm (near, nearly) famished."

_____   2. I'm afraid that my lawn will look quite (different, differently) when I return from vacation.

_____   3. Junior has been behaving quite (different, differently) since the officer reprimanded him.

_____   4. You'll very likely find that your expenses will be (considerable, considerably) higher than you had planned.

_____   5. These railings on the porch are weak; you'd better not lean (heavy, heavily) on them.

_____   6. Old Mr. Stubbs is one of the (kindest, most kindest) people I have every known.

_____   7. That untuned piano surely sounds (bad, badly).

_____   8. That piano (sure, surely) needs tuning.

_____   9. Of your two cars, which one gets the (better, best) gas mileage?

_____   10. Alice's mother squandered (almost, most) all of her money on the futile lawsuit.

_____   11. In this art appreciation class each student works (independent, independently) on a project.

_____   12. Everything on the boat seems to have been scrubbed and polished (good, well).

_____   13. "I can't take good notes. That teacher talks too (rapid, rapidly)," complained Art.

_____   14. Both of the finalists are good, but Jackman is the (more, most) experienced tournament player.

_____   15. The tent will not stay up unless the rope is pulled (tighter, more tighter).

_____   16. Mother asked Jane's boyfriend to drive more (careful, carefully) on the wet pavement.

_____   17. We all agreed that the play was (real, really) boring.

_____   18. "This wax will work equally (good, well) on your car," said the salesman.

_____   19. Grandmother looked (unhappy, unhappily) as the family departed.

_____   20. Grandmother looked (unhappy, unhappily) at the departing family.

NAME _____   SCORE _____

Directions: Rewrite the following sentences to eliminate problems with modifiers and prepositions.

1. I must confess that I felt badly when the results of the voting were announced at the meeting we were at.

   _____

2. The onlookers around the pool applauded loud when six-year-old Mark jumped off of the high-dive platform.

   _____

3. On Sunday mornings Mike starts real early and usually has delivered most all of his papers by six o'clock.

   _____

4. Lynn has responded good to all the tutoring; her grades in that course have noticeable improved.

   _____

5. Although we had washed the walls real well, they sure looked dirty when we had finished up.

   _____

6. Jim's little sister steadfast refused to tell him where she had hidden his car keys at.

   _____

7. If we try to work more faster, we should very easy finish this job in time for dinner.

   _____

8. I admit that, at the zoo, I was terrible afraid of but fascinated by the hooded cobra that was coiled at the front of the cage.

   _____

9. "I wish I could find a more easier way to fix this toy up for little Alex," said Dad weary.

   _____

10. We drove steady for five hours, but we were still real late for the meeting when we arrived at Syracuse.

   _____

11. You'll sleep good on this new mattress; it's much more firmer than the old one.

_____

12. That rose bush where you planted it at certainly complements the rest of the plantings in that impressive designed garden.

_____

13. Jackson felt surprisingly more energeticer than usual, and he worked until well after six o'clock.

_____

14. Unless traffic is unusual heavy, we should be able to get to where we need to be at by the end of the day.

_____

15. Only at that point did we full realize that we had not planned sufficient for this most difficult project.

_____

16. Jessie is a shy and quiet person with whom I rare feel comfortable with.

_____

17. "Can you tell me quick where can I buy those most tasty pastries at?" asked Julia.

_____

18. Allison's sprained ankle is bad swollen; it must be real painful to walk on.

_____

19. When the teacher walked into the classroom, the kids quieted down some, but they still whispered excited about the earlier fire drill.

_____

20. I had to work long and hard on that first essay, but more recent I have found the assignments a little bit more workable.

_____

Brief Writing Assignment: In six or seven sentences, describe yourself eating your favorite food. Include appeals to all five senses in the description. In each sentence use at least one adjective, one adverb, and one prepositional phrase.

Someone has said that the Inuit people have 18 easily differentiated words for snow, ranging from falling snow to a thin glaze of ice on water. In fact, there is considerable debate among language scholars and anthropologists about exactly how many words for snow exist in the languages that we think of as Eskimo. We need not engage in the debate about actual numbers to recognize that these people have an extensive, very precise vocabulary for what we call snow because snow is a vital part of their lives, indeed, of their survival. The choice of one word over another might, quite literally, be a matter of life and death. In English not many words have implications for survival, at least not words that we ordinarily use in polite society or more formal expressions.

But one of the beauties of the English language is its rich, broad, exceptionally precise vocabulary. In many languages one word is used to identify more than one object or condition. In Spanish, the word *piso* can mean what in English we identify as floor, the surface inside a room or building, but it can also be used to identify what in English we call ground, the level surfaces of dirt or grass that exist outside of buildings. The ability to take advantage of this rich, diverse vocabulary is one of the marks of a skilled speaker or writer of English. However, it is just this richness that sometimes requires extra attention to word choices if we are to express ourselves with precision and effectiveness, even forcefulness, to get our point across to listeners and readers.

This chapter deals with two classes of words that require some special attention if we are to be effective users of the language. The first category deals with what we ordinarily call *usage*, the standard way of expressing something in formal, academic, or business writing. This class deals with levels of language—formal, informal, colloquial, slang, and others— and it makes distinctions on the basis of appropriate word choices. For example, in informal or colloquial usage we might say that a person's performance was "pretty good," and we understand that to mean good enough, but not exceptional. In formal communication, we need to select a word that is more precise and more in keeping with the formality of the communication. So we might say the performance was adequate or acceptable.

This category also distinguishes between or among words that are similar in meaning but are used only when applied to certain words. For example, the words *number* and *amount* mean more or less the same thing, an idea related to quantity. But we usually use *amount* with materials that cannot be counted, so we say the *amount* of water in the barrel, but we say the *number* of people, because people can be counted. It is clear that we would rarely say the *number* of water in the barrel, but we sometimes hear people say the *amount* of people who came to the concert. This expression can be understood, but the use of the word *amount* identifies the user as someone who is less than careful in word choices. The goal of this chapter is to develop a sense for what is exactly right in a given situation because being exactly right conveys the precise meaning intended and shows that the person, as a regular practice, uses the language with care and precision.

The second category is more easily grasped, for it deals with words called homophones, words that sound the same when spoken but are not spelled the same way and do not have the same meaning. So the words *write*, *right*, and *rite* sound the same, a fact that requires a listener to ascertain the meaning from the context. A reader can do the same thing, distinguish among those meanings by context, but a wrong choice, especially from among more simple sets of words such as *to*, *too*, and *two*, identifies the writer, in the minds of many, as someone who is either careless or unskilled.

So then, the obvious question arises: If my reader "gets it" whether I use *to* or *too*, why are these distinctions important? They are important for two reasons:

They affect the precision and effectiveness of your writing.

They create an impression of you as a person, of your intelligence and your educational level.

Your use of language, the precision and effectiveness of your spoken and written communications, creates an impression. We can see this concept more clearly in choices of clothing. The most expensive, most stylish pair of board shorts by Billabong or Patagonia will look foolish in an uptown law office and brand the wearer as a person with some kind of strange notions about appropriate dress for an office. Likewise, a $2,000 blue pinstripe suit would probably fit in nicely in that law office but will seem completely out of place on a surfboard. So it is with language: We create an impression of intelligence, educational level, and judgment by the language we employ. The ability to use precise language, language carefully chosen for its meaning and its level, is a tool that we can use to great effect in our lives.

As soon as you move into even the lowest levels of management, you will find these language skills important.

USAGE

A, an. Use *a* when the word immediately following it is sounded as a consonant; use *an* when the next sound is a vowel sound: *a, e, i, o,* or *u* (*a* friend, *an* enemy). Remember that it is the consonantal or vowel *sound*, not the actual letter, that determines the choice of the correct form of the indefinite article: *a* sharp curve, *an* S-curve; *a* eulogy, *an* empty house; *a* hospital, *an* honest person; *a* united people, *an* uneven contest.

Ad. Clipped forms of many words are often used informally, such as *ad* (*advertisement*), *doc* (*doctor*), *exam* (*examination*), *gym* (*gymnasium*), *lab* (*laboratory*), *math* (*mathematics*), and *prof* (*professor*). Formal usage prefers the long forms.

Aggravate. In standard formal English the word means "make more severe," "make worse." Colloquially it means "annoy," "irritate," "exasperate."

> Walking on your sprained ankle will *aggravate* the hurt. [*Informal:* All criticism *aggravates* him.]

Ain't. Substandard for *am not, are not, is not, have not.*

> Am I *not* [not *Ain't I*] a good citizen?
>
> The command *hasn't* [not *hain't* or *ain't*] been given yet.
>
> They *are not* [not *ain't*] going either.

All the farther, all the faster, and the like. Generally regarded as colloquial equivalents of *as far as, as fast as,* and the like.

> This is *as far as* [not *all the farther*] I care to go.
>
> That was *as fast as* [not *all the faster*] he could run.

A lot. Always use as two words. See also *Lots of.*

A lot of. See *Lots of.*

Alright. This spelling, like *allright,* although often used in advertising, is generally regarded as very informal usage. The preferred form is *all right.*

In strictly formal usage, *satisfactory* or *very well* is preferred to *all right.*

> *Very well* [not *Alright*], you may ride in our car.
>
> The members agreed that the allocation of funds was *satisfactory* [not *all right*].

Among, between. *Among* is used with three or more persons or things, as in "Galileo was *among* the most talented people of his age," and "The estate was divided among his three sons." *Between* usually refers to two things, as in "between you and me," "between two points," "between dawn and sunset."

Amount, number. Use *number,* not *amount,* in reference to units that can actually be counted:

> the *amount* of indebtedness, the *number* of debts

And, etc. Because *etc.* (*et cetera*) means "and so forth," *and etc.* would mean "and and so forth." You should not use *etc.* to replace some exact, specific word, but if you do use it, be sure not to spell it *ect.* And remember that *etc.* requires a period after it.

Anywheres. Colloquial for *anywhere.* Similar colloquial forms are *anyways* for *anyway* or *anyhow, everywheres* for *everywhere, nowheres* for *nowhere, somewheres* for *somewhere.*

> I looked for my books *everywhere.*
>
> They must be hidden *somewhere.*

Apt to, liable to, likely to. *Apt to* implies a natural tendency. *Liable to* implies a negative outcome or result. *Likely to* suggests a strong possibility.

That car is *apt to* increase in value.

We are *liable to* have a bad leak unless we fix the roof.

The new vaccine is *likely to* cause a disappearance of chicken pox.

As, like. See *Like*.

As to whether. *Whether* is usually enough.

Awful, awfully. Like *aggravate*, these words have two distinct uses. In formal contexts, they mean "awe-inspiring" or "terrifying." Often in conversation and sometimes in writing of a serious nature, *awful* and *awfully* are mild intensifiers, meaning "very."

Because. See *Reason is because*.

Because of. See *Due to*.

Being that, being as how. Substandard for *because*, *as*, or *since*.

Beside, besides. These two prepositions are clearly distinguished by their meanings. *Beside* means "at the side of" and *besides* means "in addition to."

Lucy sits *beside* me in class.

Did anyone *besides* you see the accident?

Between. See *Among*.

Bring, take. *Bring* means to convey from a farther to a nearer place. *Take* means to convey from nearer to farther.

Bring home a loaf of bread from the store.

Take that book back to the library.

But what, but that. Colloquial for *that*.

Both sides had no doubt *that* [not *but what*] their cause was just.

Calculate, figure, reckon. These are colloquial for *imagine*, *consider*, *expect*, *think*, and similar words.

He must have *expected* [not *calculated*] that she might not be pleased to see him after he did not return her calls.

Can, may. *Can* suggests ability to do something. *May* is the preferred form when permission is involved.

Little Junior *can* already count to ten.

May [not *Can*] I borrow your pencil?

Can't hardly, couldn't hardly, can't scarcely, couldn't scarcely. Substandard for *can hardly*, *could hardly*, *can scarcely*, *could scarcely*. These are sometimes referred to as double negatives.

I *can hardly* [not *can't hardly*] believe that story.

We *could scarcely* [not *couldn't scarcely*] hear the foghorn.

Caused by. See *Due to*.

Consensus means an agreement of the majority; thus, *consensus of opinion* is redundant. Say simply, "The consensus was . . .," not, "The consensus of opinion was . . . ."

Continual, continuous. A fine distinction in meaning can be made if you remember that *continual* means "repeated regularly and frequently" and that *continuous* means "occurring without interruption," "unbroken."

Could(n't) care less. This worn-out set phrase indicating total indifference is a colloquialism. A continuing marvel of language behavior is the large number of people who insist on saying "I could care less" when they obviously mean the opposite.

Could of, would of, might of, ought to of, and so on. Substandard for *could have*, *would have*, and so on.

Couple, couple of. These expressions are fine for informal conversation but not precise enough for more formal occasions. In writing, be specific. Say "three points," for example, "four issues," rather than "a couple of points/issues."

Criteria. The singular noun is *criterion*; the plural is *criteria* or *criterions*. Such combinations as "a criteria," "one criteria," and "these criterias" are incorrect.

Data. Originally the plural form of the rarely used Latin singular *datum*, *data* has taken on a collective meaning so that it is often treated as a singular noun. "This data has been published" and "These data have been published" are both correct, the latter being the use customarily found in scientific or technical writing.

Different from, different than. *Different from* is generally correct. Many people object to *different than*, but others use it, especially when a clause follows, as in "Life in the Marines was different than he had expected it to be."

Their customs are *different from* [not *different than*] ours.

Life in the Marines was *different from* what he had expected it to be.

Different to, a form sometimes used by British speakers and writers, is rarely used in the United States.

Disinterested, uninterested. Many users of precise English deplore the tendency to treat these words as loose synonyms, keeping a helpful distinction between *disinterested* ("impartial," "free from bias or self-interest") and *uninterested* ("lacking in interest," "unconcerned"). Thus we would hope that a referee would be disinterested but not uninterested.

Due to, caused by, because of, owing to. *Due to* and *caused by* are used correctly after the verb *to be*:

His illness was *caused by* a virus.

The flood was *due to* the heavy spring rains.

Many people object to the use of *due to* and *caused by* adverbially at the beginning of a sentence, as in "Due to the heavy rains, the streams flooded," and "Caused by the storm, the roads were damaged." It is better to use *because of* or *owing to* in similar situations. *Due to* and *owing to* are also used correctly as an adjective modifier immediately following a noun:

Accidents *due to* excessive speed are increasing in number.

Note in the examples what variations are possible:

The streams flooded *because of* the heavy rains.

The flooding of the streams was *due to* the heavy rains.

The floods were *caused by* the rapid melting of the snow.

Emigrate, immigrate. To *emigrate* is to *leave* one region to settle in another; to *immigrate* is to *enter* a region from another one.

Enthuse. Colloquial or substandard (depending on the degree of a person's aversion to this word) for *be enthusiastic, show enthusiasm.*

The director *was enthusiastic* [not *enthused*] about her new program.

Everyday, every day. *Everyday* is an adjective meaning "ordinary." *Every day* is an adjective and noun combination.

Just wear your *everyday* clothes; don't dress up.

I wore those shoes almost *every day* last week.

Everywheres. See *Anywheres.*

Explicit, implicit. *Explicit* means "stated directly." *Implicit* means "implied," "suggested indirectly."

She *explicitly* told us to bring two pencils and ten pages of notebook paper.

The idea *implicit* in her statement was that we should come prepared to take the test.

Farther, further. Careful writers observe a distinction between these two words, reserving *farther* for distances that can actually be measured.

Tony can hit a golf ball *farther* than I can.

We must pursue this matter *further.*

Fewer, less. *Fewer* refers to numbers, *less* to quantity, extent, or degree.

Fewer [not *Less*] students are taking courses in literature this year.

Food costs *less,* but we have less money to spend.

Figure. See *Calculate.*

Fine. Colloquial, very widely used, for *well, very well.*

The boys played *well* [not *just fine*].

Graffiti. The singular form is *graffito.* In serious writing, *graffiti* takes a plural verb. Avoid combinations such as "a graffiti," "this graffiti," etc.

Had(n't) ought. *Ought* does not take an auxiliary.

You *ought* [not *had ought*] to apply for a scholarship.

You *ought not* [not *hadn't ought*] to miss the lecture.

Hardly. See *Can't hardly.*

Healthy, healthful. *Healthy* means "having health," and *healthful* means "giving health." Thus a person or an animal is *healthy*; a climate, a food, or an activity is *healthful.*

Immigrate. See *Emigrate.*

Implicit. See *Explicit.*

Imply, infer. Despite the increasing tendency to use these words more or less interchangeably, it is good to preserve the distinction: *Imply* means "to say something indirectly," "to hint or suggest," and *infer* means "to draw a conclusion," "to deduce." Thus you *imply* something in what you say and *infer* something from what you hear.

Incredible, incredulous. An unbelievable thing is *incredible*; a disbelieving person is *incredulous.*

In regards to. The correct forms are *in regard to* or *as regards.*

Inside of. *Inside* or *within* is preferred in formal writing.

We stayed *inside* [not *inside of*] the barn during the storm.

The plane should arrive *within* [not *inside of*] an hour.

Irregardless. Substandard or humorous for *regardless.*

The planes bombed the area *regardless* [not *irregardless*] of consequences.

Is when, is where. The *"is-when," "is-where"* pattern in definitions is clumsy and should be avoided. Write, for example, "An embolism is an obstruction, such as a blood clot, in the bloodstream," instead of "An embolism is where an obstruction forms in the bloodstream."

Kind, sort. These words are singular and therefore should be modified by singular modifiers. Do not write *these kind, these sort, those kind, those sort.*

Those kinds [not *those kind*] of running shoes sell very well.

Who could believe *that sort* [not *those sort*] of arguments?

Kinda, sorta, kind of a, sort of a. Undesirable forms.

Kind of, sort of. Colloquial for *somewhat, in some degree, almost, rather.*

They felt *somewhat* [not *sort of*] depressed.

Learn, teach. *Learn* means "to acquire knowledge"; *teach* means "to give or impart knowledge."

Ms. Brown *taught* [not *learned*] me Spanish.

Leave. Not to be used for let.

Let [not *Leave*] me carry your books for you.

Less. See *Fewer.*

Let. See *Leave.*

Let's us. The *us* is superfluous because *let's* means "let us."

Liable to, likely to. See *Apt to.*

Like, as, as if. The use of *like* as a conjunction (in other words, to introduce a clause) is colloquial. It should be avoided in serious writing.

As [not *Like*] you were told earlier, there is a small entry fee.

She acts *as if* [not *like*] she distrusts us.

Do *as* [not *like*] I tell you.

Line. Often vague and redundant, as in "What do you read in the line of books?" "Don't you enjoy fishing and other sports along that line?" It is better to say, more directly,

What kind of books do you read?

Don't you enjoy fishing and sports like that?

Lots of, a lot of. Used informally to mean a large extent, amount, or number, a usage that is enjoying increased acceptance. This usage should be avoided in formal writing.

A great many [not *Lots of*] families vacation here every summer.

The storms caused *a great deal of* [not *lots of*] damage.

All of us owe you *a great deal* [not *a lot*].

As one word, **alot** is still unacceptable spelling.

Mad. Colloquially, *mad* is often used to mean "angry." In formal English, it means "insane."

Marge was *angry* [not *mad*] because I was late.

May. See *Can*.

Media. A plural noun referring to all mass communicative agencies. The singular is *medium*. Careful writers and speakers avoid the use of *media* as a singular noun, as in "Television is an influential media." Even more objectionable is the use of *medias* as a plural.

Might of. See *Could of*.

Most. This word is the superlative form of *much* and *many* (*much, more, most; many, more, most*). Its use as a clipped form of *almost* is colloquial.

Almost [not *Most*] all of my friends work during the summer.

Nature, nurture. Nature is a noun meaning that which is inborn, inherent to the character and constitution of a person. So we say, "She is, by nature, a calm person." Nurture as a noun means training or upbringing; as a verb it means to train or educate, to further the development of a quality. "We need to nurture that attitude in her."

Nauseated, nauseous. Despite the increasingly wide use of these words as synonyms, there are still speakers and writers of precise English who insist that *nauseated* should be used to mean "suffering from or experiencing nausea" and that *nauseous* should be used only to mean "causing nausea."

Nohow. This emphatic negative is substandard.

Not all that. A basically meaningless substitute for *not very* or *not really*; it can easily become a habit.

The movie was *not very* [not *not all that*] amusing.

Nowheres. See *Anywheres*.

Number. See *Amount*.

Of. See *Could of*.

Off of. Dialectal or colloquial for *off*.

She asked me to get *off* [not *off of*] my high horse.

OK. This form calls attention to itself in serious writing. It is appropriate only to business communications and casual speech or writing. Modern dictionaries offer several permissible forms: *OK, O.K.,* and *okay* for the singular noun; *OKs, O.K.s,* and *okays* for the plural noun; and *OK'd, OK'ing, O.K.'d, O.K.'ing, okayed,* and *okaying* for verb forms.

Ought. See *Had(n't) ought*.

Ought to of. See *Could of*.

Owing to. See *Due to*.

Party. Colloquial for "individual" in the sense of *man, woman, person*.

A man [not *A party*] called while you were out.

Party is acceptable when used in reference to lawsuits, agreements, and disputes.

Percent, percentage. Use *percent* when referring to a specific number.

Ten *percent* of the class made an A.

Use *percentage* when referring to no specific number.

A small *percentage* of the class made an A.

Phenomenon, phenomena. A *phenomenon* is a single observable fact or event. *Phenomena* is a plural noun. When using either, be sure to make adjectives such as *this* and *these* and all verbs agree in number.

Plenty is a noun meaning "an abundance" and is used with the preposition *of*.

There are *plenty of* jobs available.

Do not use the word as an adverb meaning "very" or "quite."

That movie was *very* [not *plenty*] scary.

Pretty is an informal modifier. In writing, use *quite* or *very*.

The floodwaters were *very* [not *pretty*] deep.

Quote, unquote. Although these words may be needed in the oral presentation of quoted material, they have no use in written material, in which quotation marks or indentation sets off the quoted material from the text proper.

Real, really. The use of *real*, which is an adjective, to modify another adjective or an adverb is colloquial. In formal contexts, *really* or *very* should be used.

We had a *really* [not *real*] enjoyable visit.

The motorcycle rounded the corner *very* [not *real*] fast.

Reason is because, reason is due to, reason is on account of. In serious writing, a "reason is" clause is usually completed with *that*, not with *because*, *due to*, or *on account of*.

The *reason* they surrendered *is that* [not *because*] they were starving.

The *reason* for my low grades *is that* I have poor eyesight [*not is on account of* my poor eyesight].

Reckon. See *Calculate*.

Same. The use of *same* as a pronoun, often found in legal or business writing, is inappropriate in most other types of writing.

I received your report and look forward to reading *it* [not *the same*].

So, such. These words, when used as exclamatory intensifiers, are not appropriate in a formal context. Sentences like the following belong in informal talk: "I am *so* tired," "She is *so* pretty," or "They are having *such* a good time."

Some. Colloquial for *somewhat, a little*.

The situation at the border is said to be *somewhat* [not *some*] improved today.

Somewheres. See *Anywheres*.

Sort. See *Kind*.

Such. See *So*.

Suppose to, use to. Although these incorrect forms are difficult to detect in spoken English, remember that the correct written forms are *supposed to, used to*.

Sure. *Sure* is correctly used as an adjective:

We are not *sure* about her plans.

He made several *sure* investments.

Sure is colloquial when used as an adverbial substitute for *surely, extremely, certainly, indeed, very, very much*.

The examination was *surely* [not *sure*] difficult.

The lawyer's plea *certainly* [not *sure*] impressed the jury.

Sure and. See *Try and*.

Suspicion. *Suspicion* is a noun; it is not to be used as a verb in place of *suspect*.

No one *suspected* [not *suspicioned*] the victim's widow.

Swell. Not to be used as a general term of approval meaning *good*, *excellent*, *attractive*, *desirable*, and so on.

Take. See *Bring*.

Teach. See *Learn*.

That there, this here, those there, these here. Substandard for *that*, *this*, *those*, *these*.

Them. Substandard when used as an adjective.

How can you eat *those* [not *them*] parsnips?

Try and, sure and. *Try to*, *sure to* are the preferred forms in serious writing.

We shall *try to* [not *try and*] make your visit a pleasant one.

Be *sure to* [not *sure and*] arrive on time.

Type. Colloquial when used as a modifier of a noun. Use *type of* or *kind of*.

I usually don't enjoy that *type of* [not *type*] movie.

Uninterested. See *Disinterested*.

Unique. In its original meaning, the word meant either "the only example" or "without a like or equal." In modern use, it has also acquired an additional meaning: "unusual." In the first sense, it cannot be modified by an adjective.

As a politician, he is *unique*.

She gave him a *unique* [*very special*] pen as a present.

Many object to the use of a modifier with *unique*; in formal writing, it is best to choose some other adjective to convey the meaning "special" or "unusual."

Use to. See *Suppose to*.

Want in, want off, want out. Colloquial and dialectical forms for *want to come in*, *want to get off*, *want to go out*. Inappropriate in serious writing.

Ways. Colloquial for *way*, in such expressions as

It is just a short *distance* [not *ways*] up the canyon.

We do not have a long *way* [not *ways*] to go.

What. Substandard when used for *who*, *which*, or *that* as a relative pronoun in an adjective clause.

His raucous laugh is the thing *that* [not *what*] annoys me most.

When, where clauses. See *Is when*.

Where . . . at. The *at* is unnecessary and undesirable in both speech and writing.

Where [not *Where at*] will you be at noon?

Where is your car? [Not *Where is your car at?*]

-wise. The legitimate function of this suffix to form adverbs like *clockwise* does not carry with it the license to concoct such jargon as "Entertainmentwise, this town is a dud" or "This investment is very attractive long-term-capital-gainswise."

Without. Not to be used as a conjunction instead of *unless*.

He won't lend me his car *unless* [not *without*] I fill the gas tank.

Would of. See *Could of*.

WORDS SIMILAR IN SOUND

Accept. I should like to *accept* your first offer.

Except. He took everything *except* the rugs.

Advice. Free *advice* [noun] is usually not worth much.

Advise. Ms. Hull said she would *advise* [verb] me this term. (Similarly, *device* [noun] and *devise* [verb].)

Affect. His forced jokes *affect* [verb] me unfavorably.

Effect. His humor has a bad *effect* [noun]. Let us try to *effect* [verb] a lasting peace.

All ready. They were *all ready* to go home.

Already. They had *already* left when we telephoned the house.

All together. Now that we are *all together*, let us talk it over.

Altogether. They were not *altogether* pleased with the results.

Altar. In this temple was an *altar* to the Unknown God.

Alter. One should not try to *alter* or escape history.

Ascent. The *ascent* to the top of the mountain was quite steep.

Assent. The judge did not *assent* to our request.

Bare. The *bare* and leafless limbs of the trees were a dark gray.

Bear. He could not *bear* to look at the accident.

Breath. His *breath* came in short gasps at the end of the race.

Breathe. The problem is solved; you can *breathe* easily now.

Canvas. We used a piece of *canvas* to shelter us from the wind.

Canvass. The candidate wanted to *canvass* every person in her precinct.

Capital. A *capital* letter; *capital* gains; *capital* punishment; state *capital*.

Capitol. Workers are painting the dome of the *Capitol*.

Cite. He *cited* three good examples.

Site. The *site* of the new school has not been decided on.

Sight. They were awed by the *sight* of so much splendor.

Climactic. The *climactic* moment in that movie was extremely exciting.

Climatic. According to NOAA, *climatic* conditions in North America have not changed much over the past 100 years.

Coarse. The *coarse* sand blew in my face.

Course. We discussed the *course* to take. Of *course* he may come with us.

Complement. Your intelligence is a *complement* to your beauty.

Compliment. It is easier to pay a *compliment* than a bill.

Consul. Be sure to look up the American *consul* in Rome.

Council. He was appointed to the executive *council*.

Counsel. I sought *counsel* from my friends. They *counseled* moderation. He employed *counsel* to defend him.

Decent. The workers demanded a *decent* wage scale.

Descent. The *descent* from the mountain was uneventful.

Dissent. The voices of *dissent* were louder than those of approval.

Desert. Out in the lonely *desert* [noun—desert], he tried to *desert* [verb—desert] from his regiment.

Dessert. We had apple pie for *dessert*.

Device. The *device* that controls the alarm system has malfunctioned.
Devise. We should *devise* a new system to cope with that problem.

Die. Old habits certainly *die* hard.
Dye. That *dye* produced a strange color in that new fabric.

Dining. We eat dinner in our *dining* room. *Dining* at home is pleasant.
Dinning. Stop *dinning* that song into my ears!

Fair. The decision of the umpire seemed very *fair*.
Fare. By plane, the *fare* from here to Toledo is $115.67.

Formerly. He was *formerly* a student at Beloit College.
Formally. You must address the presiding judge *formally* and respectfully.

Forth. Several witnesses came *forth* to testify.
Fourth. We planned a picnic for the *Fourth* of July.

Gorilla. The zoo has built a new habitat for the *gorillas*.
Guerrilla. The *guerrilla* forces are operating in the mountains beyond the city.

Heard. I had not *heard* that news.
Herd. The *herd* of cows moved slowly toward the barn.

Hole. The *hole* in my sock is growing bigger every minute.
Whole. The *whole* office is filled with a strange odor.

Incidence. Better sanitation lowered the *incidence* of communicable diseases.
Incidents. Smugglers were involved in several *incidents* along the border.

Instance. For *instance*, she was always late to class.
Instants. As the car turned, those brief *instants* seemed like hours.

Its. Your plan has much in *its* favor. [possessive of *it*]
It's. *It's* too late now for excuses. [contraction of *it is*, *it has*]

Later. It is *later* than you think.
Latter. Of the two novels, I prefer the *latter*.

Lead. Can you *lead* [lēd—verb] us out of this jungle? *Lead* [lĕd—noun] is a heavy, soft, malleable metallic element.
Led. A local guide *led* us to the salmon fishing hole.

Loose. He has a *loose* tongue. The dog is *loose* again.
Lose. Don't *lose* your temper.

Meat. We did not have any *meat* at lunch.
Meet. We intend to *meet* you after lunch.
Mete. The judge will *mete* out the punishment tomorrow.

Passed. She smiled as she *passed* me. She *passed* the test.
Past. It is futile to try to relive the *past*.

Patience. The teacher has little *patience* for lame excuses.
Patients. Twelve *patients* will be discharged from the hospital today.

Personal. Write him a *personal* letter.
Personnel. The morale of our company's *personnel* is high.

Pore. [verb] For hours they *pored* over the mysterious note. [noun] a minute opening, as in the skin.
Pour. Ms. Cook *poured* hot water into the teapot.

Precede. The Secret Service agents always *precede* the President when he enters a building.
Proceed. They all left the building and *proceeded* immediately to the parking lot.

Precedence. Tax reform takes *precedence* over all other legislative matters.

Precedents. The judge quoted three *precedents* to justify his ruling.

Presence. We are honored by your *presence*.

Presents. The child received dozens of Christmas *presents*.

Principal. The *principal* of a school; the *principal* [chief] industry; the *principal* and the interest.

Principle. He is a man of high *principles*.

Quiet. You must keep *quiet*.

Quite. The weather was *quite* good all week.

Rain. A soaking *rain* would help our crops greatly.

Reign. Samuel Pepys was briefly imprisoned during the *reign* of William III.

Rein. Keep a tight *rein* when you ride this spirited horse.

Right. Take a *right* turn on Oak Street.

Rite. Taking that course is a *rite* of passage for many students.

Write. Please *write* me a letter when you arrive.

Scene. The last *scene* in that movie was exceptionally touching.

Seen. I had not *seen* Frank for two weeks.

Sense. That statement makes a great deal of *sense* to me.

Since. Ten more people have arrived *since* we got here this morning.

Scents. The *scents* of those flowers are not easy to distinguish.

Sent. We *sent* a copy of the report to you yesterday.

Cent. We won't pay another *cent*.

Shone. The cat's eyes *shone* in the dark.

Shown. He hasn't *shown* us his best work.

Stationary. The benches were *stationary* and could not be moved.

Stationery. She wrote a letter on hotel *stationery*.

Statue. It was a *statue* of a pioneer.

Stature. Athos was a man of gigantic *stature*.

Statute. The law may be found in the 1917 book of *statutes*.

Than. She sings better *than* I.

Then. He screamed; *then* he fainted.

Their. It wasn't *their* fault. [possessive pronoun]

There. You won't find any gold *there*. [adverb of place]

They're. *They're* sure to be disappointed. [contraction of *they are*]

Thorough. We must first give the old cabin a *thorough* [adjective] cleaning.

Threw. The catcher *threw* the ball back to the pitcher.

Through. The thief had entered *through* [preposition] a hole in the roof.

To. Be sure to speak *to* her. [preposition]

Too. He is far *too* old for you. [adverb]

Two. The membership fee is only *two* dollars. [adjective]

Waist. She wore a beautiful silver belt around her *waist*.

Waste. Save every scrap; don't let anything go to *waste*.

Weather. The *weather* last week was very cold.

Whether. Do you know *whether* Jim has arrived?

Whose. *Whose* book is this? [possessive pronoun]

Who's. I wonder *who's* with her now. [contraction of *who is*]

Your. I like *your* new car. [possessive pronoun]

You're. *You're* not nervous, are you? [contraction of *you are*]

SUPPLEMENT

Rule 1: A few common adjectives with the suffix *able* have two correct spellings:

likable/likeable, lovable/loveable, movable/moveable, sizable/sizeable, usable/useable

Rule 2: Dictionaries show two spellings for the *ed* and *ing* forms (and a few other derived forms) of dozens of verbs ending in single consonants preceded by single vowels. Some nouns also fall into this category. In general, the single-consonant spelling is usually found in American printing; some of the dictionaries label the double-consonant spelling a British preference.

biased/biassed, canceling/cancelling, counselor/counsellor, diagraming/diagramming, equaled/equalled, marvelous/marvellous, modeled/modelled, totaling/ totalling, traveler/ traveller

English Fundamentals Online

After you have completed the Practice Sheets and Exercises in this lesson, you can find additional help and drill work at **MyWritingLab.com**, in the section on Easily Confused Words.

NAME _____   SCORE _____

Directions: In the space at the left, write the expression from each set of choices in parentheses that is more appropriate for use in serious writing.

_____   1. (Unless, Without) I pay him tomorrow, Link won't have money for
_____   gas for his trip home, and he will be (aggravated, annoyed) at me.
_____   2. It would be a (grate, great) idea to invite Mike and Carolyn to the
_____   meeting; both of them are (real, really) creative people.
_____   3. If page 124 is (all the farther, as far as) you've read, you still have
_____   (lots of, a great many) pages to cover before tomorrow's test.
_____   4. (Almost, Most) all of that movie came directly from the novel, but
_____   the ending (sort of) departed (somewhat) from the end of the novel.
_____   5. We drove (farther, further) today than I thought possible, but we
_____   still have a(n) (awfully, very) long distance to cover tomorrow.
_____   6. Roberta is (not all that, not very) (enthused, enthusiastic) about
_____   sending that negative report to the boss.
_____   7. The (amount, number) of people attending last night's concert
_____   (might have, might of) exceeded the attendance in any other city.
_____   8. That one long conversation significantly (altared, altered) my
_____   opinion of Johnson's ability; I now (accept, except) him as an
_____   expert in his field.
_____   9. "(Altogether, All together) one more time on the chorus," said the
_____   director; "I'm not (all together, altogether) satisfied with your work."
_____ 10. "It is not my (nature, nurture) to be extremely critical, but her
_____   lack of preparation made me (angry, mad)," said Carlos.
_____ 11. I can (learn, teach) you to use that program, but I (figure, think)
_____   you will need about a month of practice to become really proficient
_____   with it.
_____ 12. The president did not give (ascent, assent) to our request but said her
_____   decision would not (affect, effect) any future requests negatively.
_____ 13. Can you give me some (advice, advise) about a book to read for that
_____   assignment? My last choice proved to be (pretty, very) difficult to read.
_____ 14. The cabin is just a short (way, ways) up this road; we don't have a
_____   long (distance, ways) to go before we get there.
_____ 15. Those (sort, sorts) of assignments (use, used) to take me hours to
_____   complete; now I finish them very quickly.
_____ 16. When I stepped outside this morning, the feel of the icy deck boards
_____   on my (bare, bear) feet almost took my (breath, breathe) away.
_____ 17. Those fans in the stands need to (reign, rein) in their enthusiasm, the
_____   referee is losing her (patience, patients) with their booing and hissing.
_____ 18. The (principal, principle) industry of that region is raising corn,
_____   but the drought has, as a (hole, whole), devastated this year's crop.

_____ 19. (It's, Its) very (quiet, quite) in the house. Do you think everyone
_____ has left for the day?

_____ 20. Joe (lead, led) us step by step through that long calculus problem, but
_____ five minutes later I felt (as if, like) I'd never heard a word he said.

_____ 21. The detectives (suspect, suspicion) that someone else (beside,
_____ besides) that one man must have witnessed the crime.

_____ 22. Is there (any way, anyway, anyways) that I can get an (invite,
_____ invitation) to meet that speaker when she is on campus?

_____ 23. The students (implied, inferred) from the instructor's introduction that
_____ this (coarse, course) will not be very difficult if they study regularly.

_____ 24. The reason for the competitive cheerleading squad's success is
_____ (because, that) it practices (incredibly, incredulously) long hours.

_____ 25. Do you think we (had ought to, should) (bring, take) a raincoat
_____ with us to the stadium tonight?

_____ 26. The puppy we (adapted, adopted) from the animal shelter has
_____ (adapted, adopted) well to his new home.

_____ 27. Because it is well (passed, past) 6 o'clock, everyone has (already,
_____ all ready) packed up the tools and prepared to leave.

_____ 28. Please call me (later, latter) and give me the assignment for next
_____ class so I can (precede, proceed) to work on it.

_____ 29. Joanna had not (herd, heard) the news that there had been several
_____ (incidence, incidents) of theft on the campus.

_____ 30. Before going to the game, those fans (died, dyed) their hair purple
_____ so that they could be sure of being (scene, seen) on television.

_____ 31. Anyone with any common (scents, sense) (should have, should of)
_____ known that Charlie's plan would not be very successful.

_____ 32. (Sense, Since) we missed that last (right, rite) turn, we need to turn
_____ around and make a left turn onto that road.

_____ 33. David was (plenty, extremely) excited when his boat beat all
_____ (them, those) other boats to the finish line.

_____ 34. We need a (disinterested, uninterested) person to give us an
_____ opinion so that we can choose wisely from (among, between) the
_____ three investments.

_____ 35. After falling into the river, the woman said, "No, I (ain't, am not)
_____ (alright, all right), and I want to go home immediately."

_____ 36. If we go (anywhere, anywheres) today, I want to go to that new
_____ restaurant to sample several of the delicious (deserts, desserts) the
_____ owner advertises.

_____ 37. It is important for you to write a (personal, personnel) note of
_____ thanks on special (stationary, stationery) for each of those gifts.

_____ 38. There seem to be (to, too, two) (to, too, two) many people sitting
_____ at this table for us all to be comfortable.

_____ 39. "These (criterion, criteria) for judging each player's performance
_____ are (extremely, so) complicated," said Ms. Jackson.

_____ 40. The thing (that, what) pleases me most about today's victory is
_____ that the team never went (off, off of) the game plan during the
_____ entire second half.

NAME _____   SCORE _____

Directions: When you find an incorrectly used word in a sentence, write the correct word in the space at the left. If you find an unnecessary preposition, put an **X** through it. Some sentences may have one word incorrect, some, two; some sentences may be correct.

Review: In your dictionary, look up the meaning of any words you missed on this page.

_____
_____
1. Please tell me wear you bought that incredulously beautiful saddle and bridle for your horse at.

_____
_____
2. Whose car is parked in front of the fire hydrant, and who's going to suggest that the owner might want to move it?

_____
_____
3. John was not able to tell us weather he will be here tomorrow; actually, he may have to pass us by all together.

_____
_____
4. When I herd the score of the game, I couldn't hardly believe my ears; I'm surprised we beat that team so easily.

_____
_____
5. "I'm trying to remember where I left my umbrella at; I can't afford to loose another one so soon after I bought it," said Arline.

_____
_____
6. The pitcher waisted a pitch because she had to strikes on the batter, and then she threw a drop ball for the third strike.

_____
_____
7. It was probably not there fault that they didn't find me their because the crowd was huge by the time I arrived.

_____
_____
8. Joseph is a man of short statue, but he is extremely strong and agile and has shone that he knows how to play the game.

_____
_____
9. That politician's statement made no scents to me; translating political language has become a right of passage into adult life.

_____
_____
10. The last seen of that play was riotously funny because the rein of the fictional king came to such an improbable end.

_____
_____
11. In what obscure source did you find that funny quote, the one you used to conclude your paper?

_____
_____
12. James Walton is a man of high principals, so I'm sure we can trust him to precede correctly in the matter of that anonymous donation.

_____
_____
13. The precedences for that court decision seem quiet clear; it's difficult to find fault with the court's decision.

_____
_____
14. Jim and I pored over our notes for hours, and then we proceeded to work out an outline of all the material on which we'll be tested.

_____
_____
15. As the group past the courthouse, the guide told a few stories from the passed history of the county.

_____
_____
16. Accept for Martha, no one in the room had ever read that wildly popular column of advise that appears in our local paper.

_____
_____
17. The coach needs to affect several changes in the team rules without reducing the effects of the rules all ready in place.

_____
_____
18. The assent up that mountain leads to the ruins of an alter to a god worshipped centuries ago by the original inhabitants.

_____ 19. "It is all together to early for us to know the results of that
_____ opinion poll," said Mark; "we'll probably know something defini-
tive in two days."

_____ 20. Altogether, there were twenty or twenty-five media representatives
_____ standing in that politician's driveway this morning when she tried
to effect her escape.

_____ 21. The results of that canvas of the neighborhoods in our district
_____ suggest that the newcomer will get a bear majority of the votes.

_____ 22. Alice and Marie had very little working capitol when they started their
_____ business, so it was several months before they could breath easily.

_____ 23. "Your choices for desert," read the menu, "are a slice of apple pie or a
_____ bowl of fresh strawberries; both complement the main course nicely."

_____ 24. The cite of the Blue Angels flying their fighter jets low over the
_____ sight of the stadium inspired awe and admiration in the crowd.

_____ 25. Use a course sandpaper when you begin to sand that peace of
_____ furniture, and then switch to a finer grit to finish the job.

_____ 26. Do not infer anything special from Jorge's comments; he acts like
_____ he has some special insight into problems, but his ideas are rarely
original.

_____ 27. The instructions told us explicitly that the test is difficult, but
_____ apparently all of us did just fine when we took it.

_____ 28. "Ware your every day clothes," said the boss; "we're going to call
_____ Monday a recovery day since we finished that difficult project today."

_____ 29. The committee has decided to look farther for more information
_____ because no one was satisfied by what had been taught from the
existing data.

_____ 30. Not much can be learned from these kind of study because the
_____ amount of people polled is not sufficiently large for sound judgment.

_____ 31. "May I ask Tom for help with this problem, as I can hardly
_____ understand even the basic ideas?" asked Catherine.

_____ 32. "In what store are we likely to find that album in?" asked Wilma;
_____ "I've already looked everywheres I could think of."

_____ 33. As the whole in the pipe grew larger, the flow of water changed
_____ from a constant drip to a continuous stream and soon flooded the
basement.

_____ 34. Employing a disinterested person to settle a dispute is a good
_____ idea, but an uninterested person might not give the matter very
much attention.

_____ 35. The climatic moment in that novel left almost all of its readers
_____ incredulous because no one thought such an ending was possible.

Brief Writing Assignment: In five sentences, describe yourself in action as you eat the first delicious bite of that food you described in Lesson 25. Dramatize the action as much as possible; use only multisyllable descriptive words in the passage.

Check Sheet

USAGE

☐ Using Verbs Correctly

☐ Using verb tenses correctly requires close attention to the principal parts of the verb:

> *run* (the base or infinitive)
> *ran* (the simple past tense)
> *run* (the past participle)

☐ Tense formation is almost automatic in the present and the future tense:

> I *run* that machine every day. I *will run* that machine again next week.

☐ Shifting to the past tense and to the perfect tense requires careful attention to the principal parts of the verb. The past tense is always a single word: the second principal part.

> Yesterday I *ran* that machine for two hours.

The three perfect tenses require the use of the third principal part and an auxiliary verb:

> I *have run* that machine every day for the past three weeks. By last Friday, I *had run* that machine for a total of 72 hours. By next Monday, I *will have run* that machine for a total of 100 hours this month.

☐ *Troublesome Forms*

☐ Three pairs of verbs present especially troublesome problems because their spelling is similar and their principal parts seem to overlap. Three words are intransitive verbs and three are transitive:

- I *lie* down for a nap, but I *lay* the book on the table.
- I *sit* down in a chair, but I *set* the book on the shelf.
- I *rise* from a sitting position, but I *raise* the flag.

The past tense of *lie* is *lay*; the past tense of *lay* is *laid*.

> I *lay* down for a nap an hour ago, but I *laid* the book on the table this morning.

The perfect tense of *lie* uses *lain* as its principal part; the perfect tense of *lay* uses *laid*.

> I *have lain* here peacefully for almost an hour, but I *have laid* that question to rest.

☐ *Subject–Verb Agreement*

☐ The basic rule for subject–verb agreement is that verbs agree with—that is, use the same number, singular or plural, as—the subject. This rule presents a problem only in the third-person singular present tense and in the third-person singular of certain auxiliary verbs:

> she *runs*
> she *has run*
> she *is running*
> she *does run*

☐ The problem is created by the fact that the third-person singular of these verbs ends in *s* but the other forms end without the **s**. Although **s** is the sign of the third-person singular in verbs, **s** is the sign of the plural for most nouns. Keep this concept straight, and most problems with verb forms in subject–verb agreement will solve themselves.

☐ The other problem in establishing subject–verb agreement is usually solved by determining the real subject of the verb:

- Prepositional phrases and other words that come between the subject and the verb do not dictate the number of the verb.
- The subject and verb agree in number even when the subject follows the verb.
- Compound subjects joined by **and** take a plural verb whether the nouns are singular or plural.
- When compound subjects have one noun singular and the other plural, the noun closer to the verb governs the number of the verb.
- Singular subjects joined by **or** or **nor** take a singular verb.
- When the subject of a verb is a relative pronoun, the verb takes its number from the antecedent.

☐ Reference and Agreement in Pronouns

☐ Two basic rules govern the connection between a pronoun and its antecedent.

1. Establish a clear, easily identified relationship between the pronoun and its antecedent.
   - This rule means, in its simplest form, that a noun must precede the pronoun when the pronoun replaces it.
   - Use a noun, not a clause or a phrase or an idea, as the antecedent of a pronoun.

   I was tired from the hike, which made Jan laugh at me. [It is the fact that I was tired from the hike that made Jan laugh. The pronoun *which* has no antecedent in the sentence.]

2. Make the pronoun agree with its antecedent in gender and number.
   - Singular nouns are antecedents for singular pronouns; plurals are antecedents for plurals.
   - With personal pronouns and pronominal adjectives, use the gender that matches the antecedent.

   Paul submitted *his* paper; Pauline submitted *her* paper. The car has lost *its* bumper.

☐ Two problem areas occur regularly in working with pronoun reference and agreement.

☐ Indefinite pronouns such as *everyone*, *someone*, and *each* have always been considered, at least in formal language, singular, in spite of the fact that the pronouns seem to convey a sense of group or plural number. It is probably best in academic writing to stick with the traditional usage and avoid structures that use a plural pronoun.

- Avoid structures such as *Everyone* will certainly do *their* best.

☐ This use of indefinites leads to another problem related to the gender of pronouns.

- Traditionally, sentences such as *Each student will do his best* were considered both correct and acceptable. The problem is that the use of *his* seems to suggest that all students are male—clearly an untrue idea.
- One possible solution, a sentence that reads *Each student will do his or her best*, is both correct and acceptable, but it creates a kind of stumbling awkwardness in the rhythm of the sentence. The solution to this awkwardness is to make the noun plural and provide a plural pronoun.

> *All students* will do *their* best.

Case in Pronoun Usage

☐ Certain pronouns change form to show their use in a clause or sentence.

Nominative	Possessive	Objective
I	my, mine	me
he	his	him
she	her, hers	her
we	our, ours	us
they	their, theirs	them
who	whose	whom
whoever	whosever	whomever

☐ Possessive case shows ownership. The first form is an adjective, sometimes called a *pronominal adjective* because it both shows possession and modifies a noun.

> That is *my* dog.

☐ The second form fills a noun slot and thus is a true pronoun.

> That dog is *mine*.

☐ While indefinite pronouns use an apostrophe to show possession, personal pronouns do not even if they end in *s*. Make a sharp distinction between possessive forms *its* and *whose* and contracted forms such as *it's* (short for *it is*) and *who's* (short for *who is*).

☐ Use a possessive pronoun with a gerund.

> They had not planned on *my* [not *me*] coming with you.

☐ Nominative and Objective Cases

- A pronoun is in the nominative case when it is used as
    a subject (*He* arrived early yesterday.)
    subjective complement (This is *he* speaking.)
    an appositive with a nominative noun (*We* students appreciate your help.)

- A pronoun is in the objective case when it serves as
    the object of a verb or verbal (They told *me* the story. We saw *them* yesterday.)
    the object of a preposition (Everyone but *him* left early.)
    the subject of an infinitive (They asked *him* to come early.)
    an appositive of an objective noun (Two of *us* players came back.)

☐ Pronoun case is sometimes a problem when the pronoun is part of a compound.

> Have you spoken to Juan or *her* [not *she*] today?
> Give your report to Jim or *me* [not *I*].

- Testing for correctness in these cases is simple. Omit the first noun in the compound and read the sentence. You are unlikely to say

> Give your report to *I*.

☐ In comparisons after *as* and *than*, when the pronoun is the subject of an omitted verb, use the nominative case.

> She is smarter than *I* (am).

- Most of the time, the sense of the sentence will demand a pronoun in the nominative case, but occasionally, the sentence can be taken in two ways:

> Sue loves that dog more than *I* (love that dog).
> Sue loves that dog more than *me* (more than she loves me).

Both sentences are correct, but the meanings are different. Be sure to specify your meaning by choosing the proper case for the pronoun.

☐ Who and Whom, Whoever and Whomever

☐ As an easily followed rule of thumb, remember that *who* and *whoever* can usually be replaced by *he* and *him*, or by *they* and *them* if the construction is plural. test your choices by turning the clause into a single statement and replacing the relative or interrogative pronoun with one of the personal pronouns. The correct form will be easy to recognize.

> Yesterday I saw someone with *who/whom* I went to high school.
> Yesterday I saw someone. I went to high school with *he/him*.

It's obvious in the second pair of sentences that the form needed is *him*, so in the relative clause in the first sentence the form needed is *whom*. If the sentence changes to read

> Yesterday I saw someone *who/whom* went to high school with me.
> Yesterday I saw someone. *He/Him* went to high school with me.

It's unlikely that you would choose

> *Him* went to school with me.

If you select *He* went to school, then select *Who* went to school.

☐ When *who/whom, whoever/whomever* begins a noun clause, the case of the pronoun is determined by its role within the clause.

> Give the package to *whoever* comes to the door.
> I'll work with *whomever* you designate.

Make the *who-to-him* change again.

> *He* comes to the door, [therefore the proper choice is *whoever* comes to the door].
> You designate *him*, [not *he*; therefore, the proper choice is *whomever*].

☐ When a pronoun subject is followed immediately by a parenthetical expression such as *do you think* and then a verb, choose the nominative case (*who/whoever*) for the pronoun. When the pronoun is an object of a verb or preposition, choose *whom/whomever*.

> *Who/Whom* do you think is the best choice?

Test your choice here by making the same change as above. Disregard the parenthetical expression and ask is the choice *he* or *him*? *He* is clearly the choice; therefore, the question should read *Who* do you think is the best choice?

☐ Modifiers and Prepositions

☐ Use the short forms of such adverbs as *late*, *hard*, and *near* because the *ly* forms of these adverbs have acquired special meanings. Among other adverbs, the short form serves well for informal writing, and the *ly* forms are better for more formal writing.

☐ Remember that adverbs modify verbs, adjectives, and other adverbs. Be careful to distinguish the adverb *well* from the adjective *good*, *almost* from *most*, *really* from *real*, *easily* from *easy*, and so on.

☐ Remember that *feels*, *sounds*, *smells*, and *looks* usually take adjectives, not adverbs.

☐ In English, we do not double intensifiers to make a point. We do not say *more friendlier* or *most friendliest*. If you are uncertain about the correct way to form comparatives and superlatives in adjectives and adverbs, consult your dictionary.

Plurals and Capitals; Revising, Proofreading, and Correcting

Lesson 27 *Plurals and Capitals*

This lesson covers the formation of plurals and the conventions for using capitals.

PLURALS

Plurals of most nouns are regularly formed by the addition of *s*. But if the singular noun ends in an *s* sound (*s, sh, ch, x, z*), *es* is added to form a new syllable in pronunciation:

crab, crabs	foe, foes	kiss, kisses	tax, taxes
lamp, lamps	box, boxes	church, churches	lass, lasses

Words ending in *y* preceded by a vowel retain the *y* before a suffix; most words ending in *y* preceded by a consonant change the *y* to *i* before a suffix.

toy, toys	army, armies	fly, flies	attorney, attorneys
key, keys	lady, ladies	sky, skies	monkey, monkeys

Some words ending in *o* (including all musical terms and all words having a vowel preceding the *o*) form their plurals with *s*. But many others take *es*:

alto, altos	folio, folios	tomato, tomatoes
piano, pianos	hero, heroes	potato, potatoes

For several nouns ending in *o*, most dictionaries give both forms. Here are some examples, printed in the order they are found in most dictionaries. The first spelling is the more common one:

banjos, banjoes	frescoes, frescos	lassos, lassoes	volcanoes, volcanos
buffaloes, buffalos	grottoes, grottos	mottoes, mottos	zeros, zeroes
cargoes, cargos	halos, haloes	tornadoes, tornados	

Some nouns ending in *f* or *fe* merely add *s*; some change *f* or *fe* to *ves* in the plural; and a few (*hoofs/hooves*, *scarfs/scarves*, *wharves/wharfs*) use either form. Use your dictionary to make sure:

leaf, leaves	life, lives	half, halves	wolf, wolves
roof, roofs	safe, safes	gulf, gulfs	elf, elves

A few nouns have the same form for singular and plural. A few have irregular plurals:

deer, deer	ox, oxen	child, children	goose, geese
sheep, sheep	man, men	foot, feet	mouse, mice

Many words of foreign origin use two plurals; some do not. Always check in your dictionary:

alumna, alumnae	criterion, criteria
alumnus, alumni	datum, data
analysis, analyses	thesis, theses
appendix, appendixes, appendices	focus, focuses, foci
curriculum, curriculums, curricula	fungus, funguses, fungi
memorandum, memorandums, memoranda	index, indexes, indices
tableau, tableaus, tableaux	medium, media
bon mot, bons mots	
crisis, crises	

Note: Do *not* use an apostrophe to form the plural of either a common or a proper noun.

Wrong: Our neighbor's, the Allen's and the Murray's, recently bought new Honda's.

Right: Our neighbors, the Allens and the Murrays, recently bought new Hondas.

CAPITALS

A capital letter is used for the first letter of the first word of any sentence, for the first letter of a proper noun, and, often, for the first letter of an adjective derived from a proper noun. Following are some reminders about situations that cause confusion for some writers.

1. Capitalize the first word of every sentence, every quoted sentence or fragment, and every transitional fragment. (See Lessons 14 and 19.)

    The building needs repairs. How much will it cost? Please answer me.

    Mr. James said, "We'll expect your answer soon." She replied, "Of course."

    And now to conclude.

2. Capitalize proper nouns and most adjectives derived from them. A proper noun designates by name an individual person, place, or thing that is a member of a group or class. Do not capitalize common nouns, which are words naming a group or class:

    Doris Powers, woman; France, country; Tuesday, day; January, month; Christmas Eve, holiday; Shorewood High School, high school; Carleton College, college; *Mauritania*, ship; Fifth Avenue, boulevard; White House, residence

    Elizabethan drama, Restoration poetry, Chinese peasants, Red Cross assistance

3. Do not capitalize nouns and derived forms that, although originally proper nouns, have acquired special meanings. When in doubt, consult your dictionary:

    a set of china; a bohemian existence; plaster of paris; pasteurized milk; a mecca for golfers; set in roman type, not italics

4. Capitalize names of religions, references to deities, and most words having religious significance:

> Bible,* Baptist, Old Testament, Holy Writ, Jewish, Catholic, Sermon on the Mount, Koran, Talmud

5. Capitalize titles of persons when used with the person's name. When the title is used alone, capitalize it only when it stands for a specific person of high rank:**

> I spoke briefly to Professor Jones. He is a professor of history.
> We visited the late President Johnson's ranch in Texas.
> Jerry is president of our art club.
> Tonight the President will appear on national television.

6. Capitalize names denoting family relationship but not when they are preceded by a possessive. This rule is equivalent to saying that you capitalize when the word serves as a proper noun:

> At that moment Mother, Father, and Aunt Lucy entered the room.
> My mother, father, and aunt are very strict about some things.

7. Capitalize points of the compass when they refer to actual regions but not when they refer to directions:

> Before we moved to the West, we lived in the South for a time.
> You drive three miles west and then turn north on the Pacific Highway.

Do not capitalize adjectives of direction modifying countries or states:

> From central Finland, the group had immigrated to northern Michigan.

8. Capitalize names of academic subjects as they would appear in college catalog listings, but in ordinary writing capitalize only names of languages:

> I intend to register for History 322 and Sociology 188.
> Last year I took courses in history, sociology, German, and Latin.

9. In titles of books, short stories, plays, essays, and poems, capitalize the first word and all other words except the articles (*a*, *an*, *the*) and short prepositions and conjunctions. (See Lesson 19 for the use of italics and quotation marks with titles.)

> Last semester I wrote reports on the following works: Shaw's *The Intelligent Woman's Guide to Socialism and Capitalism*, Joyce's *A Portrait of the Artist as a Young Man*, Pirandello's *Six Characters in Search of an Author*, Poe's "The Fall of the House of Usher," Yeats's "An Irish Airman Foresees His Death," Frost's "Stopping by Woods on a Snowy Evening," and Muriel Rukeyser's "The Soul and Body of John Brown."

---

*Note that "Bible" is lowercased when not used as a religious reference, as in "Chapman's *Piloting and Seamanship* is a bible for sailors everywhere."
**Capitalize titles of people when used in direct address, as in "How do you respond, Senator?"

Note: Traditionally, a capital letter begins every line of poetry. This convention, however, is not always followed by modern poets; when you quote poetry, be sure to copy exactly the capitalization used by the author.

English Fundamentals Online

After you have completed the Practice Sheets and Exercises in this lesson, you can find additional help and drill work at **MyWritingLab.com**, in the section on Capitalization.

NAME _____   SCORE _____

Directions: Write the plural form or forms of the following words in the blanks below. When in doubt, consult your dictionary. If two forms are given, write both forms.

1. analysis

2. aquarium

3. archipelago

4. assembly

5. Charles

6. commando

7. Dutchman

8. father-in-law

9. flamingo

10. folio

11. fungus

12. handful

13. inferno

14. lily

15. mouse

16. octopus

17. plateau

18. podium

19. scarf

20. sheriff

21. spy

22. thesis

23. turkey

24. vortex

25. wife

Directions: The following sentences contain 50 numbered words. If you think the word is correctly capitalized, write **C** in the space at the left with the corresponding number. If you think the word should not be capitalized, write **W** in the space.

```
____ ____ ____
 1    2    3

____ ____ ____
 4    5    6

____ ____ ____
 7    8    9

____ ____ ____
 10   11   12

____ ____ ____
 13   14   15

____ ____ ____
 16   17   18

____ ____ ____
 19   20   21

____ ____ ____
 22   23   24

____ ____ ____
 25   26   27

____ ____ ____
 28   29   30

____ ____ ____
 31   32   33

____ ____ ____
 34   35   36

____ ____ ____
 37   38   39

____ ____ ____
 40   41   42

____ ____ ____
 43   44   45

____ ____ ____
 46   47   48

____ ____
 49   50
```

(1) The guide told Mother and Aunt Mabel to walk two blocks
     1   2
farther West to reach the Museum of Modern Art.
       3   4   5   6

(2) Jerry's Uncle, who retired recently from the State Department
          7   8   9
and who had served in many Countries in the Far East,
                           10   11 12
often vacations in the South Seas.
                        13   14

(3) Last Spring our Geology Professor scaled Mt. Rainier, the
         15   16   17   18
highest Mountain in the Cascades.
        19   20

(4) Wilma, who transferred from a Junior College in the South,
                                  21   22   23
is majoring in Drama and Speech.
               24   25

(5) Did you know that Professor Fry, our French teacher, has a
                      26   27
Ph.D. degree from Princeton University?
28   29   30

(6) A Librarian told me that material on African Pygmies could
      31   32
be found in the *Americana*, the *Britannica*, or any other
                  33   34
good encyclopedia.
     35

(7) When I was a Senior in High School, our class read Holmes's
                 36   37   38
The Autocrat of The Breakfast Table.
 39   40   41 42   43   44

(8) Besides courses in Psychology and Mathematics, Jane is
                       45   46
taking Literature 326, which deals with American novels
       47   48
written since World War I.
              49   50

NAME _____ SCORE _____

Directions: Write the plural form or forms of each of the following words. When in doubt, consult your dictionary. If two forms are given, write both of them.

1. auditorium   _____   _____

2. automaton   _____   _____

3. belief   _____   _____

4. cello   _____   _____

5. census   _____   _____

6. crisis   _____   _____

7. curio   _____   _____

8. difficulty   _____   _____

9. Frenchman   _____   _____

10. grotto   _____   _____

11. journey   _____   _____

12. latch   _____   _____

13. man-of-war   _____   _____

14. moose   _____   _____

15. mutiny   _____   _____

16. process   _____   _____

17. roomful   _____   _____

18. soprano   _____   _____

19. stimulus   _____   _____

20. stratum   _____   _____

21. symposium   _____   _____

22. talisman   _____   _____

23. waltz   _____   _____

24. wharf   _____   _____

25. zebra   _____   _____

Directions: The following sentences contain no capital letters except at the beginnings of sentences and the personal pronoun *I*. Underline each letter that should be capitalized.

1. In yellowstone national park last summer, I took some very impressive photographs of old faithful and half dome, a famous climbing face.

2. My uncle jim and two of my aunts will travel to the outback of australia next summer.

3. My uncle said to me before he left, "if I can find one, I will bring you a boomerang from my trip; I'll also take photos in melbourne and sydney."

4. A friend of mine, georgette olsen, will be a rhodes scholar next year and will study in oxford, england, at oxford university.

5. There is a beautiful italian sculpture in the lobby of the parsons memorial library on our campus; the statue was donated by the members of the parsons family in memory of their grandfather, jonas parsons.

6. The renaissance is a period in european history in which many works of literature and art from ancient greece and rome were rediscovered.

7. *Brown v. the board of education of topeka kansas* is a landmark case in the civil rights movement.

8. The world cup is the world championship of soccer, or football as it is known everywhere but the united states, where the super bowl decides the champion of american football.

9. "We have a very small budget for computer purchases this year," said the dean, "but next year may be a better year for such purchases."

10. Alex's first thought on tuesday morning in his history class was, "why did I ever sign up for history 3211, anyway? I don't even like the saying, 'those who do not know history are doomed to repeat it,'" which is sometimes attributed to henry ford, the founder of the ford motor company.

Brief Writing Assignment and Review: Record a ten-line conversation between you and a friend. Include at least one double quotation. Be sure to punctuate correctly, including capital letters and quotation marks.

PROOFREADING AND CORRECTING

All of the work you have done so far in this book has been focused on developing two sets of skills.

First, everything you have done, beginning with learning to identify subjects and verbs, through the sentence building sections, and on to the word choice drills in the last chapters, offered the opportunity to become a more fluent, fluid, and powerful writer by building a broad repertoire of structures, a variety of ways of expressing an idea, so that you can say precisely what you want to say and say it in ways that will hold your reader's interest and attention.

As a simple example, one you will recognize from the sentence-combining drills, look at these two short, simple sentences:

John walked slowly down the street.
He entered a coffee shop at the end of the block.

Those two sentences are complete and correct, and they explain exactly what happened. But if you continued the rest of that narrative by writing a dozen more short, simple sentences, you would lose the attention of the reader and possibly drive the person to go off for a short nap. So instead of repeating the same construction, you vary the sentences to hold the reader's interest. Using those same sentences as a model, you can use a compound verb:

John walked down the street and entered a coffee shop at the end of the block.

You can construct a compound sentence:

John walked down the street, and he entered a coffee shop at the end of the block.

You can employ a subordinate clause:

When John had walked down the street, he entered a coffee shop at the end of the block.

You can use a participial phrase at the beginning of the sentence:

Walking (or, Having walked) down the street, John entered a coffee shop at the end of the block.

You can employ a different participial construction:

John walked down the street and entered a coffee shop standing at the end of the block.

You can switch to a relative clause:

John walked down the street and entered a coffee shop that stood at the end of the block.

By rearranging the structures in the sentences and by choosing different words, you can construct almost limitless variations on those two simple sentences. Learning to employ a variety of sentence structures will enable you to write effectively and hold the interest of your reader. In the world of publishing, the world where books and articles are printed for distribution or posted on the Internet, these skills fall under a general heading: *copyediting*. It is there that another person, a copyeditor, might make suggestions about sentence structures and word choices. Because your writing, at least in college, will not be read by a copyeditor, you will need to do that work yourself.

So as you read the first finished draft of your writing, the draft you will use for working through the revision process, follow these steps:

- Check the thesis to be sure it is accurate and explicit.
- Check each paragraph to be sure all paragraphs support the thesis.
- Check the order of the points in your outline to be sure the order of presentation is logical and effective.
- Check the development of the paragraphs (narration, description, analysis, discussion) to be sure each choice is the best choice for that spot in the essay.

Then follow the procedure discussed below to improve the quality of your sentences. (Note that by this time you will have read the paper two or three times. Please be patient and work through this final portion of the revision process. Doing so will markedly improve your paper.)

Read the paper through from start to finish; read slowly, perhaps aloud, to give yourself a sense of the sounds and rhythms of the sentences.

Read the paper again to identify the structures you have used in constructing the sentences. Where you find repetitious structures, sentences that sound the same, change some of them to different structures to provide some variety in your sentences.

Test each of the major words in each sentence to be sure that the word expresses exactly what you want to say. Make the wording as explicit as possible. Use action verbs wherever it is possible within the sense of the sentence. Avoid words that are very general in their meaning, such as *nice* and *good*. Be specific.

In the example given above, instead of saying,

John walked . . .

you might have said,

John strolled
John ambled
John strode

You might also have used an adverbial modifier such as *slowly* or *purposefully*.

Your goal in any piece of writing should be to state your idea so clearly and effectively that the reader is allowed little or no room for interpretation of your idea. This idea is, after all, yours, not the reader's. Therefore, you want to leave the reader no *wiggle room* to change your idea before it is stated completely. Once **Your Idea**, your very own special statement, is passed on to a reader, that person is perfectly free to agree or disagree with your statement. But before agreeing or disagreeing, the reader must grasp your idea. Your responsibility as a writer is to make sure that your idea is clearly stated, and stated in such a way that the reader cannot twist it or change it because of prior suppositions or biases on the part of the reader.

Examine a farfetched, even laughable example. If you say,

"I think I'll get a pickle out of that jar and eat it with my sandwich."

your listener will probably visualize your unscrewing the top and pulling out a pickle with your fingers or a fork.

But if you have a different method for getting pickles out of jars, if, for example, you empty the jar into the sink and select a special pickle or smash the entire jar on the kitchen floor to find that special pickle, ". . . get a pickle out of the jar . . ." is simply not going to convey to the reader exactly what your method of pickle extraction is.

Be specific in your word choices to make your meaning as clear as possible and to keep your reader from changing your idea before it gets a complete presentation.

The second set of skills gives you the ability to find and correct any errors in your paper before you submit it to your reader. Correctness, coming as close as you possibly can to error-free presentation, is vital to your success as a writer. When reading your paper, the reader probably reacts as follows to errors. The first error gets passed off as a simple mistake. The second error gets a flicker of attention. The third error, especially if the three occur on the same page, creates a moment of annoyance. Any additional errors will cause the reader to begin to lose faith in what you are saying. The reader loses respect for you as a writer and for your idea because the errors you left in the final draft have created a distraction.

So for the last step, you need to proofread your draft. If you made significant changes in the first finished draft, print off a new version of the paper.

This second set of skills, especially those developed in the sections on punctuation, usage, and capitalization, concentrate on helping you to submit writing that is correct and does not call unfavorable attention to itself because of errors. In order to do a successful job of proof-reading, you need to recognize something amazing that happens when you read through a piece that you have written.

If you read your own writing from beginning to end as you wrote it, the chances are excellent that you will miss errors and will even supply omitted words.

To proofread successfully, you must break the connections between the sentences, so you need to read each sentence separately, one at a time, from the bottom of the paper back to the top.

Reading in this direction, in reverse order, will accomplish several good things:

- Sentence fragments and dangling modifiers will stand out starkly because they are alone, unconnected to related ideas.
- Pronouns without antecedents, subjects without verbs, subject–verb disagreement and other errors will be much more easily identified because, again, the sentence is isolated from its context.
- Even misspelled words will be easily spotted because you have read the sentence as a single unit, disconnected from the other sentences.

You need a simple checklist that will lead from the largest elements of the sentence to the smallest:

- Sentence completeness, fragments and dangling modifiers
- Construction of clauses, both independent and dependent

- Subordination and connection of phrases
- Matters of usage such as subject–verb and pronoun–antecedent agreement
- Capitalization and punctuation

If this list raises questions, or if some of these items are not clear to you, refer to the Check Sheets at the end of each unit for a quick review.

WRITING WITH A COMPUTER

Most college writers have access to a computer with a word-processing program. For convenience's sake, we'll use the word *computer* in this discussion when we all know that it is a word-processing program that does this work. Computers have revolutionized the production of papers for college classes.

In the days before computers, students wrote papers out by hand and then typed them for submission to a college teacher. The process was laborious, painful, and frustrating. Any copies had to be made by using a black paper, called carbon paper, that was messy and complicated to correct. Producing the final draft of a paper was a long, tedious, often frustrating process.

Computers perform amazing feats with seemingly no effort at all. With one or two keystrokes, writers can perform all the operations necessary to produce a finished paper:

- Set the size and shape of the pages, usually by accepting the default margins in the program
- Establish line spacing, single or double
- Select font type and size
- Insert headers, footers, and page numbers
- Make columns
- Add bullets, lists, numbers
- Record text, the actual writing
- Add, relocate, and remove segments
- Import text from other sources
- Check spelling
- Count words
- Print a final copy
- Store the paper conveniently for future use

This list doesn't cover all the talents of a word-processing program. The list could go on and on.

But it is important for writers to see that many of the jobs performed by the computer actually interrupt the writing process.

If you look at writing as a process divided into two separate parts, composing and revising, you will see that most of the items in the list above, and most of the other functions performed by the computer are actually part of the revision stage of the process.

In composing, writers:

- Choose or identify their subject
- Gather as much information on the subject as time and resources allow

- Establish a thesis
- Select content
- Select a tentative order for that content
- Choose paragraph types, such as process paragraph, comparison/contrast, and others
- Write the first finished draft

This first draft is not the finished product, and it will probably never be seen by anyone other than yourself. It is the first, tentative version of the paper, and it needs to be added to, subtracted from, reshaped, revised, and corrected before it is ready for public viewing.

All these steps are made easier than they were years ago by the computer. The problem with the computer, with the word-processing program, is that it tries to perform all the steps of revision while the writer is still composing.

Imagine that you are writing—composing—the first draft of a paper for a history course, and you key in a sentence that begins

In the riegn of Louis XIV of France

The computer recognizes that you have misspelled the word *reign* and it underlines that misspelling in red. You immediately stop, retrace your steps, and correct the spelling. Often, the computer picks out certain structures that might possibly be incorrect or need improvement and underlines them in green. When the lines appear, you stop composing and try to correct the structure highlighted on the screen.

Whenever the highlights appear, or when you recognize a poor word choice or structure, you stop to make changes. There is almost no way to avoid the interruption. Lines have appeared under certain words in your writing, and those lines say, "Whoa. You made a mistake and you need to correct it right now." And you stop and attempt the correction.

So in the example above, you look at "riegn" and say to yourself, "Oh, yeah. That word is an exception to the old rule that says, 'Put *i* before *e* . . .'" When you stop to remember a rule and make a correction, your entire train of thought on Louis XIV stops at the same time. So you make the correction, and then you try to remember what you wanted to say about the king and his rule.

No one is suggesting that you stop using the tools provided by the computer. Those tools have literally revolutionized the writing of papers, and have made the process of producing a clean, beautiful final draft infinitely easier than it was 50 years ago. Not one of us wants to go back to the old methods.

But, and it is a very important *but*, you need to use the tools of the computer at the proper time. And the proper time is not during the composing stage of the writing process. The proper time is during the revision stage.

ONE CONCRETE SUGGESTION

Because computers can store materials very conveniently and make them available with a mouse click, it would be useful to construct a permanent header or title page for your papers. This process will work for the major word-processing programs.

Follow these steps:

1. Open the program to a blank page.
2. Click "Save As."

3. Give the page a file name, such as English Heading.

4. Type into the page the heading required by your instructor:

Your name	John Smith
Course name	English 1101
Class or reference number	Ref. 25732
Assignment	Essay No.
Date	October 5, 20xx

Set a position for the title of the paper, if the instructor requires a title. Put the word "title" at the proper place and required number of lines down the page. If the instructor specifies some different heading or asks for additional information, set up all that is asked for in this file. If the margins and line spacing for your papers are different from the default settings in the program, set them in this file.

Then, save the file with that information typed into it. When you begin an assignment, open the file English Heading. Immediately click "Save As" and rename the file, for example, Essay No. 1. Then type in the pertinent information such as the assignment number and the date due. You will then have on your screen a proper heading for the current assignment, complete with margins and line spacing. The new file will store as the current assignment, and the file "English Heading" will be available for the next assignment, complete with all the information and settings required by your instructor.

Brief Writing Assignment: Set up an "English Heading" file in your computer. After you have saved it as "English Heading," close it and reopen it. Save it as "Brief Writing Assignment"; then write an eight-sentence paragraph describing the process you just followed. Write the first version as eight simple sentences; then combine the sentences into three or four longer sentences, using compound and complex sentences.

English Fundamentals Online

After you have completed the Practice Sheets and Exercises in this lesson, you can find additional help and drill work at **MyWritingLab.com**, in the sections on Revising the Essay; Editing the Essay.

Directions: Rewrite the following short, simple sentences by making them longer, complex sentences. Use compounds, noun phrases, verbal phrases, and subordinate clauses where they seem appropriate.

It was a late autumn day. It was a bright day. It was a sunshiny day. The leaves had turned bright colors. The colors were red and orange. A group of people walked down the road. Five people were in the group. Three of them were men. Two of them were women. The three men owned a construction company. The two women were engineers. Soon they came to the river. The road ran across the river on a bridge. The bridge was beautiful. The bridge was old. It was made of wood. Some of the wood was rotten. The bridge needed to be repaired. The people walked to the middle of the bridge. The two women began to take measurements. They began to make notes. One of the men took several photographs. He used a digital camera. They all finished gathering information. They returned to their office. They made plans to repair and preserve the bridge.

_____

_____

_____

_____

_____

_____

_____

_____

_____

_____

Directions: Rewrite the following short, simple sentences by making them longer, complex sentences. Use compounds, noun phrases, verbal phrases, and subordinate clauses where they seem appropriate.

It was early Tuesday morning. Sam was walking to class. Gary was walking to class. They met at an intersection of two streets. They walked on down the street. They walked toward class. Suddenly Sam remembered something. They were supposed to take a test that morning. Sam also remembered something else. He had not brought any No. 2 pencils with him. The pencils were needed to take the test. Sam stopped short. He turned. He ran into a drugstore. He bought five No. 2 pencils. He returned to the street. He and Gary continued to walk toward class. Gary laughed for a moment. He asked Sam, "Why were you worried? We don't actually need No. 2 pencils to take this test. Any pencil will work."

_____

_____

_____

_____

_____

_____

_____

_____

_____

NAME _____   SCORE _____

Directions: Correct all the errors of grammar, mechanics, spelling, and punctuation in the following passage.

The Xerox machine is an absolute marvel of simplicity, and complexity. The machine is reletively easy to operate. Lift the cover, and place the materiel to be copied on the glass plate. Select the number of copies and any other special formating items. Push the start button, and wait for the machine to do its work. Internaly the machine is amazingly complex. Physical principals, that involves oppositly charged substinces, and an application of heat provides the capibility from making clean copies of print and pictures either black and white, or color. Earlier methods of office copying had been cumbersome and slow—assigning a monk to make a copy or messy and smelly—mimeograph and ditto machines, which use volatile chemicals to make copies. Now since the invention of the Xerox machine by Chester Carlson even the smallest bussiness and many of us at home can make copies with enormous ease. Copying is so easy that we all make copies of everything anytime the mood strikes us even if the document is unbelievable trivial. Building supply stores maintains a "bridal registry" of gifts, requested by prospective grooms. Somone on the staff will make a copy of the list if it is requested. Thus if cousin Max is marrying his true love Marcia he can go to the building supply store, and enter his request for an air compressor or a hammer drill, and you can check your copy of the registery to see what Max requested, and know imediately weather or not another friend or relative has purchased the requested gift. This ability is a wonderful thing because it will prevent needless duplication of presence. After all no bride wants a second air compressor cluttering up the floor of her guest bedroom. The Xerox machine is a truly beautiful and wonderful device.

Directions: In the following passages make all necessary corrections in grammar, mechanics, punctuation, and spelling.

Of the seven species of sea turtles the green turtle is the largest, and the most widely distributed but it is nearing endangered status because it has commercal value. It is a large turtle, measuring between 3 and 6 feet in length over the top of the shell and weighing on the average 200–300 pounds. The largest specamens are more than 5 feet in length and weigh 800–1000 pounds. The upper shell (carapace) is light to dark brown shaded or mottled with darker colors ranging to an almost black-green. The lower shell (plastron) is white to light yellow. The scales on the upper surface of the head are dark and the spaces between them are yellow on the sides of the head the scales are brown but have a yellow margin giving a yellow cast to the sides of the head. The shell is broad low and more or less heart-shaped. The green turtle inhabits most of the warm shallow waters of the world's seas and oceans prefering areas 10–20 feet deep where it can find good sea grass pastures for browsing. The turtles prefer areas that have many potholes, because they sleep in the holes for security. In numbers and population trends the status of the green turtle is in doubt. It is under great pressure in highly populated areas such as the Caribean Sea where it is avidly hunted for food and for use in making jewelry and cosmetics. However because it occurs in large numbers in remote area it is not technecally an endangered species at this time. It needs better protection in populated area so that its number will not decline any further.

On any Saturday or Sunday afternoon in the fall hundreds of thousands of americans take themselves to stadiums and millions more hunker down before television sets to witness the great american specator sport football. If one reads the simplest definition of the sport football is a game played on a large field by two teams of eleven players scoring is acomplished by carrying or throwing an oval ball across the opponents goal line, or by kicking the ball between two uprights that are called *goal posts*. Such a literal definition however scarcely does justice to the game or its impact on americans. For it is more than a game or a sport it is a happening a spectacle a ritual that is almost a relegious experience for its devotees. The game catches them with it's color a beautiful field surrounded by a crowd dressed in every color of the rainbow teams uniformed in the brightest shades ever to flow from the brush of a derainged artist. It holds these fans with its excitement the long pass the touchdown run the closing minutes drive to victory. But above all these games seem to captivate them with its violence with dangers vicariously experienced with a slightly vieled aura of mayhem. This element of danger draws casual viewers and converts them to fanatic worshipers of the great american cult-sport football.

Brief Writing Exercise: In ten short, simple sentences, tell the story of your most recent test in your most difficult class. Then, rewrite the story by combining the ten simple sentences into three or four complex sentences.

7

Progress Tests

PROGRESS TESTS

Progress Tests are designed to check your mastery of a single concept or an idea covered in a single lesson. The tests are short, usually 20 items, and they focus closely on the materials covered in one lesson. Taking the test should not be considered a threat; instead, the tests will reveal whether or not you have mastered the concept. If you need additional practice to solidify your control over the material, go to **MyWritingLab.com** and work through the material specified at the end of the lesson. Also, your instructor can give you a copy of the Test Bank page for the lesson in question. You might also need to review the lesson in the textbook to confirm the concept in your mind.

Progress Test 1

Parts of Speech

NAME _____   SCORE _____

Directions: In the space at the left of each sentence, write one of the following numbers to identify the part of speech of the italicized word:

   1. noun   3. verb   5. adverb

   2. pronoun   4. adjective   6. preposition

_____ 1. The morning *after* the game, the players *reviewed* films of the game.

_____ 2. The latest *review* of that movie was very *positive*.

_____ 3. "I will *positively* be at the *office* early tomorrow morning," said Earl.

_____ 4. Where did *you* last see *that* book?

_____ 5. I *saw* my textbook in my room *under* some papers on my desk.

_____ 6. *James* was the *first* person in line for those tickets.

_____ 7. *First*, we *went* to the library for some books on that subject.

_____ 8. *I booked* a room at a hotel on the beach.

_____ 9. The men *beached* the boat and then walked away *from* the shore.

_____ 10. Our walk across town *took us* past several historic buildings.

_____ 11. Our instructor gave *us* an *historically* correct account of those important events.

_____ 12. We *accounted* for everyone but *Maria*.

_____ 13. *Every* member of the class will be hard at work on the reports *tonight*.

_____ 14. I can *hardly* see *anything* in this fog.

_____ 15. The instructor gave us a *hard assignment* for this weekend.

_____ 16. The *instructions* for the assignment seem extraordinarily *complex*.

_____ 17. *My* math *instructor* assigned 15 problems for Tuesday's class.

_____ 18. The weather report is predicting a *clear*, cold day *for* tomorrow's game.

_____ 19. *These* predictions, however, are not *always* accurate.

_____ 20. In fact, today's weather is nowhere close to the predictions *from yesterday*.

After you have checked your answers on the test, correct each one that you missed by rewriting enough of the sentence to show your correction. Then, under the sentence, write the rule or principle that governs your error.

NAME _____   SCORE _____

Directions: Copy the subject of the sentence on the first line and the verb on the second line.

_____
_____
1. There was a large crowd of people in the plaza in front of the building.

_____
2. None of the people paid any attention to the rain clouds overhead.

_____
3. Three young boys ran down the sidewalk at the edge of the plaza.

_____
4. A hard rain began very suddenly.

_____
5. Most people walked quickly back into the building.

_____
6. On the sidewalk the three youngsters stopped their run.

_____
_____
7. Under an awning on the next building, they waited for the end of the rain.

_____
8. Finally, the rain slowed to a light drizzle.

_____
9. Two of the boys continued their run.

_____
10. The third walked slowly down the sidewalk toward his house.

_____
_____
11. By the end of the night, I will have worked on this paper for ten hours.

_____
12. Unfortunately, the paper will not be near completion by that time.

_____
13. Joan has not finished her paper, either.

_____
14. She, in fact, has only recently finished her notes for the paper.

_____
_____
15. At noon today, not even the first page had moved from the note cards to the computer screen.

_____
16. We will meet after supper tonight for a work session on these papers.

_____
17. Perhaps such a meeting will encourage the two of us in our work.

_____
_____
18. The complexity of the assigned subject for the papers has been a problem for both of us.

_____
_____
19. For the rest of the class, the assignment will be exceedingly difficult also.

_____
_____
20. In this assignment, the professor presented us all with a major challenge.

After you have checked your answers on the test, correct each one that you missed by rewriting enough of the sentence to show your correction. Then, under the sentence, write the rule or principle that governs your error.

NAME _____ SCORE _____

Directions: Each of the following sentences is a Pattern 1 sentence with an intransitive verb or a Pattern 2 sentence with a noun, pronoun, or adjective as a subjective complement. Circle the subject and underline the verb in each sentence. If the sentence is a Pattern 1 sentence, write the numeral 1 in the space at the left. If the sentence is a Pattern 2 sentence, write the subjective complement in the space at the left.

_____ 1. Because of their behavior off the field, the members of the baseball team make good representatives of the college.

_____ 2. The rest of my books and papers are probably in the trunk of Janice's car.

_____ 3. Up at the end of that long, winding trail stands a shelter with a supply of fresh water in a nearby spring.

_____ 4. After all those hours of study, we certainly felt good about our chances for success on that test.

_____ 5. April's biology project, because of its complexity, was amazingly impressive.

_____ 6. According to my sources, the next sales manager will be Joe White.

_____ 7. Joe White is an excellent choice for the job of sales manager.

_____ 8. In ability, Joe White stands head and shoulders above any other candidate for the job.

_____ 9. In a short time, he will become an outstanding manager.

_____ 10. I will be very happy with Joe White in the manager's job.

_____ 11. Yesterday it rained almost three inches during the afternoon.

_____ 12. The water in the streets rose to the bottom of the doors of the cars.

_____ 13. Yesterday's rain was the heaviest rain in the past three months.

_____ 14. The stream in the park was full of rushing water.

_____ 15. All the soil in my grandfather's garden washed away during the rain.

_____ 16. A straight line is the shortest distance between two points.

_____ 17. On my solitary hikes, I sometimes wander far from the trail.

_____ 18. The most interesting sights often stand far from the beaten path.

_____ 19. Last week during a hike, I became lost for about an hour.

_____ 20. During that time, I wandered in circles through a beautiful forest.

After you have checked your answers on the test, correct each one that you missed by rewriting enough of the sentence to show your correction. Then, under the sentence, write the rule or principle that governs your error.

NAME _____   SCORE _____

Directions: Identify the italicized word in each sentence by writing one of the following abbreviations in the space at the left:

      D.O. [direct object]   I.O. [indirect object]   O.C. [objective complement]

If the italicized word is not one of these complements, leave the space blank.

_____ 1. The sun cast beautiful *shadows* through the trees onto the road.

_____ 2. The chief financial officer read *us* a summary of his report.

_____ 3. The guide walked up the narrow trail ahead of the *group*.

_____ 4. In her anger, Jane called her boyfriend a *jerk*.

_____ 5. The athletic director introduced *John Watkins*, the new baseball coach.

_____ 6. The new coach created a positive *impression* with the players.

_____ 7. Everyone on the team considered the coach a very impressive *man*.

_____ 8. We all thought the thunderstorm a frightening *experience*.

_____ 9. Mary rolled the *baby* the multi-colored ball.

_____ 10. The *baby* squealed with delight at the sight of the ball.

_____ 11. The baby's delight at the sight of the ball amused *all* of us.

_____ 12. The grade on that last test delighted *Karen* immensely.

_____ 13. The immense size of that offensive lineman impressed *everyone* in the stands.

_____ 14. The manager promised the office *staff* a bonus for the early completion of that report.

_____ 15. Up to this point in the season, our quarterback has been very *successful*.

_____ 16. Before the end of the class, I gave my *essay* a very thorough proofreading.

_____ 17. I sent *Margie* a text message about tonight's study session.

_____ 18. The company will give us that software *free* of charge.

_____ 19. We found the search for that lost ring almost *impossible* because of the darkness.

_____ 20. Last week we rode our *bikes* down that trail for about 2 hours.

After you have checked your answers on the test, correct each one that you missed by rewriting enough of the sentence to show your correction. Then, under the sentence, write the rule or principle that governs your error.

NAME _____   SCORE _____

Directions: Copy the auxiliary verbs in the first space at the left. In the second space, write
1, **2**, **3**, **4**, or **5** to identify the sentence pattern. If there are no auxiliary verbs in a sentence,
write the base of the verb in the first space.

_____   1. The men have looked everywhere on the job site for that lost nail gun.
_____

_____   2. No one should have laughed at Max's silly joke.
_____

_____   3. You will find that extra pay in your next check.
_____

_____   4. We might have overlooked those errors in our haste to finish the job.
_____

_____   5. Because of their game that day, the women may not be able to
_____   attend that meeting.

_____   6. I did the final work on my paper last night before the beginning of
_____   the game.

_____   7. Amy did not finish her paper until very early this morning.
_____

_____   8. We have only a few days before the due date for that report.
_____

_____   9. We have not seen Barbara since yesterday morning.
_____

_____   10. I had not given much thought to that idea before today.
_____

_____   11. I had not given that idea much thought before today.
_____

_____   12. The manager would not have thought Kevin capable of such a
_____   fine job because of his earlier mediocre work on such projects.

_____   13. At least one of us group members must attend that review session
_____   for Thursday's test.

_____   14. Yes, we did exaggerate the danger of that last set of rapids on
_____   yesterday's raft trip.

_____   15. The coach was not very happy with the performance of the defensive
_____   secondary in yesterday's game.

_____   16. That rumor had run very rapidly throughout the entire office by
_____   the end of the day.

_____   17. Ordinarily, we would not have sent Jim that e-mail.
_____

_____   18. Without several hours of training, I cannot run that complicated
_____   machine with any success.

_____   19. No one could be successful in that field without years of intense
_____   training.

_____   20. No one can succeed in that field without years of intense training.
_____

After you have checked your answers on the test, correct each one that you missed by rewriting enough of the sentence to show your correction. Then, under the sentence, write the rule or principle that governs your error.

NAME _____   SCORE _____

Directions: In the first space at the left of the sentence, write the form of the base of the verb. In the second space, write any auxiliary verbs. Some sentences may not have auxiliary verbs.

_____   1. We have not seen Jill since last week.

_____   2. Everyone in the class has grown wary of that next test.

_____   3. Mark did not run in that event at the last track meet.

_____   4. The team was weary to the point of exhaustion at the end of practice.

_____   5. The fire alarm has rung several times today.

_____   6. By noon Uncle Joe and I had caught only three small fish.

_____   7. The team should have eaten lunch two hours before the game.

_____   8. I cannot put all those books back on the shelves before the end of the day.

_____   9. Joanne did all those problems in a little over 15 minutes.

_____   10. Yesterday we were doing agility drills at the beginning of practice.

_____   11. The bear has bitten a huge hole in that bag of bird seed.

_____   12. That player will probably retire at the end of the season.

_____   13. The quarterbacks and receivers are reviewing film of last week's game.

_____   14. We probably should work on that project for at least two hours this afternoon.

_____   15. Our three-person team has been making that climb once a month for the past year.

_____   16. We have also been practicing with the kayaks for several months.

_____   17. Jenny did stretch carefully before her injury in the soccer game.

_____   18. John has two copies of that history textbook.

_____   19. Perhaps you could borrow one copy for a few weeks.

_____   20. I have been studying that chapter for over two hours without much success.

After you have checked your answers on the test, correct each one that you missed by rewriting enough of the sentence to show your correction. Then, under the sentence, write the rule or principle that governs your error.

NAME _____   SCORE _____

Directions: In the blank in the sentence, supply any punctuation and a conjunction (where needed) to form the required compound verb or sentence.

1. Tom and Joan left the campus _____ walked down the street to the deli.

2. At the deli, Tom and Joan looked for Barbara _____ did not see her anywhere.

3. They sat down by themselves _____ Barbara arrived very soon.

4. The three of them ordered lunch _____ they were all very hungry.

5. Soon two other people came into the deli _____ sat down at the table with them.

6. The newscaster made a brief explanation of the current economic situation _____ her explanation should have been much more thorough.

7. I barely understand the simplest concepts in economics _____ perhaps I should take a class and increase my knowledge.

8. One of the professors on this campus is a famous economist _____ I should probably take a class with her as teacher.

9. Unfortunately, my schedule for next term is already full _____ thus I cannot take her class until a later time.

10. Until that time, I will read business magazines _____ watch a business channel on television.

11. Please tell me about your experiences on that camping trip _____ I plan a similar trip for next summer.

12. I have gone camping with my family for years _____ I plan a solo trip for next summer.

13. Fishing is one of my hobbies _____ I will arrange the trip along a famous trout stream.

14. Several of my friends are interested in fishing _____ but they prefer fishing offshore in the ocean to fishing in inland streams.

15. One day in the future, I will schedule a trip with them _____ then I can understand their fascination with that type of fishing.

16. Last fall Karen's uncle built a tennis court at his house _____ encouraged her to take up the game.

17. She had not played tennis at an early age _____ she found the game rather difficult.

18. Karen took a tennis class and then private lessons _____ she could not master even the rudiments of the game.

19. Finally she met a tennis player and dated him for several months _____ thus she kept her interest in the game alive.

20. She worked at the game for another year _____ finally developed into an adequate player.

After you have checked your answers on the test, correct each one that you missed by rewriting enough of the sentence to show your correction. Then, under the sentence, write the rule or principle that governs your error.

NAME _____ SCORE _____

Directions: In the first space at the left, write a subordinating conjunction that logically connects the two clauses in the sentence. In the second space, write one of the following numbers to identify the type of subordinate clause:

1. Time	4. Purpose	7. Condition	10. Modification of an
2. Place	5. Manner	8. Concession	adjective or adverb
3. Cause	6. Result	9. Comparison	

_____ 1. The people on our staff are delighted _____ that they will
_____ receive their year-end bonuses at the party.

_____ 2. The team will leave for the next game _____ a short practice
_____ has ended.

_____ 3. This last assignment is much more difficult _____ the previous
_____ one.

_____ 4. You will find your textbook _____ you left it in the back
_____ seat of your car.

_____ 5. At noon we left campus for the weekend _____ bad weather
_____ was in the forecast.

_____ 6. I was forced, _____ I could not find my own notes, to rely
_____ on Melanie's rather sketchy version of the lecture notes.

_____ 7. The members of the class looked _____ they had never
_____ heard the announcement of the test.

_____ 8. We all gathered up our warmest winter clothes _____ we
_____ would be prepared for any bad weather.

_____ 9. Bill was so tired after that last practice _____ he could
_____ barely drag himself off the field.

_____ 10. _____ we study very hard this weekend, we probably won't
_____ be prepared for that final exam in our history class.

_____ 11. My sprained ankle is feeling much better _____ it did last
_____ week.

_____ 12. You should go to that politician's speech _____ I can't go
_____ with you.

_____ 13. I can turn in my paper on time _____ my aging computer
_____ doesn't give me any trouble.

_____ 14. There were so many variables in our last science experiment
_____ _____ we could not draw a valid conclusion.

_____ 15. In spite of their complexity, I followed those directions as well
_____ _____ I possibly could.

_____ 16. _____ we finally got to the end of that long, difficult run,
_____ we were all exhausted beyond belief.

_____ 17. _____ Kathy barely finished that paper on time, she will
_____ probably start work earlier on the next paper.

_____ 18. Let's pack the car tonight _____ we can get an early start in
_____ the morning.

_____ 19. _____ you don't find your book on the desk, look in the
_____ living room closet.

_____ 20. _____ some kind person buys the tickets for us, we will
_____ almost certainly miss that concert.

After you have checked your answers on the test, correct each one that you missed by rewriting enough of the sentence to show your correction. Then, under the sentence, write the rule or principle that governs your error.

NAME _____ SCORE _____

Directions: Each sentence contains an adjective clause. Underline the clause. In the first space at the left of the sentence, write the antecedent of the relative pronoun. In the second space, write **N** if the adjective clause is nonrestrictive or **R** if the clause is restrictive. Place commas where needed in the sentences.

1. James is looking for a car that will have both adequate speed and high gas mileage.
2. Cars that possess those two qualities are somewhat scarce, so he is conducting a very thorough search.
3. This search which began almost two months ago has not produced any satisfactory choices.
4. James' requirements are special because he has a job that sometimes requires driving as much as 200 miles a day.
5. Because he must also take with him small pieces of equipment, he needs a car that has a fairly large cargo space.
6. So that he can buy a car that meets these specifications, James will probably have to ask his boss for a larger car allowance.
7. The other option about which the boss has some reluctance would be a company car and a gasoline credit card.
8. But only three top executives drive company cars, a benefit that would lose importance if James also received a company car.
9. Until he and his boss reach a resolution that satisfies everyone, James has requested a gasoline credit card for job-related car expenses.
10. Perhaps someday the company will be so profitable that a company car James can drive on the job will no longer be a problem.
11. In early winter, all of us students are happy to see the first heavy snow which piles up in beautiful white drifts.
12. When the snow piles up, we all borrow cafeteria trays which make excellent sleds and slide down the hills on the campus.
13. During the last snowfall, two people brought out a small plastic sled that they had bought for just that occasion.
14. They went to the top of a hill on campus, and then they slid to the bottom of the hill where there was a small stream.
15. Near the stream were many sizable rocks which were completely hidden by the snow.
16. As they slid down the hill and came near the stream, they hit a fairly large rock which catapulted them head over heels into the stream.
17. They landed in the shallow water in the stream; fortunately, they were wearing all the winter clothes that they owned.
18. Their winter clothes which were quite bulky cushioned their fall into the stream.
19. Thus, they were unhurt, but they were very cold from their fall into the water, which was only a few degrees above freezing.
20. They rose from the stream, waved at their friends, and then ran to the dorm where they took hot showers and put on dry clothes.

After you have checked your answers on the test, correct each one that you missed by rewriting enough of the sentence to show your correction. Then, under the sentence, write the rule or principle that governs your error.

NAME _____   SCORE _____

Directions: The following sentences contain a noun clause. Put brackets around the noun clause, and, in the space at the left, identify the function of the clause in the sentence by writing one of the following abbreviations:

S. [subject or delayed subject]   S.C. [subjective complement]

D.O. [direct object or   O.P. [object of preposition]

    delayed direct object]   Ap. [appositive]

Note that some clauses are within other subordinate clauses and some clauses have subordinate clauses within them.

_____ 1. Secretly, the coach thinks it unlikely that the team can win Saturday's game.

_____ 2. It is rather unlikely that the team can win Saturday's game.

_____ 3. All the fans were pleasantly surprised by the fact that the team did win Saturday's game.

_____ 4. The rest of us in the work group are unaware of what you told the managers.

_____ 5. The story of that woman's life is what has inspired us to greater efforts.

_____ 6. I can never understand how files in my computer take themselves to such strange locations on the hard drive.

_____ 7. The staff will have to seek assistance on that project from whichever people have a little free time.

_____ 8. Wherever you can find a spot that is out of the way of traffic in the lumber yard would be a good place to stack those beams.

_____ 9. Do you know whom I can ask for help in proofreading my papers?

_____ 10. The idea that you would take a job with that law firm never occurred to us.

_____ 11. It never occurred to us that you would take a job with that law firm.

_____ 12. The fact that the weather report is forecasting snow for tonight caught us all by surprise.

_____ 13. It was a surprise that the weather report is forecasting snow for tonight.

_____ 14. I do not know anyone who was not surprised by the fact that the weather report contains a prediction of snow.

_____ 15. Announce the postponement of the test to whomever from the class you see on campus.

_____ 16. Just put those books that you brought from the library in whatever little spot is available on the table.

_____ 17. Whichever driver is on the bus this morning can tell you the stop for the science classroom building.

_____ 18. Once we discover where my little brother hides his cash, we can borrow a few dollars for a pizza.

_____ 19. That short note from Sam is what we know about the contents of the next test.

_____ 20. A good student always gives a great deal of thought to what might appear on a test.

After you have checked your answers on the test, correct each one that you missed by rewriting enough of the sentence to show your correction. Then, under the sentence, write the rule or principle that governs your error.

NAME _____   SCORE _____

Directions: Sentences 1–10 contain a gerund phrase. Underline the phrase and identify its use in the sentence by writing one of the following in the space at the left:

S. [subject]   S.C. [subjective complement]

D.O. [direct object]   O.P. [object of preposition]

Sentences 11–20 contain an infinitive phrase. Underline the phrase and identify its use in the sentence by writing one of the following in the space at the left:

N. [noun]   Adj. [adjective]   Adv. [adverb]

_____ 1. Without even checking my balance, I can tell you that my account has very little money in it.

_____ 2. My friend Tom, who is a banker, has always enjoyed making furniture in his spare time.

_____ 3. Walking from her car into her apartment is the only exercise Carla ever gets.

_____ 4. One of my father's hobbies is playing fantasy baseball in a league with his friends.

_____ 5. The technician at the tire store can fix that problem by rotating and balancing the tires.

_____ 6. Running a Computer Numeric Control lathe can be a highly paid job.

_____ 7. Next month the company will begin computerizing its parts inventory.

_____ 8. The last step in the preparation of that estimate is figuring the square yards of carpet needed for the house.

_____ 9. The three of us got a great deal of satisfaction from finishing that adventure race ahead of most people our age.

_____ 10. Will would not consider leaving his good job at this time.

_____ 11. Would you like to go with me to tonight's game?

_____ 12. To duplicate that apple pie without a recipe will be a difficult task.

_____ 13. The rest of us could do nothing but cheer as you attempted that difficult path up the rock face.

_____ 14. Our next big challenge will be to hire a competent computer technician.

_____ 15. The architects are working on the plans to be submitted next Friday.

_____ 16. The girls were happy to survive that ride on the roller coaster.

_____ 17. Before we can leave for work, we will need to scrape the ice and snow off the windshield of the car.

_____ 18. To walk across the top of that waterfall is too dangerous a stunt for me.

_____ 19. Perhaps those two men would be willing to push the car with us.

_____ 20. Mark was not able to find that file because it was lost somewhere on the hard drive of his computer.

After you have checked your answers on the test, correct each one that you missed by rewriting enough of the sentence to show your correction. Then, under the sentence, write the rule or principle that governs your error.

NAME _____ SCORE _____

Directions: Each of the following sentences contains either a participial or an absolute phrase. Put brackets around the phrase. If the phrase is a participial phrase, copy in the space at the left the noun or pronoun the phrase modifies. If the phrase is an absolute phrase, leave the space blank.

_____ 1. Having exhausted all our options for entertainment, my room-mates and I decided to study for tomorrow's test.

_____ 2. With all the options for entertainment exhausted, my roommates and I decided to study for tomorrow's test.

_____ 3. My roommates and I decided to study for tomorrow's test, all our options for entertainment having been exhausted.

_____ 4. On television, I watched a video clip of a man with a metal detector searching for metal objects on a beach.

_____ 5. How can we possibly get to sleep with that man playing the drums one floor below us?

_____ 6. The two men, working diligently until late at night, managed to finish the drawings for the next day's presentation.

_____ 7. The two tired men turned out the lights and went home, the work on the next day's presentation finally completed.

_____ 8. With our hearts pounding in our throats, we watched as the BASE jumper launched himself off the top of the antenna.

_____ 9. Please give the keys to whomever you find sitting at the security desk.

_____ 10. Being a very active person, I would find a desk job a very difficult assignment.

_____ 11. It was extremely difficult to concentrate on the task at hand with all that activity going on just outside the window.

_____ 12. The annoyed professor dismissed our class, a lawnmower running just outside the window and drowning out his voice.

_____ 13. The professor, having dismissed the class, packed his briefcase and went off to lodge a complaint about the noise.

_____ 14. The man operating the lawnmower tried to explain why it was necessary to work at that time in that location.

_____ 15. Without the sun shining on the grass, it is impossible to tell what areas have been cut.

_____ 16. Johnson loves to drive through the parking garage setting off car alarms with his booming stereo.

_____ 17. With his booming stereo setting off car alarms, Johnson loves to drive through quiet neighborhoods and wake people up.

_____ 18. Cathy shivered as she walked to class in the cold, her heavy jacket hanging at home in the closet.

_____ 19. Carelessly leaving her heavy jacket at home in the closet, Cathy shivered as she walked to class in the cold.

_____ 20. Cathy, having carelessly left her heavy jacket at home in the closet, shivered as she walked to class in the cold.

After you have checked your answers on the test, correct each one that you missed by rewriting enough of the sentence to show your correction. Then, under the sentence, write the rule or principle that governs your error.

NAME _____   SCORE _____

Directions: Each item is either a sentence fragment or a complete sentence (or an acceptable fragment). In the space at the left, write **F** if the item is a fragment. Write **S** if the item is a complete sentence or an acceptable fragment.

_____ 1. Wow! What a shot! From behind the arc, nothing but net!

_____ 2. Finding Mr. Ransom the best candidate for the teaching job because of his educational background and his long years of experience.

_____ 3. James Jackson, whose skill as a sailor and navigator will make him a valuable addition to the crew.

_____ 4. The captain hired James Jackson, whose skill as a sailor and navigator will make him a valuable addition to the crew.

_____ 5. The administration, finding Mr. Ransom the best qualified person, offered him a teaching contract.

_____ 6. But we do not know the location of that building, nor do we have anyone to ask for directions.

_____ 7. The row house, standing at the end of a long line of houses, a beautiful example of that type of architecture.

_____ 8. Standing at the end of a long line of people, Joe and I waited patiently for the opening of the jetway so that we could take our seats in the plane.

_____ 9. So the two men finally came into view, wandering slowly down the road and stopping to rest frequently.

_____ 10. To find our way out of town and onto the Interstate highway was a job that took full attention from both of us.

_____ 11. To find our way out of town and onto the Interstate highway, a difficult, tricky job that took full attention from both of us.

_____ 12. Finding our way out of town and finally getting onto the Interstate highway took our full attention and easily 30 minutes of our time.

_____ 13. Finding our way out of town and getting onto the Interstate highway, we easily reached home in less than 90 minutes.

_____ 14. The top of that skyscraper, rising majestically over all the buildings in its vicinity and offering a wide view of the Gulf of Mexico, which spread itself out for miles.

_____ 15. We took the elevator to the top of that skyscraper, which rose majestically over all the buildings in its vicinity and offered a view of the Gulf of Mexico.

_____ 16. Come here and look! A herd of wild horses running down that canyon and onto the open prairie.

_____ 17. Sit here and watch that herd of wild horses as it runs down the canyon and out onto the open prairie.

_____ 18. One of those people who are always ready for any adventure, no matter the cost or the danger involved.

_____ 19. Shannon, one of those people who are always ready for any adventure, no matter what cost or danger is involved.

_____ 20. We should invite Shannon, who is one of those people always ready for any adventure, regardless of the cost or danger involved.

After you have checked your answers on the test, correct each one that you missed by rewriting enough of the sentence to show your correction. Then, under the sentence, write the rule or principle that governs your error.

NAME _____ SCORE _____

Directions: In sentences 1–10, there is a modifier in parentheses at the beginning of the sentence. In the space at the left, write **a** or **b** to indicate the logical place for the modifier.

_____ 1. (not all) Jan discovered that [a] the customers had [b] left the store.

_____ 2. (either) To get those drawings done on time, [a] you must [b] work late tonight or work on Saturday.

_____ 3. (early in the morning) Karen has decided to [a] run [b] for the next two weeks.

_____ 4. (for the entire morning) Because she needed that material [a] for her report, Jean searched the Internet [b].

_____ 5. (only) That meeting room will [a] be available for [b] two hours this morning.

_____ 6. (with a negative mind-set) Those two girls [a] undertook that project [b].

_____ 7. (on Saturday mornings) I like to [a] take a long bike ride [b].

_____ 8. (just) Andy [a] left town [b] three months ago.

_____ 9. (almost) In her attic, Aunt Martha [a] found [b] all of her grandfather's book collection.

_____ 10. (for a long time) When I missed that last bus, [a] I had to stand in the snow [b].

Directions: In sentences 11–20, there is a dangling modifier. Rewrite enough of the sentence to show how you can correct the dangling modifier.

_____ 11. We went to a play written by Arthur Miller at the insistence of my father.

_____

_____ 12. While running down the street, the trees seemed to loom darkly over us.

_____

_____ 13. Before selecting a new computer, several models should be evaluated.

_____

_____ 14. To complete that job more quickly, your keyboarding speed needs to improve.

_____

_____ 15. While still under ten years old, my parents moved my sister and me to New York City.

_____

_____ 16. Most engineers can either operate equally well in the office or the field.

_____

_____ 17. Being very early in the morning, I am not always fully awake for that class.

_____

_____ 18. The frame badly bent from the accident, Mary sent her motorcycle off on a wrecker.

_____

_____ 19. To find that lost set of keys, the entire room will need to be thoroughly searched.

_____

_____ 20. Seeing Laura Jones for the first time in years, her name slipped my mind for a few moments.

_____

NAME _____   SCORE _____

Directions: In each sentence you will find a subordinate clause or phrase in italics. In the space at the left, write one of the following numbers to identify the italicized subordinate unit:

1. Adverb clause   4. Gerund phrase   7. Infinitive phrase
2. Adjective clause   5. Absolute clause
3. Participial phrase   6. Appositive

_____ 1. Jon Jenkins, *a college football star*, has joined our high school's coaching staff.

_____ 2. *Riding my bicycle down that long hill* was one of the big thrills of my childhood.

_____ 3. *With all these recent developments overwhelming us*, we decided to reconsider our work on that project.

_____ 4. The business needs a new person *to lead the IT Division*.

_____ 5. It seems likely that, *after we have moved into the new building*, work will go more smoothly.

_____ 6. I know someone *who can do that job for us*, if we are willing to pay her well.

_____ 7. That runner *lying exhausted on the ground* just set a new state record in the 200-meter dash.

_____ 8. *To find that tiny town with any ease*, you will need both a map and a GPS.

_____ 9. I have never enjoyed *working late into the night because of a changed deadline*.

_____ 10. *After the men finish that work on the wall*, tell them their day's work is done and send them home.

_____ 11. *With the lightning flashing and the thunder crashing*, we had difficulty keeping the younger children calm.

_____ 12. The company president will introduce Walter Jones, *our new CFO*, at a meeting tomorrow morning.

_____ 13. Please tell me the name of the man *to whom the receptionist is giving an identification badge*.

_____ 14. When you arrive at the restaurant, look for a man *dressed in a gray overcoat*.

_____ 15. *With several men in gray overcoats present in the restaurant*, Jack wasn't able to decide which person to greet.

_____ 16. Every one of the freshmen *whom the coach invited to the tryouts* will probably make the team.

_____ 17. Would you mind *taking my dog for a short walk*? I'm very busy right now.

_____ 18. *After she calmed down*, my sister realized that getting angry was a waste of energy.

_____ 19. We need planning that is calm and rational *if we are going to solve this problem*.

_____ 20. *Dressed in her best business suit*, the young woman waited nervously for her first job interview.

After you have checked your answers on the test, correct each one that you missed by rewriting enough of the sentence to show your correction. Then, under the sentence, write the rule or principle that governs your error.

NAME _____   SCORE _____

Directions: Rewrite the sentences to correct the faulty parallelism.

1. Sonya is a player with great hitting skills and who also plays the outfield well.

   _____

2. Wearing an oversized shirt and with baggy jeans, Jim Smith does not look successful.

   _____

3. Janine succeeds in her sport more through hard work than having great skill.

   _____

4. Walt has a reputation as a hard worker and getting along well with customers.

   _____

5. Robert can be heard attacking the officials and constantly criticizes his teammates.

   _____

6. You need to sand that table thoroughly and then covering it with polyurethane.

   _____

7. The instructions are incomplete and with such complexity that we cannot understand them.

   _____

8. Most students would rather write a paper than making a speech.

   _____

9. Jameson has been training with weights to gain strength and increasing his power for tennis.

   _____

10. We took that course because it is required but also because of its interesting content.

   _____

Directions: Rewrite the sentences to make the comparison logical and correct.

11. The streets in the old area of downtown are much more narrow than the rest of the city.

_____

12. Alex is taller than anyone on his basketball team.

_____

13. She is unsmiling, with a constant frown and looks as if she just ate something sour.

_____

14. Her speed is equal, and in some cases faster than, the rest of the team.

_____

15. His reaction to your remark was as sharp if not sharper than any I've heard recently.

_____

16. Marcia says her work as an executive assistant is more important than the executives.

_____

17. Alicia likes her cats more than her sister. (Correct two ways.)

_____

18. Our IT technician is more skilled than anyone on the campus.

_____

19. I never suspected that the work on my first job would be so much harder than college.

_____

20. That three-hour movie was one of the most boring, if not the most boring, I've ever watched.

_____

NAME _____   SCORE _____

Directions: In each of the following sentences, two commas are missing. Add commas where they are needed. In the spaces at the left of each sentence, write the number of the rule that applies to each comma you have added:

1. Before a coordinating conjunction in a compound sentence
2. In a series
3. Between coordinate adjectives
4. After an introductory modifier
5. To prevent misreading

_____ 1. The band played, the crowd roared and the umpire shouted, "Play ball!" to begin the important exciting game.

_____ 2. When I started this job was very intricate but the new, computerized machine has made the work much simpler.

_____ 3. My car needs new tires, a new battery and a new radiator cap but, unfortunately, I don't have any money at this time.

_____ 4. After I read and outline that long complicated chapter I will study the material for another hour.

_____ 5. Riding his bike down that long tricky hill Richards fell heavily and strained his shoulder.

_____ 6. In this new and different economy skill sharp judgment and a little luck will be needed to land a good job.

_____ 7. Jackson Rhodes, and Williams came in early this morning but no one has done any real work yet.

_____ 8. Moving slowly out of the side entrance to the building the two men turned and walked slowly hesitantly down the alley.

_____ 9. In order to stop the train's engine must be shut down almost completely and the brakes applied very gently.

_____ 10. There were several people standing in the room but no one seemed to know when Jim, Robert and Paul would arrive.

_____ 11. The tall swaying mast of the sailboat cast a long shadow on the water but the boat remained totally stationary because of lack of wind.

_____ 12. After we had finished the test we all walked to the barbecue restaurant for a delicious satisfying lunch.

_____ 13. After she finished changing the tire Rachel put the flat tire in the trunk of the car cleaned her hands on an old cloth, and got back into the car.

_____ 14. My cousin Barbara has changed majors twice she has dropped out of college for a semester, and she is now working in a difficult dangerous job with the Forest Service.

_____ 15. Walking into the room and dropping her briefcase on the desk the scowling instructor suddenly looked at the class and gave everyone a wide cheerful smile.

_____ 16. Marilyn has studied ancient history modern art, and ceramics but she recently took up auto mechanics to develop a useful skill.

_____ 17. As soon as Harry entered the room grew very quiet and the people in the back of the room began to move to their seats.

_____ 18. After singing the alma mater the graduates moved the tassels on their mortarboards and then they marched in dignified fashion out of the auditorium.

_____ 19. Having failed completely to master the last obstacle the weary recruits were forced to return to the start of the difficult tricky course and begin their effort again.

_____ 20. The snow fell heavily the wind blew fiercely, and the happy exhausted skiers sat in the lodge warming their feet by the fire.

After you have checked your answers on the test, correct each one that you missed by rewriting enough of the sentence to show your correction. Then, under the sentence, write the rule or principle that governs your error.

NAME _____   SCORE _____

Directions: Insert commas where they are needed in the following sentences. Then, in the space at the left of the sentence, write one of the following numbers to indicate the rule that governs the punctuation of the sentence:

1. a nonrestrictive clause or phrase   4. a parenthetical element

2. an appositive   5. the speaker in dialogue

3. a noun in direct address   6. an absolute phrase

_____ 1. James Belson to whom we wrote that letter is coming to town tomorrow.

_____ 2. James Belson a friend of my father is coming to town tomorrow.

_____ 3. "Mark will you take this package up to the executive offices?" asked Mr. Wilson.

_____ 4. I thought that the whole project, in truth, was a great idea from the beginning.

_____ 5. "Jose believes, and I think you'll agree, that we need to move with more speed on that operation" said Mike.

_____ 6. With all the lights out and the air conditioning off because of the storm we probably should just leave for the day.

_____ 7. "I agree with the majority" said Milly "that an investment in that company's stock is too risky for us at this point."

_____ 8. "If you don't mind Jim please stop tapping your pencil on the desk," said Melanie.

_____ 9. That window the one on the south wall gives one a terrific view of the river.

_____ 10. That window which is in the middle of the south wall gives one a terrific view of the river.

_____ 11. There is no reason under these circumstances to go out on the lake when a storm is moving in from the south.

_____ 12. "Jan, Janice" screamed her father "must you play that iPod so that I can hear the speakers five rooms away?"

_____ 13. All things being equal and money being no object I would buy the red convertible with the turbocharged engine.

_____ 14. That new novel which has the spookiest ending imaginable kept me awake almost all night.

_____ 15. That book one of the last written by that author has an amazing twist in plot at the end.

_____ 16. "Alan you should read this book," said Will; "you will enjoy the intricate plot and the amazing characters."

_____ 17. That test surely you'll agree with me was one of the hardest we've taken all term.

_____ 18. "I don't believe" said Dan "that I've taken a harder test in the last two terms."

_____ 19. "With all those problems weighing heavily on my mind it's no wonder that I forgot your birthday, Marcie," said Manny.

_____ 20. That one question from the test the last question on the first page continues to puzzle me; I'm sure I got the answer wrong.

After you have checked your answers on the test, correct each one that you missed by rewriting enough of the sentence to show your correction. Then, under the sentence, write the rule or principle that governs your error.

NAME _____   SCORE _____

Directions: The following passage lacks punctuation at points where a line is introduced in the text. Enter the proper punctuation mark at each point. Do not leave blanks; each point will require a punctuation mark.

Dad, can I borrow the car tonight _ asked sixteen_year_old Janie_ _ I want to go to the mall with Margie and Sue_ _

What time can I expect you home _ asked Dad_

_No later than midnight, _ replied Janie_

_Don't the stores close at 10_00 P.M. _Where will you be between ten o_clock and midnight_ _

_We_ll probably go out for a pizza and then come home_ The other two are spending the night here_ _

This conversation is a staple of American life_ every American over the age of twelve wants to drive, does drive, or just stopped driving because of a license suspension or old age_ All Americans _ regardless of age, gender, or driving experience_ fancy themselves to be expert drivers_ But this fancy_ better yet, this fantasy_ cannot be based on reality_ Accident statistics_ not a pretty sight by any stretch of the imagination_ suggest that there must be a certain number of less_than_expert drivers on our roads_ But can we identify the qualities that are the identifying marks of a good driver_ Probably there are at least three such qualities_ technical and physical skills, proper attitude, and steel nerves to cope with the inevitable emergency, the emergency that will come to every driver at some point_ Technical and physical skills are those related to moving the car_ in addition, these involve reflexes and reaction time_ Proper attitude is based on a defensive driving posture_ the defensive driver assumes that every driver in the general vicinity is about to make a life_threatening mistake and plans evasive or preventive actions accordingly_ Steel nerves are the requirement for making the right decision and executing the right maneuver in that certain_to_occur emergency_ These three qualities are at least the beginning of expert driving.

After you have checked your answers on the test, correct each one that you missed by rewriting enough of the sentence to show your correction. Then, under the sentence, write the rule or principle that governs your error.

Using Verbs Correctly: Principal Parts; Tense

NAME _____ SCORE _____

Directions: In the space at the left, write the correct form of the verb shown in the parentheses. Do not use *ing* forms.

_____ 1. I (leave) for school after I (tell) my parents the good news.
_____
_____ 2. The wind has (swing) to the south now that the cold front has
_____   (pass) through the area.
_____ 3. "I didn't (know) that I had already read this romance novel," said
_____   Cheryl as she (fling) the book into the corner of the room.
_____ 4. "Have you (see)," asked Loretta, "that horrible furniture the
_____   college (buy) for the student lounge?"
_____ 5. Max (climb) that ladder very rapidly because his cat had gotten
_____   (stick) in the tree.
_____ 6. After my grandmother had (set) out her tomato plants, they (grow)
_____   very rapidly because the soil is very rich.
_____ 7. I (lay) my jacket on that table in the hall, but someone has (take)
_____   it and I can't find it.
_____ 8. The carpenter (draw) on all his past experience as he (build) that
_____   grand staircase.
_____ 9. The sun (rise) and the moon set long after we had (rise) to go fishing.
_____
_____ 10. The workers (lie) down for a short nap shortly after the whistle
_____   had (blow) for lunch.
_____ 11. At the end of the day, I (take) my new shirt home and (hang) it in
_____   the closet.
_____ 12. "I will (sit) here and watch you as you run by," said Arthur, "but I
_____   (be) not interested in joining you in that marathon."
_____ 13. Our company (pay) far too much in salary and benefits when it
_____   (bring) in that new executive.
_____ 14. The girl (creep) into class late because she had not (find) a parking
_____   place close to the classroom building.
_____ 15. The temperature had (fall) sharply last night, and the driveway
_____   had (freeze) solid sometime before dawn.
_____ 16. Perhaps Joan has (forget) that she (leave) her heavy coat out in
_____   the car last night.
_____ 17. "You have (deal) me a very weak hand again," said the bridge
_____   player; "I should have (withdraw) from the game long ago."
_____ 18. Mike Gonzales (find) a new job last week, but we still have not
_____   (make) arrangements for a replacement.
_____ 19. The college president has never (forgive) us for all those terrible
_____   pranks we (play) during our freshman year.
_____ 20. As Al (lay) asleep under the tree, a wasp (sting) him on his hand.

After you have checked your answers on the test, correct each one that you missed by rewriting enough of the sentence to show your correction. Then, under the sentence, write the rule or principle that governs your error.

NAME _____   SCORE _____

Directions: For each sentence, copy the correct form of the verb from those shown in the parentheses.

_____ 1. The band's plan for buying new uniforms and instruments (is, are) going to be postponed.

_____ 2. Not one of the ten people who applied for that job (was, were) qualified.

_____ 3. Within five minutes of our new offices (is, are) a beautiful city park.

_____ 4. The mayor, along with several members of the city council, (was, were) standing on the platform.

_____ 5. "(Has, Have) either of you seen my new baseball bat?" asked Charlie.

_____ 6. For next summer I'm looking at several possibilities for jobs that (pays, pay) well and have pleasant working conditions.

_____ 7. Loretta must be the only one of our friends who (pilots, pilot) a fishing boat as a weekend job.

_____ 8. Sam is one of those quiet people who almost never (speaks, speak) up about any issue in the office.

_____ 9. The costs of insuring and maintaining my motorcycles (is, are) prohibitively high.

_____ 10. My neighbors contend that the noisy parties and the late band practices in the house down the street (makes, make) life almost unbearable.

_____ 11. Reliable data (demonstrates, demonstrate) that many students change their majors during their time in college.

_____ 12. The number of teams that have rookies starting (is, are) certainly growing.

_____ 13. The winner of the race, along with two other drivers, (is, are) headed to the podium.

_____ 14. Martha is one of those people who (enjoys, enjoy) unraveling complicated plot lines in long novels.

_____ 15. Neither Mr. Jackson nor Ms. Roberts (brings, bring) any special skills to this project.

_____ 16. I don't think that $300 adequately (compensates, compensate) me for three days of work painting that porch.

_____ 17. There (stands, stand) all thirty people who have signed up for this course.

_____ 18. Apparently, there (is, are) no serious problems standing in the way of completing that project on time.

_____ 19. The combination of great speed and high quality workmanship (makes, make) that car an extremely good buy.

_____ 20. The value of those lots along the lakefront (has, have) increased greatly in the last few months.

After you have checked your answers on the test, correct each one that you missed by rewriting enough of the sentence to show your correction. Then, under the sentence, write the rule or principle that governs your error.

NAME _____   SCORE _____

Directions: In the space at the left, copy the correct pronoun or pronoun–verb combination given in the parentheses.

_____ 1. Whoever comes up with the solution to that complicated problem can certainly take pride in (his or her, their) ability in physics.

_____ 2. It takes a great deal of character for a man to admit that (he, they) made such a colossal blunder.

_____ 3. The manager decided to close the restaurant in August so the staff can take (its, their) vacation then.

_____ 4. Marlene said, "The power of that enormous waterfall shows us how insignificant (we, you, they) are in the grand scheme of things."

_____ 5. If the tennis team goes to the state finals, each girl will need to pay (her, their) own expenses.

_____ 6. That ice cream parlor is about to celebrate (its, it's, their) tenth anniversary.

_____ 7. A real craftsman will put every tool back where (it belongs, they belong) at the end of the day's work.

_____ 8. "You may use either of those boats if you promise to clean (it, them) and fill (its, their) gas tank at the end of the day," said the manager.

_____ 9. Not a single person in my class said that (he or she, they) studied for today's test.

_____ 10. Our neighborhood has raised a great deal of money to provide parks for (its, it's, their) kids.

_____ 11. A girl may sign up for white-water kayaking only if (she, they) can swim the length of the swimming pool twice without stopping.

_____ 12. It is annoying to search for an item for an hour, and then (the clerk says, they say) that the item is out of stock.

_____ 13. Students can get terrific instruction in computers at the local technical school if (you, they) take the work seriously.

_____ 14. Caroline would like to join the Air Force because it would send (her, you) to places all over the world.

_____ 15. If a person needs help with an income tax form, he can go to an IRS office where (someone, they) can help in filling out the form.

_____ 16. Our business has been very successful this year, and the prospects for (its, our, their) continued success look extremely positive.

_____ 17. The Search Committee will meet next week to decide which candidates (it wants, they want) to interview in depth.

_____ 18. All the players on the team insist that (she, they) arrived on campus in top physical condition.

_____ 19. If anyone has an A in the course at the end of the term, (he or she, they) will be exempt from taking the exam.

_____ 20. In a department store as large as this one, all customers can find clothes that suit (his or her, their) needs.

After you have checked your answers on the test, correct each one that you missed by rewriting enough of the sentence to show your correction. Then, under the sentence, write the rule or principle that governs your error.

NAME _____   SCORE _____

Directions: In the space at the left of the sentence, copy the correct pronoun given in the parentheses.

_____ 1. Jordan was with me at work all day yesterday; it was not (her, she) whom you saw at the game.

_____ 2. (Who, Whom) would you guess Jon was referring to when he used the word "beautiful"?

_____ 3. Donovan is an experienced scout; he seems to have a feel for (who, whom) the real athletes are.

_____ 4. Just between you and (I, me), I believe that we will have a new coach next year.

_____ 5. Unless those runners pick up their pace, none of them will be able to catch (us, we) leaders by the end of the race.

_____ 6. The people gossiping on that bench are trying to figure out (who, whom) Governor Landry will choose as his running mate.

_____ 7. The staff members, all the assistants, and (us, we) interns were praised by the boss for dedication to that project.

_____ 8. (You, Your) leaving us to do volunteer work in that island country is certainly a noble thing to do.

_____ 9. The planning committee members are trying to reach Charles English, (who, whom) they hear is a very interesting speaker.

_____ 10. I can't lift that book box; it is twice as heavy as (me, I).

_____ 11. I have watched that film three times, but it has never lost (its, it's) appeal for me.

_____ 12. No one else's grades are as good as (your's, yours), Arline; you certainly lead the class at this point.

_____ 13. (Who's, Whose) books are those lying on the table? I put mine in my room when I came home.

_____ 14. The technician pointed to the broken speaker wire and told John and (I, me) what he needed to do to replace it.

_____ 15. (Who, Whom) do you think could be responsible for that silly prank on the campus last night?

_____ 16. I see no chance of (him, his) reaching that goal unless he begins to work much harder than he has before.

_____ 17. Sam said, "I want to thank you for your efforts; all of you worked much harder than (I, me) today."

_____ 18. That teacher, (who's, whose) a favorite among freshman students, will be returning next year.

_____ 19. "Our firewood is soaking wet," said Marie. "Do you think the people at the next campsite would lend us some of (theirs, their's)?"

_____ 20. "Faithful, hardworking people like you and (I, me) are really the backbone of this company," said Mr. Wallace.

After you have checked your answers on the test, correct each one that you missed by rewriting enough of the sentence to show your correction. Then, under the sentence, write the rule or principle that governs your error.

NAME _____   SCORE _____

Directions: In the space at the left, copy the correct form given in the parentheses.

_____   1. If you practice (diligent, diligently), your play as shortstop should improve.

_____   2. Both my brothers are fine golfers, but Tim is the (better, best) putter.

_____   3. The car dealer and I were unable to agree (on, to) a price for that used car.

_____   4. The people in that house down the street need to keep that huge dog (inside, inside of) the fence.

_____   5. Do you think that shirt looks (good, well) with those pants?

_____   6. We will divide the money equally (among, between) the four people.

_____   7. That pizza should have been cut into eight (equal, equally) parts.

_____   8. When Sue told me about her new boat, she sounded (happily, happy).

_____   9. The grass out back (sure, surely) does need to be cut; it must have grown six inches since last Saturday.

_____   10. Who is (taller, tallest), Gina or Michelle?

_____   11. The gloom hung (thick, thickly) in our locker room after that disappointing loss.

_____   12. There has been a (slight, slightly) easing of tension since Harry was transferred to Wichita.

_____   13. That apple pie has cooled only (slight, slightly) since I took it out of the oven.

_____   14. The little boy looked quite (sad, sadly) as he watched his balloon float away in the sky.

_____   15. The return on this latest investment will be (better, more better) than the return on that last loser we chose.

_____   16. Which of those two computers can recalculate that spreadsheet (faster, fastest)?

_____   17. (Almost, Most) all the people in that class are would-be architects.

_____   18. When Mary decided to become a firefighter, her mother was (real, really) delighted.

_____   19. The ammonia that you spilled on the floor smells quite (sharp, sharply).

_____   20. Tom did very (good, well) on that test yesterday.

After you have checked your answers on the test, correct each one that you missed by rewriting enough of the sentence to show your correction. Then, under the sentence, write the rule or principle that governs your error.

Appendix A SENTENCE COMBINING

Sentence combining is a simple process designed to help you write more sophisticated and effective sentences. You began to employ combining techniques in Lesson 7 and its accompanying exercises, so the following exercises ought to be familiar to you. The exercises in Appendix A begin with the simplest kinds of combining, embedding an adjective from one sentence into another sentence, thus enriching one sentence and eliminating the other. The exercises then move through the formation of compound sentences and into complex sentences, those constructed with verbal phrases and subordinate clauses.

Every set in these exercises can be done in several ways, each one correct. The following example offers a good example of the possibilities:

> The man was tall.
> He was thin.
> He walked down the street.

The simplest combined form puts the adjectives *tall* and *thin* in the sentence immediately before the noun:

> The tall, thin man walked down the street.

But it is possible to move the adjectives into more emphatic positions:

> Tall and thin, the man walked down the street.
> The man, tall and thin, walked down the street.

Each of these options is correct, and each creates a slightly different sentence—a sentence that draws the reader's attention to the facts in slightly different ways.

These additional combining exercises will help your writing in two ways. First, they will remind you of different ways of expressing the same idea, and thus they will expand the range of constructions you employ in your writing. Second, the exercises will focus your attention on punctuation as you make up the combinations.

Remember that every set in these exercises can be done in several ways, all of them correct. For each set, test the various ways of creating combinations, and you will make yourself a more flexible and more effective writer.

Combine the sentences in each numbered unit into a single longer sentence.

1. The building stands.
   It is tall.
   It is stately.
   It stands at the end of Main Street.

   _____

   _____

2. The two men walked.
   They walked down Main Street.
   They were elderly.
   They were well dressed.

   _____

   _____

3. The elderly men walked down Main Street.
   They stopped in the middle of a block.
   They stopped beside a bench.

   _____

   _____

4. The elderly men stopped beside a bench.
   They spoke briefly to another man.
   The other man had a small leather briefcase. (Use *with*)

   _____

   _____

5. The man with the briefcase pointed down the street.
   He pointed at the tall building.
   The tall building is at the end of Main Street.
   The building has a coffee shop on the ground floor. (Use *with*)

   _____

   _____

Combine the sentences in this numbered unit into a single longer sentence.

6. John walked across the campus.
   He walked quickly.
   Cathy walked across the campus.

She walked quickly.
They went into the bookstore.

_____

_____

7. John and Cathy walked into the bookstore.
   They looked on the shelf for a textbook.
   The textbook was for their biology class.

_____

_____

8. Unfortunately, the text was not on the shelf.
   So they left the bookstore.
   They walked down the street.
   They walked to a sandwich shop.

_____

_____

9. They walked to a booth.
   The booth was beside a window.
   They sat down in the booth.
   They each picked up a menu.

_____

_____

10. The server asked them for their order.
    They could not decide on their order.
    So the server went on to another table.

_____

_____

Combine the sentences in this numbered unit into a single longer sentence.

11. Bob walked into the stable.
    Jan walked into the stable.
    Each one selected a horse.
    The horses were for a ride into the mountains.

_____

_____

12. Bob and Jan selected their horses. (Use *after*)
    They put bridles on the horses.
    They put saddles on the horses.

    _____

    _____

13. Bob and Jan saddled their horses. (Use *after*)
    Then they mounted the horses.
    They rode off into the mountains.

    _____

    _____

14. The two of them rode into the mountains.
    They found a few head of cattle.
    The cattle were lost.

    _____

    _____

15. They rounded up the cattle. (Use *after*)
    They drove the cattle down the mountain.
    They drove them down to a meadow.

    _____

    _____

Combine the sentences in this numbered unit into a single longer sentence.

16. Jo went to the team meeting late this afternoon. (Use *when*)
    The coach told her that she would be the starting pitcher.
    She would start in the next game.

    _____

    _____

17. Jo was excited by the news.
    She was thrilled by the news.
    This would be her first start of the season. (Use *because*)

    _____

    _____

18. The meeting ended. (Use *As soon as*)
    She went back to her dorm room.
    She called her parents.
    She told them the good news.

    _____

    _____

19. Her parents wanted to see Jo's first start. (Use *Since*)
    Her parents made to the trip to the campus.
    They arrived the night before the big game.

    _____

    _____

20. In the game the next day, Jo pitched beautifully. (Use relative clause)
    She struck out 10 opponents.
    She allowed only three hits.

    _____

    _____

Combine the sentences in this numbered unit into a single longer sentence.

21. Jim was exhausted from his long night of studying. (Use relative clause)
    He took his exam.
    He went back to his room for a nap.

    _____

    _____

22. Jim took a long nap.
    He woke up and went to the chemistry lab.
    He worked on a difficult report.
    The report was due the next day.

    _____

    _____

23. He finished the work on the lab report.
    He went out for supper.
    Then he went back to his room.
    He worked on a long math assignment.

    _____

    _____

24. On Friday he turned in his math assignment.
    The assignment was due that day.
    Then he went to two more classes.

    _____

    _____

25. The classes were finally over.
    Jim packed up his car for the weekend.
    He went home.
    He slept a long time.
    He ate some of his mother's good cooking.

    _____

    _____

Combine the sentences in this numbered unit into a single longer sentence.

26. The company president hired a new manager last week.
    The new manager has long experience in sales and marketing.
    She does not have much knowledge of finance.

    _____

    _____

27. Thus, the manager will need an assistant.
    The assistant must have experience with finance.
    The manager's lack of experience can be overcome. (Use *so that*)

    _____

    _____

28. Hiring a manager seems like a bad business move.
    She will need a new assistant. (Use *who*)
    The assistant will add cost in both salary and benefits.

    _____

    _____

29. There was a better option.
    The option was open to the president. (Use a colon)
    The option was finding someone who had all the necessary experience.

    _____

    _____

30. Sometimes those of us wish the president had more patience.
    We are actually working here.
    The extra costs come out of our income.

    _____

    _____

Combine the sentences in this numbered unit into a single longer sentence.

31. On the first day of class, Sara awoke suddenly.
    She realized (something).
    She did not know the room number for her calculus class.

    _____

    _____

32. She ran to her desk.
    She tried to find a paper copy of her class schedule.
    Her desk was so messy.
    She could not find anything important.

    _____

    _____

33. She booted up her computer.
    She hoped to find a copy of her schedule online.
    Unfortunately, the college's system was down.
    She was unable to get any help from that source.

    _____

    _____

34. Sara e-mailed her best friend.
    She had e-mailed a copy of her schedule to the friend.
    The friend was not at home.
    She was out of luck there, also.

    _____

    _____

35. Finally, she grabbed her backpack and her purse.
    She pulled out her cell phone.
    She called another friend.
    The friend told her the room number of the class.

    _____

    _____

Combine the sentences in this numbered unit into a single longer sentence.

36. Rain fell heavily.
   It fell for three long days. (Absolute phrase)
   All the bike trails were extremely muddy.
   The bike trails were in the national forest.

   _____

   _____

37. The two men loaded their bikes onto the bike rack.
   The woman loaded her bike onto the rack.
   The rack was on the back of an SUV.
   The three drove off to the head of the bike trail.

   _____

   _____

38. They arrived at the head of the trail.
   It was shortly after first light.
   They unloaded the bikes.
   They unrolled a map of the trail.

   _____

   _____

39. The trail was highly technical.
   It wound up a steep mountainside.
   It descended sharply into a deep ravine.
   It would provide excellent practice for the three people.

   _____

   _____

40. The three rode the trail.
   One of them fell on the way up. (Use *with*)
   The other two fell on the descent into the ravine.
   They came back tired, scratched, and a little bloody from the ride.
   They thought the ride a complete success.

   _____

   _____

Combine the sentences in this numbered unit into a single longer sentence.

41. The hour was quite late.
    Mindy and two members of her project group were working very hard on the project.
    The two other members were named Jim and Anne.
    The project was due at 8:00 A.M. the next morning.

    _____

    _____

42. The three of them were annoyed.
    The three had done most of the work on the project.
    They were annoyed by (the fact).
    The other three group members had contributed little or nothing to the work.

    _____

    _____

43. The three were annoyed.
    One of the absent members had written one page of the project.
    The other two had not even come to a meeting of the group.

    _____

    _____

44. At midnight Anne called one of the missing people.
    Jim called the other two.
    None of the three answered their phones.

    _____

    _____

45. Mindy, Jim, and Anne worked until 4:00 A.M. (Use *ing*)
    They finally finished the project.
    As they finished the project, they decided something. (Use *that*)
    They would not put the names of the other three on the finished project.

    _____

    _____

Combine the sentences in this numbered unit into a single longer sentence.

46. On Monday morning last week, Alex tried to access the Internet.
    He wanted to check his bank balance.
    He wanted to contact a friend.
    He wanted to do some research on a car.

    _____

    _____

47. Alex tried to access the Internet.
    He discovered something.
    His Internet connection was not working.
    He could not do any of the things.
    He needed to do these things.

    _____

    _____

48. Alex picked up his telephone.
    He dialed the phone number.
    The phone number was for his Internet Service Provider.
    He listened to the recorded instructions.
    He pressed the appropriate number on his phone.

    _____

    _____

49. A recorded voice on the phone told him something.
    All the technicians were serving other customers.
    His call was very important to the ISP.
    The voice asked him to stay on the line.

    _____

    _____

50. Alex put his phone on the speaker phone.
    He worked on another project on his computer.
    He wondered something.
    If he was so important.
    Why the ISP did not have enough people to answer the phone.

    _____

    _____

Appendix B   DIAGNOSTIC TESTS

Diagnostic Tests such as those in this section of *English Fundamentals* would more properly be called **Skills Assessments**. The purpose of such work is not to test or evaluate for admission to a class or for a grade. Such work serves only one purpose: identifying areas of language work you already know and areas where you need to focus your attention in order to make yourself a more powerful writer. The assessments should never be considered a threat or a negative commentary on the language skills you have developed. Rather, they are a helpful tool designed to guide you in further developing your skills. Take them in a relaxed fashion, and use the information gained to show where a little extra concentration is needed.

NAME _____   SCORE _____

Directions: Identify the part of speech of each italicized word by writing one of the following numbers in each space at the left.

1. noun	3. verb	5. adverb
2. pronoun	4. adjective	6. preposition

_____
_____   1. *Under* that stack of books on the table *I* found two letters that should have been mailed last week.

_____
_____   2. The *two* men walked *slowly* down the street toward the coffee shop.

_____
_____   3. The *blimp flew* slowly around the stadium as the crowd below watched the game intently.

_____
_____   4. The bright *red* bird perched *happily* on the bird feeder for almost five minutes.

_____
_____   5. The last five *minutes* of the class *passed* very, very slowly.

_____
_____   6. The hikers walked slowly *up* the *trail,* picking their way carefully among the rocks and roots that covered it.

_____
_____   7. The boss told *Jim* about his *promotion* early this morning; Jim was thrilled and excited.

_____
_____   8. The team scored its first two runs *easily,* but the rest of the game was a *defensive* struggle.

_____
_____   9. *I waited* for fifteen minutes in the rain for the campus shuttle, but it never came to my stop.

_____
_____   10. Please lend *me* the notes from this morning's lecture; I *slept* late and did not make it to class.

_____
_____   11. *In* the back of my refrigerator I *found* an old slice of bread; it was covered with a strange green growth.

_____
_____   12. I *had* never *seen* a sight as *beautiful* as that waterfall, with the sun shining through the mist.

_____ 13. *That* man in the back of the room is waiting for *us*; he wants to ask some
_____   questions about our project.

_____ 14. The *energy* left the *team* when the other side scored three times in the first
_____   quarter.

_____ 15. *Hastily*, the people in the meeting gathered their belongings and *walked* out
_____   to the street.

_____ 16. *According to* the most recent polls, the mayor is enjoying great popularity
_____   among the voters in *our* town.

_____ 17. The Joneses *have moved* the offices of their company *out of* this building into
_____   another one closer to downtown.

_____ 18. *Does* anyone *know* the *whereabouts* of our company's president?
_____

_____ 19. *Nobody* on the team has seen Charlie *since* early this morning.
_____

_____ 20. Tomorrow, I *will take* an *earlier* train so that I won't be late for work again.
_____

_____ 21. The *defeated* team walked *slowly* from the dugout, their heads hanging and their
_____   shoulders drooping.

_____ 22. *Beside* Joan sat a tall, handsome man; we *did* not *recognize* him as one of our
_____   fellow employees.

_____ 23. The coach *selected* Mary *in place of* Jackie as the opening day pitcher.
_____

_____ 24. The *replacements* for the firefighters arrived *at* noon, two hours later than
_____   they were expected.

_____ 25. *Kindness* and compassion are *two* of the qualities we all seek in a doctor.
_____

NAME _____ SCORE _____

Each item below contains two italicized words. Identify the italicized words by putting one of the following numbers in the blank to the left of the sentence:

1. Subject
2. Verb
3. Subjective complement

4. Direct object
5. Indirect object
6. Objective complement

7. Object of a preposition

_____
_____
1. The *plot* of that novel developed very slowly, and I soon lost *interest* in reading further.

_____
_____
2. The rainstorm was very *violent*, washing out the road to the cabin and giving *us* no option but to return to town.

_____
_____
3. The college *sent* a letter to all incoming *freshmen* and asked them to come to the campus one day before the other students for testing.

_____
_____
4. My friend calls his little brother a *genius,* but the boy *is* strong only in math and science courses.

_____
_____
5. The weather today seems *dark* and gloomy, but the *forecast* for tomorrow is for a bright, sunshiny day.

_____
_____
6. The appointment of the new coach caused great *excitement*; everyone on the team *is hoping* for a successful season next spring.

_____
_____
7. Please give the *clerk* in the post office those letters and ask *him* for a receipt for the stamps.

_____
_____
8. Once the bus driver passed the city limits, *she* drove steadily toward our *destination* for two hours without any stops.

_____
_____
9. Jim seemed very *happy* with his grade on the physics test although the grade was only a *C+*.

_____
_____
10. Although I thought Jim *was pleased* with his grade on the physics test, *it* was only a C+ and not one of the better grades in the class.

_____ 11. Please pass *me* the salt; I find this pasta dish a little *bland* for my taste.
_____

_____ 12. When I reviewed my past *efforts* in my history classes, I found the amount of
_____   work *insufficient* for making a good grade.

_____ 13. Joe's Uncle Charlie owns several antique cars, and he lavishes a
_____   great *deal* of attention on *them* to keep them in good shape.

_____ 14. The facts in that case were a little *unclear,* so the *defense attorney*
_____   was able to earn an acquittal for the accused thief.

_____ 15. Moving quickly down the *street,* the police searched all the buildings
_____   for the lost child and finally found *her* after an hour.

_____ 16. One member of my statistics class finds the work very *easy;* she seldom *studies*
_____   for more than a few minutes for tests.

_____ 17. The *two* of us were very *tired* when we finally finished the work on that
_____   project at 2:00 o'clock this morning.

_____ 18. Many of the *people* on that trip *were* better *informed* about the national park
_____   when they finished listening to the guide.

_____ 19. The entire staff in the back office *had been working* on that *problem* since
_____   they arrived early this morning.

_____ 20. I sent *everyone* in the office a *copy* of that memo late last night.
_____

_____ 21. The instructor considers *Jim* a *nuisance* because he asks many difficult
_____   questions during the class sessions.

_____ 22. *Will* you please *tell Martha* that story so that she will understand the background
_____   of this project?

_____ 23. Unfortunately the entire *class* remained *confused* by the complexity of that
_____   concept at the end of the lecture.

_____ 24. Someone *should have told us* about the change in this morning's schedule.
_____

_____ 25. I *have* never *known* anyone more *fortunate* than Jill; she seems to win a prize
_____   in every contest she enters.

NAME _____   SCORE _____

Directions: In the spaces at the left of each sentence, copy from the parentheses the word appropriate in serious writing.

_____ 1. (Rapid, Rapidly) changes in the price of gasoline (have, has)
_____   become quite common in the last few years.

_____ 2. A brisk breeze (blew, blowed) from the north, making the
_____   temperature feel much (lower, more lower) than it actually was.

_____ 3. Neither the players nor the coach (know, knows) (who, whom) we
_____   will be playing in the first round of the tournament.

_____ 4. Both the man and the two women (look, looks) (unhappily,
_____   unhappy) because the time of the meeting has been changed.

_____ 5. The fans (raised, rose) to their feet and stood silently as the soldier
_____   (raised, rose) the flag and the band played the national anthem.

_____ 6. John (implied, inferred) from the instructor's statement that the
_____   (easy, easily) part of the course was already behind us.

_____ 7. We had already (drinked, drunk) all the water well before we had
_____   (arrived, arrove) at the halfway point in the race.

_____ 8. (Fewer, Less) people have enrolled in that class than were
_____   enrolled last term, and so (fewer, less) money was collected in tuition.

_____ 9. It was (good, well) that the technician came so soon; without a
_____   working air conditioner the house heats up very (rapid, rapidly).

_____ 10. Sam is one of those people who (take, takes) great pleasure in
_____   finding new songs as soon as they (appear, appears).

_____ 11. The club (appreciate, appreciates) (you, your) working so hard on
_____   the latest fund drive.

_____ 12. (Late, Lately), it seems that there are more and more people who are
_____   taking an interest in jobs that (require, requires) physical labor.

_____ 13. The (incidence, incidents) of rear-end collisions (has, have)
_____   increased markedly since the red-light cameras were installed.

_____ 14. Most of the team members (has, have) arrived, and we're ready to
_____   begin the team meeting, whether everyone (are, is) here or not.

_____ 15. Jane observed, "That movie seemed (awful, very) familiar to me;
_____   it seems (as if, like) I read the novel on which it was based."

_____ 16. (Who, Whom) do you think will make (a better, the best) shortstop,
_____   Margie or Cathy?

_____ 17. Do you know anyone (who, whom) I could hire as a tutor in
_____   calculus? I am having (a very hard, such a hard) time in that class.

_____ 18. My father, along with three of his friends, (has, have) come to town
_____   to watch tomorrow's game and take three of (us, we) players to dinner.

_____ 19. When the lightning (striked, struck) nearby, all the golfers
_____   (seeked, sought) shelter in a small building.

_____ 20. Mike is an excellent tennis player, although he never (taked, took)
_____   many lessons in (it, the game).

_____ 21. Our team has been successful this year, and (its, our) prospects for
_____   the next two years (look, looks) extremely positive.

_____ 22. The two seats in this row are (our's ours); all four of your seats
_____   (are, is) in the next row.

_____ 23. The manager gave Sue and (I, me) tickets to tomorrow's game;
_____   both she (and I, and me) are looking forward to the experience.

_____ 24. His cough sounds (bad, badly) this afternoon; if it gets any
_____   (worse, worst) he should go to the doctor.

_____ 25. Chuck played (good, well) in today's game because he practiced
_____   so (diligent, diligently) this past week.

NAME _____ SCORE _____

One sentence in each pair has problems with incompleteness, dangling or misplaced modifiers, faulty parallelism, or faulty comparison. In the space at the left, write the letter that identifies the correct sentence.

_____ 1. a. Having gotten a late start on my history paper, tonight's work will take longer than I anticipated.
b. Having gotten a late start on my history paper, I see that tonight's work will take longer than I anticipated.

_____ 2. a. Last term's class in study skills taught us all the value of listening closely, taking careful notes, and reviewing several times before a test.
b. Last term's class in study skills taught us all the value of close listening, to take careful notes, and several reviews before a test.

_____ 3. a. When I saw the bear, I had to decide to either stand my ground or to quickly run to the nearest tree.
b. When I saw the bear, I had to decide either to stand my ground or to run quickly to the nearest tree.

_____ 4. a. I keep all the models I made as a kid in a closet under the stairs.
b. In a closet under the stairs, I keep all the models I made as a kid.

_____ 5. a. In that small town, the police chief's salary is higher than the mayor.
b. In that small town, the police chief's salary is higher than the mayor's.

_____ 6. a. Charles Anderson, a man whose integrity and credentials for that job cannot be matched by many other people.
b. Charles Anderson is a man whose integrity and credentials for that job cannot be matched by many other people.

_____ 7. a. Coming into the center of town, tall, handsome buildings rose on both sides of the street.
b. Coming into the center of town, we saw tall, handsome buildings rising on both sides of the street.

_____ 8. a. Using a bullhorn, the police officer told us as quickly as possible that we had to leave the area.
b. Using a bullhorn, the police officer told us that we had to leave the area as quickly as possible.

_____ 9. a. It is Jim's habit to on Saturday morning's take a long, relaxing run, but which seems to thoroughly exhaust him.

   b. On Saturday mornings, it is Jim's habit to take a long, relaxing run, but the effort seems to exhaust him thoroughly.

_____ 10. a. Mary Anne throws a great fastball, but, of the two girls, Judy has the best drop ball.

   b. Mary Anne throws a great fastball, but, of the two girls, Judy has the better drop ball.

_____ 11. a. The two students camped out next to the ticket office. Hoping to get good seats for the big game Saturday.

   b. Hoping to get good seats for the big game Saturday, the two students camped out next to the ticket office.

_____ 12. a. The instructor encouraged us to regularly attend class, reviewing our notes after class, and a careful review before each tests.

   b. The instructor encouraged us to attend class regularly, review our notes after class, and review carefully before each test.

_____ 13. a. The company president said that after dinner we would be shown charts and graphs that illustrate the company's progress in the past year.

   b. The company president said after dinner that we would be shown charts and graphs that illustrate the company's progress in the past year.

_____ 14. a. The new district sales manager is short and fat, and with a thin, wispy mustache.

   b. The new district sales manager is short and fat, and he has a thin, wispy mustache.

_____ 15. a. Stepping to the railing at the top of the monument, my camera dropped onto the rocks and smashed itself into tiny pieces.

   b. Stepping to the railing at the top of the monument, I dropped my camera onto the rocks, and it smashed itself into tiny pieces.

NAME _____ SCORE _____

Directions: Each sentence contains two punctuation errors, either an incorrect punctuation mark or an omitted mark. In the spaces at the left of the sentence, write the word that **precedes** the error followed by the correct mark of punctuation.

_____
_____
1. Standing on the corner in the frigid whipping wind the miserably cold couple decided to go to the car and return home.

_____
_____
2. When they had carefully checked their navigation system; the two silent men turned right and then they drove exactly 2 miles to their destination.

_____
_____
3. Having parked the truck along the side of the road the volunteers walked slowly along the road and picked all the papers, bottles and cans.

_____
_____
4. The club members were instructed to bring certain items to the next meeting, two pencils, a legal pad, and a list of their friends phone numbers.

_____
_____
5. "Dear me," said Charlie's kind, charming aunt, I don't think I would have used such harsh words to describe Cheryl who is certainly a wonderful person."

_____
_____
6. With the speaker's final words left hanging in the air the members of the audience stood and filed silently out of the room which was deathly quiet.

_____
_____
7. "Mr. Nelson please stand and give me your interpretation of the quotation that appears at the end of page 72 in the novel we are reading" said the instructor.

_____
_____
8. Should we leave do you think, a little earlier today than we did yesterday so that we can avoid the build-up of traffic at the road construction site.

_____
_____
9. Ruth moaned "Mary, please help me with this equation, I can't seem to make it work out correctly."

_____
_____
10. After I parked the car was almost immediately covered with the thick sticky pollen that was falling from the tree standing beside the driveway.

_____
_____
11. We did leave early and we made a quick stop at the grocery store for: eggs bacon, and coffee.

_____ 12. In fact the men had no way to make that repair today, so they will
_____ bring a new already-painted door to the house tomorrow.

_____ 13. That teacher takes a "Mickey Mouse approach to this course,
_____ I wish he would take the work more seriously.

_____ 14. Mr. Jones car is in the shop so he will be depending on us for a
_____ ride to work.

_____ 15. Howard Nichols, our new director of public relations has
_____ scheduled a meeting with his staff for this afternoon at 200 P.M.

_____ 16. I believe dont you, in doing some research before I make any
_____ major purchase, especially an item that must last for a long time.

_____ 17. Mr. Woods said "John I would like for you to work with Katherine
_____ on our next lab assignment."

_____ 18. When we come around that next bend in the road we should be
_____ able to see the river, the covered bridge and the small town
beyond the river.

_____ 19. With no one in the office to take my call I was forced to leave a
_____ message in Janes phone mail.

_____ 20. I always keep certain items in my truck, a first-aid kit a set of
_____ flares, and 50 feet of stout nylon rope.

_____ 21. The men walked slowly down the dark gloomy hallway, finally
_____ they found a light switch and were able to walk more quickly.

_____ 22. Tom, who works with us, Jim, who is on site as a consultant; and
_____ Mark worked through the night but they were unable to restore
our computer system.

_____ 23. It seems, dont you think that we have been very fortunate in our
_____ efforts to locate former students for the reunion?

_____ 24. With the storm clouds building on the horizon we decided to pull
_____ up the anchor and run quickly back to the harbor which was about
30 minutes away.

_____ 25. After we had finished eating the table scraps and leftovers made a
_____ healthy hearty meal for the two dogs.

NAME _____   SCORE _____

The following passage lacks internal punctuation, and it contains other problems of the sort we all make as we write first-draft material. Read the material carefully and correct all the errors by inserting punctuation where needed, and by writing other corrections in the space underneath the line where the correction is needed.

The Osprey

The osprey is one of the largest and most wide distributed birds of prey that occupy our planet. In fact ospreys can be found on every continent except Antarctica. They reproduce on all these continents but South America where they migrate to spend the winter. The birds range in size from 42 to 70 ounces in wieght are usually about 22 inches in length and have wingspans that in the largest specimens may exceed 5 feet. The birds are a dark brown on their backs and generally white on their underside. The heads are white, but the eyes have a dark almost black mask across them.

The ospreys is sometimes called the fish hawk or the sea hawk because its diet consists almost exclusively of fish. Because of their diet they generally live within a short distance of bodies of water that are shallow and contain an ample supply of fish. In North America they are especially prevalent in the Chesapeake Bay area but they may be found in any area where they can find an adequate supply of food. They hunt by soaring above the water at heights between 30 and 100 feet. When a bird sights a fish it descends hovers momenterily above the water and dives feet first usually catching the fish from behind. The birds has longer legs than most raptors, and have spiny footpads to provide a grip on a slippery fish. They also have specially adapted talons that allow it to reverse an outer toe to aid in grasping a fish. The birds can dive as much as 3 feet under the water and usually struggle momentarily to lift the fish into the air. Occasionally an osprey will catch a fish too large for it to lift, and the bird drowns when the fish goes deep into the water.

Ospreys nest in places not easily accessible to predators, choosing a steep cliff, a isolated tall tree, or a buoy or channel marker in the water. They also nest on artificial platforms situated in or near bodies of water. The nest is constructed of sticks and is lined with softer material such as seaweed, grasses, even newspapers and plastic bags. The female lays 2 to 4 eggs, one at a time over a period of 4 to 5 days. The chicks hatch in the order in which the eggs were laid and are ready to leave the nest when they are between 45 and 70 days old. Both the male and female incubate the eggs, but the male is the primary hunter of the pair.

In the period from the 1950's to the 1970's widespread use of the pesticide DDT threatened the osprey population. The chemical interfered with the bird's metabolism of calcium and caused them to produce eggs that were easily damaged. Since the use of DDT was banned in this country and many others, the population has recovered significantly.

The osprey is the provincial bird of Nova Scotia and the Seattle professional football team uses the lesser known name, Sea Hawks, as their team name.

Practice Sheet 1 Page 5

1. runs	6. was	11. are	16. was
2. works	7. seemed	12. stands	17. presents
3. chime	8. goes	13. hides	18. grasp
4. are	9. stretches	14. see	19. seek
5. appear	10. opens	15. seem	20. is

Practice Sheet 1 Page 6

1. No one	6. James	11. trail	16. purchases
2. lack	7. dogs	12. grandmother	17. brother
3. collection	8. I	13. Some	18. we
4. room	9. loss	14. women	19. uses
5. assistant	10. team	15. Two	20. car

Practice Sheet 2 Pages 15 and 16

1. 1, 6	6. 6, 5	11. 4, 1	16. 3, 4	21. 1, 6	26. 5, 4	31. 3, 2	36. 4, 2
2. 3, 4	7. 3, 4	12. 4, 6	17. 4, 2	22. 1, 1	27. 3, 6	32. 1, 3	37. 4, 1
3. 5, 1	8. 6, 4	13. 2, 6	18. 5, 4	23. 1, 2	28. 3, 6	33. 1, 5	38. 5, 3
4. 3, 4	9. 4, 6	14. 2, 5	19. 2, 4	24. 4, 2	29. 3, 1	34. 4, 3	39. 5, 1
5. 5, 4	10. 2, 3	15. 5, 6	20. 3, 4	25. 1, 3	30. 1, 1	35. 3, 4	40. 1, 3

Practice Sheet 3 Page 27

1. 1	6. agent	11. man	16. 1
2. 1	7. thin	12. 1	17. 1
3. 1	8. 1	13. 1	18. addition
4. representative	9. choice	14. 1	19. liability
5. musician	10. 1	15. 1	20. downpour

Practice Sheet 3 Page 28

1. successful	6. skilled	11. 1	16. seasick
2. 1	7. mechanic	12. off-key	17. faithful
3. 1	8. sour	13. humorous	18. ready
4. soggy	9. loose	14. colors	19. 1
5. thin	10. stale	15. shaky	20. tired

Practice Sheet 4 Page 35

1. company has provided service	11. I dropped books
2. I have added class	12. You will find notes
3. operator runs machine	13. We carried most
4. team feels confidence	14. company has ordered computers
5. Jim will have worked problems	15. Everyone will receive computer
6. we had seen race	16. we will have reached level
7. novel foretold identity	17. company has replaced computers
8. characters frightened nephew	18. two have found key
9. people attended rally	19. We will call locksmith
10. none have time	20. Neither has found solution

Practice Sheet 4 Page 36

1. O.C.	6. D.O.	11. O.C.	16. I.O.
2. I.O.	7. I.O.	12. O.C.	17. D.O.
3. D.O.	8. I.O.	13. O.C.	18. I.O.
4. D.O.	9. I.O.	14. O.C.	19. O.C.
5. D.O.	10. O.C.	15. D.O.	20. D.O.

Practice Sheet 5 Pages 43 and 44

1. will have, 1
2. had been, 1
3. has, 2
4. feel, 2
5. will, 3
6. could have, 3
7. should have, 4
8. has been, 4
9. find, 5
10. has, 1
11. should have been, 3
12. did, 2
13. has, 3
14. should have, 3
15. could have, 4
16. think, 5
17. do, 5
18. will be, 4
19. may, 4
20. should have been 3

21. has, 3
22. does, 5
23. be, 2
24. has, 2
25. have, 3
26. will, 1
27. can, 3
28. will have been, 1
29. should have, 1
30. will, 1`
31. have been, 3
32. have, 5
33. might, 4
34. try, 3
35. did, 2
36. should be, 3
37. must have, 4
38. find, 5
39. will, 5
40. should have been, 1

Practice Sheet 6 Page 53

1. 5, has been appointed
2. 4, has been given
3. 3, should be found
4. 5, will be made
5. 5, is considered

6. 4, could be sent
7. 3, will be evaluated
8. 5, was thought
9. 3, are shown
10. 3, must be doubled

Practice Sheet 6 Page 54

1. red
2. students
3. What
4. Who
5. leader

6. What
7. What
8. sales manager
9. Allison Reynolds
10. Allison Reynolds

11. qualified
12. What
13. whom
14. quarterback
15. quarterback

Practice Sheet 7 Pages 65 and 66

1. 0	6. S	11. S	16. S	21. C
2. C	7. 0	12. C	17. C	22. S
3. S	8. C	13. C	18. C	23. 0
4. C	9. C	14. S	19. S	24. C
5. C	10. C	15. 0	20. C	25. S

Practice Sheet 8 Pages 77 and 78

1. 1	6. 4	11. 1	16. 4	21. 6	26. 1	31. 1	36. 10
2. 2	7. 5	12. 1	17. 5	22. 6	27. 5	32. 4	37. 3
3. 3	8. 6	13. 2	18. 9	23. 3	28. 9	33. 6	38. 3
4. 8	9. 8	14. 3	19. 8	24. 9	29. 10	34. 1	39. 4
5. 10	10. 7	15. 6	20. 1	25. 1	30. 7	35. 1	40. 1

Practice Sheet 9 Page 87

1. someone
2. exercises
3. gate
4. Joe Mann
5. Tom Johnson
6. person
7. Senator Matthews
8. teacher
9. Allison McGuire
10. Martha James
11. sled
12. Mario Lopez
13. article
14. Aunt Autumn
15. road
16. shirt
17. photos
18. town
19. time
20. bookstore

Practice Sheet 9 Page 88

1. Jason Schmidt, who maintains our computer system,
2. Jason, whose official title is Manager of Information Technology
3. Jason whom we call whenever our computers develop problems
4. computers, which have all been around for several years,
5. problem that we cannot solve by rebooting the computer
6. computer, which is in an office in the basement.
7. solution, which is easy for Jason,
8. Jason, who is always dressed in old blue jeans and a sweatshirt,
9. directive that went against everything in Jason's makeup as an IT guy
10. neither of which was included in Jason's wardrobe
11. request, which would have choked off his thinking processes and made him ineffective,
12. image that Jason carried in his mind
13. college where he learned his computer skills
14. request, which we had always thought very silly
15. Jason, who is comfortable in his jeans and sweatshirt,
16. computer that has the problem
17. problem, which is usually fairly easy for him
18. discs that he has prepared for emergencies
19. reputation that he has been building for years
20. man who always solves our problems

Practice Sheet 10 Page 99

1. D.O.
2. S.
3. S.
4. S.
5. S.
6. O.P.
7. O.P.
8. S.C.
9. Ap.
10. S.
11. S.
12. D.O.
13. D.O.
14. S.
15. D.O.
16. D.O.
17. O.P.
18. O.P.
19. Ap.
20. S.

Practice Sheet 10 Page 100

1. Ap. that James is a good choice for that job
2. S. that James is a good choice for that job
3. D.O. where Les has been this morning
4. S. How we can work out a solution to this problem
5. D.O. which computer system is best for our purposes
6. O.P. whichever job you choose
7. D.O. you will enjoy that novel
8. O.P. whomever you think will be interested in it
9. D.O. that I could not attend that seminar
10. S. that I could not attend that seminar
11. D.O. whoever has it
12. Ap. that 97 people came for the initial tryouts
13. S. That all those people were interested in soccer
14. S. that the coach can only keep 35 players for the soccer team
15. S.C. what he told us as an excuse for his absence
16. D.O. what the real reason for his absence was
17. S. that I considered him a good source of notes for the test
18. O.P. whichever of those two people parked in my driveway
19. D.O. when Jason left for home this morning
20. D.O. whose bright idea this project was

Practice Sheet 11 Page 113

1. D.O.	6. O.P.	11. S.	16. S.
2. S.	7. D.O.	12. O.P.	17. D.O.
3. O.P.	8. S.C.	13. O.P.	18. O.P.
4. S.C.	9. O.P.	14. O.P.	19. S.C.
5. S.	10. S.	15. S.	20. S.

Practice Sheet 11 Page 114

1. N.	6. Adv.	11. N.	16. Adj.
2. N.	7. Adj.	12. N.	17. N.
3. N.	8. N.	13. N.	18. N.
4. Adv.	9. N.	14. Adv.	19. N.
5. N.	10. N.	15. Adv.	20. Adv.

Practice Sheet 12 Pages 123 and 124

1. man	11. _____	21. _____	31. _____
2. sun	12. intruder	22. photo	32. myself
3. _____	13. _____	23. someone	33. friends
4. _____	14. _____	24. _____	34. _____
5. I	15. speaker	25. system	35. I
6. man	16. person	26. _____	36. I
7. _____	17. David	27. system	37. _____
8. players	18. someone	28. _____	38. I
9. those	19. picture	29. snowstorm	39. _____
10. Louisa	20. photo	30. I	40. I

Practice Sheet 13 Pages 141 and 142

1. F	6. S	11. S	16. S	21. F	26. S	31. F	36. S
2. F	7. S	12. F	17. F	22. F	27. F	32. S	37. F
3. F	8. S	13. S	18. F	23. S	28. F	33. F	38. S
4. S	9. S	14. S	19. S	24. S	29. S	34. S	39. F
5. S	10. F	15. S	20. S	25. F	30. S	35. S	40. S

Practice Sheet 14 Page 151

1. b	3. b	5. a	7. b	9. b
2. b	4. a	6. b	8. b	10. b

Practice Sheet 14 Page 152

1. b	4. b	7. a	10. b	13. b
2. a	5. b	8. b	11. b	14. a
3. a	6. a	9. a	12. b	15. b

Practice Sheet 14A Pages 155 and 156

1. b; Inf.; To find the best route through the mountains	11. b
2. b; Part.; Looking at the horizon in the distance	12. a
3. a; Part; Running late to the meeting	13. a
4. a; Part.; Meeting the professor after class	14. b
5. a; Part.; covered with mud and dirt	15. b
6. b; Part.; Approaching the coast	16. a
7. b	17. a
8. b; Part.; Covered with mud	18. b
9. b; Part.; Opening the heavy door into the library	19. a
10. a	20. b

Practice Sheet 15 Pages 163 and 164

1. 1	5. 1	9. 7	13. 1	17. 4
2. 5	6. 1	10. 1	14. 1	18. 5
3. 2	7. 2	11. 3	15. 4	19. 4
4. 6	8. 4	12. 5	16. 7	20. 1

Practice Sheet 16 Page 171

1. b	3. a	5. b	7. a	9. a
2. b	4. a	6. a	8. a	10. a

Practice Sheet 16 Page 172

1. b	3. b	5. a	7. b	9. a
2. b	4. b	6. b	8. b	10. b

Practice Sheet 17 Pages 183 and 184

1. 3, 1 sleek, showroom,
2. 4, 2 project, cutter,
3. 5, 2 set, horseback,
4. 2, 1 hammers, drills,
5. 3, 3 handsome, strange-sounding,
6. 4, 2, car, papers,
7. 4, 1 game, stadium,
8. 4, 1 Earlier, game,
9. 3, 1 tall, wind,
10. 4, 2 then, them,
11. 2, 4 bookstore, briefly,
12. 4, 3 watched, restless,
13. 4, 3 him, mid-priced,
14. 2, 3 up, steep,
15. 4, 1 clearing, tent,
16. 4, 1 Once, menacing,
17. 3, 1 tall, booth,
18. 4, 3 door, enticing,
19. 4, 1 day, cleared,
20. 4, 3 test, hot,
21. 2, 3, site, small,
22. 4, 3 paper, long,
23. 4, 3 east, hazy,
24. 2, 1 trout, fire,
25. 5, 1 walking, bone,
26. 4, 2, car, strong,
27. 3, 1 narrow, us,
28. 2, 4 gear, lines
29. 4, 2 visit, hedges,
30. 4, 2 street, Jim,

Practice Sheet 18 Page 193

1. 6 us,
2. 2 friend, fall,
3. 5 wish, Karen,
4. 2 Johnson, photographer,
5. 3 hope, John,
6. 4 was, least,
7. 1 Smith, jacket,
8. 2 weekend, rain,
9. 3 Richard,
10. 4, morning, know,
11. 5 said,
12. 6 room,
13. 1 Williams,
14. 2 Williams,
15. 1 Williams, moment,

Practice Sheet 18 Page 194

1. R where Mr. Roberts has his office
2. R that has such good Italian food
3. R who wrote this report
4. N, who wrote this report,
5. R that appear on the cover of the report,
6. R whose names appear on the cover
7. R whom the company president named CFO
8. N, which runs north and south at this end of town,
9. R striding purposefully into the room
10. N, who is striding purposefully into the room at this minute,
11. N, which are both quite impressive,
12. R who took a class from Mr. Black last term
13. N, who took this class from him last term,
14. N, whom you met at my house last week,
15. R when my history paper is due
16. N, when my history paper is due,
17. R whose pleasing personality wins many friends
18. N, whose pleasing personality impresses many people,
19. N, shielded from the north winds by a hill,
20. R when you have about an hour to spare

Practice Sheet 19 Page 207

__C__ 1. They'll need another's opinion on that presentation; its content and data aren't familiar to most of us.

__W__ 2. "Did she say, 'Your **work's** not finished **yet'**?" asked Diane.

__W__ 3. **We're** not sure–no **one's** ever really sure–how fast that weather system will move once **it's** crossed the Mississippi River.

__W__ 4. Mark responded that she's given contradictory statements about that task, so **he's** not sure which parts are **yours** and which parts are his.

__W__ 5. The list of guests at the conference is **impressive:** the **company's** president, two past **CFO's,** and two well-known politicians.

__W__ 6. **It's** going to be difficult to find **Arlene's** replacement; her skills with computers–not to mention her easy-going personality–will be hard to duplicate.

__W__ 7. "My grades were all **A's** and **B's** last term, said Mary, "so **I'll** need to work very hard to match that record."

__W__ 8. The boss said, "**Tomorrow's** our day to finish that report; there'll be no **if's, and's,** or **but's** about it."

—W— 9. That huge heater blasts out too many **Btu's** for this room, so its always too warm for comfort in here.

__W__ 10. That's my **cousin's** brother-in-**law's** sister, but **it's** impossible to tell if **she's** really related to me.

__W__ 11. Our jackets look the same, but, since mine's at home, **that's yours** on the table.

__W__ 12. "Two things hurt my performance on that **test:** failing to study beforehand and working too slowly on the first twenty-five **questions,**" said Mike.

—W— 13. "**I** think she said, 'Meet me at the restaurant at 8:30 **tonight,'**" said Allen, "**but I'm** not really sure which restaurant **she'd** selected."

—W— 14. At five **o'clock you'll** need to check the length of the **lines** outside; perhaps **we'll** need to open a second ticket-window.

—W— 15. If **it's** true that the paper is due tomorrow, I've less than twenty-four hours time to do my research and write the **paper's** final draft.

Practice Sheet 19 Page 208

1. Harry said, "I will arrive arrive about five o'clock tomorrow afternoon, unless I get caught up in rush-hour traffic."
2. The office manager claims, "I will need to hire three additional people if we take on that new client."
3. My brother said to me, "I will need to gain about 15 pounds of hard muscle before football practice starts in August."
4. Mrs. Carlson asked us, "Would you be willing to help me move some furniture on Saturday morning?"
5. Did the dispatcher say, "All the trains are running behind schedule today"?
6. The officer told us that it would be almost an hour before that tree could be removed from the road.
7. The technician tells me that my computer will need an increase in its RAM before it can handle that new program.
8. The coach told me that my fielding is excellent, but I need to improve my ability to hit with men on base.
9. The tourists asked if we could tell them where that famous waterfall is located.
10. Sam asked the mechanic if she could tell him when the repairs on his car would be completed.

Practice Sheet 20 Page 215

1. W inside, robbery; finished,
2. W run?" Jaime.
3. W Jim's directions, confused and
4. W football, catch."
5. W GPS works?" Allison;
6. C
7. C
8. W Street, it," Ray
9. W nouns, "his" "its."
10. W dinner," Brett; "If it's, I'll, home."
11. C
12. W "AL," Alabama, "Al"
13. Mrs., garden; beautiful and tomatoes, green beans,
14. W "gift," "I 'gifted' immediately."
15. C

Practice Sheet 20 Page 216

1. Crawford, job, can't
2. There's reason, there, yours, out-of-town gas?
3. trip, Barbara, who's experienced, Rosa, Kelli, who, unfortunately, rivers but
4. office, bring a laptop, pens,
5. huge, dog, threatingly, would-be, alleyway,
6. Drs. Jameson, right, discussion, after experts', mixed-fuel
7. impressed, didn't think, players' program, didn't
8. we're face, you've changes that
9. anticipate, or . . . guess, arrive, classrooms?
10. It's, now, they'd trouble, you don't suppose, do you, they're longer?

Practice Sheet 21 Pages 229 and 230

1. ring, dragged
2. set, seen
3. laid, is
4. laid, hung
5. lain, drove
6. became, blown
7. drawn, drowned
8. torn, know
9. swum, is
10. grown, paid
11. ate, eaten
12. swung, threw
13. begun, chosen
14. brought, lent
15. thrown, spent
16. sat, caught
17. set, burst
18. sought, struck
19. grown, broken
20. fallen, sunk
21. built, sits
22. bought, laid
23. crept, stolen
24. gotten, flung
25. taught, had
26. built, been
27. bought, driven
28. taken, took
29. stung, begun
30. shook, meet
31. skinned, felt
32. burst, slunk
33. found, frozen
34. dealt, run
35. come, grown
36. shaken, began
37. shined, given
38. shone, become
39. slew, was
40. lay, leaped or leapt

Practice Sheet 21 Pages 231 and 232

1. C, lying
2. C, C
3. gotten, stole
4. raise, slid
5. are, rise
6. worn, C
7. paid, C
8. grown, caught
9. laid, walked
10. C, shown
11. slept, ran
12. C, set
13. C, C
14. sitting, ran
15. C, has been
16. C, lying
17. taken, sits
18. blew, come
19. brought, forgiven
20. built, stood
21. C, will come
22. did, blown
23. C, C
24. C, moved
25. C, C
26. C, C
27. to see, walked
28. C, walked
29. saw, knew
30. drowned, gave
31. eaten, C
32. swung, split
33. C, found
34. wore, tore
35. climbed, fell
36. hung, organized
37. written, printed
38. have been, C
39. shook, fell
40. skinned, C

Practice Sheet 22 Page 239

1. sit
2. were
3. was
4. were
5. opposes
6. oppose
7. repeats
8. were
9. are
10. is
11. fills
12. are
13. have
14. is
15. hang
16. are
17. seems
18. are
19. were
20. are

Practice Sheet 22 Page 240

1. C
2. have been able
3. is
4. have been meeting
5. works
6. is
7. C
8. work
9. runs
10. seem
11. C
12. is
13. C
14. are walking
15. has
16. C
17. takes
18. seems
19. seems
20. seems

Practice Sheet 23 Pages 249 and 250

1. b
2. a
3. a
4. a
5. b
6. a
7. b
8. a
9. a
10. b
11. b
12. b
13. a
14. a
15. b
16. b
17. b
18. b
19. a
20. b

Practice Sheet 24 Page 259

1. 4	6. 5	11. 1	16. 2
2. 3	7. 1	12. 6	17. 5
3. 6	8. 4	13. 1	18. 5
4. 1	9. 2	14. 5	19. 4
5. 1	10. 4	15. 1	20. 1

Practice Sheet 24 Page 260

1. who	6. he	11. we	16. who
2. us	7. whoever	12. us	17. me
3. Your	8. whomever	13. whose	18. who
4. I	9. me	14. I	19. me
5. yours	10. nobody's	15. whom	20. whoever

Practice Sheet 25 Page 269

1. left, Adv.	6. runs, Adv.	11. waters, Adj.
2. answer, Adj.	7. behavior, Adj.	12. followed, Adv.
3. Come, Adv.	8. manner, Adj.	13. he, Adj.
4. spot, Adj.	9. retreat, Adj.	14. Jerry, Adj.
5. sounds, Adj.	10. is growing, Adv.	15. necktie, Adj.

Practice Sheet 25 Page 270

1. nearly; man looked and said	11. independently
2. different; I (a)m	12. well
3. differently; Junior has been behaving	13. rapidly
4. considerably; You (wi)ll find	14. more
5. heavily; railings are	15. tighter
6. kindest; Mr. Stubbs is	16. carefully
7. bad; piano sounds	17. really
8. surely; piano needs	18. well
9. better; one gets	19. unhappy
10. almost; mother squandered	20. unhappily

Practice Sheet 26 Pages 287 and 288

1. Unless, annoyed	11. teach, think	21. suspect, besides	31. sense, should have
2. great, really	12. assent, affect	22. any way, invitation	32. Since, right
3. as far as, a great many	13. advice, very	23. inferred course	33. extremely, those
4. Almost, somewhat	14. way, distance	24. that, incredibly	34. disinterested, among
5. farther, very	15. sorts, used	25. should, take	35. am not, all right
6. not very, enthusiastic	16. bare, breath	26. adopted, adapted	36. anywhere, desserts
7. number, might have	17. rein, patience	27. past, already	37. personal, stationery
8. altered, accept	18. principal, whole	28. later, proceed	38. two, too
9. All together, altogether	19. It's, quiet	29. heard, incidents	39. criteria, extremely
10. nature, angry	20. led, as if	30. dyed, seen	40. that, off

Practice Sheet 27 Page 301

1. analyses	6. commandos, oes	12. handfuls	17. plateaus, plateaux	22. theses
2. aquariums, a	7. Dutchmen	13. infernos	18. podia	23. turkeys
3. archipelagoes, archipelagos	8. fathers-in-law	14. lilies	19. scarves, scarfs	24. vortices, vortexes
4. assemblies	9. flamingos, oes	15. mice	20. sheriffs	25. wives
5. Charleses	10. folios	16. octopuses, octopi	21. spies	
	11. fungi, funguses			

Practice Sheet 27 Page 302

1. C	11. C	21. W	31. W	41. C
2. C	12. C	22. W	32. C	42. W
3. W	13. C	23. C	33. C	43. C
4. C	14. C	24. W	34. C	44. C
5. C	15. W	25. W	35. C	45. W
6. C	16. W	26. C	36. W	46. W
7. W	17. W	27. C	37. W	47. C
8. C	18. C	28. C	38. W	48. C
9. C	19. W	29. C	39. C	49. C
10. W	20. C	30. C	40. C	50. C

Practice Sheet 28 has no key

There is no key for the practice sheets for this lesson as there are so many possibilities for constructing the sentences.

Index